P9-EDJ-797

This Book is Number Two of the Calafía Series.

The legend of Calafía is intimately associated with the nomenclature of California. This fanciful tale occurs in the fifth book of a popular Portuguese-Spanish cycle of the late fifteenth and early sixteenth centuries, a romance in which the knightly and heroic deeds of Prince Esplandian, son of King Amadis, who rallied to the support of the Christian faith when it was threatened by the pagan forces before the walls of Constantinople, are depicted in the elaborate manner of the period. As the battle between the Crescent and the Cross reached its zenith, the opposing armies were thrown into turmoil when Esplandian fell suddenly in love with one of the allies of the pagan King Armato, a beautiful queen who lived on an island called California, "very close to that part of the terrestial paradise, which was inhabited by black women without a single man among them, who lived in the manner of Amazons."

The name of this queen was Calafía.

DUFLOT DE MOFRAS'
TRAVELS ON THE
PACIFIC COAST

Duflot de Mofras'
Travels on the Pacific Coast

Volume I

Translated, Edited and Annotated by
Marguerite Eyer Wilbur

Foreword by
Dr. Frederick Webb Hodge

The Fine Arts Press
Santa Ana, California
1937

To Monsieur, le Marechal Soult, Duc de Dalmatie
President of the Council of Ministers
Monsieur le Maréchal,

In begging you to accept the dedication of the relation of a voyage undertaken at your orders, I am merely fulfilling my duty, for I dare hope that the public will appreciate the true spirit and motive with which this exploration has been undertaken and will not see in this volume merely my own feeble attempts to justify the confidence imposed in me by this mission, but rather the lofty spirit behind it which, having made France so illustrious during the war, is now attempting, by commercial expansion, to achieve Pacific conquests through the medium of industry and intelligence

I have the honor respectfully to be,

Monsieur le Maréchal,

Your very humble and obedient servant,
Duflot de Mofras.
Attaché of the French legation in Mexico.

(Facsimile Title Page)

EXPLORATION

DU TERRITOIRE

DE L'ORÉGON,

DES CALIFORNIES

ET DE LA MER VERMEILLE,

EXÉCUTÉE PENDANT LES ANNÉES 1840, 1841 ET 1842,

PAR

M. DUFLOT DE MOFRAS,

Attaché à la Légation de France à Mexico;

OUVRAGE PUBLIÉ PAR ORDRE DU ROI,

SOUS LES AUSPICES DE M. LE MARÉCHAL SOULT, DUC DE DALMATIE,
Président du Conseil,

ET DE M. LE MINISTRE DES AFFAIRES ÉTRANGÈRES.

TOME PREMIER.

PARIS,

ARTHUS BERTRAND, ÉDITEUR,

LIBRAIRE DE LA SOCIÉTÉ DE GÉOGRAPHIE,
Rue Hautefeuille, n° 23.

1844.

PREFACE

The meager amount of information available about the west coast of New Spain, the Vermilion Sea, the interior provinces of Mexico, the two Californias, the Russian establishments, and especially Oregon Territory, whose possession is now being disputed by the United States and England; the important future in store for the entire coast of America situated north of the equator and bathed by the Pacific Ocean; the interest already aroused in the different archipelagoes of the South Sea; the development of our shipping and whaling industry in these regions; all these are problems that for a considerable period of time have been of profound interest to the French government.

For this reason toward the end of 1839, M. le Maréchal, the Duc de Dalmatie, President of the Council of Ministers, and at that time Minister of Foreign Affairs, with the idea of utilizing what information I might have acquired either on former voyages to America or during a sojourn of three years in Spain, recalled me from the French embassy at Madrid, to which I was attached, and appointed me to the legation of the King in Mexico, with the special mission of visiting the provinces of western Mexico, New Galica, Colima, Sinaloa, Sonora, the Gulf of Cortés, Old and New California, the Russian forts adjoining, and the American and English posts situated at Astoria, along the Columbia River, and throughout Oregon, and of ascertaining finally, irrespective of its political aspect, what advantages might be afforded to our commerce and merchant marine by the founding of settlements in these regions as yet comparatively unknown in France.

The foresight of those who planned this expedition is apparent for not everyone is fully aware of the increasing importance of the Marqueses, Tahiti, the Sandwich Islands, and Oregon Territory, especially since the opening of commerce with China, which should lead to broader relations with Japan, and since intercommunication between the two great oceans seems probable through work feasible at Lake Nicaragua, and by the ease with which the Isthmus of Panamá can be pierced.

The results of this expedition are now being placed before the public, and include a geographical description, the history of early discoveries, the hydrography of the coasts, the statistics of the country, a picture of the customs of the citizens and the Indians, a survey of the influence exercised by the Spanish missionaries and establishments founded by them, details regarding the commerce that shipowners and French merchants might carry on in these countries, European commodities to be exchanged, the exploitation of precious metal and the whaling industry, points where ships can take on supplies, ports of call for whaling vessels, products of the soil and, finally, a survey of its botany and zoology. To elucidate the text there has been affixed, in addition to the sketches and drawings, the plans of the principal ports, and a large general map prepared with the greatest care, which includes all the country situated west of the Rocky Mountains, a portion of Canada, the territory of the Hudson's Bay Company, Russian and English America, the United States, Texas, the majority of the Mexican provinces, and all of Oregon Territory, a region practically unknown until our day. The present boundaries and their proposed limits have been traced on the maps, together with notes indicating the treaties of peace and conventions whereby they have been defined. This is an entirely new diplomatic departure.

This work, I might add, begins where that of M. Humboldt ends and this, to the author, would seem to afford better ground for indulgence than to have attempted to follow the footsteps and continue the work of that illustrious traveler.

Duflot de Mofras

INTRODUCTION

French exploration and colonization in America followed, originally, two main arteries. The first of these led west by way of the valley of the St. Lawrence and the Great Lakes, then south down the Mississippi to the Gulf of Mexico. The second, after following for a considerable distance the same major water route toward the west, continued in the same direction by way of the Canadian lakes and rivers to the Pacific. Over these two trails traveled some of the greatest explorers known to history. Among them were men of various ranks and creeds, statesmen, noblemen, priests, trappers, traders, and explorers who, braving untold hardships and dangers, carried the French flag into remote corners of the new continent. The tale of their achievements, their heroism, their tragedies, and their disappointments while attempting to establish a French empire in America is one of the most amazing records of all ages. That ultimately they were destined to lose the lands acquired at such peril is one of the tragedies of history.

America, historically speaking, was originally believed to be the gateway to China. Hence, for many decades this continent was regarded primarily as a convenient entrepôt, a stepping-stone to the remote and alluring "land of Cathay and Inde." This mysterious Orient with its untold riches, "the wealth of Inde and Cathay," so subtly dramatized by the Venetian writer, Marco Polo, in his epochal *Travels,* was the powerful magnet that lured the courageous Columbus and his terror-stricken sailors westward across the unknown Atlantic into awesome space and darkness. But Columbus found the supposed waterway to the Orient barred by lands, at first believed to be Cathay, which were subsequently named in honor of another great explorer of that era, Amerigo Vespucci.[1]

Columbus, by his discoveries, completely revolutionized the geographical conceptions of his age. Having proved by his voyages that the Atlantic, which appeared to dip so perilously off into space, actually led to new lands screening China, he paved the way for explorations

---

[1]For several decades the Spaniards referred to their American possessions as the "Indies," or "las Indias," the name applied by Marco Polo to the islands east of China. The name America appears to have been first used by Martin Waldseemüller, a teacher of geography in the College of St. Dié, in a treatise called Cosmographiae published in 1507.

that extended into remote corners of the world. Among those who soon followed in the footsteps of the heroic Columbus was the French navigator Jacques Cartier. After crossing the Atlantic, in 1534 this Breton navigator sailed up the St. Lawrence in the same futile search for a waterway to China. Baffled, like Columbus, in his quest, the more practical-minded Cartier recognized in the Canadian wilderness with its wealth of furs and fishes, an opportunity for a great colonial empire.

The history of French activities in America actually begins, however, not with the amazing adventures of the great Cartier and his attempts to colonize Canada, but with the comparatively unimportant visits of Breton and Norman fishermen, following the discovery by John Cabot in 1497 of the Northwest Coast of America. These obscure toilers of the sea brought back to their humble homes on the French coast, and to that of Cartier, St. Malo, not only tales full of glamor but also an exact knowledge of winds, routes, and dangers encountered on the North Atlantic.

The rôle of Cartier in the New World was primarily that of colonizer. To procure men for the Herculean task of pioneering in the wilderness Cartier, soon after reaching Canada, sailed back to France. In 1535 he returned to the New World with a group of colonists, who passed the winter in the shadow of the bleak cliffs of Quebec. A second and larger group under his leadership arrived at Quebec in the fall of 1541. These inexperienced Frenchmen, however, utterly demoralized by the hardships encountered during frigid Canadian winters, soon returned to the milder land of France.

For fifty years after Cartier's colonists disbanded no further attempt was made by the French to conquer the wilderness of the New World. The next settlement of importance may be ascribed to the activities of Samuel de Champlain who, in 1603, entered the St. Lawrence. On the banks of this river within five years this dynamic leader had founded Quebec, a port that served for the next twenty-five years as a base for extensive explorations into the interior as far as Lake Huron and Ontario. Notwithstanding the fact that from 1618 to 1648 the Thirty Years' War was being waged in Europe, that the relations between France and England were strained, and that, in 1629, a small English fleet even took Quebec; yet under Champlain's leadership France continued to retain her colonies in eastern Canada. Nor did this Thirty Years' War, with its interminable fighting, fail materially to retard French colonial development in America.

The next important step toward French colonization in America took place in 1629 when Cardinal Richelieu, following the lead of the great English and Dutch East India companies, formed what was known as the Company of New France. Richelieu's colossal scheme included the transportation of colonists, priests, and fur traders to New France and the colonization and development of the St. Lawrence Valley. Until 1663 this Company of New France remained in complete control of eastern Canada.

At the same time, Canadian explorers were gradually moving west. Radisson and Groselliers, penetrating into the wilderness north of Lake Superior, were followed by a group of Ursuline Nuns and Sulpician, Franciscan, and Jesuit Fathers whose tact and patience brought many of the more hostile Indian tribes under their benign sway, thus materially strengthening the hold of France beyond the confines of the St. Lawrence Valley.

In 1664, a year after Richelieu's charter was revoked because of the company's failure to fulfill its obligations, another vast colonization project to include not only Canada, but also West Africa, South America, and the West Indies was launched by the French Company of the West Indies. Under its auspices a group of French immigrants made their way into Canada during a period of ten years before its charter was revoked by Louis XIV. The rise and fall of these vast but unwieldly colonial companies failed, however, to affect to any considerable degree the more immediate and practical results achieved by priests and explorers. In 1661 Fort Radisson, and in 1665 a French outpost mission were established on the remote shores of Lake Superior; in 1673 Marquette and Joliet explored the upper reaches of the Mississippi.

The discovery of this Mississippi waterway afforded a definite impetus to French expansion in America. Down this vast and unknown stream in 1682 came Robert Cavalier, Sieur de la Salle, who took formal possession of the wilderness on all sides for his monarch, Louis XIV, naming it Louisiana. Some three years later this same valiant explorer founded a French colony far down on Matagorda Bay, in a region then known as Tejas.

Out of these early explorations and virgin settlements France dreamed of developing in the ensuing decades a vast colonial empire in America. But the basic obstacle to the realization of this vision of colonial expansion was the growing strength of British colonies just south of the St. Lawrence.

That the growth of these young French and English settlements in the New World should be materially affected by the political relations of their respective governments was inevitable, and when the war of the Palatinate broke out in Europe, French and English colonials fought bitterly in America. In 1690, Acadia—the French colony directly south of the St. Lawrence—fell into British hands. Finally, by the Treaty of Utrecht signed in 1713, France admitted her defeat in America by conceding to England her claims to Acadia, the Hudson Bay region, and Newfoundland.

The war had been concentrated along the Atlantic Coast and had not spread down the basin of the Mississippi or into the interior, now recognized as the most fertile area of the new continent. In the south and southwest, as an aftermath of this conflict, a new wave of exploration and colonization now began. Young explorers commenced to move up unknown rivers, especially affluents of the Mississippi, into remote regions occupied by the Spaniards, believed to contain certain mines of gold and silver.

Notable among this group of pioneers in the early decades of the eighteenth century were St. Denis, explorer of the Rio Grande; La Harpe, who traveled up the Rouge, or Red River; Du Tisné, who ascended the Missouri; and Bourgmont and the Mallet brothers who penetrated far up the main streams of the Kansas and Missouri.

At this time Louisiana, a thriving settlement between 1717 and 1731, while in the hands of the powerful French Company of the Indies, was the center of a series of new colonial enterprises, despite the infamous collapse of the Mississippi Bubble and the financial trickery of John Law and his associates. After 1700 many important settlements— New Orleans, Mobile, Natchitoches, Biloxi, and Natchez—were founded. While the south was thus attracting the interest of large colonies of French pioneers, in the north, under the leadership of La Vérendrye, a series of trading posts connecting the French settlements of the St. Lawrence Valley with the fur-trading lands beyond Lake Superior were established.

La Vérendrye's efforts, however, were largely frustrated by wars and foreign complications and ultimately the political manipulations of France, Spain, and England sounded the death knell of the French advance in America. By a secret treaty, Louisiana passed in 1762 to Spain. In 1763 France surrendered Canada and her lands east of the Mississippi to England. Then, in 1800, the tide of European politics swung back in favor of France, and Louisiana reverted to its former owner, in whose possession it remained for the brief span of three years until its rich lands, the last vestige of the French colonial empire in America, were purchased in 1803 by the United States for the trivial sum of four cents an acre.

Notwithstanding these chaotic changes, French colonists, still staunchly loyal to their own flag, carried on under alien rule, in the vain hope that the tides of fortune might again turn back to France. In the south, New Orleans and the Mississippi River towns continued to retain their distinctly French character; in Canada the French trappers, voyageurs, and *éngagés,* now largely employed by great English concerns, the Hudson's Bay and North West Companies, were pushing as far west as the Pacific Coast.

Occasionally racial loyalty, invariably keen among Frenchmen, took concrete shape. Even as late as 1837, when English trading forts dotted the west, a group of French Canadians, led by Louis Joseph Papineau, took up arms with the hope of establishing a French republic in Canada.

Papineau's revolt was significant because it occurred at a time when the ultimate ownership of vast areas of western America still hung in the balance. By the third decade of the nineteenth century it was universally recognized that the rich and untapped resources of the Pacific Coast were the loadstar of several powerful nations, notably the United States, Russia, and England.

Mexico's hold on her colonial possessions of Baja and Alta California was at this time notably weak. The fate of this land, of Texas, and of Oregon Territory was one of the burning questions of the hour. Toward the north, English holdings strengthened by great chains of forts extended across the continent and down the Columbia River. On the east was the United States, whose vanguard of trappers, traders, and explorers, already familiar with the country, were finding new and safer overland routes to the coast. Directly above San Francisco, a Russian colony, with headquarters at New Archangel, had been established.

Still another aggressive European power, France, had for many decades been approaching the west coast by way of the Pacific, seeking to replace her colonial holdings, lost in 1713 and 1763 by the Treaties of Utrecht and Paris. Among those who fought against the English in the conflict that preceded this disastrous Treaty of Paris was Louis Antoine de Bougainville, whose fervent patriotism led him on a circumnavigation of the globe, in 1766, in the hope of finding new lands to replace the colonial losses of France in America.

Bougainville, who discovered unknown islands in the Pacific, was soon followed by a new group of French explorers led by Jean François de la Pérouse, whose mission, of a semi-political character, included an inspection of the actual strength of Spain on the west coast of America. Although La Pérouse was fated to lose his life before his mission was fully accomplished, his official records were published in 1797 in Paris. His four erudite volumes[2] gave to the world at large the earliest French record of the Pacific Coast, including a comprehensive account of Monterey, which had been visited in the fall of 1786 by La Pérouse and his party. La Pérouse disclosed in his narrative the military weakness of California, a weakness verified by the records of the English navigator, George Vancouver, who visited the same coast six years later.

After the chaos brought on by the Napoleonic wars had ended in Europe, French ships began to appear more frequently among the Oceanic Islands and off the west coast of California. These ships— whalers, trading vessels, scientific expeditions, and warships—had a wide range of objectives. But behind their varied activities lay one main purpose—to pave the way for new French colonies on the west coast or the islands of the Pacific. Of these various expeditions the most notable were those of Roquefeuil, Choris, Duhaut Cilly,[3] Claudière, Morineau,[4] Dupetit Thouars, and La Place, whose narratives contributed a vast amount of scientific and historic data about California.

It was inevitable that these voyages, whose purpose was a close survey of Pacific Coast ports and a study of the opportunities these afforded, should lend credence to the belief that France had definite designs on this territory.[5] Such rumors were materially strengthened by the arrival on the west coast in 1840 and 1841 of a young diplomatic attaché, Duflot de Mofras, who had been sent out to inspect the country in the interest of the French government.

---

[2]See infra, I. 207, also note 17.

[3]Duhaut Cilly's Voyage autour du monde devoted 300 pages to California and included elaborate descriptions of Yerba Buena, Monterey, Santa Bárbara, San Pedro, and San Diego. See infra I, 262, also note 8.

[4]M. P. Morineau was believed to have visited the coast in 1833. The following year his Notice sur la California was published in Paris, and aroused considerable interest in this comparatively unknown land.

[5]See A. P. Nasatir, "French Activities in California before Statehood," in Proceedings of the Pacific Coast Branch of the American Historical Association for 1928, pp. 76 to 88.

Count Eugène Duflot de Mofras, the most important of these French explorers of the eighteenth century, was born on July 5, 1810, at Toulouse. After completing his education at Toulouse and Paris, where he specialized in science, at the comparatively immature age of eighteen he was appointed attaché to the court at Madrid. Here he came into contact with one of the leading Spanish historians of that day, Martín Fernández de Navarette. This noted historiographer was at that time a familiar figure in the intellectual circles of Madrid, having published a short time before De Mofras met him the first volume of an erudite and comprehensive work, *Colección de los viajes y descubrimientos que hicieron par mar los Españoles desde fines del siglo XV*, etc. From Navarette, who was conceded to be an authority on the voyages of early navigators who visited many islands of the Pacific as well as ports along the coast, De Mofras acquired his first definite knowledge of Spanish activities in western America. De Mofras' interest in Navarette bore fruit in his volume, written years later, on this scholar.[6]

The first published record of the young diplomat's scholastic interests, in so far as can be ascertained, is found in a letter dated Madrid, December 20, 1837,[7] addressed to Monsieur le Ministre and subsequently published in the *Journal Général d'Instruction Publique* of May 5, 1838.[8] This communication is in essence a full report of a visit to the leading Spanish archives of Saragossa, the Escorial, and Toledo, in a search for documents of historic interest; it was soon followed, on October 6, 1838, by a second article published in the same journal.

These evidences of scholastic leanings on the part of young Mofras, his knowledge of Spanish, his previous visit to America, and his obvious interest in the Northwest, soon led to his appointment as honorary attaché to Mexico, with specific instructions to conduct investigations along the Pacific slope. The magnitude of De Mofras' task is revealed in the following letter written by the Minister of Foreign Affairs, the Duc de Dalmatie, to Baron de Cyprey, French ambassador to Mexico.[9]

"In accordance with your desire I have authorized Duflot de Mofras to accompany you to Mexico as honorary attaché to the legation of the

---

[6]A brochure of 45 pages entitled **Mendoza et Navarette, Notices Biographiques** (Paris, 1845).
[7]See Duflot de Mofras, **Mélanges**, (1838-1863), I, 1-3. MS. Bancroft Library.
[8]Ibid. I, 4.
[9]**Correspondence Politique, Méxique**, Vol. XVIII, folio 38. Minister to Cyprey, Paris, November 6, 1839. Sections of this report appear in the **Proceedings of the Pacific Coast Branch of the American Historical Association**, 1928, pp. 89-90.

King, and I intend to take the first opportunity that arises to regularize
his position and to obtain for him through the good will of his Majesty
the title of paid attaché (poste d'attaché payé). I desire that he shall
utilize his zeal and scholarship during his sojourn in Mexico by making
a tour into the interior of the country and also into California, for the
purpose of procuring reliable information regarding political and commercial conditions in these lands and also the geography of ports
slightly known, or even entirely unknown. You will authorize him to
undertake this journey as soon as possible after his arrival, and give him
whatever assistance is within your power. It is principally to California,
as I have said, that M. de Mofras will direct his attention; there the
objective of his mission will be to collect as complete information as
possible about the geography of the country, its political, moral, industrial, and commercial conditions, the places it would be advantageous
for our merchants to visit, and particularly detailed information about
establishments that the Russians have founded in the neighborhood of
those posts which the North Americans have opened on the Columbia
River, beyond the Rocky Mountains."

Arrangements were then made for De Mofras to accompany Baron
de Cyprey, who planned to sail for Mexico in November, 1839, on the
Sabine. Before their departure from French soil, however, a coolness
arose between the two diplomats. Much to the indignation of the more
punctual Cyprey, Duflot de Mofras, for reasons not disclosed, non-
chalantly failed to arrive at the port until ten days after the time set for
their departure. This discourtesy caused a breach that was never
healed.[10]

During the year 1840 Duflot de Mofras traveled throughout Mexico.
After wintering at the Mexican capital, he began in the late spring the
first stages of his diplomatic journey, an inspection of the outlying
provinces of Mexico. While visiting Guadalajara, the aristocratic center
of Mexico, De Mofras unfortunately became embroiled with the local
police, who arrested him for wearing decorations rightfully worn only
by the highest officials of the Mexican army. This impudent prank, trivial
as it may seem, was the spark that ignited the embers of international
distrust.

A voluminous diplomatic correspondence between France and
Mexico now followed, a discussion wholly out of proportion to the

---

[10]Correspondence Politique, Méxique, Vol. XXI, folio 49, Cyprey to the Duc
de Dalmatie, Toulon, November 6, 1839.

seriousness of the offense. The French government held that the official standing of De Mofras should have protected him from molestation on the part of the Mexican authorities, and the Mexicans made a diplomatic issue of the affair that disclosed their fear of French encroachment in Mexico. The case was settled only after Mexico agreed to punish the querulous officials if France would reprimand De Mofras.[11]

The publicity attending this incident proved so far-reaching, and Mexican suspicions regarding the true motives of De Mofras' visit were aroused by this episode to such an extent that a local journal, *La Cosmopolite,* openly denounced his mission in a distinctly hostile manner. One aspect of the local embroglio was endless delay in issuing a passport for the French attaché to visit California, an indignity which, when brought to the attention of the French minister, caused him to decide to recall De Mofras to Paris. The official summons to return appears in the following letter, sent on January 10, 1841, by the French minister of foreign affairs to Baron de Cyprey in Mexico:[12]

"The situation of M. Duflot in respect to the French government, the real but absurd suspicions that his journey has aroused, the uneasy watchfulness that would follow him to California, and the restrictions, to say the least, that he would encounter in California, lead me to think that it would be difficult for him to carry out with any degree of success the mission that has been confided to him. I have therefore deemed it wise to terminate his mission and recall him to France, in case he has not already left Guadalajara for California."

De Mofras, however, refused to be swerved from the mission he had commenced. Despite diplomatic recalls and the embarrassing state of his own personal finances, he completed his Mexican tour. From Mazatlán, on the west coast, he sent the following report on conditions in Mexico to his home government.[13]

"I have recently visited a large part of Mexican territory and found the moral and political conditions deplorable; the people possess all the worst qualities of the Spaniards and few of their virtues. On all sides disorder, decay, and corruption to exceed anything known in Europe prevail. The North Americans, the English, and the Russians do not conceal their designs on Upper California. The British govern-

---

[11]The official correspondence regarding this affair is found in ibid, Vol. XXI, folios, 108-112; 117-121.

[12]Ibid, Vol. XX,, folio 9. Minister to Cyprey, Paris, Jan. 10, 1841.

[13]See Amérique, Vol. 43, Mémoire II, folio 108.

ment had a careful survey of this country made in 1828 and 1838 by Captains Beechey and Belcher, and a ship that came in from the Sandwich Islands a few days ago carried dispatches to the American consul from a Commodore [Wilkes] in command of a scientific expedition composed of five warships bound for Upper California and the Columbia River. Moreover, there is at Monterey an officer [Larkin] of the North American navy who acts as consular agent. The two Russian colonies on Mexican territory receive supplies from the ports of Kamchatka. All the information I have been able to gather from navigators and merchants represents New California as a land with an immense future, especially if Central America were to be traversed by a canal, or railroad. The magnificent ports of Monterey, San Diego, and San Francisco, surrounded by fertile lands, are, because of the direction of the winds, points of call for ships coming from China, the Philippines, and India. The establishment of French settlements along the northwest coast of America would probably prove advantageous for our commerce and our navy."

De Mofras' audacity in the face of official recall, and his terse letter concerning his plans that he sent to his superior, De Cyprey, which the latter forwarded to Paris, caused a definite rupture between these two officials.[14]

The agitation that arose in Mexico over the De Mofras incident served above all else to reveal the extent of Mexican fears of French, English, and American designs on the west coast. These fears were not unfounded. As early as 1836, definite evidence that the acquisition of California was agitating both French and English governmental circles appeared in the private correspondence that passed between Deffandis and Adolphe Thiers at Paris regarding Great Britain's attitude toward the Pacific Coast policy of the United States. England, these letters disclose, had a premonition that the latter power would soon expand toward the coast, absorb the whaling industry, acquire San Francisco Harbor, and ultimately take over the bulk of the trade with China.[15]

Approximately two years later, England and France again corresponded at some length on this same vital topic—the importance of the

---

[14]In Correspondence Politique, Mexique, Vol. XXI, folio 37. Cyprey to Guizot, Mexico, September 17, 1841.

[15]See ibid, Vol. X, folio 164 ff., especially letter of Pontois to Pageot, March 12, 1838.

Pacific Coast. In this correspondence the designs of Russia on California were gravely considered, and the point plainly made that the United States and England also appeared to covet these lands for themselves.

Mexican suspicions of the possibility of foreign settlements on the Pacific Coast were further aggravated to such an extent as to call for diplomatic correspondence when the French corvette, *La Danaïde*, engaged in making hydrographic surveys, reached the west coast. In fact, in the early decades of the nineteenth century several vessels had already visited the Pacific Coast without causing suspicion, notably the expeditions in command of Duhaut Cilly in 1827, Dupetit Thouars in 1837, and Cyrille La Place in 1839—but the advent of a French warship irritated Mexico, already unfavorably disposed toward France over local grievances that culminated in 1838 in the so-called Pastry War.

This irritation is clearly indicated in a letter from Baron de Cyprey to the Duc de Dalmatie, in which he writes:[16] "Mexico demands an official explanation of the presence of this ship; she suspects France of planning to recognize the independence of Texas, and believes that France intends to establish a base in California from which she can strike at the Russians near Ross."

Thus it may be seen that by 1840, as De Mofras' mission to the Far West reveals, French official circles had become fully alive to the growing importance of the Pacific Slope. They were aware that England, the United States, and possibly Russia had concrete designs on California. They knew, too, that Mexico and California were the seat of profound political unrest and that corruption, civil wars, financial crises, and a lack of sound leaders had come dangerously close to plunging these countries into chaos.

In California the problem of foreign encroachment, linked with political unrest, was at that time rapidly forcing a crisis. The first indication of dangerous international difficulties arose in the spring of 1840. Early in April of that year rumors circulated throughout Monterey that a group of traders and ex-sailors, led by a backwoodsman called Isaac Graham, were about to overthrow the governor of California, Juan Alvarado, and rob, plunder, and murder the local residents. Just how far these rumors were justified has long been a mooted question. But in any event they were sufficiently strong to arouse Governor Alvarado to immediate action. Generals Castro and Vallejo received

---

[16]Ibid, Vol. XVIII, folios 238 to 239. Cyprey to the Duc de Dalmatie, Mexico May 18, 1840.

orders to arrest all foreigners under suspicion living between Monterey and San Francisco and ship them out of the country. After a series of dramatic episodes, on April 29 a group of approximately forty of these suspects were put aboard ships at Monterey, and still other suspects were taken on the ship at Santa Bárbara, to be sent to the dungeons of San Blas and Tepic.

This high-handed act on the part of Californian officials focused international attention on California. The remaining foreigners, panic-stricken, appealed frantically to their home governments for assistance and protection. Among them was a group of Frenchmen who wrote on June 20, 1840, to Baron Cyprey[17] in Mexico requesting that a consul be sent to California to protect their interests.[18] This letter, signed by Remi Leroy Fourcade, expressed anxiety over the outcome of political intrigue in Mexico, and voiced fears that French citizens would be forced at the point of a gun to lend money, or would be herded aboard a ship and sent to Mexico.

Although no Frenchman had been arrested for suspicious conduct in California, yet this political incident called to the attention of France the extent to which the political kettle was already seething in California. On July 8, 1840, a full account of local conditions was sent by Rosamel, commander of the French corvette *Danaïde,* to Baron de Cyprey.[19] In his letter he voiced the belief that Governor Alvarado was well rid of the unwelcome foreigners, but adds significantly that many were convinced that this Governor had merely tried to give the Americans a pretext to take possession of California, that active adventurers from the United States had in mind the taking over of California, and that the French government should be so advised.

"By following these crooked paths," adds Rosamel, "the government of California has made this beautiful country as backward in its political and civil institutions as it is distant in its geographical position. Only one future," he points out significantly, "is possible for California; to become the prize of the first nation that will send two hundred armed men there." As he wrote, an American ship, the *St. Louis,* lay ominously at anchor in the harbor near his own vessel, while her commander, Captain Forrest, attempted to extract from the evasive Alvarado a reply

---

[17]Baron Alleye de Cyprey, French Minister to Mexico.

[18]Correspondence Politique, Méxique, Vol. XVIII, folio 135. Citizens of Monterey to Cyprey, June 20, 1840.

[19]Ibid, Vol. XIX, folios 138 to 140, Rosamel to Cyprey, July 8, 1840.

that would ease the strained relations existing between the United States and California, which had grown out of the Graham affair.

Definite interest on the part of England in the future of California appears to have been first aroused by an incident connected with the plot of Graham against the Alvarado government. At this time British subjects began to clamor for protection, and much to the chagrin of Eustace Barron, the British vice-consul at Tepic, England was forced to rely during the crisis upon American warships to protect British subjects in California. In the political correspondence that followed, the attention of English officials was directly focused on the value of Upper California. A concrete and forceful expression of the importance of this country is contained in the following letter, dated August 30, 1841, sent by Pakenham, the English Minister to Mexico, to Lord Palmerston in England:[20]

"It is much to be regretted that advantage should not be taken of the arrangement some time since concluded by the Mexican government with their creditors in Europe to establish an English population in the magnificent territory of Upper California . . . I believe there is no part of the world which offers greater natural advantages for the establishment of an English colony than the provinces of Upper California; while its commanding position on the Pacific, its fine forests of excellent timber for ship-building as well as for every other purpose, appear to me to render it by all means desirable, from a political point of view, that California once ceasing to belong to Mexico, should not fall into the hands of any power but England . . . in fact, there is some reason to believe that daring and adventurous speculators in the United States have already turned their thoughts in the direction of annexation of California."

Pakenham, as the result of long conversations with Forbes, who had lived in Upper California, and of correspondence with the zealous vice-consul, Eustace Barron, at length submitted a plan for the English to acquire California. The British Foreign Office, however, replied that the day for colonial enterprises had passed and that the Earl of Aberdeen[21] was not anxious for the foundation of new and distant colonies which would involve heavy direct and still heavier indirect expenditure, besides multiplying the liability of misunderstandings and collisions with other powers.

---

[20]See Ephraim D. Adams "English Interest in the Annexation of California" in **The American Historical Review**, Vol. XIV, No. 4, (July, 1909), pp. 745-763.
[21]Ibid, p. 747.

Yet this land, toward which the eyes of so many powers were turned, was almost a *terra incognita*. What few travelers had visited California reported it to be a sparsely populated and undeveloped country. Estimates of its population varied, but in all probability the inhabitants numbered fewer than 10,000, of whom several hundred were foreigners.

Santa Bárbara, the most aristocratic town on the coast, and San José each had not more than 1,000 inhabitants, while Nuestra Señora de Los Angeles had only 1,500 settlers. At Yerba Buena there were only a handful of houses and five to ten permanent residents. The capital, Monterey, had forty or fifty shabby houses and from 1,500 to 2,000 inhabitants. These poor Mexican settlements were confined to the coast and did not extend beyond San Francisco or east toward the mountains. North of the hamlet of Yerba Buena was the unprofitable Russian colony of Fort Ross, conceded to be a failure and about to be abandoned. A few scattered settlers lived in or near the Sacramento, but the majority of the interior waterways were, as De Mofras' map reveals, both unexplored and unknown. Since the secularization and plundering by the dishonest Mexican administrators of the old Spanish missions which had formed the basic wealth of California, this nucleus of wealth and culture had fallen into ruins.

Foreign interest, however, was centered on Monterey, the seat of a decadent Mexican rule, the hub of political activity in Upper California, and the home of the notorious governor, Juan B. Alvarado. To him flocked politicians seeking favors, foreigners asking land grants, and military leaders hoping to acquire material gain through the sponsoring of a civil war. That the governor was not unaware of conditions, appears in this excerpt from Dupetit Thouars' *Journal:*[22] "Alvarado," Thouar observes, "appears to feel keenly the precarious and unfortunate condition of California, too weak to be independent, and too backward in civilization to administer to its own needs."

Toward this seat of international conflict De Mofras now set sail from Mazatlán on the *Ninfa,* in command of Captain Fitch. He carried with him various letters of introduction to leading Mexican officials, prominent Californians, and important Catholic dignitaries. On May 6 his ship dropped anchor in Monterey, the point from which De Mofras began his peregrinations in California.

After spending five months in his official tour of inspection, which

---

[22]See Dupetit Thouars, **op. cit.,** II, 101.

is recorded at full length in his *Exploration,* on October 18 De Mofras left Yerba Buena, or San Francisco, on the *Cowlitz,* to inspect the English settlements in Oregon territory. After a short sojourn along the Columbia River, on December 30, accompanied by Sir George Simpson, John McLoughlin, and Horatio Hale, he returned to Yerba Buena.

Here Hale and De Mofras caught the *Bolivar* for Monterey, where the *Maryland,* Captain Pierce, bound for Mazatlán, rode at anchor. On the latter vessel De Mofras left Monterey on January 3, 1842, for Mexico, stopping en route at Santa Bárbara and San Diego.

The colorful and dynamic personality of the youthful French writer has become almost traditional in California and has given rise to a mass of conflicting rumors as to the true character of the French diplomat. He appears to have made many warm friends on the coast, but also an equal number of vindictive enemies. Among the former were the mission Fathers, whose esteem and veneration he never failed to win. He was equally popular with the Spanish señoritas, whom he won by his wit, vivacity, and charm.

Among the close friendships formed by De Mofras in California was that with Nathan Spear, at whose home on the northwest corner of Clay and Montgomery Streets De Mofras lived while in San Francisco. Spear's nephew, William Heath Davis, recounts many illuminating and amusing anecdotes of this visit in his volume on California.[23]

From De Mofras' *Mémoires* it seems obvious that largely through his influence Fort Ross, which the Russians had urged the French attaché to purchase on behalf of the French government, a purchase that De Mofras actually recommended to the French Minister in Paris, was finally acquired by a shrewd Swiss pioneer called Sutter. At this period Sutter was prone to represent himself as a French citizen, and even confided in his friend, Jacob Leese, that he would be protected by French frigates on the coast.[24]

On the other hand, the French attaché appears to have aroused the bitter antipathy of many leading Californians, especially that of the dignified General Vallejo[25] at Sonoma, of his brother, Salvador,[26] and

---

[23]William Heath Davis, **Seventy-five Years in California,** (San Francisco, 1929) p. 52 ff. He is mistaken in the year of De Mofras' arrival in California, which was not 1840, but 1841.

[24]Mariano Vallejo, **Documentos para la Historia de California,** X, (1841) no. 322, Sutter to Leese, November 8, 1841. MS, Bancroft Library.

[25]Mariano Vallejo, in his **Historia de California** IV, (1839-1845) no. 246 writes that Duflot de Mofras came west to incite the citizens of California to join in a movement to annex their land to France.

[26]Salvador Vallejo, **Notas Históricas,** pp. 128 to 129. MS. Bancroft Library.

of other leading politicians. He was accused of being a spy, the bastard son of a king, and a French traitor. He also appears to have been embroiled with the natives of Mission San Antonio, which resulted in an unpleasant scandal. Governor Alvarado, who recognized his ability, comments as follows on his arrogance:

"The Señor Conde Duflot de Mofras," he wrote,[27] "is a youth of good literary reputation, of an impetuous character and generous instincts; but unfortunately he arrived among us imbued with false ideas about our character. He believes that the inhabitants of this country are brutal Indians whose duty it is to prostrate themselves before him, and that the Count should hesitate to allow them to be honored with his presence."

Far less flattering than the mild opprobrium of Alvarado is the testimony of Señora de la Guerra Hartnell, at whose rancho, "Alisal," near Monterey, De Mofras was a guest. Señora Hartnell describes a sojourn of several days made by De Mofras at "Alisal," where he came into the *casa* without waiting outside for the customary invitation extended to strangers in a land as yet devoid of hostelries. Making himself at home with a self-assurance and boldness that included ordering of servants and the clandestine consumption of the Father Confessor's special wine, he drank himself into a state of stupor so profound that he was confined for several days to his apartment. His ingratitude toward the kindly Señora, who nursed him through his convalescence, so incensed this patrician Spanish lady that she denounced him soundly in her *Narrativa* published many years later.[28]

No hint of these escapades or of his personal relations with the prominent foreigners with whom he came into contact, appears, however, in the pages of his *Exploration*. His record is thorough and sound, the record of a scholar concerned mainly with world politics and international problems of the first magnitude. That his visit and its object did not, however, escape the attention of rival nations, appears in the political correspondence of that period.

De Mofras, in turn, was watching with keen interest all British and American manoeuvers in this important territory, for, by a curious coincidence, both the United States and England had personal representatives at this time inspecting the Far West. The former power was

---

[27]See **Historia de Alvarado**, IV (1838-1842) p. 175 ff. MS. Bancroft Library.
[28]See Señora de la Guerra Hartnell, **Narrativa**, p. 14 ff. MS. Bancroft Library.

represented by Lieutenant Charles Wilkes, who was making a five-year tour of the world; the latter in an ex-officio capacity, by Sir George Simpson, governor of the Hudson's Bay Company.

As his writings disclose, De Mofras knew these two men intimately. Accompanied by Governor Simpson, he visited the English, the American, and the French-Canadian settlements along the Willamette and heard the Englishman remark that England would go to war rather than compromise on the boundary issue. With similar frankness the American leader, Charles Wilkes, told De Mofras that the United States would fight rather than accept any boundary but the forty-ninth parallel.[29] Out of these American-British complications the Frenchman hoped a new and independent government would be formed in Canada whose sympathies would lean toward France.

The relations of Wilkes and De Mofras were, to all outward appearances, courteous and cordial. A distinct coldness appears, on the contrary, to have arisen between the Englishman and the Frenchman, a breach intensified by the unfortunate fact that they were obliged to travel together under adverse and taxing conditions from Fort Vancouver to San Francisco. Leaving the British settlement on November 30, 1841, De Mofras and Simpson with a boat and ten men descended the Columbia, swollen with early rains, to Fort George. Here on December 3 they boarded the *Cowlitz,* only to be forced to remain behind the storm-tossed bar for two weeks.

The private letters to Sir George, referring to the visit of the American, Wilkes,[30] and the Frenchman, De Mofras, to his head fort on the Columbia, throw an interesting light on the attitude of the Hudson's Bay Company toward the subtle investigations of these obviously unwelcome visitors. In an important communication, dated March 10, 1842, Sir George Simpson wrote to John Pelly as follows:[31]

"Commodore Wilkes was by no means communicative on the subject of these surveys and examinations, but I gathered from a very intelligent and confidential member of the expedition that it was the intention of Commodore Wilkes to recommend strongly to his government to claim the whole territory on the shores of the Northern Pacific,

---

[29]See **Amérique**, Vol. 44, Mémoire IX, folio 222.

[30]Wilkes held the rank of lieutenant until 1843 when he became a commander. In 1855 he was made captain, in 1862, commodore, and in 1866, rear admiral on the retired list.

[31]See Letters of Sir George Simpson, 1841-1843 in **The American Historical Review**, Vol. XIV, (October, 1908) p. 86 ff., where this letter is quoted in full.

from the Mexican northern boundary in lat. 42° to the Russian southern boundary in lat. 54° 40′ . . . . but I trust you will urge H. M. government not to consent to any boundary which would give to the U. S. any portion of the territory north of the Columbia River. This country, which is of great extent and possesses advantages of soil and climate unrivaled perhaps in any part of the world is in the hands of a very few indolent Californians. The country might become invaluable to Great Britain as an outlet for her surplus population, and as a stronghold and protection to her commerce and interests on the seas, and as a market for her manufacturers; as the principal people in the country, and indeed the whole population, seem anxious to be released from the Republic of Mexico, which can afford them neither protection nor assistance, and are apprehensive that they may fall within the grasp of the United States. . ."

Sir George regarded with equal disfavor signs of French interest in this fertile coast, as revealed by the visit of the young Frenchman.[32]

After thus successfully completing what proved to be a self-appointed mission, De Mofras was back in Mexico City by March, stopping there en route to Vera Cruz, from which port he set sail for France.[33] His appearance in Mexico revived old suspicions of his mission. The British vice-consul, Barron, wrote from Tepic in December, 1842, that De Mofras occupied himself while in Monterey in endeavoring to persuade the authorities and inhabitants of California to put themselves under the protection of the French government.[34]

Extreme as the British vice-consul's viewpoint undoubtedly was, yet in its essence Duflot de Mofras' visit may properly be considered as a quest for colonial possessions in the Far West. This was the motive behind his minute analysis of ports, resources, industries, international politics, local conditions, and future possibilities of the lands visited; this was what inspired his detailed descriptions of the Russian settlements in Alaska and on the Sandwich Islands, his minute record of English trading posts, and his study of diplomatic moves by foreign

---

[32]Ibid, p. 81, ff.

[33]**Correspondence Politique, Méxique,** Vol. XXI, folio 274. Cyprey to Guizot, March 22, 1842.

[34]For an interesting and scholarly discussion of De Mofras' rôle in the menace of French imperialism on the Pacific see Rufus Kay Wyllys, "French Imperialists in California" in **California Historical Society Quarterly,** Vol. VIII, No. 2 (June, 1929), pp. 116 to 129.

powers. What France hoped to gain is revealed in an illuminating manner by this excerpt from his *Mémoire*:[35]

"Obviously France has never been in a more propitious position than she now is to replace the deplorable loss of Canada and Louisiana. Already mistress of the Marquesas and Tahiti, she could materially enhance her power by assuring herself of one of the Sandwich Islands, by purchasing the settlement at Port Bodega, which would be a preliminary step toward acquiring the entire harbor of San Francisco, the key to the Pacific Ocean; by grouping around this the French-Spanish Catholics of the country, by opening to our countrymen who are constantly going out to settle in the United States, Buenos Ayres, and Chile, a vast field for national colonization, and by establishing on a continent over which our flag has so long floated, a *New French America!*"

Upon reaching Paris, De Mofras was honored by many of the learned societies of the day. He was asked to speak before the Société Royal de Géographie, before which, on December 30, 1842, he read an excerpt from his travels which was published in the bulletin of the Society the following year with the title *Fragment d'un Voyage en Californie.*[36]

During the next year De Mofras was engaged in revising his *Mémoires* containing information collected during his travels in America, into form suitable for publication. The work was published in two volumes[37] in 1844 by Arthur Bertrand in Paris and dedicated to the Duc de Dalmatie, former Minister of Foreign Affairs.[38] An elaborate atlas of plates and maps accompanied the volumes. His task, as indicated by the letter that accompanied the completed manuscript, seems to have been completed by the middle of the previous year.

What De Mofras brought to the attention of the French govern-

---

[35]Amérique, Vol. 44, Mémoire IX, folio 245. See also George Verne Blue, "Unpublished Portions of the Mémoires of Duflot de Mofras," in Proceedings of the Pacific Coast Branch of the American Historical Association for 1928, pp. 89-102.

[36]In Bulletin de la Société de Géographie, Deuxième Série, Vol. XIX, No. 109, (January, 1843).

[37]Exploration du territoire De l'Orégon, des Californies, et de la mer Vermeille, exécutée pendant les années 1840, 1841, and 1842. Ouvrage publié par ordre du roi, sous les auspices de M. le Maréchal Soult, duc de Dalmatie, Président du Conseil, et de M. le Ministre des Affaires Étrangères, (2 vols. and atlas, Paris, 1844). The edition is now extremely rare.

[38]See Amérique Vol. 43 Mémoire I, folios 3 and 4. De Mofras to Guizot, July 24, 1843. In the course of this letter De Mofras observes that the extra expenses entailed by the expedition and for preparing the manuscript have cost him 20,000 francs personally, but that he does not regret this sacrifice if the manuscript meets with his approbation and is of value to France.

xxxii DUFLOT DE MOFRAS'

ment in his volumes heightened its interest in the Far West. He pointed out the need for more adequate protection for French citizens on the coast, especially a consulate backed by frequent visits from French warships; he indicated the commercial possibilities for French vessels in Pacific waters; and he suggested ways and means whereby France might acquire possessions on the Pacific. At the same time he clearly exposed the power and political ambitions of England, also the steady influx of Americans toward the west.

Although certain sections dealing with French imperial designs were omitted from the published volumes,[39] yet De Mofras' mission, and his *Mémoires* supplemented by the diplomatic correspondence of the period,[40] unmistakably reveal that by the time these volumes were published, French designs on the Pacific, especially on Mexico, California, and the Hawaiian Islands, were both concrete and definite.

How extensive and far-reaching these designs had grown is succinctly set forth in the correspondence of Baron de Cyprey, French ambassador to Mexico, and Guizot,[41] Minister of Foreign Affairs for France. After discussing what they called France's mission to regenerate Mexico and give her the government she needed and the benefits of their own superior civilization, they visualized the easy conquest of California, to be accomplished by sending French soldiers from the Marquesas and Society Islands, and around the Horn from France, also the ultimate extension of French sway to other Pacific Islands.

De Mofras' official report, however, came too late. The tide of American emigration was already engulfing the west, sweeping over Texas, California, and Oregon Territory.

The publication of his volumes raised De Mofras to a prominent place in the realm of historical writing. Here, for the first time, was a complete, concise, and scholarly survey of the entire Pacific Coast, based on first-hand observation and personal experience. In a review of his volumes published in the *Journal des Débats* for February 26, 1845, the critic, F. Barrère, wrote, "He is a man of sound judgment and keen

---

[39]See infra, p. 1*.

[40]See Abraham P. Nasatir, "The French Consulate in California," in **Quarterly of the California Historical Society**: Vol. XI, No. 3 (Sept. 1932) pp. 195-223; No. 4 (Dec. 1932) pp. 339-357: Vol. XII, No. 1 (March, 1933) pp. 35-64); No. 2 (June, 1933) pp. 155-172; No. 4 (Dec. 1933) pp. 331-357: Vol. XIII No. 1 (March, 1934) pp. 56-79; No. 2 (June, 1934) pp. 160-175; No. 3 (Sept. 1934) pp. 262-280; No. 4 (Dec. 1934) pp. 355-385.

[41]**Correspondence Politique Méxique** Vol. XXVI, folios 291 to 296. Cyprey to Guizot, Mexico, May 21, 1844.

intellect, a courageous traveler, and an enlightened observer." In America the leading historians of California, Hubert Howe Bancroft and Theodore Hittell, also speak in terms of highest praise of his *Exploration*.

The success of his published volumes gained for De Mofras a widespread recognition as an able writer on political topics of his day. In 1845 *La Presse,* and in 1846 *La Revue Nouvelle,* carried articles by this rising young diplomat, who soon became a regular contributor to leading French journals.[42] Interest in foreign affairs led him to travel extensively, especially in Italy and Germany and even as far as Rio de Janeiro, where some of his most interesting letters were written.

Many of De Mofras' trips were of a semi-political nature, for during his absence he sent back to France extensive reports of political conditions in these various countries. Some insight into the breadth of his interests is afforded by the wide variety of titles found among his writings for the year 1850, which include *Mémoire on the State of Upper Italy, Notes on the Armament of Germany and Russia,* and a letter to Princess Mathilde in Paris describing a visit he had made to her uncle, the King, in Germany.

Many articles, book reviews, and essays on literature and travel by De Mofras also appeared in the Paris *Moniteur,* to which he contributed regularly a column called Correspondances Étrangères. Later a series of his political articles dealing with Spain, Portugal, Cuba, Belgium, Prussia, Russia, and Morocco appeared in *La France,* the official journal of the French empire, and in *Le Moniteur*. A departure from his purely political writings are his translations from the Spanish of the *Romances Históricos* of the Duque de Rivas, former Spanish ambassador to Paris.

Throughout these years De Mofras' interest in the Far West never waned. The gold-rush brought forth some vigorous articles on California from his fluent pen, and in *Le Constitutionne* for January 29, 1849, he warns his government of the danger of sending ships to California. Two months later, in a long article entitled *La Californie* that appeared in the *Journal de Toulouse* for March 28, 1849,[43] he gives at considerable length for the benefit of emigrants a survey of conditions in the gold

---

[42]See his "Saint Domingue" in La Revue Nouvelle, Vol. VII, (March 1, 1846) pp. 451-464; "Le Méxique et Les Etats Unis" in Vol. IX, (June 1, 1846), pp. 1-51; "La Grande Bretagne," Vol. X, (Sept. 15, 1846) pp. 606-626; and L'Esprit du Siècle," Vol. XII, (Dec. 15, 1846) pp. 165-179.

[43]"La Californie" appeared in the Journal de Toulouse, March 28, 1849; "l'Orégon" in ibid, April 25, 1849.

fields, warning travelers of the costs, hardships, and doubtful outcome of a journey to El Dorado.

Then, for a time, from 1862 to 1863, his interest was concentrated once more on Mexico, and he wrote extensively for the columns of *Le Moniteur* of this period on the political, economic, and historic interest of the country, possibly in preparation for another volume which, however, was never published. His final work was a compilation of his various articles and reviews into two volumes that appeared in 1878 and 1880.[44] In 1880 De Mofras had reached the age of seventy and about this time his literary activities appear to have ceased. His death occurred in 1884.

The following English rendition has been based on Duflot de Mofras' *Exploration du territoire de l'Orégon, des Californies, et de la Mer Vermeille,* collated with a transcription of his ten original *Mémoires,* on which the French publication was based, now housed in the office of the Ministère des Affaires Étrangères, in Paris, and further compared with a supplementary holographic manuscript of certain portions dealing with Fort Ross, found in his *Mélanges,* Volume II. Any changes and variations from the French publication have been so indicated in footnotes and in important unpublished sections from the *Mélanges* arranged to form appendices.[45]

Collateral material has been found in the official French diplomatic correspondence covering the period of Duflot de Mofras' explorations, in the manuscript narratives of Mariano Vallejo, Salvador Vallejo, Juan Alvarado, Señora de la Guerra Hartnell, in the Departmental State Papers in the Bancroft Library, and in contemporary volumes in the Huntington Library.

In the preparation of these volumes for the press, invaluable assistance has been received from many sources. First and foremost was the generous offer of Dr. Abraham P. Nasatir of the State Teachers' College in San Diego, of his English translation of the complete file of the French-Mexican consular and diplomatic correspondence covering the period from 1836 to 1846. This material, procured by Dr. Nasatir dur-

---

[44]For a complete list of his published works see **Catalogue Général de la Bibliothèque Nationale Auteurs**, Vol. CXVI, pp. 250-254, and Duflot de Mofras' **Mélanges,** MS. Bancroft Library; also Appendix D.

[45]Duflot de Mofras' personal scrap books, nine large volumes known as Duflot de Mofras' **Mélanges,** containing clippings of his own writings, as well as information on important topics of the day, were presented by the French historian to Hubert Howe Bancroft, and are now housed in the Bancroft Library at Berkeley, California. See Appendices A, B, and D.

ing a two years' residence in Paris, has been extensively drawn upon for this Introduction.

Appreciation is also hereby expressed to Count Serge Fleury, who supervised the transcription of the original Mémoires of Duflot de Mofras, housed in the office of the Ministère des Affaires Étrangères in Paris.

The rare volumes of De Mofras' *Exploration* were generously loaned through the courtesy of Miss Susanna Ott and Miss Laura C. Cooley of the Los Angeles Public Library. Members of the staff of the Henry E. Huntington Library at San Mariano have also rendered constant assistance on various points connected with the editing of these volumes, and have made available many rare volumes dealing with this same period, including the De Mofras atlas.

Mr. H. D. Parizeau, of Victoria, British Columbia, head of the Canadian Hydrographic Service, has supplied important data, not otherwise procurable, regarding the history and location of ports on Vancouver Island. Information regarding Russian activities in Hawaii has been given by A. P. Kashevaroff, curator of the Territory of Alaska Historical Library and Museum at Juneau, Alaska, and Russian spelling has been checked by Mr. George Kern, Mrs. N. Kovediaeff, and Mr. Elijah Avin of Los Angeles. Considerable information about the ownership of ranchos in the vicinity of Los Angeles has been furnished by Mr. C. Palmer Connor. Among others who have proved helpful are Dr. and Mrs. Henry R. Wagner of San Marino, Dr. Garland C. Greever and Dr. John C. Parish of Los Angeles, and Miss Mabel R. Gillis of the State Library at Sacramento.

The task of reading the entire manuscript was generously undertaken by Dr. Frederick Webb Hodge, Director of the Southwest Museum and a noted authority on the history of the Southwest, whose courteous coöperation is deeply appreciated. Miss Margaret Baker of Pasadena has also kindly read the entire manuscript and made constructive criticisms and suggestions.

In the editing of any work, especially one written in a foreign language, difficult problems invariably arise. The De Mofras writings have proved unusually complicated because of the wide variety of foreign names—French, Spanish, and Russian—involved. To retain them as originally written would have entailed a large number of cumbersome explanatory brackets. In an effort to make the narrative as simple as possible, the plan followed in the accompanying translation was to render all names into their English equivalents wherever possible, or in some instances into the Spanish form used throughout the West. For instance, De Mofras, as a French writer, uses the French form for all western missions and towns, but these have been rendered into their Spanish equivalents, by which they are now universally known. Where identification of names was doubtful, the original French form has been retained and an explanatory footnote given.

MARGUERITE EYER WILBUR

Pasadena
April, 1937

FOREWORD

The author of this important work was an acute observer who embraced every opportunity to acquire knowledge that would add to the interest of his quest. Perhaps chargeable with prolixity, due probably to his training in diplomacy from the time he was eighteen years of age, it was the evident intention of young Eugène Duflot de Mofras to err on the side of fulness rather than to omit anything of potential usefulness to his native France or to one reader or another. Consequently he embodied in his work a very wide range of information, gathered from personal observation or derived immediately from the people of the vast territory which he traversed, or from authoritative books of the period. In this way our author gathered information on a great variety of subjects pertaining to Mexico, California, the Northwest Coast, and Russian America. He was interested in everything from the physical features of the land to the prospects of trade and commerce, natural history, the character of the people, political intrigue, diplomatic relations, the Californian missions, before and after their secularization; the native tribes, their customs, beliefs, and languages, together with a host of other matters, of great practical importance at the time, which, moreover, have lost nothing of their historical significance even today.

This brief Foreword should not be closed without a word regarding the translator and editor, whose previous works of a similar tenor are now known to a wide audience. In the present volume she has performed her task in the same excellent manner. Students are indebted to her for making this addition to her considerable list of worth while productions.

F. W. HODGE

Southwest Museum
Los Angeles

CHAPTER CONTENTS

LIST OF ILLUSTRATIONS

DUFLOT DE MOFRAS'
TRAVELS ON THE
PACIFIC COAST

In this work a geographical order, from north to south, has been followed and, after a brief survey of the circumstances that led to the separation of the provinces of New Spain from the yoke of the Catholic Kings, the section of Mexico and the Northwest Coast that extends from the Isthmus of Tehuantepec to Bering Strait will be described.

CHAPTER I*

INTRODUCTION

Status of Mexico under Spanish rule. History of the revolution. Present conditions. Political problems.

Mexico has suffered far more deeply from the tragic effects of the new political era known as Independence than any of the old viceroyalties of Spanish America. In fact, the prosperity and tranquillity that at one time were universal throughout New Spain have now been superseded by constant unrest, widespread misery, and definite signs of disintegration. After 1824, in the wake of the ephemeral reign of Emperor Iturbide,[1] calamities bred of the struggle against the mother country were augmented by the disasters born of civil wars waged by the rebels.

The final blow to Mexican prosperity fell in the year 1827 when the Federal Congress decreed that Spanish Europeans who had escaped assassination should be expelled. With them disappeared the captains of industry, men who represented the backbone of commerce and the wealth of the land. Driven out by this fatal law, the leading merchants left the country and remained permanently abroad. Wealthy landowners and important officials who possessed vast wealth sent their capital to England, France, Spain, and the United States. All developments of any importance were thus suspended; the rich land of Mexico, with her

---

*Duflot de Mofras' ten **Mémoires**, on which the published volumes were based, are housed in the office of the Ministère des Affaires Étrangerès in Paris. These are found in Volumes 43 and 44 entitled **Mémoires et Documents Amérique** (hereafter cited as Amérique). The first six **Mémoires** (vol. 43), correspond to Vol. I, and the last four (vol. 44), to Vol. II, of the published version or **Exploration.** Except for the first two chapters of Vol. I and the first chapter of Vol. II, the manuscript **Mémoires** do not differ materially from the **Exploration.** For chapters I and II, see Vol. 43, **Amérique,** folios 30 to 50. These have been completely rewritten and the published version contains an elaborate historical background not found in the **Mémoires.**

[1]Agustín de Iturbide (1783-1825) was a colonel in the Spanish army. His manifesto, or edict, of February 24, 1821, known as the Plan of Iguala, proposed that Mexico become independent under a Spanish prince. Many revolutionists favored this plan, but Ferdinand VII declined to accept the crown. For a time Iturbide served as emperor, only to be deposed by the republicans led by Santa Anna. For Iturbide and other Mexican leaders mentioned throughout this chapter see H. H. Bancroft, **History of Mexico (6 vols. San Francisco, 1883-88);** H. G. Ward, **Mexico in 1827 (2 vols. London, 1828);** Lucas Alamán, **Historía de Méjico (5 vols.** Mexico, 1852); and Alexander von Humboldt, **Political Essay on the Kingdom of New Spain (4 vols.** London, 1811).

mineral wealth, favorable geographical situation, and ports on the two major oceans, now became largely sterile. What was left to this impoverished country by way of compensation for its disasters and errors, was nothing more than an idle and sonorous word called liberty.

The Spanish régime, on the other hand, brought prosperity to Mexico by establishing certain basic conditions that tended to create a stable government and a thriving race. A large navy, adequate fortifications, a well-disciplined army, a sound and vigilant government, salutary municipal laws, a sound financial position—these were her achievements and the foundation of her strength.

Hernán Cortés[2] and Charles V[3] promulgated the first sound laws governing colonization. Philip II,[4] whose political views were both sound and broad, subsequently laid the foundation for the Laws of the Indies. Perfected by Philip V, the work was gradually continued until, under the glorious reign of Charles III, amazing development was achieved. Finally, a powerful minister, the Count of Aranda,[5] became alarmed when he saw the United States throw off the yoke of England and declare its independence. Aware that the Spanish colonies, inspired by this example, might at some future time sever their own bonds with the motherland, at the risk of incurring royal disfavor he called this perilous situation to the attention of his sovereign. Guided by his wise arguments and clear foresight, Charles III seriously considered the advisability of incorporating the American viceroyalties into kingdoms and placing on these thrones the infantes of Spain. By reserving for himself the title of Emperor of the Indies, he could thus place the kings of his family in the position of vassals and, by retaining in Spain all future regulation of their interests, Madrid could be made the supreme center and seat of authority.

----

[2]The Spanish conqueror, Hernán or Hernando Cortés (1485-1547), landed at Mexico in 1519. For a time the natives revered him as a supernatural being; but he soon proved his mortal vein by throwing their leader, Montezuma, in irons, only releasing him upon payment of heavy ransom. By 1521, after a series of battles, he had conquered Mexico. The tale of his amazing achievements has been aptly told by a fellow-soldier, Bernal Díaz del Castillo, in his **Historía Verdadera de la Conquista de la Nueva España** (Madrid, 1632).

[3]Throughout his reign, Charles V (1500-1558) kept in close contact with the conquerors of America, attempting above all else to protect the natives and prevent slavery. The organization of Spanish America is one of his greatest achievements.

[4]Under Philip II (1527-1598) laws covering many decades were compiled in 1680 into what was known as the **Recopilación de Leyes de los Reinos de las Indias,** a monopolistic code designed for the administration of the colonies.

[5]Pedro Pablo Abarca y Boleo, Count of Aranda (1719-1799), was a prominent Spanish statesman and diplomat who served as president of the Council of Castile.

Unfortunately this plan, so pregnant with possibilities—since it would have rendered unassailable at all times Spanish control over its colonies in America—was abandoned. To Charles III neither the time nor the opportunity seemed ripe for its execution. The policy of this prince, notwithstanding, was constantly directed toward achieving a closer union between Spanish America and the motherland. With this end in view a personal bodyguard composed exclusively of young Americans belonging to distinguished families was created. This move, irrespective of the advantages it afforded in the event of a revolution in Mexico to Charles III by having in his ranks the flower of young manhood from Spanish America, had the important advantage of initiating the latter into European manners and of establishing a closer bond between the two races. Unfortunately the successors of Charles III inherited his power without his ability, and under Ferdinand VII this guard ceased to function.

The tempest that broke over the peninsula as the result of the French Revolution, the feeble administration of Charles IV, and, above all, the intrigues of England and the United States in America, imperceptibly weakened the ties between New Spain and the Old World.

The first cry of independence, raised in 1810, was easily stifled.[6] In 1814, however, the movement became more pronounced. Finally, in 1820, it acquired definite force when several Spanish generals, Xavier Mina,[7] Echeverría,[8] Arana,[9] and Negrete,[10] deserted the royal flag and supported the insurgents, who thus received the benefit of their vast military knowledge and the discipline so direly needed. The direct respon-

---

[6]Mexican independence was an aftermath of the French revolution, with its new doctrine of "liberty, equality, and fraternity," and was directly caused by the placement by Napoleon of his brother Joseph on the Spanish throne. Politicians of New Spain, aided by the priest Hidalgo, attempted to secure certain rights and privileges for the lower classes. A revolution ensued, but was put down in 1811 and its leaders executed. Hidalgo's cause was embraced by Morelos, who was able to assemble a congress, issue a declaration of Independence, and draft a constitution. By 1820 a definite break with Spain was imminent.

[7]Francisco Xavier Mina (1789-1817) was a noted Spanish leader who in 1814 rose against Ferdinand VII. Organizing, in England and the United States, an expedition to aid Mexican patriots, in 1817 he reached Mexico and defeated the Spanish forces.

[8]José Antonio Echeverría, at one time an ally of Iturbide, formed and became president of a revolutionary military junta, but was later forced into exile.

[9]General Gregorio Arana also belonged to this Spanish group, and was executed for his political activities.

[10]Another royalist leader was Pedro Celestino Negrete, noted for his zeal and severity. Negrete subsequently joined the revolutionists under Echeverría, with whom he was later exiled.

sibility for this fiasco may be laid at the door of Ferdinand VII[11] who, deposed for a time in Spain, had welcomed the absolutist party with open arms, exiled the liberals, turned against his most devoted generals, and abused the very men who had rallied to the support of his throne.

Spanish officials who happened to be living in Spanish America during these persecutions were indignant at a system that served to stifle the glories of the realm. This sentiment won them over to the ranks of the insurgents, and while it did not exonerate their conduct, yet at least it provided extenuating circumstances. Many of the generals vainly attempted to remain loyal to the cause of their motherland. Don José de la Cruz,[12] Calleja,[13] Novella,[14] Venegas,[15] and Trujillo[16] all waged a futile fight to save the throne. But fortune favored the revolution, and, early in 1822, the definite break came.[17] This was a day crowned by folly and expiated by years of disaster.

An entirely new status of affairs was now essential in order to mitigate the stigma of what had occurred. Incorporated in an edict promulgated against Spain were bitter accusations to the effect that American-born Spaniards had received scant consideration; that favoritism was shown to Spanish Europeans. Most of these charges, however, were false. Self-protection, irrespective of justice, had compelled the government at Madrid to avoid any semblance of favoritism in order to create a closer relationship between the two races. Sensing the wisdom of such a course, Spain put this policy into effect. Definite proof of the wisdom of this move is revealed by the fact that even at the present day many

---

[11]Ferdinand VII (1784-1833), who had been forced to abdicate in 1808 by Napoleon, returned to power in 1814. He abolished the liberal constitution of 1812, restored the Inquisition, and embraced the absolutist or apostolical party.

[12]José de la Cruz was one of the associates of Venegas by whom he was made comandante general of New Galicia. He took an active part against the revolutionists.

[13]Calleja del Rey (1750-1820), who defeated Hidalgo near Guadalajara and subsequently Morelos at Cuantla, served from 1813 to 1816 as viceroy of Mexico.

[14]Mariscal Francisco Novella, a grandee of Old Spain, became viceroy in 1822. Bancroft discusses his career at length in **Mexico**, IV, 718-731.

[15]Francisco Xaviêr de Venegas reached Mexico in 1810, where he entered upon his duties as viceroy. For many years as lieutenant colonel in the Spanish army, he had been conspicuous as a leader. Though an honest, capable, and energetic viceroy, he arrived in New Spain too late to attempt to stem the revolution already fomented by Hidalgo.

[16]Torcuato Trujillo who had accompanied Venegas to Mexico, was in charge of stemming Hidalgo's advances, but proved a failure as a soldier. His conduct during campaigns against the revolutionists brands him a villain and a traitor. These leaders were unable to save the royalist movement. On July 21, 1822, Iturbide became emperor.

[17]Royalist control, however, was soon lost. On February 24, 1822, the first Mexican Constituent Congress convened.

eminent men who were born in America are taking an active part in the affairs of the Spanish government.

The claim of imaginary cruelties inflicted on the Indians is of as little weight. Although during the early days of the conquest, a certain amount of violence was inevitable, subsequently the Spanish régime faithfully endeavored to spread among the natives the teachings of Catholicism, the fundamentals of instruction, and the blessings of tranquillity. In fact, in the most important Mexican centers royal colleges called *Reales Colegios de Indios nobles* were founded for Indians of noble birth and here sons from families of leading chiefs were educated at the King's expense. Even today throughout New Spain village Indians educated, happy, and governed in a fraternal manner by the local Fathers, will be constantly encountered. Often in the immediate vicinity villages of half-breeds exist where the natives live in abject poverty with arid lands on every hand. Lacking the restraint of wise laws, morals have grown extremely lax; and misery, linked to a false patriotism, tends invariably to breed vice.

Furthermore, Spain did not inflict cruel treatment on her colonies, but was, on the contrary, kind and tolerant. Whereas the Anglo-Saxon race annihilated the unfortunate natives of Pennsylvania, New England, and the Carolinas,[18] Spanish missionaries substituted the priest's staff for the conqueror's sword, and civilized the Indians on behalf of Spain by the sheer force of religion, intelligence, and mercy.

Europeans have no conception of the grandeur these Spanish-American cities have retained despite the depredations of war and the neglect to which they have been subjected by a political situation devoid of stability. They have even preserved some semblance of order and civic government. This fact is readily explained by recalling that in Spain, as in her colonial possessions, central power was limited in scope. The provinces themselves administered their own revenues and their interests were safeguarded by admirable municipal laws. To know Spain at the peak of her affluence, traces and indications of her power must be sought in her American colonies. Upon viewing what remains of her remarkable prosperity, it would seem that this nation, groaning under

---

[18]When the Europeans arrived, the Indian population of English-speaking America was sixteen millions; today [1840] it is two millions. (D. de M.). As a matter of fact, at about the time of the discovery of America the total Indian population of America north of Mexico was only about one million. Initials here and throughout the volumes indicate notes by Duflot de Mofras in the original French text.—ed.

the weight of her own wealth, had been forced to find an outlet abroad
for her excess strength and vitality. Such, in brief, was the status of
New Spain under central control. A discussion of Mexico during the
days of independence now follows.

Not long after Iturbide entered Mexico at the head of a rebel army,
the Constituent Congress convened and in May, 1822, nominated this
general emperor. Soon, however, the jealousy of his comrades-at-arms
conspired to cause his downfall. After a few months of power, he was
dethroned, exiled, and outlawed. A supreme triumvirate, composed of
Generals Bravo,[19] Michelena,[20] and Victoria,[21] now retained control
of Mexico until the latter was elected the first president.

At Victoria's request, Iturbide, who although in exile cherished hope
of regaining power, left Europe and in July, 1824, disembarked near
Tampico. There he placed himself under the protection of the local
governor, General Lagarza,[22] The latter gave him a hearty welcome,
showered him with favors, invited him to sit at his table, and then, an
hour later, called a priest to hear his last confession. Victim of his own
credulity, the unfortunate Iturbide was now dishonorably shot to death.

General Victoria continued to hold the presidency until 1828 when
he was replaced by Pedraza,[23] who had been legally elected to office.
Surrounded by constant intrigues and fierce rivalry, the latter, however,
was soon deposed and forced to escape. With a price on his head he now
fled from Mexico, disguised as a monk. Pedraza was succeeded by
Guerrero,[24] who was elevated to the presidency by the federalist party. In

---

[19]Nicolas Bravo (1787-1854) espoused the cause of Morelos and resisted the
Spaniards until 1817 when he was captured. In 1821 he joined Iturbide, only to
become his enemy and aid in his downfall. For a time he served as vice-president
of Mexico, but upon leading a rebellion against President Victoria was captured
and banished. He later returned and joined Santa Anna's council.

[20]José Mariano de Michelena was closely associated with Bravo and Negrete
in governmental offices. For a time during the absence of Victoria, he was in
charge of the government and under Bustamante held the portfolio of war and
navy.

[21]Juan Felix Fernández, known as Guadalupe Victoria (1789-1843), aided the
War of Independence, later assisting in the overthrow of Iturbide. From 1824 to
1829 he served as the first president of Mexico.

[22]Apparently an official of minor importance; he is not mentioned in contemporary annals.

[23]Manuel Gómez Pedraza (1788-1851) was a popular Mexican general and
statesman who served as Secretary of War under Victoria. From December 26,
1832, to April 1, 1833, he was president of Mexico. Later he served in the cabinet
of Santa Anna.

[24]Vicente Guerrero (1782-1831) joined Iturbide's cause, but later turned
against him. From 1824 to 1828 he was vice-president of Mexico, subsequently
opposing Pedraza. Because of his political opposition he was ultimately captured
and shot.

1829 he was replaced in turn by the vice-president, Bustamante,[25] instigator of the revolution known as Jalapa. Like Iturbide, Guerrero with his life at stake fled precipitately toward the south, gained the coast, and took refuge on a Sardinian brig commanded by a Genoese captain, Picaluga. The latter, to whom he unwisely entrusted his safety, delivered him to the authorities at Acapulco, who ordered his execution. Picaluga received fifty thousand piasters as the price of this betrayal, an act that the citizens of Genoa in a laudable burst of indignation later branded as infamous.

During the course of these hideous dramas and transient régimes the country suffered acutely. Laws were not enforced, corruption flourished, and commerce dwindled. Occupied solely with thoughts of their own self-preservation, these various leaders rose to power without time or thought for constructive measures. Until 1833 Bustamante, however, retained the presidency. At that time Santa Anna,[26] who ranks as one of the most audacious participants of the revolution, relying on his personal popularity, rose against him, met him in battle, and forced him into exile. Pedraza was appointed in his place, thus giving control into the hands of the federalist party.

Weary of service in the interests of other politicians, General Santa Anna now concluded to promote for a time his own personal interests. In 1834 he upset the federation and seized the presidency, remaining in office until 1836. Hostilities having broken out at that time between Mexico and Texas, he was forced to relinquish executive power to the vice-president, General Barragán.[27] Santa Anna now assumed command of the army and during the war fell into the hands of the Texan forces. In the meanwhile, Bustamante returned from exile. As his party had regained control, he was again raised to the presidency, an office he retained for the next five years.

---

[25]Anastasio Bustamante (1780-1853) was a Mexican politician and soldier who opposed the early revolutionists, subsequently joining Iturbide. After a series of military and political embroglios, leading in 1832 to banishment, he was recalled and made president of Mexico, only to be forced in 1841 to return governmental control to the ever-active Santa Anna.

[26]Antonio López de Santa Anna (or Ana) was born at Jalapa February 21, 1795, and died at Mexico City, June 21, 1876. In his youth he served in the Spanish army, later aiding Iturbide. After leading several major revolts, he finally became president of Mexico in 1833. In 1836 he led an army against the Texans who were in revolt. Captured at the battle of San Jacinto, he was finally released. By 1843 came his bitter opponent. In April, 1833, he became president of Mexico.

[27]Miguel Barragán (1789-1836) was one of the Mexican generals who in 1821 supported Iturbide. In 1825 he forced the last Spanish stronghold at Vera Cruz, San Juan de Ulúa, to capitulate. Until 1835 he served as vice-president under Santa Anna.

However, Santa Anna, who with his customary dexterity had obtained his freedom from the Texans on the basis of an ephemeral promise to make them independent of Mexico, deemed the time opportune to retire and so settled on his properties near Vera Cruz, where he waited until the political tide turned once more in his direction.

During the absence of Santa Anna, other ambitious men came to the fore. General Urrea[28] rose against Bustamante and in 1840 made him a prisoner in the palace, elevating Gómez Fariás[29] to the presidency. The deposed president escaped, joined the insurgents, and rallied to his support a few loyal troops. Hostilities ensued, and for two weeks spectacular but sporadic firing succeeded merely in damaging a few houses and one pavilion of the government palace.

This simulated warfare that terminated in the downfall of Gómez Fariás, afforded some of our fellow-countrymen an opportunity to display extraordinary energy, and entailed several calamities in the French colony. Doctor Plane was killed while on his way to visit a patient. Another doctor, De Villette, owing to conscientious devotion to duty displayed during the fray by ministering to a Mexican general was offered the title of colonel, which he declined; while the courageous editor of the *Courrier français,*[30] M. Thivol, hit by a bursting shell as he was about to go out and warn our merchants to close their shops, had his leg broken.

Invested once more with the presidency, Bustamante, after decreeing that all past acts should be forgotten, annulled all laws promulgated during his captivity, declaring that during this interval the republic had been acephalous,[31] a word that, incidentally, no one understood, and whose explanation Mexicans were forced to seek from cultured foreigners.

---

[28]José Urrea, a famous Mexican general, assisted Santa Anna in his campaign in 1836. His political and military career was singularly tempestuous and his rise and fall from power always meteoric. In 1846 he took an active part in the war against the United States. See Bancroft, **Mexico, V, passim.**

[29]Valentin Gómez Fariás, a physician of Guadalajara, and a champion of reform and progress, was one of the few Mexican leaders who revealed courage, honesty, and moderation in office. Originally sponsoring Iturbide, he later became his bitter opponent. In April, 1833, he became governor of Mexico.

[30]The **Courrier français,** a journal published in French at Mexico City, is extremely valuable for our merchants scattered throughout the interior of the country. Moreover, members of the Spanish legation, aware of the advantages of such a publication, since their arrival have brought out a journal called **La Hesperia,** with the dual purpose of strengthening relations between Spanish residents of Mexico and their motherland, and of renewing contacts between the inhabitants of New Spain and their former metropolis. (D. de M.).

[31]Acephalous: meaning ''headless.'' Any body of men not acknowledging a leader or chief.

A year elapsed and on August 8, 1841, General Paredès,[32] governor of New Galicia, issued an edict at Guadalajara against Bustamante, assembled 2,000 men on the road and marched on Mexico City, before which, as the result of a concerted movement, Santa Anna had already stationed his troops. After thirty-five days of skirmishing, the latter was proclaimed provisional president by the army. On October 6, he made a solemn entrance into Mexico City. At the same time Bustamante, bound for Europe by way of Vera Cruz, was carrying away the spoils of his office and the memory of his glorious past. Since that time Santa Anna has guided the destinies of Montezuma's empire with a free hand; recently he was elected president for another five years. Many, however, attribute to him the same lofty ambitions that led to the downfall and death of Iturbide.

Yet Santa Anna seems far too shrewd to allow himself to be blinded by a mere title that would entail peril without augmenting his power. If he remains in office it will be less for the acclaim it brings than for the advantages it affords. A soldier of fortune, he has espoused a series of causes, according to his personal needs at the moment. Originally a subordinate officer in the Spanish army, in 1820 he joined the insurrectionists who were then gaining favor with the public. Through Iturbide he soon obtained command of a regiment of infantry, and the post of brigadier.

Santa Anna enjoys adventure, has some military ability, adapts himself readily to conditions, and is unusually resourceful. To the latter trait, revealed when on the ill-fated expedition of General Barradas, may be attributed his prestige and popularity. Of Spanish-Indian ancestry, Santa Anna has the cunning of one and the energy of the other. His black eyes sparkle with craftiness and fire; and at the age of fifty he is still in his prime. Often cruel to the point of barbarity, in 1835, in defiance of all conventions, he ordered the Texan troops who had been captured to be shot. Courting popularity, he invokes every means to preserve it; he is often seen mixing with the crowd at cockfights and placing a piaster on the winner like the lowest *lepero*.[33]

His dictatorship, furthermore, appears to be on the wane. Even now germs of profound discontent are appearing on all sides. The military leaders who aided him to overthrow Bustamante have already become his

---

[32] The Mexican general Mariano Paredès y Arrillaga (1797-1849) led the revolt against Herrera. After De Mofras' narrative was published in France, he served for six months, in 1846, as president of Mexico.

[33] A term applied to mestizos or Mexican half-breeds. (D. de M.)

enemies, and will soon be his rivals.[34] The most dangerous as well as the most courageous of these men, General Paredès, who recently fomented another revolution, has been removed in disgrace, and is now confined in a small village in the interior.

In the south, near Acapulco, General Bravo has succeeded in establishing an independent group, while General Urrea, the leader in the rich states of Jalisco, Sinaloa, and Sonora, has revived a plan to bring about the separation of these states from the central government and the founding of the Free States of the West. Bustamante, on the other hand, will seize the first opportunity to regain power, and is confident that he will be recalled by popular opinion from Italy where he is now living in retirement. Generals Valencia,[35] Gómez Farías, Tornel,[36] and Pedraza also secretly aspire to the presidency in the future.

Moreover, even Santa Anna has slight faith that his power will endure. Neither does he entertain false hopes of the future, but directs his main efforts toward augmenting his already considerable fortune. By so doing he has acquired, either personally or through his confidential agents, enormous perquisites from the various branches of government. He has received from the tobacco monopoly alone 200,000 piasters,[37] another 100,000 more from the sale of licenses to English firms, and an additional 200,000 of the million partially spent in the last year to purchase arms in Europe.

Such an example, which high officials do not hesitate to set, is invariably imitated by minor officials. Hence unbelievable disorder prevails in the Mexican government. Armed attacks and assassinations occur at frequent intervals throughout the provinces, especially along the main routes. Week after week stages leaving Mexico City or Puebla are raided even on the outskirts of these cities. Certain officers, moreover,

---

[34]Duflot de Mofras could not foresee the dramatic career of this Napoleon of the West. In 1845 Santa Anna was exiled; in 1846 he returned to fight against the United States, only to meet defeat at the siege of Mexico City. Again exiled, in 1853 he once more occupied the presidential chair, then returned to exile, finally dying in obscurity.

[35]Gabriel Valencia, one of the leading generals under Santa Anna, who put up a stubborn defense against the American armies and subsequently incurred this leader's disfavor and abuse.

[36]José Mariá Tornel y Mendívil was a leading figure in the revolutions of this period. At one time he was Mexican minister to the United States. Later he served as Minister of War. His death occurred in 1853.

[37]Piaster (or piastre): the equivalent of the peso or dollar. Originally used in the Orient, it became the standard coin of the Spanish Americas, where it was subject to wide fluctuations in value. In 1840 the piaster, often called **piaster forte,** had an average value of 5 francs, 35 centimes.

have their soldiers commit robbery in order to divide the spoils taken in this manner from travelers. A typical instance is that of Colonel Yañez,[38] whose band in 1835 killed and robbed M. Mairet, the Swiss consul at Mexico City. Yañez, incidentally, was the friend and aide-de-camp of General Santa Anna, who was president then as he is today.

The general character of the Mexican army adequately explains these almost unbelievable facts. Soldiers are recruited largely from the peasant class, and from Indians removed by sheer force from their villages, with the addition of criminals who have been confined in prisons and bagnios. A Mexican colonel at Guadalajara is responsible for the statement that in order to replace deserters he was forced to resort to lining up the 800 criminals housed in the public prison in squads and select the finest and most robust men. This accomplished, the length of their sentence was ascertained and convicts condemned to serve ten years in the galleys were then released from serving the remainder of their sentences with the understanding that they would enlist for five years in the army.

What can Mexico expect with soldiers of this character? In Europe a military uniform is a badge of distinction and merit, and the army is purged of inferior persons who are removed for purposes of discipline. In Mexico, however, the difference between a soldier and a galley slave is imperceptible, since Mexican regiments, as already indicated, augment their ranks by bringing in the lowest type of bandit. Naturally desertions are numerous in an army where military discipline is ignored and authority lax. Peasants escape and return to their farms, while criminals rejoin their bands, or hide on the outskirts of the cities.

Officers who, under the royalist régime were recruited from the most distinguished families, are now drawn from inferior ranks, or selected from a class of parvenu soldiers whose ignorance is matched only by their perversity. Furthermore, at a typical military school recently transferred to Chapultepec, not even a pretense is made of providing instruction. The Mexican troops, moreover, include four or five young officers trained in Europe and several officers and generals who have some knowledge of military technique. But the former constantly arouse the jealousy of their comrades, and the others should be dishonored for having betrayed their mother country and borne arms against her.

Despite the efforts of the new president to increase the military strength of Mexico, up to the present time he has been able to assemble

[38]José María Yañez, a prominent politician and rebel.

an effective force of only 20,000 ragged troops, most of whom are bare-
foot and armed with inferior English rifles. These troops are distributed
as follows: Mexico, 8,000; Guadalajara and the state of Jalisco, 2,000;
the northern division opposing Texas, 1,500; the southern division, 600;
the expeditionary cantonment of Jalapa, at one time operating against
Yucatán, 2,400; the fortress of Perote, 200; Vera Cruz and San Juan de
Ulúa, 1,000. The remainder are scattered throughout the various states.

Regiments of infantry usually consist of two battalions in command
of a colonel. Each battalion is directly in charge of a lieutenant colonel
and often of an honorary colonel. These units include at the outside
300 men, while many have as low as 150. Companies of 25 or 30 men are
in charge of a lieutenant colonel, or chief of a battalion, assisted by a captain, two lieutenants, and two junior officers; in brief, one officer for
every four soldiers. A similar lack of proportion and disorder exists
in the cavalry, and squads of 50 horse have six or seven officers. That
the artillery could muster thirty field pieces in repair and of the same
calibre appears doubtful; while batteries suitable for siege, mountain,
or coast work, and laborers or crews trained to erect bridges or assist
with the artillery, are absolutely unknown. Most of their powder is even
purchased in the United States and England.

The actual equipment of the artillery is as inferior as that of the
engineers. Its strength is based on a battalion of 200 men stationed at
Matamoros, and a company occupying barracks ironically known as
the Citadel of Mexico.

In addition to these forces there exists what are termed rural police,
a weakly-organized and poorly-equipped band which the peasants are
reluctantly forced to join. Judging by the number and character of the
leading states, the Mexican army should outrank the combined forces
of Europe, for it has fewer than 20,000 soldiers under the command
of 24,000 officers! If individual courage at times seems lacking among
them, this is counterbalanced by a patriotic fervor that inspires them
to endure with the utmost patience suffering, privation, and even re-
verses, and makes important problems appear simple.

For instance, when dissention arose between Mexico and England,
General Santa Anna went in person to Jalapa to review the troops. Unaware of the true object of this meeting, when he appeared his men began to shout that they refused to march to Yucatán where most of them
would probably be killed or defeated like the soldiers who had already
gone out into this territory. Santa Anna, without losing poise, replied

that he had come to Jalapa to encourage them valiantly to defend their own country now menaced by English invasion. His words were then confirmed by a proclamation. This bold gesture of the young republic was observed by Lord Aberdeen with considerable amusement.

Mexico with her 6,000,000 inhabitants is exposed to the intrigues of 7,000 or 8,000 officers; and although by the immoderate extension of suffrage the states as a whole appear about to succumb to mob domination, yet this fine country, a contented and thriving land when known as New Spain, is also honeycombed with military despotism.

Mexican warships at Vera Cruz include only two new steam vessels, an old unseaworthy ship, and a schooner equipped with four guns of 150 tons burden. On the Pacific Coast there are only three schooner-brigs available as coast guards. These, armed with four small guns, are in command of Mexican officers, but are manned by sailors from various countries. The two steamers, on the contrary, have English crews, officers, and commanders. The officers belonged at one time to the royal navy, but left the service at the end of one year.

Throughout the land the staunch fortifications erected at heavy expense by the Spaniards are falling into decay. The northern frontiers lie unguarded, and the southern states have been devastated by savage hordes that have advanced to within 30 leagues of the capital. During the days of centralized rule, a wise combination of missions and presidios checked Indian depredations and spread the teachings of Catholicism and the light of civilization among the native tribes. A strategic line of settlements extending for more than 1200 leagues started at the ports of San Francisco and Monterey in Upper California, descending toward the south as far as San Diego.[39] From there a double line reached down each coast of Lower California. Another line stretched across the Colorado River, skirted the Gila River, crossed the Sierra Madre and, after protecting New Mexico and Texas, terminated at the far side of the Floridas, thus bisecting the width of America and establishing communication between the Atlantic seaboard and the South Sea.[40]

Within this line the governors and indefatigable missionaries attracted colonists and founded pueblos or villages composed of Spaniards and Indian converts, whom they taught to cultivate the soil, exploit the mines, and become acquainted with mechanical arts. These various

---

[39]The distance mentioned is more than five times too great.

[40]South Sea: The term originally used to define the seas of the southern hemisphere, especially the South Pacific Ocean.

centers, protected by presidial companies, were self-supporting and formed a complete system of colonization and defense. To the Jesuits belongs the initial glory of having conceived and partially executed this remarkable system, a project wholly worthy of the vast enterprises that invariably characterize this illustrious order.[41]

What now remains of this strong and efficient organization? Only ruin and anarchy. Thus, at the present time when a traveler pauses before the remains of ancient edifices and inquires about their history, invariably he is told, "That was a college, a church, or a barracks—in the days of the king."

From a financial angle the present status of Mexico is equally deplorable. Her revenues total scarcely 15,000,000 piasters, whereas expenses exceed 18,000,000.[42] Oddly enough, of this budget the army alone absorbs 13,000,000. Mexican creditors cherish vain hopes of reimbursement; but under present conditions this is impossible. The internal debt, in fact, exceeds 14,000,000 piasters. The amount due England exceeds £10,750,000—270,000,000 francs—while a considerable sum is also owing France and the United States. So acute is the financial situation of the government that her employés cannot exist without accepting fees, and her diplomatic envoys in Europe are frequently compelled to meet the exigencies of their official rank from their private purses.

During the Spanish régime such financial distress was unknown. Revenues in those days exceeded 20,000,000 piasters; and an annual subsidy of 4,000,000 was sent to Havana and the Philippines, while Spain received a liquid surplus of 6,000,000. Thus, what Mexico lost as a result of the new conditions that made her independent of the motherland, is apparent.

Throughout the remainder of this chapter a survey of the future prospects, as well as of the political relations of this country with the United States, France, and Great Britain, will be given.

As soon as the first of these three powers was established, her policy of invasion was clearly defined by the repeated excursions made by her

---

[41]In 1571 Philip II requested the Jesuits, who were already laboring in Peru and Florida, to enter Mexico. In 1572 the first Fathers reached Vera Cruz. So active was this Order that within the next hundred years their missions had spread to the remote frontiers. By mandate of February 27, 1767, Charles III expelled the Jesuits from his dominion in Europe, America, and Asia.

[42]The status of Mexican finances fluctuated widely. Many authorities placed expenditures at double the income. Two large foreign loans covering these deficits were floated in London in 1824 and 1826. So much dishonesty entered into these transactions and bonds sold so low that less than half the amount of the loans ever reached the Mexican treasury.

countrymen into Spanish territory. In 1803 Colonel Aaron Burr, who had succeeded Jefferson as vice-president of the United States, publicly announced his intention of invading and revolutionizing New Spain. Having been arrested upon the demand of the viceroy, Burr was tried and, in October, 1805, acquitted. A transient period of peace followed in the wake of this doubtful satisfaction. Then, several years later, Washington made overtures to Madrid to establish her American boundaries at the mouth of the Rio Bravo del Norte, extending these as far as 31° north latitude, and from there to draw a direct line as far as the Pacific Ocean. This plan would have conceded control of the provinces of Texas, New Santander, New Vizcaya, New Mexico, Sonora, and Upper California to the Union.

The Spanish government indignantly rejected these overtures and soon sporadic but persistent hostilities began. Officially disavowed, but secretly encouraged, American agents now took possession of Bahía and San Antonio de Béjar. A signal victory on the part of General Elizondo,[43] who routed and drove back their forces into Louisiana, finally checked these encroachments.

In 1819 the Treaty of Florida[44] was signed and further clashes did not occur until toward the end of royal rule in Mexico. Citizens of the United States succeeded, however, in obtaining many land concessions which were likewise granted by Iturbide and his successors. Unwilling to relinquish their ideas of conquest, the United States labored incessantly to realize their objective. In 1842, during a period of peace, an American commodore in command of a station in the South Sea, without preliminary declaration of war, seized the port of Monterey, capital of New California.

The Mexican government, unfortunately, is misled by the moderation her weakness has inspired. However, a decree of Santa Anna, dated August 8, 1843, has materially aided in planting the seeds of animosity between these two powers, since by closing without reservation the customs on the northern frontier, all overland American commerce was definitely checked.

Of late the question of the incorporation of Texas into the great American federation has also added new confusion to a situation al-

---

[43] General Ignacio Elizondo, by means of treachery and strategy, captured Bustamante, Hidalgo, and other leaders of the revolutionary movement. See Bancroft, Mexico, IV, 273-275.

[44] By the Treaty of Florida, signed in 1819 and ratified in 1821, East and West Florida were ceded by Spain to the United States.

ready fraught with peril. In fact, M. de Bocanegra,[45] Minister of Foreign Affairs in Mexico, informed the plenipotentiary from the United States that the Mexican cabinet would view this union as a declaration of war. To these veiled protests Washington fearlessly replied that France, England, and the United States had agreed to recognize the independence of Texas;[46] that the republic from that time on was free to choose its own course; and that, finally, if the union should take place it would be peacefully accomplished, and since Mexican claims to this land were not recognized, full responsibility for any resistance offered would be placed directly on the shoulders of the offender.

Inasmuch as the Texan Congress had just voted for annexation to the United States, it can be readily imagined how this measure, if carried out, would have endangered the position of Mexico. She would have found herself thus secretly threatened on the south by invasion by the Americans of a new state; on the north by those who had already attempted the conquest of New Mexico; and on the west by those who had recently tried to turn Upper California into another Texas.

Furthermore, it is interesting to view the various territorial losses that within a few years the ancient Spanish viceroyalty, during its transition into the Republic of Mexico, will have experienced. On the south and east she will have lost the important states of Guatemala, Yucatán, Chiapas, and Tabasco; on the north and west, Texas, Coahuila, Chihuahua, New Mexico, Sonora, and the two Californias. What the illustrious Marquis de Bedmar[47] said of his possessions on Venetian terra-firma—"the republic only preserves its authority in the absence of someone to assume the role of usurper"—might be aptly said of the majority of her provinces. A regiment of 3,000 infantry and a few warships sent out to the two oceans would be adequate to subdue Montezuma's empire, and its conquest would be relatively easier today than at the time of Hernán Cortés.

---

[45] José María Bocanegra was sent as a delegate to the first and second constitutional congresses. Later he became a member of the cabinets of Guerrero and Farías. For five days, in 1829, he served as president ad interim of Mexico.

[46] Texas at this time was experiencing the growing-pains of youth. For some time American and Spanish settlers had clashed; and in 1830 the former were barred from entering. In 1835 a provisional government was inaugurated under Henry Smith, which was rendered ineffectual by war with Mexico. Then in 1836 Santa Anna defeated the Texans at the battle of the Alamo. The following year her independence was recognized by France, Great Britain, Belgium, and the United States.

[47] Alfonso de la Cueva, Marquis de Bedmar (1572), was a noted Spanish diplomat and prelate who served as ambassador under Philip III to Venice. In 1618 he conspired to destroy the republic.

And yet there are still several ways whereby this land might avoid this tragic future. First of all, Mexico should decrease its financial indebtedness, thus escaping the domination of foreign powers. To eliminate graft and inefficiency, employés should be paid regular salaries. Sufficient troops should be maintained to repulse Indian invasion, and the northern frontiers should be fortified to check encroachment from neighboring states. However, to achieve these results, merely introducing order within the administration and formulating an intelligent economic system are not adequate. The mineral wealth should also be considerably developed. This can be accomplished by the Mexican government only through the medium of applying on a vast scale and popularizing by every means at its command, the scientific process of M. Becquerel.[48] This would eliminate the costly method involving mercury and would permit the nation to profit from some of the immense stores of minerals throughout Mexico as yet unexploited.

At the same time, if the form of government remains the same, these improvements will prove either impracticable or superflous. There are no indications at present that the establishment of a European monarchy will be adequate to end these catastrophes and crush the factions that are destroying this vast land. In 1834 M. Zavala,[49] Mexican Minister to London, had already opened negotiations with this end in view, and toward the latter part of 1840 one of the most distinguished men of Yucatán, M. Gutiérrez Estrada,[50] braved the clamors and possibly the daggers of certain radicals by boldly publishing at the capital a book in which he proposed as the only available means of safety, restitution of the monarchy under some foreign prince.

The Republican party, moreover, which is without actual strength, is divided into two factions: the Centralists, or Scottish Rite Masons, and the Federalists, or York Rite Masons.[51] Lodges of the latter group

---

[48]Henri Becquerel, a French physicist, best known for his researches in the field of uranium and its compounds.

[49]Lorenzo de Zavala (1788-1835) was a distinguished statesman and historian who held many posts of honor, among them governor of the state of Mexico, and leader of the first Mexican Congress.

[50]Gutiérrez de Estrada, recognizing the need of a firm government, proposed a plan to establish a monarchy, and enlisted the support of many property owners and industrialists whose interests were being jeopardized. So much antagonism, however, was aroused that Estrada was forced to leave Mexico. Estrada's book referred to in the text was in all probability his Impugnación á las cartes de, sobre al projecto de establecir en Méjico una monarquía moderada. (Mexico, 1840).

[51]In Mexico during the decade 1824 to 1834 two Masonic organizations supplanted the Centralist and Federalist parties. The Conservatives, Monarchists, and Centralists rallied around the Scottish Rite Masons or Escoceses, and the Liberals, Republicans, and Federalists supported the York Rite Masons, or Yorkiños.

were introduced into Mexico in the first days of Independence by Mr. Poinsett,[52] an American envoy who, faithful to the instructions of his cabinet and in favor of federal ideals, recognized that by dividing this country into small free states, it would be easier for the Union to achieve its dismemberment. Events have justified his foresight.

There are few reputable men in Mexico who do not belong to the ecclesiastical-royalist party of Europe, called the clerico-español group. all families who place value on the fine old Spanish virtues of loyalty Mining men, landowners, sound business leaders, the ancient nobility, and honor, favor the old form of monarchical government, and secretly hope this will be re-established. The fact that American republics tend to favor monarchical rule is worthy of profound consideration. Although exhausted by the struggle of introducing an independence that has proved disastrous, yet no substitute has been found; and this land now finds itself embarrassed by the liberty so dearly purchased.

Without taking into consideration the United States where the tendencies of the loyalist party are well known, since 1828 everyone has been aware that the liberator, Bolivar, has negotiated with one of our envoys in an effort to establish a French prince on the Colombian throne! At Montevideo similar desires have been expressed. These, for the last ten years, have been shared by Mexico, and of late similar demands have been made by the republic of New Granada.

The assumption with respect to Mexico is that only princes of families professing the Catholic faith who have had connections with the former rulers of this country will be considered as suitable candidates to re-establish a monarchical government in Mexico. The infantes of Spain, the French princes, and the Austrian archdukes all fulfill these conditions; but it appears obvious that in whatever way the competitor is presented, he will be unanimously welcomed by the Mexicans.

What interest at the present time has France in these questions? The establishment of any kind of stable monarchy in Mexico should form the basis of our policy; for obviously the instability attached to the existing form of government entails grave disadvantages to our commerce and serious inconveniences for our countrymen. However, should Mexico retain her status as a republic, incorporation of her lands into the Union of the North would seem to offer more advantages to France

---

[52]Joel Roberts Poinsett (1779-1851) was an American diplomat who served as United States Minister to Mexico from 1825 to 1829. See his **Notes on Mexico,** (London, 1825).

than her present organization, since our commercial transactions could not fail to acquire, under the administration now strongly entrenched in the United States, considerable development. In that event our compatriots would enjoy the protection of liberty, security, and justice which they have demanded in vain from the Mexican cabinet, notwithstanding the fact that our government has done everything possible to promote their interests by vigorous protests which, there is every reason to believe, cannot indefinitely be evaded.

England, on the other hand, will not profit by a situation favorable to French interests. The type of political sovereignty that would be imposed on Mexico would at the same time destroy what commercial monopoly she controls. She would weaken in proportion to the new forces that the absorption of this power and that of Texas would add to the United States. Furthermore, the latter country, whose population has already reached 18,000,000, owing to this double amalgamation would be increased to 25,000,000 and perhaps some day she might succeed in realizing the foremost dream of her presidents and extend her frontiers as far as the Isthmus of Panamá.

Should this occur, the Union would command the Pacific Ocean throughout whatever section of Oregon Territory she might acquire mainly by absorbing California, and the western coasts of Mexico, Guatemala, Central America, and New Granada. On the east she would be mistress of the Atlantic from Canada to the Isthmus of Darien, and would thus menace all the many groups of islands situated at the entrance to the Gulf of Mexico, and in the Antilles Sea.

England has been aware for some time of the possibility and peril of such advances; thus there is basis for the belief, which recent events tend to corroborate, that she will oppose the admission of Texas into the Union. In fact, she has protected this republic from its infancy. By the treaty of 1840 she succeeded in procuring consent to the right of search; she has assumed charge of debt amounting to £1,000,000 owed by Mexico to Great Britain; and it was largely through the intervention of her diplomatic agents that an armistice was concluded last year between Texas and Mexico.

The opposition of England to the amalgamation of Texas with the Union might have disastrous consequences for the great American confederation, since, within a comparatively few years, the population of English emigrants will exceed by a considerable proportion the total number of United States colonists established in Texas; and 4,000 or

5,000 new British voters, who were legal citizens of Texas, would hold the balance of power in the elections and subsequently influence the government of the country in its foreign policy.

Texas has neither navy nor capital. England supplies her with whatever she consumes and, by a strongly developed colonization system, the latter power might obtain from Texas in exchange for her products, all the cotton India is unable to supply, which is now being purchased from the United States.

The non-annexation of Texas by the Union, moreover, would leave the western frontier of the United States entirely exposed and, not to mention the enormous amount of contraband English merchandise that could pass through Texas, the free navigation of the lower waters and mouth of the Mississippi River would be endangered from the day when England succeeded in occupying the Sabine, the Arkansas, and the Colorado River of the West.

As for Mexico, this would mean only a change of neighbor, and the example of Balize[53] in Yucatán indicates that nothing of importance would be gained by this substitution. England, who appears as quick to take umbrage in political situations as she is tenacious in her ambitions, has raised innumerable obstacles to the aggrandizement of the United States. She has even attempted to exaggerate its importance, indicating that it is as vital to France as to other European powers to prevent too widespread an extension of the democratic principle throughout America, since at some time this might spread from the New World to the Old and thus place in jeopardy the existence of all thrones.

The fact should be stressed that if the monarchical form of government fails to be revived in the Spanish republics, France will be able to derive inestimable advantages from their absorption by the United States. However, whatever form the destinies of Mexico may assume, our government should invariably maintain favorable relations with this country and, in order to preserve a market so valuable for our commerce, should also maintain able representatives in that land to defend our interests.

This latter point is vital, for affairs are not transacted throughout the republics of Spanish America as in Europe. Haughtiness and vehemence should be studiously avoided. To be wise, to write little and talk much, to possess a fluent knowledge of the language of the land,

---

[53]Belize, or Balize, is now the capital of British Honduras.

to have honorable antecedents, and a character that is serious without being pedantic and firm without being acrimonious, to be well informed at all times without loss of dignity, to be adaptable to the easy familiarity of Spanish customs—this combination of qualities is indispensable to our European representatives.

Certain men sent to Mexico, trained to other ways and in the habit of concealing the private citizen under the diplomat, bring with them into this land an excess of etiquette and a Germanic aloofness. This unsympathetic attitude tends to isolate them in Mexican society and in the end to deprive them of their prestige. Statesmen of the Spanish race are inclined to introduce and discuss state problems in intimate and informal conversations which, if in any way checked, or if the personal influence is not effective, cannot later be rectified through official channels. The only recourse then left open for foreign governments is intimidation, or the use of force. Of this England and the United States are fully aware, and this knowledge assures the two nations an inestimable advantage in that land.

By way of concluding these preliminary observations and the rapid survey that has just been presented in this chapter of the military, financial, and political status of Mexico, it would be well to add that, although somewhat severe, yet this summary is at the same time entirely just, for, since it is entirely speculative, neither the personal merits nor the private virtues of the inhabitants are mentioned. For three years very corner of this vast country was explored and carefully studied; its material resources, institutions, and government were observed, and its most eminent men visited; and because it has appeared obvious that Mexico, backed by the wealth with which the land is endowed, and the basic elements of strength possessed can some day reconquer the prosperity she deserves, the only sound way appeared to be to speak the unadorned truth, and, by indicating the abyss, aid her to avoid this danger.

CHAPTER II

Commercial and financial status of Mexico. Production and exportation of precious metals. Budget of receipts and expenditures. Foreign debts. French population and interests.

As a result of the treacherous and disastrous measure that culminated, as already shown, in the expulsion of all European-born Spaniards, the richest merchants left Mexico and located in Havana, Cadiz, Bordeaux, and Paris. Thus funds that were sent to France at this period attained considerable proportions. In 1828, they reached nearly 21,000,000; in 1829, in excess of 13,000,000; and, in 1830, more than 10,500,000 francs. Since that time the average yearly amount of specie returned exceeds 3,500,000 francs. Amounts considerably in excess of these were sent to the United States, Spain, and England.

This enormous exportation of precious metals, which cannot be replaced by English capital obtained by the Mexican government, has caused consternation that explains the state of unrest now affecting commerce.[1] Although what silver is now produced is exported, yet this is barely adequate to pay for foreign goods. So little currency remains in circulation that the legal rate of interest on money in Mexico is one per cent a month, and this has even risen at times as high as three per cent without damage to commercial transactions.

At all times the production of metals has been an accurate barometer of Mexican prosperity. Annually from 1801 to 1810, prior to the War of Independence, the mint in Mexico City produced, on an average, 22,000,-000 piasters. In 1805, at the peak of her prosperity, 27,165,888 piasters were coined in Mexico; but by 1837 only 561,730 piasters were being put into circulation. For many years during the Spanish régime there was only one mint—that in Mexico City—which also maintained an assay and shipping office. The mint of Zacatecas was not established until 1810. Today several more are in operation, namely, at Guadalajara, San Luís de Potosí, Guanajuato, Chihuahua, Durango, and Hermosillo

---

[1]For a full discussion of the mineral wealth of Mexico see Alexander von Humboldt, op. cit., III, 119-454.

in Sonora. The latter, opened in 1838, has coined somewhat less than 70,000 piasters that contain gold, for, after the furnaces and scales were damaged, the mint was abandoned for several years. By a decree of February 16, 1842, orders were issued for this plant to be reopened, and placed in charge of Mm. Duport and Bellangé, French engineers and chemists. In September, 1842, a second edict issued by President Santa Anna, ordered, among other things, the establishment of two mints, one at Culiacán, Sonora, and the other at Guadalupe y Calvo in the state of Chihuahua.

In several other cities, only the assay offices owned by the government were closed. On January 1, 1842, the shipping offices were ordered discontinued and in February, 1843, the government bought for 60,000 piasters the commodious establishment of Mm. Duport and Bellangé in Mexico City. The unsatisfactory condition of the plant and the ignorance of the assayers, together with a lack of accurate instruments, prevented them from standardizing with any degree of accuracy the content of bullion and gold and silver coins in common use throughout Mexico. The standard of the old Spanish piaster in the colonies was 917 M; that of the Mexican piaster with the eagle has a present-day value not to exceed 903 M. The gold standard is 0,875.

The majority of the piasters shipped to Europe were sent for testing to Paris, and it is unnecessary to call attention to the many frauds perpetrated at plants in Mexico City that went unpunished. At Guadalajara 60,000 piasters were coined in 1838 which, when analyzed, were found to be four per cent under the legal standards. Even today at a certain plant in Rosario, Sinaloa, a government employé is substituting lead for bullion and is stamping out coins marked to represent those of higher value. Complaints frequently made by foreign business men at the port of Mazatlán fall on deaf ears, and this man quietly continues his scandalous labor, for no one has been able to secure his dismissal.

Throughout government plants, the coinage of gold and silver bullion costs the management about four and one-half per cent. At Paris piasters vary in value according to the plants in which they are made. For instance, those from Durango and Mexico City are worth from 5 francs, 34 centimes, to 5 francs, 35 centimes; those from Zacatecas, 5 francs, 30 centimes, to 5 francs, 35 centimes; those from Potosí and Guadalajara, 5 francs, 35 centimes, to 5 francs, 37 centimes; and in China, where piasters constitute legal tender, they command a premium of six per cent over Mexican piasters. Gold coin is depreciated to such an extent that while

Spanish doubloons are worth 84 francs, 60 centimes, those of the independent states have a value of only 82 francs, 20 centimes.

The average production of precious metals in Mexico during 1840, 1841, 1842, and 1843, as represented by coin from the mint, is approximately 13,000,000 piasters. To this should be added 3,000,000 in gold and silver bullion secretly exported. The total amount is thus 16,000,000, the ratio of gold to silver being one to sixty. As already indicated, the country has made no attempt to exploit its wealth. The accompanying tables will indicate the amount exported to France to be converted into French merchandise, as well as general trade with Mexico. To this is added, for general information, a table showing the distribution of the gold and silver coined between 1800 and 1840 at the mint in Mexico City.

Throughout America the withdrawal of Spanish capital, the war, and the establishment of Independence, proved disastrous for the development of mineral wealth, decreasing rather than increasing production. The principal mines were flooded with water. Mercury, indispensable at the mines, was either not procurable or was to be had only at exorbitant prices. English companies believed for a time that by using steam-engines they could soon reclaim the flooded shafts; but this process proved practicable only in a few localities, for in most instances the lack of fuel, added to the difficulties of transporting engines, proved insurmountable obstacles. For this reason reclamation has been gradually abandoned by these companies and during the present decade English companies are mining only about one-tenth of their properties.

A shortage of capital prevents the wholesale development of new enterprises. Undoubtedly the discovery of an extraordinary rich vein accounts for the recent formation at Guadalupe y Calvo of an English company. This mine, situated in the Sierra Madre south of the city of Chihuahua, was not worked until 1837, and has already yielded 6,000,-000 piasters, two-thirds in silver and one-third in gold. Annual production exceeds 1,000,000, although the English company has a capital of only 2,000,000 piasters.

The German companies which are working various mines are under-capitalized and unable to operate on a large scale, although the improvements in chemical and mechanical processes, and the recent introduction of the economical methods used at Freiburg, Saxony, involving a mixture of mercury, allow them to realize satisfactory profits.

With wise foresight the Spanish government has established, independent of its excellent School of Mines in Mexico City, a fund for

GENERAL TABLE OF COMMERCE BETWEEN FRANCE AND MEXICO

	Importations from Mexico to France			Exportations from France to Mexico	French Ships						Mexican Ships Departing		
				Merchandise	Entering			Departing					
Year	Mdse.	Gold & Silver	Total	Total	Ships	Tonnage	Crew	Ships	Tonnage	Crew	Ships	Tonnage	Crew
1827	5,447,148	6,289,500	11,736,648	14,925,348	21	4,388	284	34	7,514	505	None		
1828	6,762,603	20,709,640	27,472,243	9,992,017	32	7,659	523	36	8,903	552	"		
1829	8,089,419	13,482,461	21,571,880	9,734,072	37	9,396	583	34	8,706	525	"		
1830	5,899,688	10,585,050	16,484,738	23,226,747	34	8,776	503	32	7,824	486	"		
1831	3,705,846	5,158,350	8,864,196	20,353,235	29	7,095	459	29	6,838	435	"		
1832	7,876,760	3,404,310	11,281,070	13,399,956	25	5,398	371	24	5,702	351	1	294	14
1833	5,340,807	5,552,035	10,892,842	15,026,670	17	3,709	234	30	5,686	369	None		
1834	6,743,862	4,529,260	11,273,122	12,040,799	35	7,854	449	29	5,312	351	1	87	6
1835	7,093,052	3,652,182	10,745,234	17,300,858	36	7,269	429	36	6,524	425	None		
1836	8,703,985	3,231,750	11,935,735	9,499,806	39	7,762	473	25	4,902	306	"		
1837	7,111,974	4,247,710	11,359,684	9,637,652	23	4,530	283	27	4,994	334	"		
1838	4,415,076	2,297,714	6,712,790	8,106,536	20	3,955	253	21	3,994	254	"		
1839	4,578,585	5,232,950	9,811,535	11,342,314	9	1,963	114	31	5,371	360	1	195	9
1840	7,388,789	2,749,475	10,138,264	13,994,084	36	6,557	428	34	6,201	422	1	57	10
1841	5,946,718	2,929,740	8,876,458	12,652,501	29	5,142	352	37	7,206	457	None		
1842	5,253,627	1,469,760	6,723,387	11,407,300	28	4,532	321	27	4,599	318	"		
Total	100,457,939 fr.	95,541,785 fr.	195,979,826 fr.	212,639,895 fr.	450	95,984	6,059	486	102,276	6,450	4	633	39

MINTAGE

Year	Silver, piasters	Gold, piasters	Total, piasters
1800	17,898,510	787,164	18,685,674
1801	15,958,044	610,398	16,568,442
1802	17,959,477	839,122	18,798,599
1803	22,520,856	646,050	23,166,906
1804	26,130,971	959,030	27,090,001
1805	25,806,074	1,369,814	27,165,888
1806	23,383,672	1,352,348	24,736,020
1807	20,703,984	1,512,266	22,216,250
1808	20,502,433	1,182,516	21,684,949
1809	24,708,164	1,464, 818	26,172,982
1810	17,950,684	1,095,504	19,046,188
1811	8,956,432	1,085,364	10,041,796
1812	4,027,620	381,646	4,409,266
1813	6,133,983	000,000	6,133,983
1814	6,902,481	618,069	7,520,550
1815	6,454,799	486,464	6,941,263
1816	8,315,616	960,393	9,276,009
1817	7,994,951	854,942	8,849,893
1818	10,852,367	533,921	11,386,288
1819	11,491,138	539,377	12,030,515
1820	9,897,078	509,076	10,456,154
1821	5,000,022	303,504	5,903,526
1822	5,329,126	214,128	5,543,254
1823	3,276,474	291,408	3,567,882
1824	3,267,000	236,944	3,503,944
1825	3,235,045	2,385,455	5,620,500
1826	2,998,411	218,592	3,217,003
1827	2,868,624	590,597	3,459,221
1828	1,385,505	111,776	1,497,281
1829	898,350	380,996	1,279,346
1830	881,339	221,776	1,103,115
1831	973,932	291,217	1,265,149
1832	1,057,059	308,915	1,365,974
1833	1,152,515	76,904	1,229,419
1834	937, 054	23,938	960,992
1835	537,900	00,000	537,900
1836	734,007	20,160	754,167
1837	516,354	45,376	561,730
1838	1,088,520	00,000	1,088,520
1839	1,742,915	79,314	1,822,229
1840	1,917,617	71,207	1,988,024

furnishing aid to mining. The basic idea of this fund is to advance to mine-owners whose lodes are temporarily unproductive or who have limited capital, a considerable sum of money amounting in certain instances to as much as 100,000 piasters. Furthermore, since 1776, the government has sold from its own office situated at the most important mines in Mexico, Almadén[2] mercury at a price of 42 piasters for each Spanish hundredweight (46 kilograms). Today mercury is worth at the ports from 120 to 130 piasters; at Mexico City, 115 piasters; at Zacatecas, 165 piasters; and in the remote mining camps the excessive cost of transportation places a value on this metal, bought in lesser quantities by the small operators, of 200 piasters. Thus at the present more than 3,000 mining camps may be cited where work has been abandoned because costs materially exceed the value of the metal extracted.

Control of the mines at Alamadén is held by the Rothschild family; these mines produce yearly on an average of 20,000 to 21,000 hundredweight in metals. Spain, financially embarrassed, has steadily advanced the price of quicksilver. Thus, in 1839 her contract with the Rothschilds fixed the price at 51.25 piasters; later this was raised to 59; and, finally, in the agreement of June, 1843, the price of metal at Almadén was advanced to 82.50 piasters. These excessive increases cannot fail to react disastrously on Mexico, which is now replacing the benefits Spain at one time derived from coinage in her old colony.

The price of mercury has undergone a series of fluctuations, having increased from 4 or 5 francs to 22 francs a kilogram. However, prior to the present century Spain held mercury to the flat rate of 4 francs 84 centimes by governmental contracts with leading markets in Europe—Idria and the Palatinate—reserving for her exclusive use a monopoly of their output and agreeing to protect her colonies from any advance in price beyond that figure. Soon after the split between Spain and the mother country, however, the price began to advance until mercury is now worth from 10 to 11 francs the kilogram. Europe produces annually 1,400,000 kilograms. Of this amount, 1,000,000 comes from Almadén, the remainder being supplied by the mines in Idria[3] and a few important centers in the Palatinate. The annual consumption in America is some

---

[2]For centuries the Almadén mines in the southwestern part of the province of Ciudad Real, Spain, worked by convict labor, have been one of the leading centers for the production of cheap mercury.

[3]Idria, near Triest, was famous for the quicksilver mines discovered in 1497. The Palatinate, or region near the Rhine, had developed many mines in the Harz Mountains.

850,000 kilograms. The remainder is used in Europe and also to a minor degree in India.

After Almadén, the most important properties are the mines at Idria. Their production, however, never exceeds 300,000 kilograms, even under the most favorable conditions, and to all appearances this is daily on the decline. These mines, although discovered as early as 1497, have not been actively exploited since 1506. The Almadén mines, on the other hand, are so rich that they have been worked continuously, although during twenty-five centuries they have not sunk shafts below 300 meters. These same mines have been exploited since the early ages. According to Pliny, the Greeks extracted lead from these veins seven centuries before our era, and the same writer also adds that they furnished annually to the Romans 10,000 pounds of cinnabar.

In Mexico the annual consumption of quicksilver is approximately 20,000 hundredweight;[4] of this amount 12,000 disappears entirely in the handling, representing, at an average price of 150 piasters, a loss of 1,800,000 piasters, or 9,000,000 francs. The royal government was wrongfully accused of having prohibited the exploitation of the quicksilver mines in New Spain. On the contrary, Spain encouraged this development, at the same time controlling the sale of the output. Where mines have been abandoned it is because production costs have been exorbitant, making them unprofitable, and because the output of the Almadén was considerably less costly for the consumers. Notwithstanding the fact that the mines of Durasno,[5] near Tasco, were exploited before the days of Independence, yet what mercury they produced cost 60 piasters, whereas that imported from Spain could be sold for 42 piasters, delivered at the royal depositories.

At the present, foreigners are carefully attempting to locate deposits of mercury. Already at San Luís Potosí several veins of cinnabar have been found. In the vicinity of Guadalajara a deposit is being worked that yields annually four or five hundredweight. Recently a vein has been discovered at Zacatecas with so rich a showing that in July, 1843, a company formed to promote these holdings was able to raise on the Exchange in Mexico City 200,000 piasters, divided into twenty units of 10,000 piasters each.

When the independence of New Spain was recognized in 1836 by

---

[4]Hundredweight: Originally the equivalent, in England and the United States, of 112 pounds.

[5]Durasno lies near the town of San Luís de La Paz in the state of Guanajuato. See Humboldt, op. cit., III, 301-302.

the mother country, the Mexican government should have offered the cabinet at Madrid some special concessions that would have assured the closing of the mines at Almadén, thus acquiring for herself the enormous profits that the house of Rothschild derives from this monopoly. What would be the effect on Mexico if the mines at Almadén should cease to produce, or if, in the event of war, the supply of mercury should be checked? Quicksilver produced in Carniola is used in Transylvania and Saxony. But this output is so limited that it would be impossible to export any to Mexico. Into what confusion European commerce would be thrown by the interruption of an annual product bringing in 24,000,000 francs in actual currency is self-evident. In Mexico, where industry is a negligible factor, where agriculture is virtually at a standstill, where exportation of products is highly restricted, what would be the outcome if European merchandise, which her population can scarcely forego, were not purchased, but the enormous total of its debts owed foreign powers were cleared instead?

The exportation of coined metals is subjected to outrageous laws. By orders incorporated in a single ordinance issued by the Minister of Finance that went into force recently on August 29, convoys of specie are not allowed to leave the Mexican gulf ports of Tampico and Vera Cruz except once every three months—on January, May, and September first. All money sent from the interior to the port is inspected as if destined for export, and is forced to pay in advance the costs of exportation, whether or not it actually leaves the country. These duties, amounting to eleven per cent, are divided as follows: four per cent circulation tax; six per cent export tax; one per cent mining tax. This ordinance obviously nullifies a decree, published by the president on the tenth of last March, that establishes definitely the distinction between the laws governing circulation from one department to another, and that of foreign exportation.

Prohibited in Atlantic ports under penalty of confiscation and fine, the exportation of gold and silver bullion is now allowed in the three principal ports on the Pacific Ocean open to commerce, San Blas, Mazatlán, and Guaymas. Formerly this exportation, according to law, was required to cease from the day when offices of the banks at Hermosillo and Culiacán were open for business, and from that time on, from these same ports, only specie could be exported. The execution of these measures, however, is wholly impracticable, for the majority of the mines are situated two or three hundred leagues from the cities of

Culiacán and Hermosillo, and no doubt owing to the poor condition of the roads, and the bands of robbers that ravage the country, the owners, unwilling to ship their precious metals such distances, prefer to send their wealth to the nearest port to be shipped as contraband.

The government is fully aware that for its own protection the exportation of gold and silver bullion should be encouraged by suitable laws that would decrease the amount of contraband by removing many of its chief advantages.

Although the legal rate on silver bars is seven per cent, in accordance with an agreement made with the Spanish firm of Rubio frères in Mexico City, only four per cent is collected. The English warships stationed constantly in the harbors of San Blas, Mazatlán, and Guaymas, which leave every six months for England, charge two per cent for freight. This is divided as follows: one per cent for the officer in command of the ship; one-half per cent for the commodore in charge of the squadron in the South Sea; one-half per cent for the Marine Hospital at Greenwich.

Insurance at Paris on English warships bound for the three designated ports is one and one-fourth per cent, and funds deposited at the Bank of London that are transported as far as Paris average one-third per cent, or three francs in every thousand.

Freight on goods or coin via commercial vessels is one and one-half per cent, while insurance is two and one-half per cent. Thus the latter method of transportation costs one and one-quarter per cent more than by warship and does not offer nearly so much security.

English warships stationed on the west coast of Mexico are built from poor designs but are armed with sixteen carronades of twenty-four calibre and manned by crews of 100 men. These ships are relieved every six months and sent back to London with specie. The following table, based on the most reliable documents available, indicates the exact amount of money exported during the last four years in the form of coin or bullion from the ports of Guaymas, San Blas, and Mazatlán.

By English warships Guaymas................................ 800,000 piasters
                    San Blas................................1,200,000 piasters
                    Mazatlán ....2,000,000 piasters
By commercial vessels (from the three ports)...........1,000,000 piasters

                                    ——————————
                                    Total 5,000,000 piasters

The ports of Acapulco and Monterey in Upper California which, together with the three preceding points, are the only ports open to foreign commerce on the west coast of Mexico, report only a small amount of commerce, and do not export metal.

In the Gulf of Mexico, specie is usually put aboard English steamers that leave once a month from Vera Cruz and Tampico; these carry from 400,000 to 500,000 piasters on each voyage. The rest of the money included in the 16,000,000 piasters annually produced is exported by French, Hamburg, Spanish, and other vessels.

With a sloop of war of twenty-four cannon and two brigs that appear only at infrequent intervals in regions where English and American groups constantly sojourn, our station in the Gulf of Mexico is quite inadequate to guard our interests. However, the growth of our station in the Pacific Ocean which possesses eight ships affords our commerce a protection and prestige that are invaluable. At the same time the mere presence of our ships in Mexican ports does not fulfill our needs. To prove of the utmost value these should be stationed there at definite intervals, like English vessels, and should return directly to France so that they might carry not only the funds of our merchants, but also those of foreign tenders. According to reliable reports probably half the sums herein indicated are destined for France. The Paris firm of Aguirre Vengoa receives annually by way of London more than 1,500,000 piasters from the South Sea, while more than 1,000,000 is shipped to other houses at Bordeaux and Havre.

Thus if our ships had proper authority, and were placed in charge of our consuls, they might be able to handle Spanish business whose total amount is considerable, as well as some for the United States, Hamburg, Belgium, Sardinia, Germany, and Switzerland. Without supplying further details, the many advantages that would accrue from this activity of capital, exchange, commissions, and brokerage is obvious. Personal profits should be barred to our French officers, although this is contrary to the custom followed by captains of the English navy. The latter, in fact, pose as agents to the merchants at the ports in order to procure for their ships, in a fraudulent manner, the business of handling their specie. Our country should prevent this lust for profit from inciting our officers to demonstrations that the mercantile spirit of the English is able to tolerate.

As a matter of fact, the profit that is derived from this traffic is enormous. Here is a typical instance: According to Mexican law, the duty for exporting bars of metal along the Pacific Coast is four per cent; freight on English ships amounts to another two per cent. However, commanders of English vessels make a charge for loading contraband that averages three and one-half in place of the stipulated two per cent. In this way two and one-half per cent is saved, which is divided by the merchants and the captains. That large sums are thus realized by officers as well as firms whose transactions total many millions of piasters annually is obvious. Should the French government decide to deduct the freight tax on precious metal transported by our warships, this revenue might appropriately be applied to aid men invalided from the navy.

Undoubtedly considerable impetus would be given our Mexican commerce by the introduction of trans-Atlantic steamers, for whose construction 28,000,000 francs have already been appropriated. These boats might also be used for some basic purpose. By appearing once a month in foreign ports, they would provide less costly protection than permanent stations and would further afford an excellent training school for sailors and mechanics for our own navy vessels which, as is commonly known, have special requirements. One of these large steamers, the *Gomer,* has just returned from a voyage to America and the Antilles to establish ports of call, and her agents were able to place favorable mail and shipping contracts with several American governments.

Although auriferous silver has always been present in the lands east and south of New Spain, as well as in the states of Chihuahua and especially upper Sonora, where traces of rich gold deposits are also present, the production of gold, oddly enough, is extremely limited. North of the towns of Hermosillo and Arizpe, in the streams adjoining the Gila that empties in turn into the Colorado River near the head of the Vermilion Sea [Gulf of California], nuggets of pure gold weighing several kilograms, that equal those recently discovered in the Ural Mountains, are found during the rainy season near the surface of the ground. At Hermosillo one of these *pepitas,* or nuggets, on exhibition was so heavy that its value was estimated at 10,000 piasters—50,000 francs.[6]

With mineral resources of such magnitude, Mexico should enjoy unlimited prosperity; however, her financial status, the backbone of

---

[6]Near the present Arizona-Sonora boundary many rich mines were discovered in the eighteenth century. What were known as **bolas de plata**, enormous pieces of pure silver were often found, especially from 1736 to 1741, near Arizonac, just south of the Arizona line. See Hubert Howe Bancroft, **History of Arizona and New Mexico** (San Francisco, 1889), pp. 12, 345, 362.

government, is in a state of chaos. This is clearly indicated by the following table showing the approximate budget of receipts and expenditures.

STATE REVENUES

	Piasters forte
Naval customs and frontiers	9,000,000
Circulation taxes and exports on money, gold and silver bars, and bullion	1,200,000
Departmental revenues	2,000,000
Postage for letters and couriers	200,000
Lottery	55,000
Salt	25,000
Stamped paper	100,000
Discounts for pawn-shops	90,000
Miscellaneous revenues, hotel licenses, vice fines, etc.	100,000
Consumption taxes	1,500,000
Receipts, general total	14,270,000

EXPENSES

President and ministers	360,000
Senate, chamber of deputies, secretaries	340,000
Supreme court of justice	90,000
Legations, consulates, and boundary commissions	150,000
Financial officers	260,000
Pensions for retirement	290,000
Subsidies for pawn-shops	200,000
Departmental expenses, juntas, secretaries, prefects, and sub-prefects	900,000
Administration of justice	1,350,000
Bishoprics and missions	50,000
Public instruction	65,000
Hydraulic works of (Desague de) Huehuetoca	50,000
Prisons and jails	150,000
Army, navy, and military activities	10,500,000
Generals, leading officers of the army, and extraordinary expenses	2,500,000
General Total	17,255,000

Annual deficit—2,985,000 piasters

ALLOTMENT OF REVENUE BY PERCENTAGE

Per cent

20 For payment of interest on the English debt.

10 Salaries for the garrisons at Vera Cruz and Acapulco.

5 For the purchase in Europe of arms and Paixhans cannons.[7] (Guns are bought in London and cannon at Liége by a friend of Santa Anna.)

25 For amortization of all other credits and general claims.

40 Liquid fund for the central government to cover all general expenses.

——

100

Since January, 1842, twenty per cent of the total revenue derived from the customs has been applied to payment of the interest on the English debt. A commissioner of the British government who resides at Mexico has special charge of collecting this sum. Formerly the English took only sixteen and two-thirds per cent, but the twenty per cent now collected yields from 600,000 to 700,000 piasters annually, and provides in the neighborhood of twenty per cent of the interest. Mexican loans, which are never listed at our commercial houses, are divided into two series.[8] The active bonds drawing five per cent have a value on the London exchange of thirty-two or thirty-three for each hundred shares, equivalent to one hundred pounds, but they have fallen at times as low as twenty-eight. Deferred bonds have almost no supporters and are worth only eight or nine per hundred. Their coupons do not draw interest, but are allotted to holders of the old debt in a certain ratio as compensation for past amounts where payment has been suspended on old loans, and where the initial capital has in consequence been reduced to the vanishing point, a method often used by bankrupt governments of the new republics of Spanish America with the single exception of Chile, which invariably pays her debts. The second type of Mexican loan is classed only as a postponed loan, and has more or less chance of recovery owing to the fluctuations of the exchange. Like the five per cent active loan, demand here, as everywhere, is what determines its rise or fall.

The house of Lizardi frères in Europe handles Mexican loans. In 1842 Lizardi senior, prior to his death, adjusted the budget and the

---

[7]The Paixhans gun was invented by a famous French general of artillery, Henri Joseph Paixhans (1783-1854), who wrote many volumes on military tactics.

[8]See supra, I, 14, note 42.

amount due was fixed at £10,000,000. At that time it was agreed that, until conditions improved, half of this amount would not bear interest and that only £5,000,000 would pay their coupons. At the beginning of the present year the firm of Lizardi frères in an attempt to recuperate considerable sums, placed an issue on the London exchange, unauthorized at the time, of £720,000 whose coupons were admitted to participate in the twenty per cent that was originally reserved for the £5,000,000 of active debt. Blocks of the old bonds have been recalled; but General Santa Anna has not favored their reclamation since he shared in the lucrative manipulation that netted the firm of Lizardi a personal profit of 1,200,000 piasters.

In February, 1844, the total amount of back claims of the United States was fixed at 2,100,000 piasters, payable every three months. The first payments of 260,000 piasters each were collected by the agents of the federal government, who had charge of distributing these amounts to private individuals. To procure this large sum the Mexican government was compelled to float a special loan, a procedure that has encouraged other countries to revive back claims. However, no action was taken in their behalf by Mexico who stands so much in fear of the United States that she yielded to their firm and open threats.

With a desperation born of despair the Mexican government is employing every means within her power to supplement her financial deficit. Thus her agents boldly seized the property of the Californian missions, valued at some 2,000,000 piasters, which was then sold to the firm of Barrio. The proceeds of the national lottery met a similar fate, for although the administration guarantees to pay the holder of winning tickets upon presentation, yet the treasury is often unable to meet even this trivial obligation.

French interests in Mexico are protected by our legation at Mexico City, by our consuls at Vera Cruz, Campêche, Mazatlán, and Monterey, by our vice-consuls at Tampico, Zacatecas, Tehuantepec, Guaymas, Tepic, and the port of San Blas, and by consular agents at La Laguna del Carmen, and San Juan de Tabasco.

The value of the industrial and commercial properties owned by our countrymen does not exceed 8,000,000 piasters. Several firms have personal investments of large amounts in the country. The various ventures of the Lestapis frères involve more than 500,000 piasters, not to mention other properties, such as plants for spinning linen and cotton cloth, and paper factories, distilleries, and mulberry plantations, situated in Mexico

City, Puebla, Tlizco, Zacatecas, Orizaba, Durango, Valladolid, Guadalajara, and Colima. Throughout the length of Mexico from 4,000 to 5,000 Frenchmen reside; these men control capital that averages from 5,000 to 10,000 piasters. All conduct their affairs with the idea of retiring some day, after they have amassed a comfortable fortune, with their capital to France. Good workmen, especially those with mechanical training, can earn a daily wage of four piasters.

The French population of Mexico, consisting at the lowest estimate of more than 3,000 individuals, derives annual profits in excess of 2,000-000 piasters. During a ten-year period, from 1830 to 1840, our laborers and petty merchants sent more than 20,000,000 francs of capital alone back to France. Furthermore, merchandise received, drafts, and currency put another 20,000,000 or 25,000,000 francs into circulation. Although our commerce with Mexico within the last few years has experienced a marked decrease, yet this country remains our leading market in Spanish America, being twentieth in order of importance out of a general list of forty-eight countries with which we have commercial dealings. Goods exported from 1839 to the present day have attained a total of nearly 12,000,000 francs annually. Nevertheless, Mexico occupies only the twenty-ninth place among nations to which we send goods and her last five-year average has scarcely exceeded 5,000,000 francs. Our commerce with Mexico usually has a favorable balance of exports over imports, which is covered by drafts or specie sent to us from England. It is reasonable to assume, however, that an advantageous treaty of commerce would make our exports with that country regain the level reached in 1830 and 1831. In the first of these two years our commerce exceeded 23,000,000 francs, and in the second, 20,000,000. Subsequently, after a series of fluctuations, in 1838 our exports fell to 8,000,000 francs. In 1840 these again climbed to nearly 14,000,000, but since then have steadily declined. France is still fortunate, however, in having a favorable balance of exports over imports with Mexico.

Obviously any cessation in shipments of such precious metals as this land exports directly to France could not fail to entail financial distress for from 1827 until the present, our land has imported directly to Mexico 100,000,000 francs in bars or in gold and silver specie.

Commercial relations with that land are of equal importance from a militaristic standpoint, for the bulk of our transactions have taken place almost without exception under the French flag. Year after year approximately thirty ships have departed from France for Mexico, while an equal number have returned to our ports. These ships combined represent a total of some 12,000 tons burden and are manned by 700 or 800 sailors. Mexican ships, on the contrary, play a relatively minor rôle in this transportation; from 1827 to 1843 only four were so engaged, whereas during this same period France devoted to this particular commerce 936 vessels.

These sail almost exclusively from the ports of Bordeaux and Havre, which dispatch and receive an equal number of French ships. Marseilles and Nantes, however, have sent out only a few ships. Four-fifths of our commerce is destined for the port of Vera Cruz, but ships returning to France often travel via Havana or Laguna del Carmen in Yucatán, or stop to take on dyewood at Campêche.[9]

Unfortunately, although our merchants are able to derive a certain amount of profit from Mexico, yet this is achieved at the cost of burdensome taxes and constant annoyances. All that the expedition from San Juan de Ulúa accomplished was to afford temporary relief to our fellow-countrymen. The Mexican government, moreover, has been quick to subject Frenchmen to an arbitrary and hostile system, for Santa Anna, aware of the sacrifices that expedition entailed, believes, although erroneously, that France will recommence hostilities only after serious difficulties and repeated affronts.

The conditions stipulated on March 9, 1839, have not as yet been executed, nor have the obligations recognized by this treaty been liquidated. The French are not treated as a favored nation; and although our merchants cannot obtain payment for legitimate sums due them within the last few years from the Mexican government, yet the English firm of Montgomery Nicod & Co., supported by the British cabinet, forced Mexico, on December 1, 1843, to sign an agreement in London by virtue of which this house will be wholly reimbursed to the amount of 941,500 piasters, the amount lent Mexico. In the current year, 1844, the firm of Montgomery will receive forty per cent in specie, while the rest of this amount will draw twelve per cent interest; to cover this, there have been alloted two and one-half per cent of the revenue of all the Mexican customs, and a part of the bonds selling at twenty-five mentioned in the general budget.

A careful examination will now be made of the outrageous decrees of the Mexican government against which the French minister has protested with almost constant vigilance.

---

[9]What was known as campêche-wood, or logwood, came from the southern shores of the Gulf of Mexico.

1. Decree of December 7, 1841, imposing another tax of two per cent on the import tax, attributed to the *juntas de fomento*[10] and the commercial tribunals.

II. Decree of May 31, 1842, placing on merchandise imported via the port of Vera Cruz, a tax of eight per cent in addition to the import taxes already in force, the proceeds to be applied to the construction of a railroad five leagues in length from the port as far as the San Juan River, traversing the property of President Santa Anna, called Manga de Clavo, and obviously having no aim but to increase its value.

III. Decree of October 25, 1842, fixing another supplementary tax on merchandise imported via Tampico, funds so derived to be used to create a road between the port of Tampico and the village of San Luís de Potosí.

IV. Decree of December 2, 1842, carrying an increased taxation on cotton goods, affecting especially our printed cottons from Alsace.

V. Decree of March 16, 1843, concerning the extraction, circulation, and exportation of legal tender, and increasing the taxes from five and one half to eleven per cent.

VI. Decree of April 17, 1843, ordering that for the duration of war between Texas and Yucatán—an armistice exists between these two countries, but war has not been terminated—all taxes on imports, international trade, consumption, and other duties shall be increased by twenty per cent.

VII. Decree of August 14, 1843, prohibiting the entry of a large quantity of articles which are not made in Mexico, and never will be made there, since their consumption is not in line with the capital necessary for their manufacture.

VIII. Decree of September 23, 1843, prohibiting foreigners from engaging in retail trade and allowing them only six months to terminate their affairs; this seems especially directed against France.

IX. New customs tariffs, published October 5, 1843, including a decree ordering the re-exportation, after an interval of one year, of merchandise already introduced, which has discharged the import taxes, now prohibited by the decree which Santa Anna determined to make retroactive.

The Mexican government vainly pretends to apply a principle that permits each nation to modify its tariffs; and it is equally contrary to the basic rights of men to attempt to prevent the citizens of a friendly nation

---

[10]**Juntas de fomento**, councils or assemblies with the function of protecting industry and commerce.

from engaging in certain industrial occupations. What is equally at variance with the simple tenets of justice, is the obligation imposed on the holders of merchandise henceforth prohibited, to re-export them at such short notice, without making any distinction between merchandise imported before or after the publication of the decree, and without allowing any reimbursement of taxes or expenses paid by the importers, although these taxes often increase by five or six times the original capital invested. Although the prohibited articles have been designated in the decree without reference to their nationality, yet they have been chosen in such a manner that their disposition touches particularly French commerce, notably the retailers and the factories of Paris, and if this edict regarding re-exportation is executed, a certain number of our fellow-countrymen will be irrevocably ruined.

Article XIII of the new tariff reaches much of our merchandise, especial discrimination being made against our wines and brandy. Thus French red wines in barrels will be admitted only by weight, and by payment, including the barrel, of nine piasters the quintal;[11] the tax on white wine is ten piasters; wines in bottles or kegs, twelve and thirteen piasters. Moreover, this does not take into consideration any waste, loss, or leakage of liquids.

Certain specified articles not included in the tariff, in place of paying twenty-five per cent on the value of the invoice, as provided by the decree of March 2, 1842, are to pay thirty per cent at the discretion of local appraisers, *aforo del vista,* which leaves the importer wholly exposed to the arbitrariness and greed of the employés.

Cotton goods mixed with silk, however slight the amount of the latter, enter as pure silk fabrics, and pay a tax of three piasters a pound. This clause has been inserted in order to double and triple, on some of these mixed goods, the amount of tax to which they were previously subjected. Fabrics from Roubaix, Lille, Amiens, Nîmes, and those from Lyon will suffer especially from this increase.

Nevertheless, other foreign merchants are not forced to submit to similar treatment. The Mexican government tacitly retains the right to issue licenses for prohibited merchandise, and since the publication of the tariff President Santa Anna has granted to five foreign houses, four English and one Spanish, the right to import 700,000 pounds of cotton thread, an article definitely prohibited. These houses are allowed to import this in bobbins, skeins, and small balls in thread of thickness

---

[11]Quintal, or hundredweight.

from number 22 as high as number 200, with an average tax of two reals the pound, which brings the president 175,000 piasters, or 825,000 francs.

Of these various decrees, those of September 23 and October 5 are especially fatal, and if accepted will demoralize our commerce. The Mexican government, aware that it would be impossible to attempt to execute the second edict, submitted to congress, by which it was passed, a proposal to postpone for a three-year period the re-exportation of merchandise. The juntas have failed to retard the execution of the decree of September 23, that vitally affected the French and prevented them from carrying on retail business. By an inexplicable contradiction, on the one hand foreigners are granted a long period in which to re-export merchandise, and on the other hand their shops are closed and the only means of selling goods removed.

On March 23 last the six months' period fixed by the decree of September 23, 1843, for the cessation of retail trade expired. From that date the majority of our citizens, in the belief that the law would be invoked against them, closed their doors. Others, rather than face ruin, timidly renounced their French rights and became naturalized Mexican citizens. Despite equable representations, General Santa Anna has persisted in his haughty attitude.

If the Mexican government remains deaf to our just claims, if she unwisely persists in refusing again to retract this decree of expulsion, then—independently of the indemnities that our citizens have the right to exact—after having exhausted with an unparalleled patience all means of conciliation, France no doubt will be obliged to throw on Mexico the full responsibility for her barbarous and unintelligent policy.[12]

Throughout this volume an attempt will be made to indicate how a question so vital to French industry and commerce is apt to terminate.

In Mexico, French creditors of the government fall into four distinct categories:

1)   For expulsion after the capture of San Juan de Ulúa.
2)   As a result of fire in the customhouse at Vera Cruz.
3)   For the reimbursement of consumption taxes illegally levied.

---

[12]Duflot de Mofras fails to explain how this situation arose. The grievance was deep-seated, dating back to the so-called Pastry claims, arising out of difficulties with a French baker in 1838 which aroused France to the inadequacy of Mexican protection for French subjects. Finally, after a series of unfortunate episodes, France dispatched a squadron of 26 ships and 4000 men to Vera Cruz, blockading the customs and finally, on November 28, 1838, taking possession of the fortress of San Juan de Ulúa near Vera Cruz. By the Treaty of Vera Cruz, Mexico guaranteed to pay back claims of 600,000 piasters within six months, and to grant all French citizens the privileges accorded the most favored nation.

4)   For the non-reimbursement of the value of copper money withdrawn from circulation, where the payment had been made by our
fellow-countrymen.

These debts do not take into consideration operations or supplementary contracts amicably concluded, but merely events of major importance, illegitimate measures, or formal engagements not executed.

As the result of the affair at Vera Cruz the expulsion of the French
was ordered while our troops were occupying the chateau of San Juan
de Ulúa. At that time our citizens were not granted the delay stipulated
by the commercial treaty existing between England and Mexico—a
treaty that regulated and governed our rights in the latter country, although France expects to be treated in this respect on a footing with the
most favored nation.

In the Treaty of Vera Cruz it was admitted as a basic principle that
France and Mexico would accord the citizens of the other power in-
demnitites as compensation for damages caused either to Frenchmen by
expulsion, or to Mexicans by the blockade and capture of their ships.
This question, which at first was to be submitted to the King of Holland
for arbitration, was left to the decision of England; however, the Mexican government delayed so long that it has been only within the last few
months that the information supplied by it has been received at London.

The origin of the claims of our merchants based on the destruction
by fire of the customhouse at Vera Cruz is as follows: At the time the
treaty of March 9, 1839, was signed, all merchant vessels held by our
cruisers which were found in the proximity of Vera Cruz were admitted
and allowed to discharge cargo; the merchandise thus unloaded was
stored in the warehouses by the customs officials pending appraisal and
delivery to their consignees. This operation was conducted by the Mexican officials in so leisurely a manner that on April 8, the day when the
fire broke out, the customs at Vera Cruz still contained much imported
merchandise removed either from ships entering after the blockade had
been raised, or from those which had already had time to arrive at the
port from New Orleans or Havana. The only aid rendered to check the
fire was supplied by French warships, for the customs had taken no
precautions to avoid such a disaster.

A few days after the catastrophe, French merchants at Vera Cruz
acting not only as individual citizens but also as representatives of their
correspondents in the cities of the interior, addressed a letter to the
Minister of Finance at Mexico City declaring that since they had been

forced by him to place the merchandise that had been consigned to them in this depository, and since no precautions had been taken by the customs at Vera Cruz to check or stop the fire, they were holding the Mexican government responsible for the disastrous results of April 8. The English, American, and German merchants, victims of this disaster, wrote in turn to the Minister of Finance, who failed to reply to their charges.

Notwithstanding, the Honorable Mr. Pakenham,[13] Minister of His Britannic Majesty, refused to ignore this silence and readily refuted the ineffectual arguments that M. de Bocanegra, Minister of Foreign Affairs in Mexico, incorporated in a note dated March 21, 1843, addressed to the English legation. The Mexican government subsequently attempted to force the foreign merchants to bear the loss suffered by fire, on the theory that they were responsible for the accident, the fire, according to rumor, having been caused by a tin of nitrous acid contained in a box. Under these circumstances Mexico held that our interests were not open to arbitration, although our claims, totalling 500,000 francs, exceeded those of England.

With equal ineffectiveness, for more than three years our merchants have been negotiating for the reimbursement of taxes illegally and violently levied. Their amount exceeds a total of 834,000 piasters—more than 4,000,000 francs!

While the Mexican government has not failed within the last two years to admit the justice of the claims and recognize in principle the right of reimbursement, yet no action has been taken in the matter. The fact, moreover, should be stressed at this time that certain taxes covering the Mexican tariff are interpreted in a manner entirely unknown in Europe. Thus the ten per cent tax, illegally levied, is not based on its nominal total, but is multiplied by three and one-third, thus raising the tax from ten to thirty-one per cent.

The last tragedy, caused by the demonitization of copper money, merits the same attention as the preceding problems. Throughout the Spanish régime, in Mexico as in Havana at the present time, copper money was in circulation. But soon after the creation of the republican government, contraband was introduced by Americans, especially to-

---

[13]The popular Irish diplomat, Sir Richard Pakenham (1797-1868) was first attached to the Mexican legation in December, 1826. On March 12, 1835, he became English minister to Mexico, where he served as intermediary during the French-Mexican Pastry War. In 1843 he was appointed minister to the United States.

ward the end of 1830, on a large scale. By bringing in enormous quantities of illegal pieces in tin chests that could be verified only with considerable difficulty and somewhat later by the establishment of shops for manufacturing counterfeit coin which were established by deputies of congress and high officials, especially at the ports of Mexico, at Tacabaya, and San Angel, copper money suffered heavy depreciation in value. Notwithstanding, in 1834 copper coins still retained a fictitious value four times in excess of their intrinsic worth. Then, about 1837, discount on this money soared to forty per cent.

The law of March 8 of that same year, making its circulation obligatory, was only partially executed; retailers, as a matter of fact, asked two prices for their merchandise, one payable in copper, the other in silver. In stores supplies sold for twice as much when bought with copper, as when purchased with silver money. Fearing a new reduction would be announced by the government, or that the law would be rigidly enforced, hoarders of wheat and other supplies refused to bring these commodities to the capital. These conditions lasted until a proclamation on November 24, 1841, by the president, ordering the introduction of a new copper coin worth .96 of a piaster. Heavier than the coins already in circulation, this new money had an actual value much nearer its nominal worth. This law was to go in force within thirty days in the department of Mexico City, and sixty days in other states, a delay granted to turn coin into the coffers of the government, which declared that it would withdraw from circulation copper money held by private individuals, under penalty of losing the benefit of the reimbursement. The latter was to be effective within six months from the day of notification, according to the decrees, by means of the new money. A series of decrees, too long to enumerate, prolonged the time of payment and provided various methods for redemption, among them new money, the sale of national resources, stamped paper, and a tax on patents.

These various projects might actually have indicated on the part of the government the intention to cancel the debts contracted, if in place of carrying out these decrees, it had only applied some of its national wealth, the bulk of the new money which had been coined, and the proceeds from the lump sale of old copper money, of which 35,000 quintals were sold at the rate of 10 piasters, to the French firm of Duport and Bellangé who sent it to France where they extracted from 90 to 95 francs a quintal, realizing from the transaction a profit of 40 per cent. However it may be, our commercial houses have had considerable skill in handling money, since for more than two years, when controlled by agents for Mexican treasure, the value of the copper on which they have not yet received three per cent, and have not drawn any interest exceeded 17,000 francs.

The total amount to be reimbursed is about 3,000,000 piasters, whereas now the receipts which the commission of amortization has at its disposal scarcely exceed annually 150,000 piasters, with the result that fifteen or twenty years would be required to handle the reimbursement of a debt that, according to the terms of the law, should have been liquidated in behalf of our merchants shortly after July 15, 1842.

The following table will indicate the amounts due French merchants by the Mexican government, exclusive of those submitted for arbitration to England, already mentioned in enumerating the character of the various claims.

SUMS DUE FRENCH MERCHANTS BY THE MEXICAN GOVERNMENT
During the presidency of General Bustamante:

	Piasters
To seven French houses, for the compulsory and illegal levying of various assessments	734,349
To various Frenchmen, for merchandise burned at the fire that destroyed the customhouse at Vera Cruz in 1839	100,000
Total	834,349

During the presidency of General Santa Anna:

	Piasters
To nine leading houses and several Frenchmen for the non-reimbursement of copper money which they turned into the government treasury	344,925
General total	1,179,274

or nearly 6,000,000 francs capital, an amount that would be more than doubled if, according to the legal usage of the country, compound interest had been added over the last three or four years, for which the rate is never less than one per cent a month.

These sums do not belong in their entirety to merchants residing in Mexico, but the latter represent a large number of houses in Paris, Bordeaux, Havre, Lyon, Elbeuf, Mulhouse, Rouen, and Saint Etienne.

The seriousness of these problems, the invariable unjustness of these measures, the constant violation of promises, have aroused to a high degree the solicitude of the French government, and undoubtedly energetic measures would promptly end a state of affairs that compromises the fortune and safety of our merchants. As a matter of fact, if the attitude of hostility and surreptitious pilfering were to endure, our citizens would be compelled to withdraw from business in New Spain. Nor should our population in Mexico, any more than that of Buenos Ayres and Montevideo, deserve to be abandoned to their fate, or neglected.

CHAPTER III*

History of the Spanish Voyages of Discovery along the west coast of America north of the equator.

Before describing the west coast of America that borders on the Pacific Ocean, the Spanish expeditions leading to its discovery and the repeated attempts made to find a northwest passage will be summarized. Between 1498 and 1502 Christopher Columbus made his epochal voyages.[1] During his third voyage, in 1498, the American continent was discovered. In 1502, while on his fourth expedition, Columbus atttempted to find a strait that might facilitate navigation into the South Sea and establish a new route to the land of spices. From Indians along the coast of Veragua and Nombre de Dios where he hoped to find this passage, he undoubtedly procured a certain amount of vague information about the South Sea and the narrowness of the Isthmus of Panamá that separated the two oceans. From this arose the belief in the existence of a strait that led to his indefatigable explorations along the east coast and adjoining regions.

In 1513 Vasco Nuñez de Balboa,[2] governor of the Spanish colony at Darien, crossed the mountains, definitely proving the existence and lo-

*This corresponds almost verbatim to Mêmoire III, Vol. 43, Amérique, folios 116 to 129. This Mêmoire was written from the port of Mazatlán on March 22, 1841, and addressed directly to the Minister of Foreign Affairs. Omitted from the printed volumes are folios 110 to 113 telling of the need for a Mexican consul and ships on the west coast, describing in detail English battleships in Mazatlán harbor, and reporting the strength of the American forces on the coast.

[1]Apparently De Mofras disregards the momentous voyage of 1492. Columbus was seeking a new route to the spiceries and died in the belief that the lands he had discovered were Asia. The life and travels of Christopher Columbus (1446-1506) were first recorded by his son Ferdinand; and in 1867 were finally published in English in London. Historians, notably Bartolomé de las Casas in his Historia de las Indias (Madrid, 1876), have drawn heavily on this record. In 1893 the Hakluyt Society published the journal of his first voyage under the editorship of C. R. Markham. Among recent volumes on Columbus is that of John Boyd Thatcher, Christopher Columbus (New York, 1903-1904).

[2]Vasco Nuñez Balboa (1475-1517) came to America about 1500 with the expedition of Rodrigo Bastidas, residing for a time at Española. In 1510 he went to Darien, where he served as alcalde. After a series of expeditions made with local Indians, on September 25, 1512, he sighted the Pacific—or Great South Sea—reaching its shores four days later. As he was preparing ships to explore this new ocean, he was arrested, after a brief voyage, by the new governor of Darien, whose enmity he had incurred, and beheaded.

cation of the South Sea, so long a matter of conjecture. In 1519, Magellan[3] discovered the passage that bears his name. By Magellan's voyage
one of the problems that perplexed geographers—whether the globe
could be circumnavigated—was definitely solved. Throughout this period Spanish mariners did not venture on this route that presented
grave dangers, especially in the Strait of Magellan, where the wind
blows constantly from the east and where the distance from Europe
to the Indies is nearly as great as by the eastern course.

In the meanwhile Cortés, after conquering the Aztec empire, assumed charge of several expeditions that were being prepared along
the coast of Mexico near the South Sea. In a letter written from Valladolid on June 6,[4] 1523, Emperor Charles V ordered Cortés to search for a
passage along the shores of the two seas.[5] While the latter was sending
three caravels and two brigantines out to explore the northern coast
of the Atlantic from Florida to Newfoundland where the strait was
believed to exist, other mariners conducted a search along the coast of
Panamá, exploring the shores of Soconusco, Tehuantepec, and New
Galicia.

In 1528, during the absence of Cortés, who had been forced to make
a trip to Spain to refute certain slanderous reports that were being circulated about him, his nephew Don Diego Hurtado de Mendoza and
Captain Don Cristóval de Olid, with five ships and a brigantine, continued these explorations. Accompanied by a force of 400 men, adventurers and artisans of all kinds, in 1530 Cortés returned to Mexico.

The following year Cortés outfitted several ships at Tehuantepec and
Acapulco. This new expedition set sail on June 30, 1532,[6] under the leader-

---

[3]Fernão de Magalhães, known as Magellan (1480-1521), had served with the
Portuguese in the East Indies, but turned to Charles V of Spain for assistance
in finding a western passage to the Moluccas. With five ships and 265 men, he
passed through the straits, reaching the sea, which he called Pacific, on November 20, 1520. The following March he discovered the Philippines. Here, on one of
the islands, he was murdered by the natives.

[4]The five letters sent to Charles V between 1519 and 1526 by Cortés during the
course of his explorations, recount in a graphic manner his experiences in the
New World. See **Hernán Cortés, Five Letters,** edited by Ross and Power (London, 1928).

[5]Gómara, **Crónica de Nueva España** (D. de M.). De Mofras refers to Francisco López de Gómara (1510-1560), a noted historian and close friend of Cortés
in Seville. In 1552 he published the **Historia de las Indias,** and its sequel **Crónica
de la conquista de Nueva España,** the latter dedicated to the son of Hernán
Cortés.—ed.

[6]Cortés was constantly thwarted by Spanish officials in his attempts to build
ships, his difficulties arising primarily out of the use and abuse of native labor.
According to Bancroft, **Mexico,** II, 421, two ships of this expedition set sail in
May, not June.

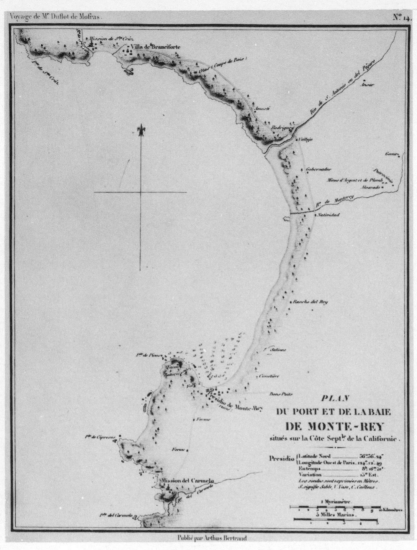

PLAN
DU PORT ET DE LA BAIE
DE MONTE-REY
situés sur la Côte Septle de la Californie.

PLAN OF THE PORT AND BAY OF MONTEREY

ship of Hurtado de Mendoza, who was ordered to reconnoiter the west coast of New Spain and the islands of the South Sea. Although this navigator reached 27° north latitude, yet, because of the mutiny of his crew, he was separated from his fleet and perished with his ship on the rocks near the Tres Mariás Islands, which he had discovered and of which he had taken possession. The remaining vessels of this expedition were wrecked off the shores of Culiacán, where the governor, Nuño de Guzmán[7] seized the cargo and indicted those who had escaped in the disaster.

Hernán Cortés, courageous in the face of disaster, now proceeded in person to Tehuantepec and outfitted two more vessels, entrusting the command to Don Hernando de Grijalva[8] and his lieutenant, Captain Don Diego Becerra. Having departed on October 30, 1533, the expedition discovered and took possession two months later of the islands of Socorro and San Benedicto. Commander Becerra, who had preceded the captain, was now assassinated by his pilot, Ximénez. The latter, after setting a course toward the west, was the first to land in Lower California where, with twenty-two members of his crew, he was killed by the Indians. When the ship returned to the coast of Jalisco, the pearls brought back so aroused the cupidity of Governor Guzmán that he seized the ship with its cargo.

When this act became known, Hernán Cortés, aware that orders issued in his behalf by the audiencia[9] had not been executed, outfitted three ships at his own expense at the port of Tehuantepec and sent them on to Chametla.[10] There Cortés, traveling overland with a train of cavaliers and foot soldiers composed of 400 Spaniards and 300 negroes, joined them in the month of August. The flotilla set sail on April 15,

---

[7]Nuno, or Núñez, Beltran de Guzmán (1485-1544) was a Spanish lawyer and soldier who was sent to govern Pánuco in northwestern Mexico. Here he came in conflict with Cortés. As virtual ruler of Mexico from 1528 to 1531, he incurred hatred and enmity by his harsh acts, especially by his enslavement of Indians. In 1531 he was deposed, disgraced, and fined. His life and activities are discussed at considerable length in Bancroft, **Mexico**, II, **passim.**

[8]Grijalva, in charge of the **San Lazaro,** discovered what are now known as the Revilla Gigedo Islands. Becerra on the **Concepción,** with **Fortún** Ximénez as pilot, was murdered soon after leaving port by the latter. Ximénez now sailed on and discovered Lower California, where he was killed by the natives. The cupidity of Guzmán was later punished. See Bancroft, **North Mexican States and Texas,** 2 vols., (San Francisco, 1884) I, 45-47.

[9]Audiencia: Literally, a hearing given by men in power to those who have something to propose or present; in Spanish America, a court or council.

[10]This was late in 1534, or early in 1535. In the spring of the latter year Cortés started overland to join them at Chametla. De Mofras incorrectly observes that the forces met in August, but Cortés undoubtly reached the coast in the spring.

1535, and on May 1 sighted the coast of California. On the third, anchor was dropped in the bay of La Paz. There on the neighboring shores the shields, swords, and bones of Ximénez and his comrades were discovered. The expedition had been divided into three units, for Cortés had intended to make several trips across the gulf that bore his name to assemble his men. However, upon learning of the arrival in Mexico of Don Antonio de Mendoza,[11] the first viceroy appointed to New Spain, he hastened to the capital to defend his interests, which were being seriously menaced.

Disembarking at Acapulco, he dispatched two ships to Peru to assist Pizarro. He then began the construction of four new vessels to conduct further discoveries. The year following, having recalled Captain Don Francisco de Ulloa[12] from California, he entrusted to him the command of an expedition that departed on June 8, 1539, from Acapulco to continue explorations up the Gulf.

Ulloa, after reconnoitering the entire coast from La Paz to the mouth of the Colorado River at the head of the Vermilion Sea, felt confident that the two coasts were connected, and that California was a peninsula, and not an island. Having returned to Cape San Lucas, he traveled north once more as far as the thirtieth parallel, visiting Magdalena Bay and the islands of Cerros and Santa Margarita. Upon reaching this latitude, the expedition was forced by contrary winds and a shortage of provisions to retrace its course. Toward the end of May, 1540, Ulloa returned to Acapulco.

These various explorations were conducted with such care and skill that the map of California drawn in 1541 by the pilot Domingo del Castillo[13] differs but slightly from the maps drawn in our own day. However, these discoveries aroused so little interest that in the account of his voyage printed at Amsterdam in 1716, Woodes Rogers[14] appeared

---

[11]Antonio de Mendoza served as viceroy from October, 1535, to November, 1549, later holding this same office in Peru. In Mexico he was instrumental in extending colonization toward the north and discovering the mineral resources of Mexico. See **A. S. Aiton, Antonio de Mendoza, First Viceroy of New Spain** (Durham, N. C., 1927); C. Pérez Bustamante, **Don Antonio de Mendoza, Primer Virrey de la Nueva España,** (Santiago de Chile, 1828).

[12]Francisco de Ulloa, who had assisted Cortés in the conquest of Mexico, was one of his most able leaders. He was now given charge of the **Santa Agueda,** the **Trinidad,** and **Santo Tomás,** 60 soldiers, and three Fathers. He left on July 8, not in June. For his voyage see Henry R. Wagner, **Spanish Voyages to the Northwest Coast of America** (San Francisco, 1929), pp. 11-50.

[13]Castillo's map is reproduced in Bancroft, **North Mexican States,** I, 81.

[14]Woodes Rogers and his fleet left England in August, 1708. En route to their piratical activities they rescued Alexander Selkirk, better known as Robinson Crusoe, who was marooned on Juan Fernández Island. See his journal entitled **A Cruising Voyage round the World** (London, 1712).

to be in doubt whether California was an island or part of the main continent.

However, Hernán Cortés, by his success, had incurred the jealousy of the viceroy who personally dispatched two expeditions toward the northwest, one overland in command of Captain Francisco Vásquez [de] Coronado,[15] and another led by Hernán [de] Alarcón, by water. The latter, who left Acapulco in 1540, traveled as far as the head of the Vermilion Sea, ascended the Colorado River in two boats, for a distance of eighty-five leagues, and, having failed to find Coronado, returned after an absence of several months. The explorations of Hernán Alarcón extended over a period of two years. Although reaching as far north as forty degrees, yet Alarcón found no trace of those fabled cities of Cíbola and Quivira that Father Marcos de Niza[16] claimed to have discovered on his earlier travels.

In 1540, Hernán Cortés, exhausted by controversies with the viceroy and embittered by the unjust manner in which the court of Madrid rewarded his loyal services and epochal discoveries, returned to Spain.

Two years later Don Antonio de Mendoza went down to the province of Jalisco, or New Galicia, preparatory to sending out new expeditions. Of these, one under the leadership of Ruy López de Villalobos[17] was dispatched to colonize the Mariannes and Philippine Islands; the other, headed by Juan Rodríguez Cabrillo,[18] set sail on July 27, 1542, from the port of Navidad. This latter expedition explored in consider-

---

[15]Francisco Vásquez de Coronado (1510-1549), came to Mexico in 1535 with Mendoza. Four years later he was appointed governor of New Galicia. In April, 1540, he started overland on an expedition of discovery that carried him into Arizona, New Mexico, Texas, and Kansas. For the tale of his amazing adventures see George Parker Winship, **The Coronado Expedition, 1540-1542**, 14th Report Bureau of Ethnology (Washington, 1916). Alarcón left Acapulco on May 9, 1540, with two small ships. Having ascended the gulf, he then made two futile attempts to ascend the Colorado and join Coronado.

[16]Marcos de Niza (1510-1570) was a Franciscan priest who in 1539 undertook a journey of exploration north of Culiacán, finally reaching the Zuñi pueblos which he called Cíbola. Rumors of golden cities circulated upon his return to Mexico led to Coronado's expedition in which he participated. See G. P. Winship, **op. cit.**; Fanny R. Bandelier, **The Journey of Alvar Núñez Cabeza de Vaca** (New York, 1922), which includes a translation of the report of Father Marcos.

[17]In November, 1542, a fleet in charge of Ruy López de Villalobos, accompanied by 370 men and several friars, set sail to colonize Cebu. The Philippines were named by this expedition. After many vicissitudes the colonists returned to Spain in 1547. See Wagner, **Spanish Voyages**, pp. 99-100, and **passim**.

[18]Juan Rodríguez Cabrillo was a soldier who came to New Spain in 1520 where he served under Cortés and Alvarado. The narrative of his voyage of 1542, resulting in the discovery of California, is the first account of this land, its inhabitants, and its future prospects. He was the forerunner of the Spanish advance toward the northwest. For the diary of that voyage, see Wagner, **Spanish Voyages**, pp. 72-93.

able detail the coast of Lower California, the islands lying north of this
land, and the Bay of Pines, subsequently known as Monterey.

On January 5, 1543, Juan Rodríguez passed away on San Bernardo
Island, inhabited at that time solely by Indians. The head pilot, Bartolomé Ferrelo, who now assumed command, sailed north to 43° where,
encountering foul weather, he was forced to turn south once more. At
latitude 40° a lofty promontory was discovered which was later named
Cape Mendocino, by the expedition of General Vizcaíno, in honor of
the viceroy, Mendoza.

In 1564 the viceroy, Don Luís de Velasco, dispatched another expedition to California.[19] Simultaneously a second attempt was made to
take formal possession of the Philippines.

Lured by the urge for loot, in 1575 a party of English pirates led by
John Oxenham[20] crossed the Isthmus of Panamá, built a ship on the
Pacific Ocean and raided the Spanish Main. Within a short time these
outlaws were captured and summarily executed. Then, in 1579, after
devastating the coast of Guatemala, Sir Francis Drake[21] appeared off
the shores of New Spain, sailing up as far as 45° or 46° north latitude.
Approaching the coast, he dropped anchor in a small bay, not clearly
defined, where he failed to find supplies. Forced as a result to turn back
as far as latitude 38°, he anchored in Los Reyes Harbor, between the
ports of Bodega and San Francisco, of whose existence he was in ignorance. Although reaching California thirty-seven years after Cabrillo's
voyage, the English leader did not hesitate to name the land New
Albion, thus attempting to claim the honor of being its discoverer.

In the summer of 1582, Captain Francisco Gali[22] left Manila on a
voyage of discovery. Sailing north of Japan, he explored the coast of

---

[19]Luís de Velasco, Count of Santiago, was second viceroy of Mexico from
1550 to 1564. He proved an able and constructive leader. The expedition sent out
at his order was in charge of Miguel López de Legaspi. For a full account of his
régime see Bancroft, **Mexico**, II, 565-599.

[20]John Oxenham, a comrade of Drake, with 70 men conducted raids off the
Pearl Islands, frequented by Lima-Panamá ships. Loot taken was later recovered
by Spanish owners, while the gang was forced to hide in the mountains, where
they were ultimately captured and executed.

[21]For many years Francis Drake (1545?-1595) had traveled extensively along
the Spanish Main, bent on plunder. Under the auspices of Queen Elizabeth he
left England in December, 1577, with 166 men and five ships. While attempting
to find a passage leading west into the Atlantic, he sailed up the west coast.
The narrative of his voyage, **The World Encompassed**, was first published in
1628 in London. A modern edition was published by the Hakluyt Society (London,
1854). See also Henry R. Wagner, **Sir Francis Drake's Voyage Around the World**
(San Francisco, 1926).

[22]Francisco Gali left Acapulco for Manila in 1582. See Wagner, **Spanish
Voyages**, pp. 133-138.

America as far as 57° north latitude, then, having visited Capes Mendocino, San Lucas, and Corrientes, sailed south to Acapulco.

On November 15, 1587, Thomas Cavendish,[23] who had set boldly forth to loot the rich coastal towns of the Spanish Main, appeared off Cape San Lucas to await the approach of the *Santa Anna,* a Philippine galleon of 700 tons burden carrying a cargo valued at more than 5,000,-000 piasters, which, after a brisk fight, was captured.

Less than a year had elapsed when another adventurer, Lorenzo Ferrer Maldonado,[24] asserted that he had passed through a strait leading into the South Sea that would enable ships to travel in three months from Spain to China. For many years this imaginary passage, known as the Strait of Anián and believed to connect the two oceans somewhere above Newfoundland, baffled geographers. The apocryphal voyages of Maldonado and Admiral Pedro Bartolomé Fonte,[25] who in 1640 was believed to have passed through this same strait, do not merit consideration. The voyage of Juan de Fuca[26] will be discussed in a future chapter.

In 1595 Gómez Pérez Dasmariñas,[27] governor of the Philippine Islands, ordered the ship *San Agustín,* in command of Sebastián Rodríguez Cermeñon,[28] to explore the coast of California, and especially the port of San Francisco. Unfortunately a squall carried the ship on the rocks, where she was wrecked in the bay she had come to reconnoiter.

---

[23]Thomas Cavendish (1555?-1592) was a seasoned mariner who in 1585 had sailed to Virginia. On July 21, 1586, he left Plymouth with three small ships bound for the Pacific. His capture of a Spanish galleon on November 15, 1587, was incidental to his achievement as the second mariner to circumnavigate the globe.

[24]Lorenzo Ferrer Maldonado was the third of this trio of doubtful voyagers. See Henry R. Wagner, **Apocryphal Voyages to the Northwest Coast of America** (Worcester, Mass. 1931), pp. 42-58; and **infra,** I, 60, 61, II, 73.

[25]Pedro Bartolomé Fonte, a Spanish navigator, probably made certain discoveries and in 1640 was supposed to have sailed from Callao up the Californian coast. The inaccuracy of reckonings and the lack of definite records, however, have caused this voyage to be regarded as apocryphal. See **infra,** II, 69, 73.

[26]The discoveries of the Greek pilot, Juan de Fuca, were never substantiated, although Michael Lok, patron of navigators of that era, was among his supporters. See Henry R. Wagner, **Apocryphal Voyages,** pp. 7-20. See also **infra,** II, 63, 64.

[27]Gómez Pérez Dasmariñas died in 1593. This was probably his son, Luís, who succeeded him. For a full account of his rule see De Morga, **The Philippine Islands,** edited by Henry Stanley (London, 1868), pp. 38-87.

[28]Sebastián Rodríguez de Cermeño or Cermeñon was a pilot on the Manila-Acapulco route. In this decade, when the Manila trade was absorbing the interest of the Spanish crown, a port of call somewhere in California was imperative to break the voyage, for the Philippine galleons lost many men from malaria and scurvy. Sailing from Manila on the **San Agustín** in 1595, Cermeñon landed on November 4 near Cape Mendocino, which he called La Baya de San Francisco. Wagner identifies this as Drake's Bay. See his abstract of Cermeñon's voyage in **Spanish Voyages,** pp. 156-167, and **passim.**

For some time the depredations of English freebooters in the South Sea had been arousing the consternation of King Philip II. As a result of these raids the Count of Monterey,[29] viceroy of New Spain, was ordered to send Don Sebastián Vizcaíno[30] to California to explore its harbors and take possession of the country. General Vizcaíno left Acapulco in the spring of 1596, returning toward the end of the same year. Six years later, in 1602, the viceroy sent Vizcaíno with a squadron of five ships and a large retinue that included Carmelite Fathers, pilots, and cosmographers, on a second voyage to California. It was during this expedition that the Port of Pines was first named Monterey. One of Vizcaíno's lieutenants, Martín de Aguilar,[31] who sailed as far north as latitude 43°, discovered Cape Blanco which Captain Cook[32] subsequently renamed Cape Gregory, just as Vancouver gave the English name of Oxford [Orford], to Cape Diligencias which had been discovered many years before his day by Vizcaíno. Early in 1603 the latter returned to Mexico.

Between 1616 and 1635, during the régime of the Marquis de Guadalcazar, then viceroy of New Spain, Don Juan de Iturbi, Francisco Ortega, and the pilot Carbonel,[33] while conducting explorations in the Vermilion Sea, brought back some pearls of rare beauty and immense value.

Under Admiral Pedro Porter[34] several more expeditions were made, between 1635 and 1640, to California. Soon after, in 1642, the new viceroy,

---

[29]This was Gaspar de Zuñiga y Acebedo, Count of Monterey, who in 1595 became Mexico's ninth viceroy. He proved an able and sane ruler. Because of his interest in colonization, Monterey in Mexico and Monterey in California were named in his honor. His ancestral palace and the family chapel where he lies buried are in Salamanca, Spain.

[30]This famous Spanish mariner, Sebastián Vizcaíno (1550?-1628?), came to Mexico about 1585 to engage in trade, especially the pearl industry. On his first important expedition, that of 1596, he left Acapulco in June with three ships, and founded a settlement that was later abandoned at La Paz. On his epochal voyage of 1601-1602, notable for its discovery of Monterey Bay, he sailed to, or possibly beyond, Cape Mendocino. A full account of this voyage is found in Wagner, **Spanish Voyages**, pp. 171-285. See also Bancroft, **California**, I, 13-14, 97-104.

[31]Martín de Aguilar, who had charge of the **Fragata**, was separated from Vizcaíno's ships and reached a northerly point that has not been definitely ascertained.

[32]For Captain Cook's activities see **infra**, II, 38, 53, 70, 81.

[33]Cardona and Iturbi sailed up the gulf to 34°, not in 1615, but in 1616. It was in 1631 that Estéban Carbonel, financed by Francisco de Ortega, sailed to the peninsula, searching for pearls. His second voyage took place in 1633-1634, and a third in 1636.

[34]Pedro Porter y Casañate, who was licensed by the Spanish government to survey the coasts of the South Sea, made several expeditions at this time and in 1640 was given the exclusive right to navigate in the gulf. See Bancroft, **North Mexican States**, I, 177-180. In 1642 Luís Cestín de Cañas, accompanied by Father Cortés, conducted extensive explorations near La Paz.

the Duke of Escalona,[35] sent the governor of Sinaloa, together with several members of the Jesuit Order, into this new land to establish missions and to christianize the natives. Later, between 1665 and 1668, Admiral Piñadero and Captain Lucenilla,[36] at the instigation of the Spanish government, led expeditions along the west coast of Mexico.

The Jesuits extended their activities in 1683 when Admiral Otondo,[37] accompanied by Fathers Juan María de Salvatierra[38] and Eusebio Francisco Kino,[39] a noted astronomer from Ingolstadt, crossed over to La Paz. From this time onward the religious orders were invested with the ecclesiastical, civil, and military administration of the missions. Their goal was to win over to the faith within a relatively short period, the natives of Lower California. The methods used in this task might serve at all times as models.[40]

A year later, in 1684, Dampier[41] and the English pirates who had established headquarters at the Galápagos Islands, continued their notorious raids along the Spanish Main.

In 1701, and again in 1703, Father Kino conducted his epochal explorations north of California and along the Colorado River. The Jesuit missions in California were now awarded an annual subsidy of 13,000 piasters by Philip V.

---

[35]Diego Pacheco Cabrera y Bobadilla, Duke of Escalona and Marquis of Villena, was a Spanish official who became viceroy of Mexico on August 28, 1640. Quarrels with the visitador led to his arrest and removal from Mexico two years later.

[36]In 1667 Bernardo Bernal de Piñadero, commissioned by Philip IV to reduce California, sailed to Lower California. Captain Francisco Luceñilla y Torres explored the peninsula in 1668, searching for pearl fisheries.

[37]In the Spring of 1683 Isidro Otondo y Antillon, accompanied by the Jesuit Fathers Kino, Copart, and Goñi, attempted to establish a colony on the peninsula at a point called San Bruno near La Paz. Soon Indian hostility forced the colonists to return to Mexico.

[38]The Jesuit, Juan María de Salvatierra (1648)-1717), was the founder of the peninsular missions that paved the way for those in Upper California. His first church was Loreto, founded in 1697. Contemporary Jesuit activities are fully discussed by the Spanish historians, Venegas, Clavijero, Alegre, and Ortega. See supra p. 113, note 32. See also Venegas' Juan María de Salvatierra, edited by Marguerite Eyer Wilbur (Cleveland, 1929).

[39]Eusebio Francisco Kino (1644-1711), one of the most noted Jesuit pioneers of the Southwest, spent more than twenty-five years in southern Arizona and northern Sonora, exploring, converting, and founding missions and pueblos. Kino left many letters and diaries, the most important of which have been published by Herbert E. Bolton as Kino's Historical Mémoir of Pimería Alta (2 vols., Cleveland, 1919). See also his Rim of Christendom (New York, 1936).

[40][Miguel] Venegas, Noticia de la California escrita por el R. P. Andrés Burriel [3 vols.], Madrid, 1754 [1757]. See infra, I, 244, note. (D. de M.).

[41]William Dampier (1652-1715) was an English freebooter and explorer, who sailed on several piratical cruises to the Spanish Main. After circumnavigating the globe, he published A New Voyage Round the World (3 vols., London, 1697). This was subsequently published in four volumes in various editions.

During the activities of the English pirates, Rogers and Dampier, that extended from 1709 to 1711, one of the rich Philippine galleons, bound for Acapulco, was captured off Cape San Lucas.

In 1719, and again in 1721, the domains of the Jesuits were extended by a series of overland explorations conducted by Father Ugarte[42] and Father Guillen [43] in [Lower] California.

Then, in 1743, Admiral Anson[44] captured a Spanish galleon carrying 4,000,000 piasters that was returning to Acapulco from the Philippines and China. These repeated raids by pirates along the coast finally caused the government to prepare to erect fortified settlements and to found Spanish colonies in California. Warships were now sent out to patrol the coast and to ward off such attacks. As a result, the missions, after being established, were afforded the security needed for their development.

In 1746 Father Consag[45] explored the Colorado River with the object of organizing other missions and opening an overland route from Sonora to California. The Jesuits, by their explorations, subsequently extended their domains, governing their missions in a paternal manner until 1767, when they were succeeded by a group of Franciscans from the Royal College of San Fernando in Mexico. In 1768, the visitor general, José Gálvez,[46] accompanied by the engineer Miguel Costansó[47] visited

---

[42]Juan de Ugarte (1662-1730) was one of the most noted Jesuit Fathers of the west. In 1700 he went over to the peninsula to join Salvatierra, where he founded the mission of San Xavier and the pueblos known as San Pablo, Santa Rosalía, and San Miguel. Much of his time was spent in putting the missions on a firm basis, in introducing various fruits and grains for native use, and in teaching agriculture, spinning, and weaving. A man of robust health, untiring industry, and unfailing enthusiasm, to him is due, after Salvatierra, the credit for the Lower California missions. He left a **Diarios, relaciones, y cartas de las cosas de California,** which was used by the historian Venegas. See also Juan José Villavicencio, **Vida y Virtudes del Venerable y Apostolico Padre Juan de Ugarte** (Mexico, 1752).

[43]Clemente Guillen, founder of Mission Dolores del Sur, south of Loreto, was one of the earliest explorers of the peninsula; in 1719 he reached Magdalena Bay.

[44]George Anson (1697-1762) was the English admiral sent out in 1640 to attack the Spanish possessions in South America. After many vicissitudes, on June 20, 1643, he captured the Spanish galleon **Nuestra Señora de Covadonga,** subsequently selling her cargo in Canton.

[45]Fernando Consag (1703-1759) was a Jesuit Father in charge of Mission San Ignacio, above La Paz. In 1746 he conducted important explorations up the Gulf to the Colorado River.

[46]José de Gálvez Gallardo (1720-1787) was one of the ministers under Charles III. From 1761 to 1774 he served as visitador-general to Mexico and the Indies and later as viceroy. He also organized and led the first expedition to California. See H. H. Bancroft, **History of California** (7 vols. San Francisco, 1884-1890), I, 113-136, and **passim;** also Herbert I. Priestley, **José de Gálvez** (Berkeley, 1916).

[47]Miguel Costansó was the cosmographer of the Portolá expedition. His diary, edited by Frederick J. Teggart, has been translated and published in the **Publications of the Academy of Pacific Coast History,** II, No. 4 (San Francisco, 1911).

California in person. Then, in November, 1769, an overland expedition that had traveled by way of Sonora, reached Monterey. Through the efforts of the thirty Franciscans Fathers who had arrived from Spain on the ships *San Carlos* and *Concepción,* five new missions were founded within a short time along the banks of the Colorado River and in Upper California.

The sloop of war *Santiago,* in command of Juan Pérez,[48] left San Blas in January, 1774, and reconnoitered the coast as far north as latitude 55°. Upon her return voyage, the port of Nootka, which Captain Cook pretended to have been the first to enter—although the fact has been definitely established that he did not stop there until 1779, several years later—was discovered.

The success of Pérez' first voyage induced the viceroy, Antonio Bucareli,[49] again to send out the sloop *Santiago,* in charge of Captain D. Bruno de Heceta,[50] together with the brig *Felicidad,* with Captain Juan de la Bodega y Quadra.[51] On September 16, 1775, these ships set sail from San Blas. At 41° north latitude, Port Trinidad was discovered. Foul weather now forced the sloop to return to Monterey, but the officers of the brig, in their youth and enthusiasm, refused to obey signals and sailed on boldly toward the north. On August 17, the brig sighted a vast bay which was named Heceta's Strait in honor of their captain. Into this bay empties the San Roque River, designated by the triple title of the Oregon, the Columbia, or the Asunción River. Eventually, twenty years later, this northern entrance received from Vancouver[52] the name of Cape Disappointment.

The brig continued on as far as 58° north latitude, sighting en route Mount Jacinto, named Mount Edgecumbe by Cook in 1779. Scurvy having broken out on board ship, Juan de la Bodega was forced to retrace his route to Monterey, but before turning back, a port which he named Port Bodega was discovered. In this same region the Russians now own a settlement which they frequently refer to as Romanov.[53]

---

[48]Juan Pérez, a Mallorcan, was captain of the **San Antonio** on her voyage of 1769. On the expedition of 1774, on the **Santiago,** he discovered the northwest coast. For the diary of this journey see Herbert E. Bolton, **Palóu's New California** (4 vols., Berkeley, 1926), 147-206.

[49]Antonio María Bucareli y Ursua (1717-1779) served for a time as governor of Cuba, and from 1771 until his death, as viceroy of New Spain.

[50]For Heceta see **infra**, II., 17, also **note** 9.

[51]For Bodega y Quadra see **infra**, I., 58, 61, II, 52, 71.

[52]For George Vancouver see **infra**, II., 41, **note** 17.

[53]Romanov (Romanoff or Romanzoff.) For the Russian settlements in California see **infra**, II, 1-28, also appendixes A and B.

In the year 1777, [1776] two Franciscans, Fathers Vélez and Escalante,[54] explored the lands west of the Sierra Madre, and the upper waters of the Colorado, Navajo, and Gila rivers.[55]

On February 11, 1779, the war sloops *Princesa* and *Favorita,* commanded by Ignacio Arteaga and Juan de la Bodega y Quadra, who had received orders to ascend as far north as 70° latitude, carefully explored the coast, leaving a record of their voyages which is of absorbing interest.[56]

Another notable voyage was that of the illustrious La Pérouse[57] who, in 1786, after discovering and naming Port des Français, a bay site above 56° north latitude, visited Monterey.

Since the year 1779 the Spaniards had failed to dispatch any expeditions to the Northwest Coast. But the encroachment of the Russians and the importance of the voyages of Captain Cook, as well as several other English and American captains, soon aroused the cabinet of Madrid from its lethargy. As a result, on March 8, 1788, Don Estévan Martínez[58] and Don Gonzalo López[59] with two brigs, the *Princesa* and *San Carlos,* sailing north from San Blas, explored and visited several Russian settlements on the Aleutian Islands, among them Unimak, Kodiak, and Unalaska. Having learned from Commander Izmaïlov[60] at the latter port that three ships were soon due from Kamchatka and that plans had been made to take possession the following year of the port of Nootka, where two frigates from St. Petersburg were to join them, Martínez hastened preparations for his return voyage to San

---

[54]Father Silvestre Vélez de Escalante was a Spanish Franciscan who came to Mexico in 1768, subsequently traveling extensively in the Southwest, searching for a route from Santa Fé to Monterey. For the interesting diary of his explorations of 1776-1777, in company with Francisco Atanasio Domínguez, see W. R. Harris, **The Catholic Church in Utah** (Salt Lake City, 1909), pp. 125-242. See also H. E. Bolton, "Escalante in Dixie and the Arizona Strip," in the **New Mexico Historical Review,** III, No. 1, (Santa Fe, January, 1928).

[55]See Crónica [serafica y] apostólica del Colegio [de propaganda fide] de la Santa Cruz de Queretaro, Mexico. 1799. [1792] by [Juan Domingo] Arricivita. (D. de M.). This is a history of missions and colonization in Mexico, Arizona, and California.—ed.

[56]**Relacion del Viaje de la Fragata Princesa,** from the archives of Mission Santa Clara in Upper California. (D. de M.). The **Princesa** made four voyages along the Northwest Coast. The narratives of these voyages are found in Wagner, **Spanish Explorations, passim.**—ed.

[57]La Pérouse: See **infra,** I, 207, also **note 17.**

[58]Martínez: See **infra,** II, 63, 71.

[59]Gonzalo López de Haro, who was in command of the **San Carlos,** accompanied Martínez to Alaska in 1788 and to Nootka in 1789.

[60]This was the explorer Gerasim Grigorovitch Izmaïlov, then in charge of a small Russian colony at Three Saints Harbor.

Blas, where he landed after a brief sojourn at Monterey early in December.

When the viceroy of New Spain, Don Manuel de Flores,[61] was informed of these Russian movements, he immediately dispatched Martínez to Nootka to prevent not only the Russians, but also the English, from founding the first settlements on the island, Spanish claims to this island being incontestable since Captain Pérez, in 1774, had anchored near Nootka Harbor.

Martínez reached Nootka on May 5, 1789, and immediately dispatched the ship *Gertrudis,* in command of Don José Narvaez,[62] to verify the existence of the Strait of Juan de Fuca. Narvaez spent six months in these explorations. On July 6, an English ship, the *Argonaut,* came into port. She was commanded by an English officer, James Colnett,[63] who carried official orders to take possession of Nootka. This officer, who did not appear to be in full possession of his mental faculties, refused to show his credentials and indulged in such excesses that Martínez, who felt compelled to make him a prisoner, sent him to the viceroy for further action. Since the frigate *Nuestra Señora de Aranzazu* had brought orders to the Spanish ships to return to San Blas, Martínez, after removing the guns he had set up for defense and destroying the ramparts, left Nootka in September.

On February 3, 1790, the viceroy, Count Revilla Gigedo,[64] sent another expedition, in command of Don Francisco Elisa,[65] composed of the frigate *Concepción* and the bilanders *Princesa* and *Argonauta,* well armed and adequately supplied with munitions and troops to this new settlement. Reaching Nootka on March 4, they took possession without delay and set up batteries.

On May 4 of the same year, Don Salvador Fidalgo[66] set sail with

---

[61]In 1787 Manuel Antonio Flores, an officer of the royal navy, became viceroy of Mexico. Two years later he resigned and returned to Spain.

[62]José María Narvaez was pilot in charge of the schooner **Santa Saturnina,** dispatched to explore the Northwest Coast in company with Martínez. See also **infra,** II., 63, 64.

[63]James Colnett, of the **Argonaut,** was an officer of the East India Company who had been sent to America to found a trading post. He reached Nootka on July 4, 1789, where he was captured by the Spaniards. A full account of his experiences is found in Bancroft, **Northwest Coast,** (2 vols., San Francisco, 1884), I, 210-212, 217-233; and in Wagner, **Spanish Explorations in the Strait of Juan de Fuca,** (Santa Ana, 1933), pp. 155-156.

[64]In 1789 Revilla Gigedo succeeded Flores as viceroy. He at once decided to reoccupy Nootka, recently abandoned by his predecessor.

[65]See **infra** II, 73, **note** 20.

[66]Salvador Fidalgo in charge of the **Filipino,** accompanied Lieutenant Elisa.

the packet *San Carlos,* to explore the coast as far as 60° north latitude.
A thorough exploration was conducted, during which, near 61° north
latitude, an active volcano was discovered which was named in his
honor.

Within a short time, on May 31, Don Manuel Quimper,[67] of the
bilander *Princesa Real,* founded a colony at the port of Nuñez Gaona
at the southern entrance of the Strait of Juan de Fuca. Subsequently
the English renamed this port Neah Bay. This strait was again explored in considerable detail in 1791 when Elisa returned with the
packet *San Carlos* and the small brig *Santa Saturnina.*

During the course of a scientific expedition around the world, the
sloops *Descubierta* and *Atrevida,* in command of the able hydrographers
Malaspina[68] and Espinosa, put in at Acapulco. The Spanish court had
requested them to make a thorough inspection of the Northwest Coast.
The aim of many expeditions of this time was definitely to prove the
reality of the evasive northwest passage whose existence M. Buache,[69]
geographer to the King, relying on the idle claims of Lorenzo Ferrer
Maldonado, had announced in September, 1790, to the Academy of
Sciences at Paris. The sloops reached Bering Bay in June, 1791. After
examining in some detail all openings and all neighboring ports, they
felt convinced that Maldonado's belief in the existence of a passage in
these higher latitudes should be discredited.[70]

Inasmuch as the Strait of Juan de Fuca could not be fully explored,
since the ships sent out for this purpose were too cumbersome for the
task, in order to navigate among the innumerable islands that dot the
Northwest Coast which might conceal some inner sea or the mouth
of some important river, the Spanish government outfitted two small
brigs at Acapulco especially designed to conduct a minute search for
this passage.

Leaving San Blas in February, 1790, the vessel reached Nootka early in April.
Here the men began to repair the old fort, finally taking formal possession on
April 10. Many of the letters, diaries, and instructions relating to this expedition
have been published by Wagner in his **Spanish Explorations.**

---

[67]Manuel Quimper, in charge of the **Princesa Real,** accompanied Elisa.

[68]Alejandro Malaspina with the **Descubierta** and **Atrevida,** after engaging in
a scientific voyage around the world, was sent in 1791 to Alaska to seek the
strait supposed to have been discovered by Maldonado.

[69]Jean Nicolas Buache de la Neuville (1741-1825) was a noted French geographer and writer whose **Géographie élémentaire ancienne et moderne,** was
widely known.

[70]See his **Mémoirs** published in 1798 at Madrid by Captain Don Ciriaco
Cevallos. (D. de M.). This appears in a collection entitled **Disertaciónes sobre
la navegación á las Indias Occidentales par el norte de la Europa,** 1798.—ed.

On March 3, 1792, this expedition, led by the able officers Alcalá Galiano and Don Cayetano Valdés, left Acapulco. On the twelfth of the same month anchor was dropped at Nootka, where two frigates and a brig in command of Captain Don Juan de la Bodega lay at anchor. Bodega had arrived to assume charge of carrying out the agreement made by the English to withdraw from Nootka as signed on October 28, 1790, between this power and Spain.

The frigate *Nuestra Señora de Aranzazu* reached San Blas on May 13, but left within a short time on a voyage of exploration north of Nootka. On June 2 the schooner in command of Galiano and Valdés entered the strait, visiting the settlement at the port of Nuñez Gaona. After spending at least three months exploring the strait, they departed, convinced that the assertions of Juan de Fuca carried no more weight than had those of Maldonado.

At the same time Vancouver's expedition consisting of a sloop and brig was cruising through these same waters prior to exploring the shores and taking over from the Spaniards the port of Nootka, so unjustly wrested from Spain by England through the Treaty of Escorial. At the time these two commanders met, the large island which together with the continent formed the Strait of Juan de Fuca, received the name of Quadra and Vancouver Island.

Toward the end of August, Galiano and Valdés sailed south from Nootka. Having explored the mouth of the Columbia River and skirted the coast of California, at the close of November, 1792, they reached San Blas. This voyage brought to a close the series of scientific expeditions sent out by Spain to the Northwest Coast. From then on her interests were centered on the settlements of Upper California, since this land afforded ports of call for ships coming from the Philippines.

Frequently the question has been raised whether the Spanish government always published a complete record of all voyages of exploration made under the leadership of noted astronomers and skilled navigators. The comprehensive volumes published by the Bureau of Hydrography at Madrid would seem to afford, however, an adequate answer to this query. Even if the Spaniards had failed to reveal portions of their documents, would such an act justify reproach? From the day these colonies were discovered, it is a well-known fact that intrigues have been incited by foreigners in an effort to bring about an insurrection against the mother country.

CHAPTER IV*

A description of the Isthmus of Tehuantepec. Plans for inter-communication between the Atlantic and Pacific Oceans. Port of Acapulco.

The idea of linking the Atlantic with the Pacific, after its discovery by Nuñez de Balboa, aroused the interest of the earliest Spanish conquerors. In fact, as early as 1520 Angel Saavedra advised Charles V to cut a passage through the Isthmus of Darien. In his correspondence with the emperor, Hernán Cortés referred to this projected passage as the Secreto del Estrecho, or the secret of the strait. After the conquest in 1521 of Michoacan and Oajaca, this great captain ordered Don Gonzálo de Sandoval[1] to explore the Province and Isthmus of Tehuantepec. Since that time, the relatively short distance across the Isthmus has proved of absorbing interest to the viceroys of New Spain, for this route was constantly used by merchants traveling from Acapulco to the Gulf of Mexico.[2]

Toward the end of the eighteenth century, when the able viceroy, Don Antonio de Bucareli attempted to ascertain how some bronze cannon cast at Manila had been transported to the citadel of San Juan de Ulúa, the discovery was made in the *Crónica imperial de la Ciudad de Tehuantepec,* that these pieces had been brought from the Pacific Ocean to the Gulf partly by land, but mainly by way of the Chimalapa, Mal Paso, and Coatzacoalcos rivers. This country was inspected at a later date by two engineers, Don Miguel del Corral and Don Agustín Cramer, who believed that a canal approximately eight leagues in length connecting the Chimalapa and Mal Paso rivers would establish direct communication between the two oceans.

At the time when the political embroglios of 1814 were stirring Europe, the Spanish Cortés issued orders to the Mexican viceroy to carry out the project of cutting through the Isthmus.

---

*This chapter is a continuation of **Mémoire I** and is found in **Amérique,** Vol. 43, folios 52 to 69. The first paragraph of this has been radically changed.
[1] Don Gonzálo de Sandoval, the valiant and benevolent conqueror with Cortés of Mexico, later turned his energies toward exploring Central America.
[2] Since the distance from the Bay of Campêche to that of Tehuantepec is only 130 miles, many projects were advanced to link the two oceans. In 1774 Miguel Corral and Agustín Cramer, young Spanish engineers, inspected the ground and proposed a route via the Chimalapa and Mal Paso rivers.

The unexpected revolution of 1821 failed to deter the Spanish general, Don Juan de Orbegoso,[3] from making a careful survey of the situation and drawing a map which, however, was not published until 1839. Although geologically somewhat incomplete, yet the work was adequate to convey an accurate idea of the character of the country and the difficulties it presented.[4]

By virtue of the decree of March 1, 1842, President Santa Anna granted the right to establish this line of communication to one of his friends, Don José Garay,[5] a business man and capitalist, who finally became involved with the government. In May, 1842, a new and so-called scientific expedition left to complete the work of General Orbegoso and to begin actual operations.

The topography of the Isthmus having been briefly indicated,[6] the privileges defined in this concession and the benefits to be derived from establishing direct communication will now be examined. The Isthmus of Tehuantepec lies within the states of Oajaca and Vera Cruz. At its narrowest point—a direct line drawn from one sea to the other—it has a minimum width of fifty leagues. The Isthmus is crossed by the Sierra Madre,[7] or main chain of the Cordilleras, that flatten out in these regions. Upon leaving the sea, this mountain chain rises on the south in a series of ranges that extend throughout the entire length of the Isthmus, whereas the two ranges toward the north gradually become lower as they approach the Gulf of Mexico. Through this region the Coatzacoalcos, that plays a major part in connecting these two bodies of water, flows.

The Coatzacoalcos rises in the Sierra Madre that traverses the provinces of Tabasco, Chiapas, and Oajaca. Its headwaters are formed by a series of small streams, the most important among them being known

---

[3]In 1821 General Orbegoso surveyed Tehuantepec, but his map remained unpublished eighteen years, as herein stated.

[4]See Resultado del Reconocimiento hecho en el istmo de Tehuantepec por el general Orbegoso, and Diario del Gobierno de la Republica Mexicana, March 3, 1842, and map No. 3 of the atlas. (D. de M.).

[5]Santa Anna's edict, as well as a full description of the local topography, is published in a pamphlet of 128 pages by José de Garay, entitled An Account of the Isthmus of Tehuantepec (London, 1846), pp. 104-107. Garay completed his survey in 1842-1843 but, failing to fulfill the terms of his contract, his grant was declared forfeited in 1851 by the Mexican Congress.

[6]Map 3 of the atlas accompanying the original French edition of Duflot de Mofras carries a detailed plan of this territory. José Garay, op. cit., reproduces a detailed map of this country drawn in 1847 by Commodore M. C. Perry.

[7]The Isthmus of Panamá extends between 16° and 18° n. lat., and 97° 30' w. long., Paris time. (D. de M.).

as the Guelaguesa[8] and the Almoyola rivers. Since the country is full of impenetrable forests, the source of the Coatzacoalcos cannot be accurately ascertained. As the river approaches the sea, innumerable side streams empty into its channel. After following a tortuous course for more than fifty leagues, the river empties into the Gulf of Mexico.

According to reports, the bar, which is available for deepening, has a depth not to exceed four or five meters. However, on beyond, the river is extremely broad and of sufficient depth to accommodate ships of all sizes. The tides are scarcely noticeable at the bar, while the depth of the channel does not fluctuate. Since ports are not available along the coast in the immediate vicinity, a ship caught in a northerly squall would undoubtedly perish if blown toward the mouth of the river.

The first settlement of importance in the mountains near the source of the Coatzacoalcos is Santa María de Chimalapa, situated at an elevation of 286 meters above sea level. Not far beyond the village an ill-fated attempt was made by M. Laisné de Villévêque to establish a French colony. One of the streams that descends from the Sierra is bordered by superb pines. In fact, the Spanish government has sent wood cut from the forest of Tarifa to be used in its lumberyards at Havana. The timber, tied together to form rafts, was floated downstream to the mouth of the river.

Ten leagues north of the hacienda or property of Chivela, the river is joined on the left by a fork called the Alamán, which is formed in turn by the junction of Malatengo and Guelaguesa rivers. This river is also augmented by the waters of the Almoyola, described in the proposed plan as the highest point north of the Sierra Madre where the waters of the Coatzacoalcos could be stemmed. Some four leagues below the Alamán, the channel of the river is blocked by the Mal Paso, a slate-colored bank that almost wholly obstructs navigation. Two leagues below—again on the left—the Sarabia River is encountered, then at fairly regular intervals the de la Puerta, or Jumuapa,[9] and the Mijes or Jaltepec; and, on the right the Chalchijapa,[10] Tecolotepec, and the Sugillaga.[11]

Below this main stream for a distance of nine leagues the channel divides, forming the Island of Tacamichapa. On the left, at the tip of the island, the Monzapa, which rises in the Sierra of Acayucan, joins

[8]The Guelaguesa is probably the Chichihua.
[9]Jurumuapa in the French text.
[10]Chalchijalpa in the French text.
[11]This appears to be the Suchiata.

the main stream. Four leagues below, along the right bank the Coachapa[12] and Chichijapa rivers empty and, on the left, the lagoon of Tlacojalpan, which adjoins a village of the same name. Small schooners are able to ascend as far as this point. El Paso de la Fabrica, situated below the lagoon which is dotted with tiny islands, is somewhat dangerous. The river, however, now broadens and grows deeper. On its left, a league before the mouth is reached, a navigable stream, the Calzada, is absorbed. Where it joins the main river, whose mouth is known as La Barrilla, an island rises.

The banks of the Coatzacoalcos are low and semi-inundated during the rainy season. The shores are filled with enormous trees suitable for building, cabinet work, and woodwork. Markets and labor being unavailable, however, this timber has not been exploited. After leaving El Paso de Sarabia, the river winds through gorges formed of slate-colored mountains. Navigation is feasible for large ships for seven or eight leagues up the river, to the vicinity of the lagoon of Tlacojalpan. From this point on, the channel becomes shallow, averaging slightly more than fifteen feet. At Mistan Grande the banks of slate and clay are first met. These shoals become so numerous that from Piedra Blanca as far as El Paso de Sarabia—a distance of some thirty leagues or more— twenty-one falls and cascades are encountered. These are frequently a meter high and have so little water at certain seasons that in the month of May General Orbegeso was forced to have his canoes carried even though they drew only one foot of water. In order to eliminate the bends in the river, a subsidiary canal might be built as far as Piedra Blanca. Undoubtedly several of these shoals or clay banks could be excavated. The slate banks above and below Sarabia, however, would require the construction of locks.

The land lying between the sea and Sarabia consists primarily of sandy clay, alluvial deposits, and crushed rock that prevents the waters from flowing north of the Sierra Madre In the vicinity of these mountains the soil is composed of slate, chalky deposits, and granite. South of the Cordilleras, porphyry striated with azure, crystals of feldspar, and hornblende are present, but no part of the Isthmus reveals evidences of deposits of volcanic origin.

The Sierra Madre continues on beyond the states of Puebla and Vera Cruz, crossing, from northeast to southwest, the province of Oajaca. Having reached the Isthmus, it bends north upon approaching the

---

[12]Cuachapa in the French text.

Pacific Ocean. From there, after passing between the haciendas of Chivela and La Venta de Chicapa, the chain runs northeast toward Guatemala. The depression becomes extremely flat and low near the Isthmus. At the entrance to the port of Guie Vichi[13] the average height does not exceed 583 meters and, in the gorge of the Chivela, approximately 241 meters. At this point the two watersheds divide. North of the Cordilleras the rise is gradual, extending over an area of some fifteen leagues. Toward the south, on the other hand, the slope is abrupt, dropping nearly 200 meters within a space of three leagues, then merging into an immense plain that extends as far as Tehuantepec and the large navigable lagoons that terminate toward the south at the sea.

Throughout this plain the soil is composed of alluvial deposits, pieces of rocks, and especially of hills of slate that extend to the sea and over to the neighboring islands. The distance from the Sierra to the lagoons is six leagues. The inner lagoon, called La Boca de Santa Teresa, is four leagues wide at its mouth. A distance of three leagues separates this from the bar that blocks the entrance to the lagoons near the sea. The outer lagoon, measuring approximately forty leagues in length from Tilema as far as Tonolá, has a depth of some five meters along the route used by small craft. The bar of San Francisco, called Boca barra del mar, is covered, on the other hand, with breakers, and lies less than two or three meters from the open sea.

Most of the streams north of the Cordilleras empty into the Coatzacoalcos, whereas on the southern slope the small streams flow in every direction. Although dry during the summer season, later in the year they pour down into the inland lagoons. The streams on the east flow toward Tonolá, while those on the west swell the Tehuantepec River. In addition to the fact that for part of the year they are dry, they are too far from the Coatzacoalcos and too inaccessible from the Sierra to afford the desired communication. The stream that flows past San Miguel and La Venta de Chicapa has its source near the headwaters of the Coatzacoalcos, but is so dry for one-third of the year and its slate-impregnated soil is so porous and full of fissures, that it would require to be reinforced with masonry. These streams also rise so high up in the mountains that reservoirs could not be devised.

The upper forks of the Coatzacoalcos near Santa María de Chimalapa might prove of value if some gorges affording a natural opening were found on the east. But the nature of the soil obviously presents serious

---

[13]This appears to refer to Mt. Guie Viche near the town of Tehuantepec.

obstacles, and whether the advantages derived would be commensurate with the enormous expenditures involved in such a project appears doubtful. However, if a decision were made to establish communication, the San Miguel, which empties into an upper lake, should be made available. In any event the rivers would require considerable excavation and need to be provided with locks.

This information, supplemented by a careful examination of the map, would indicate that the difficulties encountered in attempting to build a canal would be almost insurmountable. Although flat-bottom boats can ascend in the rainy season as far as the Almoyola north of the Sierra, and to the Juchitan and Chicapa rivers that empty into the upper lagoon on the south, yet this route, open only a few months annually, does not afford uninterrupted travel. A plan based on making the Coatzacoalcos navigable for some forty leagues to the confluence of the Malatengo would be preferable; for beyond this point a canal only twenty-two leagues in length would need to be cut before the end of the lagoon was reached.

The soil does not present any special obstacles to opening a route, nor would the topography prevent the construction of a railroad. However, at the lagoon two grave problems arise. Where the inner lagoon communicates with the outer, the passage is obstructed by the Santa Teresa bar, while the passage from the outer lagoon to the sea is almost wholly obliterated by the shoal of San Francisco. Thus these two bars would have to be removed and harbors made for ships drawing fifteen feet of water near the embarcadero. Nor should the fact that such a project would entail tremendous expenditures be disregarded. Even if the route were opened up as far as the village of San Dionisio, there would still remain the problem of the constant sanding-up of the bar by the sea to be surmounted. Neither would it be possible in this instance to use the small anchorage on the coast west of the bar of San Francisco, and east of the entrance to the Tehuantepec River, for the bed and mouth of this stream change constantly. Twenty years ago the river emptied into the lagoon below Huilotepec, but since that time it has reverted to its old channel. During the rainy season, however, some of its branches empty into the Tilema lagoon, inundating all the adjoining lands which are low and marshy. It was at the small port of Tehuantepec, called on old Spanish maps Barra de la Ventosa, that Hernán Cortés constructed and equipped the first ships used in his explorations in the South Sea.

At the summit of the Sierra Madre pines and oaks abound. Through-out the Isthmus the soil is extremely fertile and adapted to the cultiva-tion of coffee, sugar cane, cocoa, indigo, and cotton. But along the coastal regions, especially near marsh or waste lands, maladies fatal to natives and deadly to Europeans lurk. The only healthful localities are the villages and plateau country of the Cordilleras that are remote from the two oceans, even though their elevation above sea level, as indi-cated in the following table, is inconsiderable.

Table of elevations of various points on the Isthmus of Tehuantepec from north to south across the Sierra Madre. Although these figures do not claim to be strictly accurate, yet they are close enough to serve this particular purpose.

	meters
From Sarabia on the Coatzacoalcos River	45
Vicinity of Sarabia, the road from Guichicovi	79
San Juan Guichicovi	265
Santa María Petapa	229
Cerro Pelado	615
Santa Mariá Chimalapa	286
Highest point between Santa María and the Coatzacoalcos	322
Altitude near San Miguel	392
Coatzacoalcos River, three leagues east of Chimalapa	160
Farm or hacienda of Tarifa	264
San Miguel Chimalapa	173
Highest point between Tarifa and San Miguel	357
Hacienda of Chivela	241
Plain of Chicapa by way of San Miguel	112
Venta de Chicapa	54
Village of Juchitan	30
City of Tehuantepec	41

The major articles of the edict issued by General Santa Anna where-by Don José Garay was granted the exclusive right to make a cut through the Isthmus of Tehuantepec are as follows.[14]

Article 2.—Communication shall be established by water, or by means of railroads and steamships.

---

[14]De Mofras does not quote these paragraphs in full. See Garay, op. cit., pp. 105-106.

Article 3. The passage across the Isthmus shall be a neutral zone and open to all nations at peace with the Republic of Mexico.

Article 4. M. Garay guarantees to complete at his own expense and within eighteen months, as part of the present concession, a survey of the Isthmus and shall designate ports and possible routes. If within eighteen months construction has not been started, he shall lose his concession. Any construction of land passages or waterways shall be made by means of steam engines. The contractor shall erect at designated ports fortifications and stores, but must compensate individuals for all lands condemned for use. However, the sale of land larger than one-half league in width must not be required.

Article 5. The concessionaire, or those to whom he entrusts his powers or privileges, shall enjoy the following rights: For fifty years they shall retain all transportation taxes levied on merchandise and passengers, but after this period has elapsed the government of the republic shall have the exclusive right to exploit traffic by steamer or railway. During the fifty-year period of exploitation, the company, after deducting all costs of maintenance and administration, shall give the government one-fourth of the net profits, and, for the next seventy years, the government in turn shall reciprocate for the benefit of stockholders. The government grants full rights to the company over ten leagues of waste lands belonging to the state on each side of the route or canal along its full length.

Article 6. Any foreigner is allowed to acquire lands fifty leagues beyond each side of the line of communication and to engage in any industry, even the exploitation of mines. This land shall become the fatherland of all who come here to settle and who abide by the laws of the republic.

Article 7. The government guarantees to afford the company all aid and protection possible in the execution of its project, and not to impose any taxes or assessments on goods or passengers in transit during the first fifty years of its existence, nor to impose on the management or its holdings any forced loans or assessments.

Article 8. The government shall maintain, along the route and at the ports, customs officials to apprehend contraband goods, but these men shall not interfere in any way with the administration of the company. Special legislation shall be enacted to cover this situation.

Article 9. When the construction has been completed, the work shall be checked by two engineers who shall determine whether all requirements of the contract have been met.

Article 10. If the linking of the two oceans seems feasible and if some company or individual offers to undertake the project, such offers cannot be accepted for the duration of the fifty-year concession granted M. Garay, except with the full consent of the latter, or his legal agents and representatives.

Article 11. By virtue of this basic agreement the conditions stipulated by the government and Don José Garay shall be notarized and registered with all the formalities required by law.

Certain articles of the agreement filled, according to the custom of the country, with obviously extravagant phrases that promised to make Mexico not only the center of world commerce, but also the emporium of power and wealth, have been suppressed. The fact should be observed that article six, granting foreigners the right to purchase lands fifty leagues beyond the line of communication, should be annulled, since it comes into direct conflict with the decree of the same president, Santa Anna, dated March 11, 1842, that allows foreigners to locate at will throughout the department of Mexico and to own real estate, on the single condition that they locate five leagues from the frontier or the sea.[15]

Don José Garay hopes to secure stockholders at London. But whether English firms will be willing to risk their capital in an enterprise that offers such uncertain chances of success seems doubtful. Stockholders in English companies that were formed to exploit Mexican mines have lost large sums of money; and all signs indicate that this lesson will have made them cautious.

However, the conversion into a canal of a river throughout most of its length, the creation of two ports on the Gulf of Mexico and the Pacific Ocean, and, finally, the removal of two bars that are constantly sanding up, as well as the mortality that decimates European colonies, are almost insurmountable obstacles to the creation of a passage through the Isthmus of Tehuantepec.[16]

An examination of the map, as well as this topographical description, will demonstrate the futility of a canal passage, while land transportation would prove valueless for goods carrying heavy freight charges. The

---

[15]See **Diario del Gobierno de la República Mexicana, March 15, 1842, articles 1 and 10.** (D. de M.).

[16]By a decree issued in October, 1843, President Santa Anna ordered the construction of a prison on the Isthmus of Tehuantepec, adequate to hold 300 culprits who were to be supported at the expense of the contractor of the project and were to be used by him on the canal work, if that were undertaken, which appears doubtful. (D. de M.).

inhabitants of the provinces of Yucatán, Tabasco, Chiapas, and Oajaca can, as a matter of fact, procure their supplies direct at their local ports, and it would be more satisfactory for these various states to establish wagon routes leading from their main villages down to the coast.

Of the various methods of communication possible between the Atlantic Ocean and the South Sea, that of bisecting the Isthmus of Tehuantepec seems to be the last that should be adopted. The passage across Panamá and especially the lake of San Juan de Nicaragua appears far easier to execute, for the latter affords an adequate port on the Atlantic, and an excellent harbor on the Pacific—Nicoya or Realejo. Moreover, the lakes of León and Nicaragua are navigable by large vessels.

This idea of direct communication has been under investigation at various periods.* In 1780 a French officer, Martin de la Bastide,[17] submitted to the court at Madrid a plan for linking the oceans, by way of the Partido River, an intermediate canal, the lake of San Juan de Nicaragua, and the San Juan River. Again, in 1781, the engineer Don Manuel Galisteo,[18] made a complete survey of conditions at the order of the Spanish government. Although the new valley recently discovered on the Isthmus of Darien which, because of its levelness, was called to the attention of the Academy of Sciences in 1842 by the scholarly M. Arago[19] combines invaluable conditions for establishing a railroad, yet ports are lacking at the mouth of the Chagres, whereas the relative simplicity of the hydraulic work at Nicaragua will always give the latter route an added advantage over that through the Isthmus of Panamá. However, the superb harbor of Puerto Bello on the Atlantic could be made the terminal of a railroad that crossed over from the Bay of Panamá. But a canal of large capacity, or any other means of transit for ships of large tonnage is obviously preferable to a railway.

In addition to the Franco-Granada Company, backed by the firm of Salomon and Company of Guadalupe, Baring Brothers of London have estimated the amount required to make a cut through the Isthmus of Panamá. Their figure places the total cost at 3,475,000 piasters, and the

---

*Pages 72 to 75 do not appear in the Mémoire. See Amérique, Vol. 43, Mémoire I, folios 64 and 65.

[17]H. H. Bancroft, History of Central America (3 vols., San Francisco, 1883-1887) III, 695, note, assigns 1791 as the date of Bastide's plan, but adds that the French revolution caused it to be abandoned. Bastide's project was elaborate, calling for the widening of rivers and the construction of large canals.

[18]However, Galisteo, a royal engineer, declared that such a plan was impracticable.

[19]Reports read at the meetings of the Academy of Sciences in December, 1842. (D. de M.).

annual profits at some 764,610 piasters, a return of approximately twenty-two per cent.

The French government, fully aware of the importance of this problem, sent M. Garella,[20] of the Royal College of Mines, to examine the Isthmus of Panamá, and the reports of this well-known engineer on this matter, which have been of the utmost importance for several years, will undoubtedly be made public.

In the accompanying table, the distances and traveling time for steamers leaving the central point of the Isthmus—without reference to Chile or Peru—to reach all important points in the Spanish American countries north of the equator, the principal archipelagoes of the South Sea, and a few points on the coast of Asia, are correctly indicated.

Table of distances in nautical miles and number of hours required to travel by steamer from Panamá to the following points.

Points of Departure	Miles	Hours
From Panamá to the Gulf of Nicoya	435	48
Gulf of Papagayo	590	65
Realejo	680	75
Sonsonate	847	94
Soconusco	1095	121
Tehuantepec	1210	134
Acapulco	1495	166
Manzanillo	1780	197
San Blas	1962	218
Mazatlán	2091	232
Guaymas	2448	272
Colorado River	2793	310
San Diego (Via Mazatlán	3016	335
(Direct	2760	306
Monterey (Via Mazatlán	3376	375
(Direct	3120	346
San Francisco (Via Mazatlán	3456	384
(Direct	3200	355
Bodega (Via Mazatlán	3514	390
(Direct	3258	362

[20]In 1843 two engineers, Garella and Courtines, commissioned by the French government, advocated an elaborate plan involving sluiced canals across the Isthmus of Panamá.

Columbia River (Via Mazatlán	4034	448
(Direct	3570	385
Bering Strait via Columbia River	5970	663
Honolulu (Sandwich Islands)	4620	513
Petropavlovsk, Kamchatka, via the Sandwich Islands	7380	820
Tahiti	3540	381
Marquesas Islands	3150	347
Japan, via the Sandwich Islands	7950	883
Canton, China, via the Sandwich Islands	9540	1060

Direct route to China from Europe via the Isthmus of Panamá.

Points of Departure	DISTANCE IN NAUTICAL MILES	NUMBER OF OF DAYS BY SAILING VESSEL	NUMBER OF DAYS BY STEAMER
From Havre to Chagres	4830	43	26
From Chagres to the Sandwich Islands	4540	41	25
From the Sandwich Islands to Hong Kong	5160	46	27
Total	14,530	130	78

By way of the Cape of Good Hope, the distance is approximately 200 miles shorter, and a sailing-vessel traveling at a speed of five miles an hour can make the trip in 121 days. This route, however, presents more dangers and greater difficulties.

From Acapulco, the following distances and time are correct.

Points of departure	MILES NAUTICAL	DAYS BY STEAMER
From Acapulco to Honolulu (Sandwich Islands)	3,000	10
From the Sandwich Islands to Guam (Mariannes Islands)	3,100	10
From Guam to Macao or Canton (China)	1,600	5
Total	7,700	25

From Guam to Singapore, at the tip of the Malay Peninsula, the distance is 2,300 miles, and from there to Calcutta or Madras, 1,200, making a total of 3,733 nautical leagues as the distance from Acapulco[21] to Calcutta.

[21] Port of Acapulco: 16° 50′ 28″ n. lat.; 120° 12′ 44″ w. long.; time 6h 48m 50s; declination, 8° 17′ N. E. (D. de M.).

In 1838, the *Compagnie de la Navigation á vapeur dans l'Océan Pacifique,* an organization capitalized at £250,000 and whose steamers plied between ports at Chile and Panamá, was formed in London. The company hopes to send its boats farther north as commerce expands and business with Peru, the countries near the Equator, New Granada, and Mexico, assumes wider importance.*

That direct connection between these two vast oceans would infuse new life into this useful venture is obvious, and our transatlantic steamers should be encouraged to take an active part in this maritime development which cannot fail to prove advantageous to our colonies in the Antilles Sea and the Pacific Ocean.

The lands of New Spain that touch the South Sea will profit in many ways if the American continents are severed. Should this occur, Acapulco would derive the major benefit, for, given the impetus of expansion and security, this port, being the nearest point to Mexico City, from which it is separated only by one hundred leagues, would be in an advantageous situation. How opulent Acapulco became under the Spanish régime when the Philippine galleons brought in their rich cargoes, is known to the world at large.

Thus, the Mexican government should pay particular attention to this port for both the coast east of Acapulco known as the Costa Chica, and that called Costa Grande, which extends as far as Manzanillo, enjoy extraordinary fertility, yielding among other products a superior grade of cotton which might later become, like that produced in Colima, an important export.

The city of Acapulco has lost much of its former grandeur. Its population which, after the arrival of the Spaniards, increased to 9,000 inhabitants has, at the present time only 2,000. Her foreign trade in the meanwhile has dwindled to a few exchanges with countries along the equator and Peru, and a limited coastal commerce.

The Spaniards knew the vital importance of ready contact with Acapulco; and in addition to constructing a fine road between Vera Cruz and Mexico City, they had even mapped out a route and assembled the necessary materials for a road that would link the capital to Acapulco by way of Cuernavaca and Chilpancingo. In fact, immense piles of

---

*The balance of this chapter is found in **Mémoire II, Amérique** Vol. 43, folio 65.

[22]An excellent contemporary account of Acapulco is that of Admiral Dupetit Thouars. See his **Voyage,** II, 197-215. (D. de M.) De Mofras was undoubtedly familiar with these volumes, which cover much of the ground over which he traveled.—**ed.**

stones lying along the present roads are still visible. However, deep-rooted unrest and constant revolutions in Mexico will, it is to be feared, never allow this superb country to execute projects that require a wise and sane administration, or depend on the viceroys of New Spain for their conception and execution.

CHAPTER V*

*Territory and City of Colima. Volcanoes. Port of Manzanillo, Valla-
dolid, New Galicia, Guadalajara, Tepic, Jalisco, San Blas, Mazatlán,
and Guaymas. Commerce along the coast.*

Upon leaving Acapulco, the coast, which is flat and formed of what
are known as the sands of Coyuca,[1] bends toward the west. After Point
Jequepa[2] is passed, the coast bends slightly northward, then twenty
leagues beyond approaches Morro de Petatlán,[3] a lofty mountain readily
recognized by the surrounding islands.

Between this point and several white islands lies the small port of
Sihuantanejo. The entire coast is dotted with villages and salt-works
that are exploited by the inhabitants. The approach is reasonably safe,
but firm anchorage is not obtainable. There are no rivers of importance
in the vicinity. The Zacatula[4] that rises near the volcano of Jorullo,[5]
as well as the Camuta and Coalcomán rivers are unnavigable. Tejupán
and Santiago bays, located north and east of the promontory called
Mamelons de Tejupán, can only be classed as open roadsteads.

From this point the general direction of the coast is almost directly
north for half a league. After bending west, the shore then passes the
estuaries of the Coaguanaja,[6] Apiza, and Armería rivers as far as the
point of San Francisco or Ventanas. This is a landmark for the southern
entrance of the port of Manzanillo which is defined on the north side by
the two conspicuous hillocks of Juluapa and a coast fringed with palms.

---

*This corresponds to the first section of **Mémoire II, Amérique** Vol. 43, folios
70 to 92.

This **Mémoire** was written from Mazatlán, Dec. 29, 1840, and contains brief
information [see folio 72] of De Mofras' travels up to this period. Sections appear
to have been rewritten, but not materially altered. Pages 145 to 154 are not in
the **Mémoire** and have been added to the published version.

[1]The sands of Coyuca extend for 25 leagues beyond Acapulco.

[2]Apparently Point Japutica.

[3]Morro de Petatlán, 170° 32′ n. lat.; 103° 40′ 54″ w. long. (D. de M.). This lies
northwest of Acapulco in the state of Guerrero.—ed.

[4]Sacatula in the French text.

[5]The Jorullo volcano, 1,300 meters high, lies 28 leagues south of Morelia.

[6]Probably Coahuayana.

Although the port of Manzanillo or Salagua[7] has never received particular notice, yet at some future date it should acquire considerable importance. By glancing at the previously unpublished map that accompanies this chapter, it is obvious that this port is infinitely superior to the open roadsteads of San Blas and Mazatlán, since it affords four excellent anchorages where ships of large tonnage can anchor at all seasons on one of the approaches.

Upon arriving at the entrance to Manzanillo Harbor, ships should keep well out at sea and then head directly in toward land, using as a guide—but setting a course to arrive slightly further west—the double-peaked volcano of Colima. Upon approaching one finds the port, whose entrance is large and spacious, separated into two bays by Point Audiencia stretching toward the south. The eastern bay is called Manzanillo; the western, Santiago. The latter has the best anchorage. When the wind is from the south, anchor should be cast in the eastern harbor. This is reached from the entrance by steering a course past the entrance north 52° east and then dropping anchor in twelve or fifteen meters beyond the mouth opposite the rock called San Pedrito. The west bay may be reached by steering north 42° west, after passing the rocks called Los Frailes which rise off the second point of Juluapa. Anchorage is available only a few feet offshore in the lee of the mountains where the water is five or six fathoms deep. Given a favorable wind, to approach the moorings of Santiago or Salagua, a course should be set northward a few degrees east or west to avoid the rock Estrada situated at the tip of Point Audiencia, which, as already indicated, rises directly opposite the entrance. The tide rises every twenty-four hours, receding in the morning and returning in the evening. The rise is about two meters and the currents flow toward the south.

At Salagua wood and water are abundant and cattle cheap. Vanilla, fine tortoise-shell, superb pearls, shells with a purple color, and various kinds of rare woods such as ebony, mahogany, and granadilla, may also be procured at this port. At one time the port of Manzanillo was open to foreign ships and received many rich cargoes from Europe. But in 1836 the influence of merchants at Tepic and San Blas caused it to be made a closed port like Mazatlán which, however, was later thrown open to foreign commerce. Salagua is advantageously situated to serve as the natural base of supplies to the exclusion of other ports, for the provinces

---

[7]Port of Manzanillo or Salagua; 19° 6' n. lat.; 106° 48' 15" w. long.; declination 8° 15' N. E. (D. de M.) According to De Mofras' map, the Salagua empties into Manzanillo Bay.—ed.

of Colima, Michoacan, and Jalisco can all send merchandise to Guadalajara and the famous fair at San Juan del Rio easily and at slight cost.

Manzanillo lies about twenty leagues from the village of Colima, capital of the state of the same name. The road leading to the sea can now be used by carts, while the overland journey will soon be shortened by seven leagues through a cut-off that will connect the port with the salt lagoon of Cuyutlán,[8] navigable by large flat-bottom boats.

Freight shipped from Mazatlán to the interior of New Galicia[9] does not pass through San Blas; for the tariff from one port to the other is 1½ piasters a bale, and the tariff overland from San Blas to the fair at San Juan, for example, is 14 piasters, making a total of 15½ piasters a bale, or 31 piasters for each mule-pack. Mules, furthermore, are extremely difficult to procure at the latter port, whereas they are not scarce at Salagua. From Mazatlán to Manzanillo freight charges amount to 2 piasters a bale, and from the port to San Juan, 9 piasters. Thus a load costs 22 piasters in place of 31, an appreciable saving for firms who send out 10,000 or 12,000 bales each year.

The inhabitants of Colima are still bringing pressure to bear on the government to reopen their port, which is of major importance to all commerce throughout the western provinces. Manzanillo consists of three small settlements, a guard of four soldiers, and a customs employé who has charge of the small villages of Salagua and Santiago, where ships frequently anchor. Commercial contact exists only between such Mexican ports as San Blas, Mazatlán, and Guaymas.

The territory of Colima is rich and extremely fertile. Although supporting only 50,00 inhabitants, yet the annual consumption of European merchandise is approximately 1,000,000 piasters. The principal products of Colima are: salt, which is exported from the majority of Mexican mines and reaches the enormous total of 500,000 quintals, representing a value of about 1,200,000 piasters, since it sells at Zacatecas and Guanajuato for 4 piasters a quintal; 100 quintals of indigo, valued at 1½ piasters the quintal; 500 quintals of cocoa; 8,000 of rice; 5,000 of sugar, and a large quantity of soap. All grains yield abundant harvests, and more than 500,000 coffee plants flourish.

Within the past few years cotton has become an important article

---

[8]Cuyutlán, or de los Caimanes, is an extensive lagoon stretching along the coast of Colima.

[9]Nueva, or New Galicia: One of the ancient provinces of Spain; now included in the states of Aguascalientes, Jalisco, a large part of Zacatecas, sections of Durango, San Luís Potosí, and Tepic.

of commerce. The crop produced is of excellent quality, being white and compact. It grows on a bush that is not more than a meter and a half high. Planting takes place annually in September, the first crop maturing in February and the second toward the end of May. From 75 to 80 quintals are produced yearly which is sold off the bush at 4 or 6 piasters. When cleaned this shrinks two-thirds, and the net price then increases from 12 to 18 piasters for a quintal weighing 46 kilograms.

Transportation for a load weighing three quintals as far as Mexico City costs 16 piasters, and to Manzanillo, 2 piasters. This price, increased by some 2 francs the kilogram, does not justify at the present time the exportation of cotton to Europe. An excellent French firm, that of François Meillon, is established at Colima, and Mm. Lestapis and Corbière have created large plantations equipped to sort and clean cotton. A spinning mill has also been organized. The total value of these plants exceeds 200,000 piasters. Except for the frequent earthquakes, and the goiters with which many of the inhabitants are afflicted, the village presents no remarkable features. The population—some 20,000 inhabitants—thrives exclusively on agriculture and commerce.

Eight leagues northeast of the city lies the volcano of Colima, the most northerly of its kind in Mexico. Towering to a height of 3,656 meters, it is still active, throwing out sulphurous vapors, cinders, and stones, although for a considerable length of time lava has not been visible. The diameter of the crater, whose edges are cut and ragged, is 150 meters. The slopes of the mountain are arid and steep, and even the sulphur is poor in quality. A league north of the volcano towers an extinct crater that exceeds by 212 meters the height of its neighbor. The elevation above sea level of this volcano is 3,868 meters; its crest, topped with snow, is visible far out at sea. When the sky is clear this affords an excellent landmark for navigators bound for the harbor of Manzanillo.

The valley in which Colima is situated appears to be composed of volcanic deposits and decomposed lava mixed with detritus. Minerals seem to be absent, but fragments of exquisite porphyry appear. The vegetation consists of palms, aloes, pomegranates, and delicious oranges. On the upper plateaus, however, the graceful trees of the tropics are replaced by somber forests of pines covering the section of the Sierra Madre that extends to Valladolid. In this village a Frenchman, M. Guinot, has charge of an extensive industry. By means of a capital of 100,000 piasters, furnished in part by stockholders, the latter has established the cultivation of mulberry bushes on a vast scale, and is now raising silkworms.

Beyond Manzanillo as far as Cape Corrientes,[10] the coast, which stretches northward, affords three anchorages—Autlán,[11] Navidad, and Tomatlán—that are seldom used. After leaving Cape Corrientes, a point which ships outbound from Europe to San Blas are invariably careful to reconnoiter, off toward the east at a distance of twelve or fifteen leagues, the vast bay of Ameca and Banderas Valley open. Here foreign vessels frequently stop to take on cargoes of brazilwood that abounds along this coast.

On approximately the same parallel, but across and slightly south of Point Mita that forms the northern extremity of the large bay, appear three small islands called Las Marietas, and a fourth off toward the west known as Roca de la Corvetena.[12] Since this group lies only one league away from the Tres Marías, a slight error in latitude would tend to confuse one with the other. This mistake, however, would not occur if the fact were recalled that the Tres Marías are considerably larger and lie on the same line whose general direction is north-northwest; whereas the Marietas and La Corvetena are quite small and are on a line bearing east and west.

Above Point Mita the coast bends slightly east for a distance of twenty leagues. Near Point Tecusitán and south of the small Point Custodios which mark the southern entrance of the roadstead at San Blas, the anchorages of Chacala and Matanchel are encountered.

The port of San Blas lies in New Galicia. However, it seems unnecessary to comment on the cities of Vera Cruz, Puebla, Mexico City, Guanajuato, Querétaro, Celaya, León, Valladolid, or Oajaca, since they have already been described in many volumes. But Guadalajara,[13] at the present time the second largest city in Mexico, and a center that plays a leading rôle in the revolutions throughout the country, merits more consideration. This city, the capital of a former province of the same name and New Galicia, is now in the state of Jalisco which has a population of 600,000 and an area of about 9,000 square leagues. Guadalajara is situated 150 leagues west of Mexico City. The road that connects these two cities, although poor, is open to travel. Notwithstanding, it swarms with robbers and assassins. At Guadalajara the governor, the *comandante general,* and the bishop reside. Innumerable churches are

---

[10]Cape Corrientes: 20° 25′ 30″ n. lat.; 107° 59′ 31″ w. long. (D. de M.).
[11]Apparently Guatlán.
[12]The form Corventana appears in the original version.
[13]Guadalajara lies in 20° 41′ n. lat., and 105° 14′ 15″ w. long. (D. de M.).

scattered throughout the city, not to mention eleven convents and monasteries for nuns and priests.

Through lack of contact with foreigners and a dearth of cultural institutions, development in this city has been extremely backward. There is only one mediocre press functioning, and public libraries or instituations of higher learning do not exist. What training is given a limited number of pupils in the ecclesiastical seminaries is distinctly inferior. Only the art school and the free primary schools appear to flourish.

The province is primarily agricultural in character. Indians out on the plains live by cultivating the soil, the produce harvested consisting for the greater part of wheat, corn, rice, beans, oats, cocoa, cochineal, cotton, and maguey.[14] From the latter an intoxicating liquor known as mescal is distilled. Agricultural products have an annual value of 3,000,000 piasters. On the other hand, industries enjoy a certain amount of prosperity. This is based mainly on the manufacture of woolens designed for daily use, such as *serapes, coberturas,* and simple cotton materials used for *mantas, rebozos,* and *zarazas.*[15]

At Guadalajara excellent pottery is produced. Several hat factories, tanneries, and soap plants are also in operation. Work at the latter is considerably simplified since the fields in certain localities are covered with efflorescent carbonate of soda. The Indians call this *tequesquite*[16] and during the month of October collect it with great care. In the state of Jalisco alone the total value of industrial products amounts to 4,000,-000 piasters .Of this amount the soap industry represents 1,000,000 and cotton goods 2,000,000 piasters.

Cigar manufacturers employ about 800 workers, 600 of whom are women. Inasmuch as the cultivation of tobacco is prohibited, a large supply of this is sent in from the department of Orizaba. The sale of this is under lease and brings into Guadalajara an annual revenue of

---

[14]Maguey: Any species of the **agave**, especially the common century plant.

[15]**Serapes** or shawls; **coberturas**, coverlets; **mantas**, wraps; **rebozos**, shawls; **zarazas**, printed cottons.

[16]Tequesquite is carbonate of soda in its natural state of efflorescence, and is valued at one-half piaster a fanega, or 15 pounds. The analysis made by Professor Berthier, of the Royal School of Mines at Paris, is as follows:

Carbonate of anhydrous soda	0,516
Sulphate	0,153
Sea salt	0,045
Water	0,246
Earthly substances	0,030
	0,990

(D. de M.).

2,000,000 piasters. No flax, cotton, or silk is grown in this department.

The bulk of all gold and silver bullion coined at the mint comes from the famous mines of Bolaños and Hostotipaquillo.[17] However, there are more than twenty other localities where mining is carried on on a small scale, but where work is suspended when the price of mercury soars.

Coins struck off at Guadalajara are readily recognized, for they carry on the reverse side the letters GA. Houses that refine metal in France should attempt to procure them, since they contain a large amount of gold. At Guadalajara the assay and smelting plant, *Casa de ensayo y apartado,* is handled in a most inefficient manner. Neither the correct instruments nor the necessary tests are used, while managers entirely ignore the accurate method devised by Mm. Gay-Lussac and d'Arcet. Coins from this mint, and nuggets or bars of gold and silver, are sent to San Blas and Tampico, where they are loaded on English warships and commercial vessels.

The department of Jalisco has some copper mines, but these have not as yet been developed. Near Tepic small quantities of iron are obtainable and near Guadalajara a limited amount of mercury; but since the extraction of gold and silver by amalgamation is the simpler procedure, miners here prefer to employ this method.

Guadalajara, situated on a vast plain, is without means of defense, having neither walls nor moats. The entire garrison consists of only 800 poorly-armed guards. The city, furthermore, is at all times the seat of innumerable intrigues and political conspiracies. The uprising of Iturbide, the downfall of Bustamante, and the rise of Santa Anna, all centered at Guadalajara. Moreover, the Federal Congress of Jalisco was the body that issued the destructive decree expelling all Spaniards. The morals of the people are wholly deplorable and their ignorance is appalling. Robberies and assassinations occur daily; often many of these, which are committed openly and brazenly, go unpunished. The prisons contain more than 1,000 criminals. In addition to this number, 1,200 more criminals are confined in a prison that has been established on the small island of Mescala in the center of Laka Chapala, fifteen leagues southeast of Guadalajara.

This lake, that lies some 2,000 meters above sea level, is about 120 leagues in circumference and presents a phenomenon analagous to that

---

[17]The pueblo and mining camp of Bolaños lies 188 kilometers north of Guadalajara. Hostotipaquillo, situated in the barrancas, is 45 kilometers northwest of Tequila and supports 27 mines.

of the Rhône in Lake Geneva, being fed by the Rio Grande de Santiago that empties into the Pacific Ocean near San Blas. Throughout its course of 200 leagues the river is nowhere navigable.

At Guadalajara and the adjoining country more than 60 Frenchmen are engaged in industrial pursuits. Many have established important enterprises, among them being two large bakeries and flour mills, a brewery, a distillery, and a complete plant for dyeing and printing fabrics. What Frenchmen have assembled in the department to participate in its benefits belong to the laboring class of miners, carpenters, mechanics, and locksmiths. France is not represented at Guadalajara by any commercial house of importance. All major activities are concentrated in the hands of four firms—three Spanish and one English.

Like the route between Mexico and Guadalajara, the road leading to Tepic, San Blas, Rosario, and Mazatlán is infested with bandits who collect in bands of 30, 40, and even as many as 150 well-mounted, heavily-armed men. Organized in psuedo-military fashion, these groups attack travelers and kidnap their guards, pillage farmhouses and small establishments known as ranchos and haciendas, and even levy assessments on large villages.

The distance of 90 leagues between Guadalajara and Tepic must be made by horse over the worst road in all Mexico, a route that traverses immense ravines which stretch as far as the sea and are filled with trees suitable for shipbuilding. Tepic, which has fewer than 8,000 inhabitants during the hot season, numbers more than 10,000 residents during the rainy period. All officials and employés connected with the custom-house at San Blas live here and travel to the port only when a ship is expected.

A league from Tepic lies the village of Jalisco, a settlement built on the ruins of an ancient Indian village of that name which was rich and powerful at the time of the Conquest. Excavations made nearby have led to the discovery of various kinds of utensils and weapons, and idols of ancient Mexican deities.

The climate of Tepic is healthful, its elevation being 885 meters above sea level. Commercial activity is centered in the hands of five Spanish firms: M. Menchaca; M. d'Anglada, vice-consul of Spain; M. Castaños, vice-consul of the United States; Mr. Barron, consul for England; and M. Yruretagoyena, whose nephew, M. José Calvo, is vice-consul for France. M. Calvo is a young man who was reared in Paris, who is wholly devoted to our interests, and who has rendered valuable services to several Frenchmen and captains of merchant vessels hailing from Bordeaux.

On the outskirts of Tepic a large plant for spinning and weaving cotton is situated. The machinery is operated by a stream of water diverted from the Rio Grande de Santiago. The proprietor is an Englishman, Mr. Forbes,[18] who is associated with the firm of Barron. Only two or three Frenchmen reside at Tepic, and the spinning plant is the only industrial enterprise that has been established.

The actual route from Tepic to the port of San Blas is 22 leagues, whereas in a direct line the distance is not more than 8 leagues. Not long ago M. Castaños, a rich Spanish merchant of Tepic, made a proposal to the Mexican government to construct a wagon road at his own expense. This was to cost in the neighborhood of 50,000 piasters, and M. Castaños asked only the right to levy a modest toll during a period of twenty years. The apathy of the present officials has prevented the acceptance of this advantageous offer. The ancient Spanish route, known as El Camino Real—the King's Highway—which traversed the lowlands has almost entirely disappeared.

At San Blas the fortifications and the citadel that defend the approach to the port—called El Castillo de la Entrada, or the castle at the entrance, on old Spanish maps—rises 32 meters above sea level. The supply shop, the hospital, the docks, and the arsenal are in ruins; only the débris of the fine buildings erected during the Spanish régime remain. Not a battery, not a soldier, not a piece of wood, not a workman at the port where the Spanish navy once employed 3,000 men, and where her frigates were constructed, is visible.

The settlement of San Blas,[19] numbering fewer than 800 inhabitants, is situated on a small hill, one league from the sea. Along the shore are a few shabby huts occupied by fishermen, sailors, and muleteers. At this place, called La Playa, an English consular agent, Mr. Saunders, who is a retired sea captain, resides. Ships should avoid taking on local water, which is brackish and unhealthful. Supplies brought from Tepic are high, the price of cattle varying from 8 to 12 piasters.

---

[18]Alexander Forbes was a Scotch merchant whose **History of California,** published in 1839, is one of the classics of that period. See also **infra** I, 222, **note** 69.

[19]San Blas, situated on the ruins of the arsenal at sea-level, lies in 21° 32′ 34″ n. lat., and 107° 35′ 48″ w. long., Paris time. Declination 9° 12′ N. W. The average temperature throughout November, taken at noon, is 25° centigrade. The barometer falls to zero at sea-level; average 761m 5, maximum 765m 5, minimum 764m, 5. Prevailing winds: south to east. High tide, 9h, 45m. Height at the equinox, 2 meters, 40 centimeters. (D. de M.). For the port of San Blas see **Dupetit Thouars, op. cit.,** II, 185-196.—**ed.**

San Blas has only an open roadstead, but anchorage is comparatively safe during the dry season and less dangerous, during the rainy season, that that at Mazatlán. The extent and shape of the roadstead and the currents make getting under sail comparatively easy. However, ships should avoid remaining here during the time of the *cordonazo,* a periodic storm that will be subsequently described.

San Blas has the inestimable advantage of possessing a small anchorage, El Pozo, that is enclosed and sheltered on the ocean side by a natural breakwater of rocks. El Pozo is an excellent place to careen ships, but unfortunately in the cove only five or six ships with a draught not to exceed ten feet can enter and find shelter in bad weather. Furthermore, a bar obstructs the entrance to the harbor. During the Spanish régime this was kept clear of sand and the jetty was repaired sufficiently to allow frigates to anchor in safety at El Pozo. A fork of the Rio Grande de Santiago emptied at one time into the lower end of the harbor, and this heavy flow of water carried the sand and mud away from the port. During the War of the Insurrection, the Spanish commander at San Blas, in an effort to isolate the port and prevent entrance by way of the river, ordered a ship laden with stones to be sunk at the mouth of the fork that emptied into the harbor. This obstacle, however, could be removed at the present time, and the inner basin deepened.

The anchorage of San Blas can be readily sighted by several landmarks that serve to indicate its position. After rounding the Tres Marías Islands, which lie 30 leagues offshore on the coast toward the east, the mountain of San Juan[20] comes into view. This rises to a height of 1,900 meters and in clear weather may be sighted twenty leagues off at sea. Behind this mountain the city of Tepic[21] is hidden. When steering for San Juan, an enormous white rock called La Piedra Blanca del Mar— the white stone of the sea—or de Afuera—afar—which has a height of 46 meters, is soon visible. Passing somewhat south of this rock and continuing eastward, a new rock resembling the former, called La Piedra de Adentro, is sighted. This is smaller than the former rock and serves to indicate moorings. Anchorage should be sought east of the latter in 15 or 16 meters of water.

This anchorage can be reached by night as well as by day, for the two rocks that lie on the east and west are approximately 11 miles

[20]Summit of Mt. San Juan: 21° 26′ 15″ n. lat.; 107° 21′ 3″ w. long. (D. de M.).

[21]Tepic is also fully described by Captain F. W. Beechey in his **Narrative of a Voyage to the Pacific** (2 vols., London 1831), II, 325-326. Beechey touched there in February, 1828, and took on a load of specie for London.

apart. The entire coast is quite free from rocks, and the depth of
the sea is uniform. If sails are not reefed, allowance should be made
for the currents which flow with considerable force toward the south.

During the rainy season San Blas is unhealthful, for pernicious
fevers rage and the port is infested by millions of mosquitoes ,whose bites
cause skin diseases, ophthalmia, and various serious inflammations. Captains of vessels should not permit their sailors to sleep on deck or to
spend the night on shore. What merchandise arrives at the port of San
Blas supplies New Galicia and the territory of Colima. Certain shipments are sent on to Mazatlán, Durango, San Luís Potosí, and Zacatecas.
In normal years from eighteen to twenty foreign merchantmen put
in at San Blas with cargoes valued approximately at 2,000,000 piasters.
These ships then proceed to return, first taking on brazilwood at Mazatlán or Banderas Valley.

When arriving at San Blas in July, August, September, or even
later, ships can readily dispose of their cargoes to good advantage by
sending them on to the fair at San Juan de los Lagos, and thus pay *fifty-
three per cent less* on import taxes. Unfortunately this favorable opportunity is apt to be overlooked by shipowners at French ports. The small
village of San Juan de los Lagos is situated on the direct route from
Mexico City to Guadalajara, 40 leagues from the latter city. Annually
on the 5th of December a fair lasting eight days is held. Not only do
merchants from all over Mexico congregate at this time, but many even
arrive from Guatemala. Usually business amounting to 2,000,000 piasters
is transacted.

Parallel with San Blas, but 30 leagues out at sea, lie the islands discovered in 1532 by Mendoza, called the Tres Marías,[22] and the small
island of San Juanico. Often these remote and uninhabited islands have
served as a rendezvous for pirates and might prove of strategic importance if an attempt were made to blockade the northeast coast of
Mexico and capture ships coming from the Sandwich Islands, China,
and Upper California. A superior quality of tortoise shell is found
nearby, as well as game, sponges, wood, and pure water. Ships can sail
safely between the central and northwestern islands, and find anchorage west of the latter where the depth always exceeds 20 fathoms.

Twenty leagues northwest of San Blas, opposite the mouth of the

---

[22]Southern extremity of the most easterly of the Tres Marías: 21° 16′ n. lat.,
108° 35′ 5″ w. long. Islet of San Juanico off the northwest tip of the Tres Marías:
21° 45′ 30″ n. lat., 108° 59′ 18″ w. long., declination 8° N. E. La Bayona: 22° 25′
Isla Isabele: 21° 50′ 30″ n. lat., 108° 14′ 48″ w. long. (D. de M.).

San Pedro River, towers Isla Isabela, which is uninhabited. Soon the low hills of La Bayona come into view. Here near the northwest point and sheltered from the northeasterly winds anchorage is available in 8 fathoms. The mouth of La Bayona is known as Boca de Teacapán. Eight leagues beyond, toward the north, the low hills of Chametla are passed. Here in the tiny harbor formed by deposits from this same stream[23] Hernán Cortés set sail on April 15, 1535, to discover California. A mile offshore the depth varies from 15 to 16 meters.

Just beyond San Blas there are several large farms along the shore. These are the haciendas of Del Mar, San Andrés, Santa Cruz, Teacapán, and Del Palmito. There beef may be purchased for 8 piasters a head, and also vegetables. The water in all the rivers is pure and the firewood invariably abundant.

Inasmuch as hydrographical descriptions of the shores of San Blas, Mazatlán, and Guaymas are not available, it seems advisable to insert, in addition to information furnished by well-informed officers, the result of personal observations. Beacons, signals, and buoys do not exist at any point along the coast. However, the shore is entirely safe and may be approached within a short distance. The year is divided into a dry and a rainy season. The transition, however, is gradual, and the time of year frequently varies. During the dry season the weather is invariably fine, and gentle winds blow during the day from northwest to west, following the direction of the coast. These are replaced, during the night, by a light land breeze, or a calm. The rainy season that begins in June is ushered in by calms and light squalls. As the season advances the force of the rains increases and in place of occurring only at night the rains start in the afternoon, and end in violent storms accompanied by sharp claps of thunder and violent winds blowing from every direction. This weather continues until the latter part of September when the season often ends with a sharp hurricane that occurs between the 1st and 5th of October—the feast-day of St. Francis. These hurricanes that invariably blow in from the southeast or southwest are of brief duration. Yet they are so violent and pile up the seas to such heights that no ship can survive. In this country they are known as *El Cordonazo de San Francisco*.[24] A vessel taken by surprise while at anchor is in grave danger of foundering, or of dragging its cables and running aground. As the season of the

---

[23]The western tip of the Chametla or Rosario River lies in 22° 50′ s. lat., and 108° 18′ w. long. (D. de M.).

[24]Cordonazo de San Francisco: a name given by Spanish sailors to the autumnal equinox, occurring near the time of St. Francis day, October 4.

cordonazo approaches, ships are advised to head out to sea; or, if forced to remain in port, to anchor well offshore so that sail can be run aloft at the first indication of a hurricane. These observations do not apply to open moorings where ships should avoid stopping during September and October. However, occasionally the *cordonazo* will defy the foresight of navigators and arrive later than the day of St. Francis. For instance, on November 1, 1839, a dozen mariners who considered that the dangerous season for their vessels was over, were caught without warning in the harbor of Mazatlán, and most of the crew and cargoes were lost. On November 1, 1840, three ships went down in the port of San Blas, and since it was impossible to go to their rescue, several lives were lost.

Along the northwest coast of Mexico and in the Gulf of California, a meteorological phenomenon, known as the trade-wind inversion, is at times experienced. The northeasterly winds that blow almost constantly across the Atlantic and the waters north of the Equator, moreover, are replaced out here by southwesterly winds, or those that blow directly from the west. The inversion, which takes place only above the Vermilion Sea, is not felt on the Californian Coast along the Pacific Ocean above 23° north latitude.

San Blas lies 60 nautical leagues from Mazatlán, the trip requiring at the outside from two to five days. The climate is entirely healthful along the coast. Near the shore a depth of 12 to 40 meters is found, and several miles out at sea a fluctuation of 70 to 100. Like San Blas, the port of Mazatlán is nothing more than an open roadstead; although in the dry season ample protection from the prevailing winds that blow steadily from the northwest and from offshore is afforded. When the rainy season is at its peak, the harbor is unsafe and extremely perilous. A ship blown up on shore stands in grave danger of losing both men and cargo, for the coast is fringed with rugged rocks against which the sea breaks violently.

The anchorage of Mazatlán in the department of Sinaloa is fully exposed to the dangerous storms that occur in the rainy season. The port itself is formed by a recession in the land in which the village is situated. Only small ships, however, can approach land. Large vessels are forced to anchor toward the south where Crestón, a small lofty island forming the north side of the anchorage, affords shelter. Crestón is separated from a neighboring island by a narrow channel only a few fathoms deep. The latter in turn lies only a cable's length from the mainland. When approaching by the sea, the traveler sees the distinguishing landmark of

Crestón, which appears to stand out sharply from the mainland. North of this island rise two small islands, Los Pajaros, and Los Venados. These also serve to indicate the moorings, since this is the only place along the coast where a group of islands is visible. The moorings used at the present time are south of Crestón.

The intervening islands, originally used by the Spanish, afford, however, another shelter. The latter is preferable during the rainy season. Here shelter may be found.from the southerly and southwesterly gales that blow up with sudden fury. This point has the added advantage of allowing ships to get under way by sailing between the islands, or the islands and the mainland. However, since the prevailing northwesterly winds sweep through here in full force during the dry season, and the heavy seas make the unloading of merchandise hazardous, ships usually prefer to remain south of Crestón, thus avoiding these difficulties.

After Crestón has been sighted, the course should be set for this island, for a short distance south of this point anchorage is available. Care should be exercised to avoid sharp squalls that imperil navigation. The most favorable location to anchor is the passage between Crestón and the neighboring island. Here a depth varying from 16 to 20 meters is available for moorings. If anchor is dropped at night, a lookout should be kept for a flat rock that protrudes 4 or 5 feet above water; this lies a quarter of a mile southeast of Crestón and may be approached at close range.

Mazatlán[25] has been open to foreign commerce for several years. Officially the port is known to the Mexican government as La Ville de los Costillas. The total population of this city is about 8,000 inhabitants during the rainy season. However, during the dry season, or when ships come into port, this increases to 12,000, especially when merchants from the provinces of Chihuahua, Jalisco, Sonora, Colima, Sinaloa, and Durango arrive to make purchases.

Commerce is concentrated almost wholly in the hands of foreigners, who have grown prosperous. The leading concerns are: the North American firm of John Parrot, United States Consul and associate of M. Valade; Scarborough and Company, of New York, with whom is as-

---

[25]According to Dupetit Thouars, op. cit., II, 165-176, who visited Mazatlán in December, 1837, on the **Vénus**, within eight years Mazatlán had developed from a "triste pueblo" (sad little village) with a few huts, into a flourishing commercial center. Much of this growth was due to the activities of M. Machado, a Spanish banker and merchant who had developed commercial relations with China, Peru, Chile, the United States, and Europe.

sociated the English vice-consul, Mr. Talbot; the Prussian vice-consul, Kayser Hayn, and Company, of Hamburg; M. Denghausen of Hamburg who acts as vice-consul of Hansetown; M. Castaños, Spanish vice-consul; M. Granados, a Spaniard; Mm. Penny and Vega, the former an Englishman and the latter a Mexican; Mm. Machado and Yeoward, a Spanish-English firm.[26] All these commercial houses are capitalized at from 100,000 to 300,000 piasters each, while a few control as much as 1,000,000.

French firms are four in number: Mm. Patte and Sellier; M. Gaucheron; M. Vial; and Mm. Fort and Serment[27] who have a house in Mexico City and also transact a large business in gold and silver bullion.

At Mazatlán and throughout the department of Sinaloa more than 200 Frenchmen are engaged in commercial and industrial activities, in addition to the 150 sailors and carpenters in this vicinity who are employed in the coastal trade, and who are primarily recruited from our warships and merchant marine.

Our fellow-countrymen unanimously desired and with obvious pleasure welcomed the installation of M. Valade, an estimable business man who at our suggestion was chosen vice-consul, and the creation of a consulate, whose protection cannot fail to prove invaluable.

The city of Mazatlán is exposed on all sides, and has neither fortications nor batteries along the coast. The garrison consists of 15 or 20 poorly-mounted dragoons and 60 infantry. Two small cruisers, carrying four cannon and 15 marines complete the military forces.

Ships should take on water, which is brackish at other points, at the peninsula that forms the southern end of the harbor. A sojourn at Mazatlán, furthermore, might prove less healthful than at San Blas, for during the rainy season, malignant fever prevails. Inasmuch as there are no hospitals in the city, captains should attempt to prevent their crews from indulging in excesses. This port, moreover, is the only point along the North American coast above Guayaquil where large vessels can lay in a full stock of provisions. Cattle sell locally at 8 to 12 piasters. Guaymas flour, which is superior in quality, is worth from 12 to 14 piasters for 12 arrobas[28] (300 French pounds); and Bordeaux wine

---

[26]In addition to this list, the names of Mm. Moller and Becker of Hamburg also appear in the original **Mémoire**.

[27]The name of Serment is omitted in the original **Mémoire**; that of M. Pagés, a Catalonian, acting as Spanish vice-consul, is substituted.

[28]Arroba: a measure of weight used in Mexico and Spanish America, equivalent to 25.36 pounds.

may be had at 35 or 40 piasters a barrel. In the shops, extra equipment, such as new sailcloth, tar, tallow, cordage, chains, anchors, and pieces of wood—salvaged in part from wrecked vessels—is available.

In 1840, 28 ships, four of which were French vessels laden with foreign merchandise, entered this harbor and disposed of their cargoes to good advantage. Throughout 1841, no French vessels arrived. However, within the last two years ships have begun to reappear. There is less activity in the harbor of San Blas than at Mazatlán;[29] the latter is expanding, whereas the former appears to be on the decline.

Ten leagues west of the city and three leagues from the sea, on the road that comes in from San Blas and Tepic, lies the ancient presidio of Mazatlán. This settlement is largely in ruins, since trade has been diverted to the coast, and the fort no longer has military significance. All traces of the old fortifications have been obliterated and the fine barracks built by the Spaniards now shelter a small detachment of cavalry. The inhabitants number approximately 500. The Mazatlán River that flows past the presidio toward the sea, is unnavigable.

Approximately 150 leagues northwest of Mazatlán lies Guaymas; no other villages exist along the intervening coast. Near the shore the depth varies from 7 to 8 meters; however, 15 or 20 miles out at sea this increases to 80 or 100 meters. No banks or exposed reefs have been charted.

The most important rivers north of this point are the Piastla, whose mouth forms the small anchorage of Navachiste, the Tavala,[30] the Culiacán, that empties near a small port called Altata—at its mouth the water is shallow and large ships should keep 5 or 6 leagues out at sea— the Tamazula, the Macapule,[31] and the Sinaloa. North of the latter lies the Cape of San Ignacio, where a sheltered mooring, protected on the northeast, is available in 7 fathoms. The reef of San Ignacio lies 3 miles south of this point. Farther north the Santa María de Aome[32] is encountered. Upon nearing the Fuerte, anchor should be cast a mile north or south of its mouth. Five miles northwest, where the depth is some 10 or 12 meters the Mayo River affords anchorage in 7 fathoms. Near shore the tiny deserted island of Lobos Marinos is visible. Four

---

[29]Mazatlán, situated at sea level, is in 23° 12′ n. lat., and 108° 42′ w. long. Paris time, 7h. 14m. 48s. Declination 8° 33′ N. E. Average temperature at noon in November and December 22° centigrade. Prevailing winds, S. W. and S. E. High tide at the equinoxes 2m. 3. Establishment of the port, 9h. 45m. (D. de M.).

[30]Apparently the Lorenzo.

[31]Modern maps show this as the Macorita.

[32]Ahome, in the French version.

leagues south of the entrance to Guaymas Harbor flows the Yaqui, whose banks are inhabited by an Indian tribe of the same name.

Although none of these rivers is navigable, yet their mouths are adequate to shelter coastal vessels. What merchandise they handle comes from Mazatlán, Guaymas, and occasionally even from San Blas. This is then shipped on pack-mules to Culiacán, Villa Feliz de Tamazula, Sinaloa, Villa del Fuerte, and Alamos.

The port of Guaymas may be recognized from afar by a mountain capped by two peaks resembling a goat's udders; these are called Las Tetas de Cabra. As soon as the mountain hoves into view, ships should head in toward shore, bearing slightly toward starboard. Soon the island of Pajaros that forms the northern side of the entrance to the port will be seen. By setting a course to pass this island on the starboard side and entering the channel lying between it and the mainland, the port and village will soon appear. The mainland should be kept off port, thus avoiding a bank lying east. After the entrance to the harbor has been passed, two islands are visible in the bay. Ships should pass between them in order to anchor close in toward shore where the depth is adequate for ordinary vessels. Ships of 100 tons burden can tie up at the wharf, but those drawing from 12 to 15 feet should anchor a quarter of a mile away where the water is 7 or 8 meters deep. Large sloops and frigates are forced to anchor beyond the islands in 7 or 8 fathoms. The harbor can safely accommodate a large number of ships at all seasons, has a firm floor for anchorage, and is sheltered on all sides from the winds. Having the form of a vast basin dotted with islands, the sea never becomes rough. The shoal lying opposite its narrow entrance is the only danger to be avoided by navigators. However, given favorable winds this can readily be skirted by keeping well offshore. Notwithstanding, if a ship is forced to tack, care should be exercised to keep far enough way from land to avoid running on the shoal.

The city of Guaymas has fewer than 5,000 inhabitants during the dry months of the year. During the rainy season more than 2,000 retire to small villages in the interior. As at San Blas and Mazatlán, the Mexican government has no small ships available for war. This, however, does not prevent them from having numerous officers. In fact, at the three ports several captains of vessels and frigates were seen, although the ships were conspicuous by their absence. Most of the commerce is controlled by the firm of Don Manuel Inigo and Company, a concern capitalized at 2,000,000 piasters. All foreign vessels arriving at

Guaymas are advised to employ them as factors, in order to dispose of their cargoes to the best advantage. In 1841 this firm acted as agents for four large vessels whose cargoes had a total value of 600,000 piasters.

At the town of Hermosillo or Pitic, forty leagues northeast of Guaymas, a large factory for spinning and weaving cotton that cost in excess of 200,000 piasters has been established. The primary purpose of this enterprise, like those at Guadalajara and Tepic, is not so much to promote the introduction of foreign products as to check the contraband trade in cotton yarns and English textiles, with which the local manufacturers are unable to compete. At Guaymas there are four second-rate merchants: Mr. John Robinson, a North American, who acts as consul for England and vice-consul for the United States; Mr. MacAlpin, an Englishman; and Mm. García and Esprio, Spaniards. Several Frenchmen are engaged in retail businesses, and the total number residing in the district of Sonora, including 50 sailors employed at Guaymas, is approximately 200. Spain maintains a vice-consul, M. Lousteauneau, who is connected with the firm of Inigo. Our country is fortunate in having for French vice-consul, M. Cubillas, who for many years held this same office at Tepic. This young man, who is devoted to our interests, was educated in France and is now associated with the firm of Inigo. He has proved especially well qualified to deal with merchant vessels and to protect our countrymen.

Frenchmen residing in the departments of Sinaloa and Sonora suffered heavily during the expulsion. Several of them, about to lose the fruits of many year's labor, became naturalized Mexican citizens. Others, notably the Basques and Bearnais, posed as Spaniards.

About 500 Frenchmen, who control capital estimated at 2,000,000 piasters, are scattered throughout these two provinces. All are eager to have French warships sent to this coast in order to ship their wealth home to France. The French flag rarely appears on the west coast of Mexico. The first warship that visited these waters in many years was the *Vénus* which came out in 1838 in command of Dupetit Thouars, at that time captain. A year later the *Danaïde,* carrying De Rosamel, reached the coast. But since these ships were not returning directly to France, they were unable to take on specie. However, the *Danaïde* carried merchandise for several Philippine firms, and the house at Mazatlán that made the consignment was agreeably surprised to find in the commander an impartiality unknown among English captains. However, if our ships stationed at Peruvian or Oceanic points could be sent here, before returning to France, to look after the gold and silver interests at the three Mexican ports, undoubtedly business men of all nationalities—even the English themselves—would ship their funds by them, to avoid paying the two per cent tax required by the royal British navy.

The low price and excellent quality of the flour sold at the port of Guaymas offers valuable opportunities to ships taking on supplies. A load weighing 12 arrobas—138 kilograms—costs only 8 or 10 piasters. The *Danaïde* placed an order while in port for biscuits to the amount of 15,000 francs. Flour is shipped to Mazatlán, San Blas, Loreto, and La Paz on the coast of Lower California. The price of beef is usually 12 piasters. Vegetables, on the other hand, are scarce and extremely high in price, and the water at the port is so poor that small boats have to be sent for fresh water, either up the Yaqui or four leagues south. Guaymas,[33] being encircled by lofty mountains, is extremely warm during the rainy season, and, as at Mazatlán and San Blas, fevers are prevalent.

Even though the number of ships coming from France is negligible, yet the value of French merchandise used on the coast is of extreme importance. At the minimum its cost in Europe is 5,000,000 francs, and after all expenses are deducted this commands at least 1,500,000 piasters out in this country. One-eighth of most shipments coming out from England and one-fourth of those from the United States, Lima, Valparaiso, and especially from Hamburg, consist of French products, and undoubtedly their sale would considerably increase if our manufacturers, following the example of those in Silesia, Saxony, and England, would consent to make articles expressly for this country whose consumption is much like that of Spain.

Here are some suggestions as to the type of merchandise that would find an extensive and ready market. The fact should be recalled that after August 14, 1843, most of this was prohibited by an edict of Santa Anna. Ecru calicoes, or *manta*,[34] and white or imperial calicoes in three-quarters size—Rouen cottons are unknown on this coast—might compete to good advantage with those from England. Alsatian products and Indian prints would undoubtedly prove salable, since their designs are superior and their colors fast. However, their cost would tend to

---

[33]Guaymas is situated at sea level. Observations taken on the small island of Morro Almagre give 27° 53′ 50″ n. lat., and 113° 9′ 35″ w. long. Time, 7 h. 32 m. 38 s. Declination 12° 4′ N. E.; average height of barometer, irrespective of daily fluctuations, is 760 mm; average temperature at noon in December, 25° centigrade; prevailing winds beyond the port, south to west. Establishment of the port, 9h. 40m. Rise of the sea at the equinoxes, two meters. (D. de M.).

[34]Manta: ordinary cotton cloth, such as sheeting.

prevent widespread use. Factories at Mulhouse, and especially those at Rouen, should attempt to make a cheaper grade of cotton prints like those sent out by English and Swiss merchants. Our red cotton prints have proved popular, but our pattern-lengths are too large. India prints in half-lengths at a low price should be offered. Elaborate India shawls and imitation Madras handkerchiefs will sell to good advantage. It would also be advisable for our manufacturers to attempt to make shawls called *rebozos,* which are universally used in this land. This article offers an opportunity for a wide margin of profit. Percales, Mada-pollams,[35] and muslins of fine quality are in demand as well, but the possibility of being unable to compete with English fabrics cannot be disregarded. Otherwise, our muslin prints would be given the preference, owing to their elegance and originality of design.

Velveteen commands a steady market, but the only colors used are plain blues and blacks of good quality. Cotton lace is supplied by England; however, this is consumed only in limited amounts. Lace embroideries from Nancy and Saint-Quentin could probably supplant them, if shipped out in limited quantities. Cotton hose, plain, openwork, and what is known as cotton-thread hosiery, are supplied by Saxony and England. Fabrics of cotton and flax, or wool and cotton mixtures, such as Lille and Roubaix fabrics, are entirely unknown; and it seems reasonable to expect that if sold in limited quantities, these goods might prove profitable.

Among the most important articles manufactured are linens. Yet the fact must be reluctantly admitted that the negligence of French manufacturers has unfortunately allowed the cloth of Ireland, Saxony, and Silesia to supplant all other linen fabrics. Our manufacturers should refrain from manufacturing these goods except in amounts and quantities that would have an assured market in Spanish America.

Despite foreign imitations, cloth made in Brittany—such as *Bretañas legítimas, Pontivi,* and *Platillas* materials from Pontivy, made with flat thread, and goods from Lille and Valenciennes; batistes and linens from Cambrai, such as *olan, linon, cambrai, and estopilla,*[36] sell readily, as does white and tan canvas from Laval, suitable for trousers, and heavy duck in red and blue stripes used by sailors. Linen tape, linen thread,

---

[35]Madapollams: cotton cloth, heavier than ordinary cotton, made originally in Madapollam, India.

[36]Bretañas legítimas, fine Brittany linen; Pontivi, cloth from Pontivy France; Platillas, Silesian linen; olan, old Holland linen or batiste; linon, lawn; estopilla, fine cloth such as lawn, batiste, or cheesecloth.

and flat and round linen twine are supplied exclusively by Silesia. Saxony furnishes all table linen and several grades of linen known locally as *ginga, rusia, and cotense*.[37] Woolen hose from Chemnitz and England are also carried.

English, German, and Belgian goods offer the most serious competition to French materials. For this reason it might prove advantageous to send out only small quantities of medium grade goods. Black, various shades of blue, dark green and brown, are the only colors in demand. Materials from Sedan and Elbeuf are too expensive to sell well, and their value is not appreciated. Light-weight woolens from the south, especially those of Castres and Carcassonne should prove popular. Since merinos, cashmeres, and neapolitans have a limited market in this country, comparatively few patterns should be shipped. This is equally true of flannels, baizes, bombazines, and similar materials. The latter should be extremely supple in imitation of silk. Dark shades are fashionable, especially dead-black for the priests and a rich blue-black for women. Plain black woolen hose are worn exclusively by the men, and their use is quite restricted. Limited amounts of crêpe, stiff woolen voiles, serges, and other materials from Rheims, Arras, Amiens, and Beauvais should also be stocked. Carpets in all styles, in large sizes and by the piece, materials to cover furniture and drape over pianos, and bedside rugs, especially if bright in color, have a ready market.

Silk and cashmere shawls are not used. Among articles sold in large quantities is sewing silk. Unfortunately our manufacturers of this line will have to compete with products from Piedmont and especially those from China. Our silks, however, have the advantage of being made of fast dyes, but the torsion and weight of the Chinese skeins should be carefully imitated.

The choice of plain fabrics requires considerable care because of the popularity of Swiss and German products. Taffetas, serges, and satins should be supple both in texture and appearance. The most popular colors are dead-black, a lustrous blue-black, dull white and silver-white, sky-blue and king-blue, lilac, and violet. Chinese satins, highly prized because they have more body and strength than those from Europe, are used especially for making slippers for the women who wear only this type of footgear.

---

[37]Ginga, possibly goods made in Ginchy, France; rusia, either a corruption of the French term Rusie, meaning Prussian goods, or referring to Ruse, in Bulgaria; cotense, cloth probably from Constance, Germany.

Velveteen should be plain, but superior in quality, and blue, black, green, or a delicate crimson in color. Velvets, gold brocade, silks, or any fabrics suitable for waistcoats, such as are manufactured at Lyon, sell without difficulty. No doubt the silk *rebozos* made in Mexico could be imitated to advantage; several such attempts have already met with signal success.

Ribbons, chiefly of satin or whatever is in fashion, should be narrow and light. Galoons, cords, laces, gimps, and passementarie are assured of a market. Cravats, scarfs, neckerchiefs, gauze articles, and fashionable sundries are equally certain to attract sales. Merchants should not send out too many plain or brocaded shawls, since the Chinese have a decided advantage over our nation in these articles, but should include instead damasks and coverings for furniture.

Ladies' silk stockings are used in enormous quantities and should be pure white and plain or with openwork. Only a few black hose should be sent, unless for the men, for they are used exclusively by clergymen. The essential point, however, is to have them extremely fine in quality. The use of the Spanish mantilla[38] is gradually disappearing, and only a limited amount of laces, shawls, and light-colored scarfs should be included. Certain church ornaments such as chasubles, banners, and altar ornaments can still be marketed advantageously.

The firm of Rothschild in London sends out annually to the three ports of San Blas, Mazatlán, and Guaymas from 4,000 to 5,000 quintals of quicksilver. In 1841, 600 were received at Mazatlán; of this amount 500 were consigned to the English concern at Guadalupe y Calvo in the state of Chihuahua. Mercury is shipped in tightly-sealed containers that hold three arrobas, or 75 pounds of metal which, being easy to stow away, make excellent ballast for vessels.

An entire shipload of paper is consumed annually by the manufacture of cigars at Guadalajara. Although this article has an assured sale, yet our factories at Angoulême do not recognize the need of making a perfect imitation of the Spanish grades as the *florete* and *medio florete*[39] of Catalonia and Valencia. The Genoese have profited from our apathy and send over shipments that bring in a wide margin of profit. Letter paper and colored paper are usually salable, but the market for bond paper is limited.

---

[38]Mantilla: the graceful shawl worn over the head and held in place by the tall comb once universally used in Spain and Spanish America.
[39]Florete: superfine; medio florete, medium grade.

The use of pianos is becoming widespread. All English and Hamburg ships carry them to Mexico and dispose of them to good advantage. Square and upright models are to be preferred to grand pianos. Only a limited number, however, should be exported. A piano that costs 500 francs in Paris can be sold for 400 or 500 piasters at Mazatlán. All other musical instruments, with the exception of harps, are in demand, as well as printed music.

Clocks, bronzes, mirrors, common weapons, chandeliers, fans, perfume, jewelry—especially imitation jewelry—ornamental porcelains, hardware, gloves, embroidered batiste handkerchiefs, wearing apparel, shoes and slippers, metallic laces, harnesses, fashionable accessories, and the many articles and miscellaneous products known as Parisian novelties, have an assured sale, and return profits commensurate with their exclusiveness. Several of these articles are prohibited by the customs regulations; however, these may be modified, or arrangements might be made with subordinate officials, many of whom, by their tolerance, derive an annual income of 30,000, 40,000, and even as much as 100,000 piasters.

Among wines and liquors consumed in quantity are Bordeaux wines and champagne of medium grade, cognac, Bordeaux and Marseilles liquors, and some sweet wines, among them Roussillon and Frontignan. Certain houses at Hamburg that handle shipments of white Rhine wine are apt to compete with shipments of an ordinary grade of Sauterne. Bordeaux wines ferment too rapidly to withstand the sea.

Olive oil, dried fruits, brandy, boxes of conserves prepared for long voyages, and all the common commodities of Europe, should sell at a profit. If to the products valued at 12,000,000 francs that France exports annually direct to Mexico, are added the 5,000,000 brought into Pacific coast ports by foreign vessels, together with a similar amount brought into Gulf ports, the total exports would amount to 22,000,000 francs. This should be brought to the attention of the French government, which should put forth every effort possible to retain a market so valuable to our commerce, industries, and shipping.

The ports of San Blas and Guaymas do not produce any articles for the export trade. The limited amount of pearls found in the Gulf of California are sold in Sonora and Sinaloa at exorbitant prices. The only article available for exportation is found at Mazatlán. This is dyewood, called brazilwood, which sells, laid down at the port, at one piaster the quintal, or 20 piasters a ton. Mazatlán exports an annual average of 90,000 quintals. In 1841, two large English ships of 700 tons were sent from Europe, via the east, to take on brazilwood at Mazatlán, having first discharged their cargo at Sydney, in New Holland.[40] Inasmuch as large quantities of wood will never be brought into Mazatlán because of the cost of transportation, a landing has been established at the port of Banderas Valley where ships can take on cargo.

At rare intervals small quantities of tortoise shell, valued at 16 or 18 piasters a quintal, are available at Mazatlán. Occasionally ships bound for China take on several tons of mother-of-pearl shells at La Paz in Lower California; however, the Chinese usually prefer their own quality, which is superior and a clearer shade of white. Since these miscellaneous products do not make up a full cargo, foreign ships often proceed to Guaymas to take on cocoa, or to Valparaiso for hides, before returning to Europe or the United States.

Precious metals continue to remain the leading articles exported from the west coast of Mexico. For general information the taxes levied upon entering France are as follows: Gold coin, 10 centimes, and silver coin 1 centime a kilogram; gold bullion, 2 francs, 50 centimes; silver bullion, 5 centimes a kilogram. This applies to all nations and vessels.

Notwithstanding the importance of San Blas and Guaymas, Mazatlán ranks as the commercial center of Mexico in the South Sea, and the attention of all French business concerns should be called to this port whose prosperity is increasing daily, and which may rightfully be termed the Vera Cruz of the Pacific Coast. Mazatlán receives and ships the bulk of all precious metals sent from the departments of Durango, Sinaloa, Sonora, and a considerable amount from New Galicia and Chihuahua. Because of its geographical situation, this port is the clearing-house for the Northwest Coast of America, and its commercial contacts extend to Europe, the United States, Chile, Peru, Ecuador, Central America, the Vermilion Sea, Upper California, the Sandwich Islands, the Philippines, and even China.

After leaving France, the captains of merchant vessels should always include among their ports of call the four ports of Acapulco, San Blas, Mazatlán, and Guaymas. If they wish to avoid having their papers viséd by Mexican consuls residing at Bordeaux and Havre, they can designate Valparaiso, Lima, or Guayaquil as the destination of their voyage. In this manner they will put in only at the ports that, due to prevailing winds, are the most favorable for navigation. When ships

---

[40]New Holland: New South Wales.

are consigned to a certain firm, the latter will settle all difficulties and supervise the handling of the cargo. Customs officials, however, will not accept drafts in Mexico, but require all duties and gratuities to be paid in local currency. Thus a ship always needs from 40,000 to 60,000 piasters, according to the value of its cargo, upon arrival.

The presence on the Northwest Coast of Mexico of our consuls and warships, irrespective of their political significance, will tend to prevent desertions to foreign vessels, will maintain discipline aboard ship, will afford our countrymen what protection they require, and will undoubtedly encourage more shipowners to send expeditions into Pacific waters whose shores and archipelagoes in the future will prove of vital importance.*

---

*This final paragraph does not appear in the Mémoire. In its place is a discussion of the various points of residence suitable for a vice-consul, and expenses entailed by such an office.

CHAPTER VI*

The Vermilion Sea. Sinaloa. The Colorado River. Indian Tribes. Lower California.

Geographically speaking,† the entrance to the Gulf of California is defined by Cape Corrientes in the department of Jalisco, which forms part of the former province of New Galicia, and by Cape San Lucas, situated at the southern tip of Old California.[1] Because of the color of its waters and its resemblance to the Red Sea of Arabia, the Gulf was known to the earliest Spanish explorers as the Mar Rojo or Mar Vermejo—the Red or Vermilion Sea.[2] Through the activities of Jesuit missionaries this entire sea was explored and renamed Seno, or Mar Lauretaneo—the Gulf or Sea of Loreto—in honor of the holy Virgin, patroness and protectress of their apostolic labors.

The Gulf is some 300 leagues long; its widest point, which is approximately 60 leagues, is found at its entrance. Throughout its entire length, the distance from coast to coast varies only from 25 to 40 leagues. Above 31° north latitude this width rapidly decreases as far as the Colorado River, which separates Old California from the northern part of Sonora. A comparison with the Adriatic Sea gives a fairly accurate idea of the Sea of Cortés.

An extraordinary phenomenon has been observed in these regions, one without scientific explanation, and one that has been found only in a few other instances: Rain falls when the atmosphere is clear and the sky bare of clouds. The scholarly M. Humboldt[3] and Captain

---

*A continuation of **Mémoire** II, found in **Amérique**, Vol. 43, folios 93 to 146.

†The geographical description of the west coast of Lower California that appears in **Amérique**, Vol. 43, folios 130 to 132, has been revised and inserted here and in the first section of Chapter VII.

[1]The terms Alta and Baja California, rather than their English equivalents, Upper and Lower California, were generally used in 1840; De Mofras, however, uses the latter form.

[2]Because of its reddish waters, the Gulf of California was originally known on Lok's map of 1582 as Mare Bermeio; on the Wytfliet-Ptolemy map of 1597 as Mar Vermeio; and subsequently as the Mediterranean Sea of California, the Sea of Cortés, and Mar Rojo. De Mofras calls it Mer Vermeille, the Coral or Vermilion Sea, and the Gulf of Cortés.

[3]See **supra**, I, note 1.

Beechey[4] have already commented on this fact, the former having witnessed it inland, and the latter out at sea.

Since our visit to the shores of the Vermilion Sea occurred during the winter season, we hoped to witness a display of shooting stars such as are seen annually at various points along the east coast of America on the nights of the 12th and 13th of November. The heavens were also carefully watched from the 8th to the 20th of November, but no phenomena occurred except what are present every night in all lands; in other words, at every point in the firmament, but especially in the vicinity of the constellation León, where, at frequent intervals, shooting stars appear whose direction is often opposite to the earth's rotation. These meteors have a speed that at times approximates 10 or 12 leagues a second.

Tides are prevalent throughout the Gulf of Cortés, their height varying according to the direction of the winds along the coast. Thus at Mazatlán the rise is 7 feet near the open roadstead; but off Guaymas, where the harbor is dotted with islands that afford shelter from the winds, this does not exceed 5½ feet.

Upon attempting to ascertain why this Gulf was called the Vermilion Sea, only two reasons could be found: the reddish colors of its waters during the rainy season that were caused either by the rivers that flow down through ferruginous soil, especially the Colorado River; or more probably because of the gorgeous phosphorescent colors of the waves at sunrise and sunset. During the day, however, the waters appear blue or green according to the way the clouds intercept or modify the sun's rays in conjunction with the character and depth of the ocean floor. The discoloration of the water might also be caused by shoals near the surface of the water formed by myriads of tiny red crustaceans which are provided with tentacles much like our prawns.

Irrespective of the large numbers of fish of various kinds that are prevalent in the Gulf, two species of enormous sharks, called *el tiburón* and *la tintorera,* which frequently devour pearl divers, are found. Whales abound in large numbers; but until the present time whaling ships have made no attempt to find them, for the inhabitants along the coast have entirely overlooked this lucrative branch of the fishing industry. On the islands live large numbers of sea wolves[5] and seals with thick

---

[4]This was Captain F. W. Beechey whose **Narrative of a Voyage to the Pacific in the Blossom in 1825-1828** is among the best of the early voyages. See supra, I, 86, note 21.

[5]De Mofras calls these **loups de mer**, probably a misnomer for sealion, **Zalophus californianus**, abundant along the Pacific Coast.

fur,[6] but comparatively few beaver. Further information about the pearl fisheries will be given later while the islands will be described in conjunction with the adjacent coast.

The two shores of the Vermilion Sea lie parallel to one another in a northwesterly direction. They are low and fringed by salt marshes which are inhabited by alligators, reptiles, and insects. The general aspect of the country is repulsive; the imagination can picture nothing more barren or more desolate. There is a total dearth of water and vegetation, so that only mangrove trees, a few thorny bushes such as the cactus and maguey plant, and a few acacias—*Cactus opuntia,*[7] *Agave americana,*[8] *and Mimosa gummifera*[9]—can survive. Palms and orange trees seldom thrive near the sea. Vegetal soil is found only several leagues inland. The shores are composed of sand and calcareous soil unsuited to navigation. On the eastern side of the entrance to the Gulf the peaks of the Sierra Madre that separate the provinces of Jalisco, Sinaloa, and Sonora from those of New Mexico, Chihuahua, and Durango, tower off in the distance.

The coast of Old California is covered by an unbroken series of rugged peaks, volcanic in origin and devoid of all growth. This chain of mountains ascends from the north and extends throughout the entire length of the peninsula to its southern tip, growing gradually lower as it nears Cape San Lucas.

The departments of Sinaloa and Sonora are bounded on the south by 23° and on the north by 34° north latitude, from the Bayona River that separates them from Jalisco as far as the Colorado and Gila rivers. On the west these lands are bounded by the Vermilion Sea, on the east by the Sierra Madre. Their inner boundaries are defined by the Del Fuerte River. Each state has its own prefect, or civil governor, but both are under the joint control of a *comandante general.* During the Spanish régime these states were administered as a single unit. Under federal rule, however, they became the Free State of the West. This comprised more than 20,000 square leagues, and had a population of 120,000 inhabitants, including 60,000 Indians. The climate is mild, while the soil in the interior is fertile. The main source of wealth is derived from the gold and silver mines. More than two hundred claims are now being worked, and undoubtedly more mineral deposits will be found through-

[6]Veaux marins are seals with soft fur under the hair.
[7]Commonly known as the tuna, or prickly pear.
[8]The Century plant.
[9]Also called cat-claw, a low shrub with hooked spikes.

out the country.* In these states such ores as contain less than three or four parts of silver, which is always auriferous, to the metric ton, are considered of no value. That vast profits await those who first introduce into Mexico the Becquerel process[10] that extracts everything down to one-half part of the metal at slight cost, is obvious. All silver mines in this country are auriferous, and although assay offices are in operation at Rosario, Cosalá, Alamos, Hermosillo, and Guadalupe y Calvo, yet they are so obsolete that the ingots brought into them for assay are invariably superior to the analyses made by the assayer. Our refining houses should make every effort to secure from London metals taken out from this locality. No one except M. Brasdefer, head of the mint at Durango, supervises metallurgical tests with the accuracy of a chemist.

In these two departments there are no large cities.† The principal center in Sinaloa is Culiacán. This has a population of 5,500 inhabitants, and is the official residence of the governor, prefect, and bishop. Rosario, where the departmental countinghouse is situated, has fewer than 3,500 inhabitants. Approximately 200 mediocre soldiers are stationed at this point. The general of this brigade, who is *comandante general* of Sinaloa and Sonora, usually resides at Rosario, but is living at the present time at Mazatlán. The richest mine at Rosario is flooded with water. The only important concern at the latter town is the assay office.

Another, however, is in operation at Cosalá, a town of 3,000. Near this village the Iriarte mine, whose output has been so much exaggerated, is situated. Although a considerable amount of gold is present with the silver, yet the profit does not exceed 40,000 piasters annually. The small villages of Sinaloa, San Sebastián, Tamasula, and Villa del Fuerte, which have an average population of 2,500 inhabitants, are comparatively uninteresting.

Sonora[11] is divided into an upper and a lower department which are named for the Pima Indians, being called Pimería Alta and Baja—Upper and Lower Pimería. The former extends from the Colorado and Gila rivers as far as the city of Hermosillo and De los Ures River; while the latter lies beyond this boundary as far as Del Fuerte that separates it

---

*An unimportant section of folios 95 to 97, dealing with methods of mining has been omitted at this point.

[10]See **supra**, I, 17, **note** 48.

†At this point the **Mémoire** continues to follow the printed text.

[11]The boundaries of Sinaloa and Sonora have been materially changed since that time.

from Sinaloa. As late as 1839 the capital of the state was Arizpe,[12] in 30°
36′ north latitude, a town supporting several years ago more than 7,000
inhabitants. Today this number, through emigration and fear inspired
by the constant depredations of the Apache Indians who frequently
enter the town bent on plunder and murder, has dwindled to 1,500.
The seat of government has now been moved 40 leagues south to the
former mission of San José de los Ures,[13] whose population is less than
1,000. The governor usually resides at the latter settlement. The villages
of San Miguel de Horcasitas[14] and Oposura[15] each have 2,000 inhabitants.
Alamos,[16] credited with 3,000, also owns an assay office.

The port of Guaymas, which has already been mentioned, is the
center of all maritime activities in Sonora. Of secondary importance is
the city of Hermosillo,[17] formerly the presidio of Pitic, which has 8,000
citizens, and is situated in the center of a vast and pleasant plain of
extraordinary fertility. Here all kinds of European fruits are produced,
as well as what wine is used throughout the country. The land is watered
by several small rivers that supply power for mills. This section of
Sonora exports the wheat that is sold at Guaymas and then shipped to
all coast ports as far as San Blas, including Lower California.

Hermosillo is the center of commerce and wealth in Sonora. An official survey indicates that in 1839, 600 bars of silver and 60 bars of gold,
having a combined value of more than 1,000,000 piasters, passed through
the assay office. Probably an equal amount was shipped out, without being listed, to avoid payment of taxes, which amount to 5 per cent on
silver and 4 per cent on gold. Several rich copper mines are also being
worked; but operators as a whole are inclined to disregard metals except those bearing pure gold.

---

[12]Arizpe lies in Sonora on the upper fork of the Sonora River. Coronado
passed through the place in 1540 when it was an Opata settlement. Later it was
a Jesuit mission and the residence of the **comandante general**. For the mission
and presidio of Sonora see Herbert E. Bolton, **Kino's Historical Mémoir; Rim of
of Christendom.** and Frank C. Lockwood, **Spanish Missions of the Old Southwest**
(Santa Ana, 1934).

[13]San José de los Ures is on the Sonora River above Hermosillo. Nearby
was a rich grazing country.

[14]San Miguel Horcasitas is on the north fork of the Sonora River.

[15]Oposura or Montezuma lies on the northern fork of the Yaqui River, near
the thirtieth parallel, in Sonora. In Father Kino's day it was a favorite seat of
the Jesuit Fathers.

[16]Los Alamos lies on the Alamos River halfway between the Fuerte and the
Mayo. Rich mines had been discovered in this vicinity.

[17]Since De Mofras' day, Hermosillo, near the confluence of the Sonora and
San Miguel de Horcasitas rivers, has become the capital of Sonora, and a leading
commercial and industrial center, with a population of some 15,000.

No other country in the world possesses such rich and extensive auriferous outcroppings and gold placer mines. The metal is found in alluvial deposits, often in ravines after rains, and usually on the surface of the ground or only a few feet below. North of the town of Arizpc, the outcroppings of Quitovac and Sonóitac[18] which were discovered in 1836, produced daily for three years 200 ounces of gold. Gold-seekers confined themselves to removing the dirt with a pointed stick and extracting only what grains were visible. However, if the stream were to be diverted and the soil thoroughly washed, the profits would be materially increased.

Often gold nuggets are found, weighing several pounds, which have inestimable value as scientific specimens. M. Zavala, formerly ambassador from Mexico to London, owns a gold nugget worth more than 9,000 piasters. The king's cabinet at Madrid has several magnificent specimens of this character. Unfortunately, for the last three years the Pápago Indians have been raiding this country and have carried off and massacred many who have gone out into the Sonóitac country. The commerce of Sonora has suffered from this decrease in mineral revenue, but the belief prevails that peace will soon be made with these tribes. Up to the present time the Indians have been ignorant of the value of gold, and have not attempted to keep it.

In addition to these villages, in Sonora and Sinaloa several large villages or pueblos, missions, and presidios exist, from whose inhabitants are derived the nomadic groups of workmen and merchants who congregate in the vicinity of every important mine that begins operation and return to their homes when the veins are exhausted. These miners assemble in a place known as the *Mineral,* or *Real de Minas,*[19] and if the mine shows promise of being productive for a long period, the group will locate in the neighborhood. Zacatecas, San Luís de Potosí, Durango, Guanajuato, and several other Mexican towns originated in this manner.

Miners earn considerable sums of money without difficulty, and this explains the enormous consumption of European merchandise in these provinces. Frequently humble rancheros will spend within a few days four or five pounds in gold which often represents not more than a

[18]Quitovac, a rich gold mine, lies 36 miles northwest of Altar in northern Sonora. Sonóitac is Sonoyta, in the district of Altar in northern Sonora. These mines were not worked extensively because of their proximity to the barbarous tribes of the Colorado.

[19]Mineral, mining center; real de minas, a town having mines in the vicinity.

week's labor. A fatal passion for gambling prevents important mine owners from amassing large fortunes, a situation that retards extensive development.

In Sonora and Sinaloa assassins and robbers are not so numerous as in the other states of Mexico. The roads are also safer, and it is only north of Guaymas and Hermosillo that Indians are apt to prove troublesome.

Comparatively few priests reside in these provinces; convents do not exist; and public instruction is so negligible that as late as 1840 there was no school at Mazatlán, the free school existing today being opened largely through the donations of foreign merchants.

Sonora has five distinct tribes of Indians, the Yaquis, Mayos, Opatas, Gileños, and Apaches.[20] The Yaquis and Mayos inhabit lands south of Guaymas as far as the Del Fuerte, and are farmers, servants, miners, masons, and divers. The total number of the latter group is about 40,000. In 1827 they revolted, proclaiming one of their chiefs emperor. After certain concessions were granted, the uprising was quieted, and since that time the Indians have lived at peace in their villages.

The Opatas live in the lands bordering the San Miguel de Horcasitas, Arizpe, De los Ures, and Oposura rivers. They make good laborers and reliable soldiers. Long bitter enemies of the Apaches, this tribe has invariably served the Spanish or Mexican government faithfully and loyally. By their efforts alone the province of Sonora upon several occasions has been saved from devastation. The Opatas have approximately 20,000 members.[21]

The Gileños, who inhabit the valleys of the Gila and Colorado, together with the Acaxées [Axuas] and Apaches from the Sierra Madre, are grouped under the general name of Pápagos.[22] These natives live by hunting and robbery. Although nearly four years have elapsed since their last uprising, they are not yet pacified. However, the governor of Sonora has at his disposal only 400 regular soldiers, most of whom are

---

[20]De Mofras is mistaken in regard to the Apaches. This term included several tribes which formed the most southerly group of the Athapascan family. The Apaches were a savage tribe of buffalo hunters, and roamed throughout Texas, northern Mexico, and Arizona. See Frederick W. Hodge, **Handbook of Indians North of Mexico** (2 vols., Washington, 1907-1910), I, 63.

[21]Modern authorities differ considerably as to the numbers of these tribes. De Mofras' estimate, however, is probably right.

[22]The Pápago, or bean-people, were a minor tribe of Piman stock and lived near the Gila and southward in southern Arizona and Sonora. They were a tribe of agriculturists, raising beans, maize, wheat, and cotton. They lived in commodious flat-roofed lodges built of saplings roofed with mud. The Acaxée and the Apache are not related to the Pápago.

Opatas, and a few poorly organized militia. The combined military forces controlled by the *comandante general* of Sinaloa and Sonora do not exceed 600 infantrymen and 200 cavalry, without field equipment.

Near the town of Hermosillo is a mission that has under its control 500 Séris Indians, while a 1,000 more live along the shore north of Guaymas and on Tiburón Island.*

The tribes of Chihuahua and Sonora have been forced south and west as the Americans and Texans have encroached on Mexican territory. They are equipped with a large supply of firearms acquired at settlements along the banks of the Arkansas, Missouri, and Bravo del Norte, in exchange for furs and pelts.†

Up the coast of Sonora toward the north, four leagues beyond Guaymas, lies an excellent harbor, Port Escondido. Near by are the small islands of San Pedro Nolasco, Tortuga, and, in 29° north latitude, Tiburón Island. The latter is inhabited by the Séris Indians who also have several settlements on the main coast. Tiburón, which is 10 leagues long, is the only inhabited island in the Gulf. Together with the coast, Tiburón forms a narrow and dangerous channel, El Canal Peligroso, that terminates in Duck or de los Patos Island. This section of the coast is entirely barren and is frequented only by a few poor Tépocas[23] Indians. The crumbling mission of Caborca is situated 22 leagues inland, in 31° north latitude, on the bank of a small river.

North of the Concepción de Caborca River lies the Bay of Santa Sabina, the tiny island of Santa Inés, the Santa Clara River, and the moorings known as Tres Ojitos. As far up as the Colorado River the coast, which is arid and extremely low, is swept by winds and clouds of fine sand.

The stream known as the Colorado River of the West to differentiate it from the river that flows down into the Gulf of Mexico, rises in the Rocky Mountains near north latitude 41°. The French residents of Louisiana and Canada, who have been familiar with this stream for many years, refer to its upper reaches as the Spanish River. The Colorado

---

*Sections of the **Mémoire** dealing with the Indians of these regions and Spanish methods of control through the mission-presidio system have been omitted at this point in the published version.

†The French text follows the **Mémoire** from this point.

[23]The Tépocas, a treacherous tribe which, together with the Séris lived on the coast above the Yaqui River. They steadily resisted conversion, although Mission San José de Guaymas was established among them. Caborca, site of a mission founded in 1654, lies near the Gulf on the lower end of the Altar River in northern Sonora. Bolton's **Kino op. cit., passim,** frequently mentions this post.

River, which bends slightly west as it traverses the western slope of the vast mountain ranges, flows from north to south. The course is approximately 300 leagues in length, while the shores are inhabited by several tribes of Indians. The river bed is shallow, and can be forded at almost any point throughout its entire length during the dry season. But when the rains descend and the snows melt, its banks overflow, inundating the flat lands adjoining. Where it empties into the Vermilion Sea the Colorado broadens to a width of 2 leagues. Near north latitude 32°, two islands called Islas de los tres Reyes divide the mouth into three channels. The tides have a rise of 6 or 7 meters, causing swift currents whose velocity is often from 12 to 15 miles an hour. At its mouth the river is extremely shallow. When searching for the channel that contains at all times only 5 or 6 feet of water and is quite narrow, ships should sail close to the Californian shore. The river bed is also covered with shoals that are exposed at low tide.

Eight leagues above its mouth, the Colorado is joined by the Gila, which ascends from the east after uniting with its fork, the De la Asunción, which is formed in turn by the union of the Green and Salt rivers.[24] These various streams rise in the foothills of the Sierra Madre, and although not deep, yet, during the rainy season they inundate the surrounding country. The banks of the forks are remarkably fertile, and nuggets of pure gold have, moreover, been found in large numbers. These lands are inhabited by Indian tribes known as the Yumas, Acaxées, Cocomaricopas, and Apaches, all of whom belong to the Pápago family.[25] These tribes must amount altogether to 20,000 members.

A few years ago a plan was formulated in the United States for establishing contact between the Gulf of Mexico and that of California by connecting the Colorado and the Arkansas that flows into the Mississippi, by means of a canal. The originators of this project, however, did not know that these two rivers had their sources on opposite slopes of the Rocky Mountains, and that the Colorado River contained only a few feet of water in the dry season.

---

[24]In 1699 Father Kino named the Colorado the Río de los Mártires; the Gila, Río de los Apostólicos; and its four forks—the Salado, Verde, Santa Cruz, and San Pedro—Los Evangelistas. The main fork of the Gila is not the Asunción, but the Salado, or Salt River. The Asunción empties into the Gulf directly above 30° n. lat.

[25]The tribes mentioned are in no way related to the Pápago, who belong to the Piman stock, whereas the Yuma and Cocomaricopa (Maricopa) are of Yuman stock. The Acaxée do not belong in this unit, as they lived far southward in Mexico. See Hodge, **op. cit.**; Thomas and Swanton, **Indian Languages of Mexico and Central Mexico**, (Washington, 1911).

Since the majority of the missions have been destroyed, the journey overland from Sonora into California is not only extremely difficult, but so unsafe that a large caravan is required. Twenty leagues or more from the Colorado River stands Mission Santa Catalina,[26] the most northerly of all those in Lower California. This has only a few inhabitants and lies about six days' march from the port and mission of San Diego, situated on the Pacific Ocean.

The dividing line between Old and New California commences near the mouth of the Colorado River and terminates south of Mission San Diego, following the thirty-second parallel on which Mission San Miguel is situated. The peninsula that forms Old, or Lower California, is bounded on the north by Upper, or New California, on the south and west by the Pacific, and on the east by the Vermilion Sea.

Between the western slope of the Anahuac Mountains, the eastern slope of the Sierra Nevada, the northern offshoot of this chain, the Gila River and Pimería Alta, the most northerly part of the province of Sonora, stretches the great American Desert, a region of vast sandy plains, unsuited to cultivation, which is traversed throughout its entire length by the Colorado River of the West. This portion of the new continent offers little of interest. Inhabited solely by tribes of unintelligent Indians, this desert affords no support to trains crossing from New Mexico and the United States into California and Oregon Territory.

Upon following the eastern shores of the Gulf from north to south the traveler finds lagoons extending as far as the Cape of San Buenaventura, the anchorage for San Felipe de Jesús, San Fermin, Santa Isabel, La Visitación, San Estanislao, the Bay of San Luís de Gonzaga, San Juan y San Pablo, Los Remedios, the Bay of Los Angeles, the capes known as San Miguel and San Juan Bautista, Isla San Barnabé, Cape Trinidad, Santa Anna Island, and finally Cape Virgines, which is the last extinct volcano in Lower California. In 1746, according to Jesuit records, this volcano was still active. Near its crater considerable sulphur is apparent. Situated on the same parallel as the volcano, but 5 and 8 leagues inland, lie the missions of Santa María Magdalena[27] and Nuestra Señora de Guadalupe.[28]

----

[26]Mission Santa Catalina Mártir, founded under the auspices of the Dominicans on November 12, 1797, lay between San Vicente and Santo Tomás and was designed to minister to the Colorado River country. It was not, as De Mofras says, the most northerly mission.

[27]Mission Santa María Magdalena, which stood 16 miles northwest of Santa Rosalía, was one of the missions founded in the early part of the eighteenth

On the twenty-ninth parallel, the island of Angel de la Guardia, which is long and narrow, forms, together with the mainland, the channel of Ballenas where cetaceans are found in large numbers. Opposite the island, 9 leagues from shore, Mission San Francisco de Borja is situated.[29] Toward the south lie the islands of Salsipuedes, Las Animas, and San Lorenzo—all dangerous to navigators. South of Cape Virgines are the Bay of Santa Agueda, Galapagos Island, and the cape and island of San Marcos, which, together with Tortuga Island and Cape San Miguel, form Mulégé Bay.

Across from San Marcos Island, 6 leagues from the shore, stands Mission San Ignacio.[30] That of Santa Rosalía[31] is situated one-half league from the sea on the banks of the Mulégé River. This point is readily recognized when approaching from afar by a small hat-shaped mountain called Sombrerito. The bay is extremely shallow, only ships of 15 or 20 tons being able to navigate. Here a few pearls are found, while along the banks of the river wheat, vines, olives, figs, and dates thrive.

From the Bay of Mulégé as far as Loreto, the depth close to shore is never less than 40 or 50 meters. The coast affords good harbors at the points called Concepción, Santa Teresa, Colorado, Púlpito, San Juan, the anchorage of San Juan, that of Los Mercenarios, Point Manglares, and the anchorage of San Bruno. Three leagues beyond Loreto the small island called Coronados affords shelter from northeasters. Offshore, close to the mission, the depth is 4 fathoms, and in the lee of Carmen Island, from 15 to 18 fathoms.

The anchorage at Loreto[32] is indicated by the church and a clump of palms, and may be sighted far out at sea by a lofty peak surrounded by smaller peaks. This mountain, called El Cerro de la Gigante, is the loftiest peak in Old California, with an elevation above sea level of

---

century among the Temoris Indians. It was originally in charge of Fernando Pecora, a Jesuit of Sicily.

[28]The first mission of Nuestra Señora de Guadalupe was founded near Santa Cruz Bay by Otondo in 1683, but later abandoned. The Guadalupe to which De Mofras refers was established in the mountains 10 leagues west of Mission Magdalena early in the eighteenth century, by Father Everhard Helén. This should not be confused with Frontizera de Guadalupe, or Huasinapi, begun in the north in 1795 by Cayetano Pallas.

[29]San Francisco de Borja was begun in 1762 by a Bohemian father, Winceslao Link. To the Indians it was known as Adac.

[30]Mission Nuestro Padre San Ignacio was established in 1728 by Bautista Luyando.

[31]Mission Santa Rosaliá was founded in 1705 by Juan Basaldua.

[32]Loreto was founded in 1697 by Father Juan María de Salvatierra. For a century it was the most important point in Baja California.

1,388 meters, trigonometrical measure. Like the entire chain that traverses the peninsula, the peak is of volcanic origin. The anchorage[83] at Loreto is exposed to northwesterly and southwesterly gales. When these rage in full force, ships are advised to head out to sea to avoid being blown ashore. If a ship is small, the course should be set for Port Escondido, 14 leagues toward the south.

The settlement of Loreto has approximately 200 inhabitants. At one time this mission was the capital of Lower California, but it has fallen into decay and its prestige transferred to the Real de San Antonio.[34] The presidio, mission, and church are now slowly crumbling away, although the buildings were constructed in a substantial manner by the Jesuit Fathers, being designed to afford shelter, in case of attack, to the colonists. They were also surrounded by a thick wall that diverted the waters of a mountain stream which upon several occasions destroyed the houses and submerged the lands under cultivation.

The presidio has a small esplanade defended by two bronze swivel-guns whose breeches are now wide open and whose gun carriages are missing. The church still contains a large number of paintings, silver cases, and some valuable jewels belonging to the Virgin. Although these objects are placed in the altar and in the sacristy, the doors are never closed, for no one would dare commit a sacrilegious theft. Loreto is without a garrison, and the resident priest governs the inhabitants in a paternal manner. Fifteen leagues inland, toward the west, the missions of San José de Comondú[35] and San Francisco Xavier,[36] were founded. Loreto has a few gardens; but water is not abundant, and what comes from the wells is salty and unpalatable.

During the Spanish régime, a messenger left Guaymas once a month, crossed the Gulf in a small boat, and landed at Loreto. From there letters were carried overland to the various missions as far as Monterey. This service has been discontinued for some time, and frequently an entire year passes without news from California.

South of Carmen Island lie Los Danzantes, the pearl banks, Las Galeras, La Catalina, Monserrate, San Marcial, Santa Cruz, La Morena, San Diego, San José, San Francisco, Espíritu Santo, and Cerralvo. Along

---

[83]Loreto lies in 25° 59″ n. lat.; 113° 20′ 37″ w. long., Paris time. (D. de M.).

[34]Real de San Antonio, a small settlement of fewer than 1,000 residents, lies below La Paz. There are many mines nearby. San Antonio, however, was never the capital. In 1829 the seat of government had been moved to La Paz from Loreto.

[35]San José de Comondú was started in 1708 by Julian de Mayorga.

[36]San Francisco Xavier was founded in 1699 by Juan de Ugarte and Francisco Picolo.

the coast are the anchorage of Tripuy, the harbor of Agua Verde, the mooring of Santa Marta,[37] the roadsteads of San Carlos, Tembabiche,[38] Dolores, Los Burros, the points known as San Abarito, Mechudo, San Lorenzo, the anchorage of La Paz or port of Pichilingue, Point San Gonzalo, the anchorage of Cerralvo, Port Arena, Muertos Bay, Capes Palma, Porfia, San José, and San Lucas, which forms the western entrance of the Vermilion Sea. The only points at which ships touch are the ports of La Paz and San José del Cabo.

At La Paz,[39] where on May 3, 1535, Hernán Cortés landed,[40] anchorage is available in Pichilingue Bay east of the island of San Juan Nepomuceno at a depth of 5 or 6 fathoms, 2 leagues from the settlement and approximately the same distance from the island called Espíritu Santo and Point San Lorenzo. Only small ships are able to approach the settlement. La Paz has a population of 400 inhabitants, the majority being descendants of foreign sailors. A retired French captain of wide experience, M. Bellot of Bordeaux, is comfortably established at this port. Our vessels rarely visit La Paz; none has put in since 1830 when the three-master *La Félicie* dropped anchor. Commercially this is the most active port in Lower California, being frequented by ships from San Blas, Mazatlán, and Guaymas, which put in for tortoise shell valued at 16 to 18 piasters a quintal, and mother-of-pearl that commands 6 piasters for 100 pounds.

At La Paz a fleet of eight or ten small boats varying from 15 to 40 tons has been outfitted to ply on the Yaqui and Guaymas rivers. These boats are manned by 200 divers, all of whom are Yaqui Indians. The fishing season opens in May and ends in October. Until the close of the last century this was quite remunerative. However, times have now changed. The amount of capital invested annually in this industry is approximately 12,000 piasters, but the pearl beds are being rapidly demolished. Although 800 divers were once employed in the pearl-fishing industry, it is now difficult to find Indians for this task, since each season several of these poor creatures are devoured by sharks and *Manta rayas,*[41] a kind of giant skate some 4 inches long.

---

[37]San Marcial in the French text.

[38]Tembabiche and Tripuy do not appear on modern maps and were probably minor anchorages. The San Abarito of De Mofras is probably Point Nopolo near Mission Dolores del Sur.

[39]La Paz lies in 24° 10′ n. lat.; and 112° 20′ w. long. (D. de M.).

[40]For Cortés at La Paz see **supra,** I, 48-50, also **notes** 5, 6, and 10.

[41]Mantas rayas: a marine monster frequenting the Gulf whose body attained a length of 12 feet and the tail, 15 feet. The species is now almost extinct.

Divers often descend to a depth of 10 or 12 fathoms. Great strength is required to extract oysters from the crevices of the rocks, and workers frequently emerge with hands and feet bleeding. The expression "pearl banks"—*placeres de perlas*—is somewhat misleading. The shells are never superimposed or scattered over a horizontal surface, but are usually hidden in an opening in the rock, so that a diving bell is useless.

In 1827 a company formed in London known as the General Pearl and Coral Fishery Association sent an agent to Guaymas. After a minute examination of the various banks in the Gulf, he was convinced that the diving suit with which he was provided could not be used. The two ships under his command collected only a small supply of pearls of an inferior quality and failed to find coral. Thus the company was forced to abandon the attempt. The richest banks are found in the Bay of La Paz near Loreto, the southwest point of Carmen Island, Port Escondido, Los Coronados, Los Danzantes, and the islands of San Bruno and San Marcos. The shores of Tiburón Island are reputed to abound in shells, but no expeditions have been sent out according to all reports, for the Séris Indians who reside there are extremely cruel. Mr. Hardy,[42] an English officer who landed on the island, sent out divers, but discovered only a few pearls of slight value. Farther north in Mulégé Bay Yaqui divers also failed to find pearls.[43]

At Loreto a certain portion of the pearls is reserved for the Virgin. The divers, too, received their share, in addition to money, clothes, and food that are furnished by their employers. When the ships return to port, the pearls are sold in one lot from 1,500 to 1,800 piasters a pound, and are then sold at retail throughout the country. The inhabitants of Sonora and Sinaloa ask such high prices for pearls that they are more expensive at Guaymas and Mazatlán than at Mexico City where pearls from India and Panamá may also be purchased. After all expenses have been deducted, the pearl fisheries clear an annual profit of 12,000 or 14,000 piasters. Pearls that are entirely black are especially prized.

From San José del Cabo, La Paz, Loreto, and Mulégé, coastal vessels are sent to ports along the coast of Mexico to procure flour and European wares in exchange for cheese, jerked beef, butter, oranges, dates, raisins, and dried fruits. Near Mulégé and Real de San Antonio, a few leagues

---

[42]During July and August, 1826, Lieutenant R. W. H. Hardy in the **Wolf** and **Bruja** explored the coast above Guaymas, searching for pearls and gold. See his **Travels in the Interior of Mexico** (London, 1829).

[43]See Henry R. Wagner, "Pearl Fishing Enterprises in the Gulf of California," in **Hispanic-American Historical Review** Vol. X, (May, 1930), pp. 188-220.

from La Paz, silver mines are being worked, but the output is negligible. However, by a comparison of outcroppings it appears that the geology of Lower California is similar to that of Sonora and Sinaloa, and that this peninsula was abruptly severed from the mainland at some remote period. Thus, if the rocks exposed on the two shores lying in practically the same latitudes have the same formation, the auriferous outcroppings would probably be the same. Upon approaching the sea near Cape San Lucas, this chain gradually forms a fertile plateau where, surrounded by twelve or fifteen small hamlets, the Real de San Antonio, the actual capital of the district, the ancient mission of Santiago de los Coras,[44] and those of Todos los Santos[45] and San José[46] have come into existence.

At the latter mission the noted Chappé d' Auteroche[47] whom the Royal Academy of Sciences had sent out to observe the passage of Vénus across the disk of the sun, a phenomenon that occurred on June 3, 1769, passed away. The French Academician was accompanied by two distinguished officers of the Spanish navy who determined with scientific accuracy the position of Cape San Lucas that serves as a reconnoitering point for ships bound for China and Europe.

The Indians of Lower California are now thoroughly subjected and any distinction between Coras, Edués, Pericúes, and Cochimiés has been largely obliterated.[48] The Mexican government does not station troops in this country and all authority is vested in a Dominican Father, the president of the apostolic prefect of the missions, in a civil prefect, and in a justice of the peace. The *comandante general* of the two Californias resides at Monterey. The entire population of Lower California does not exceed 4,000 inhabitants. Of these, one-third, as indicated in the following table, belong to the white races.

---

[44]Santiago de los Coras was founded in 1721 by Ignacio Nápoli.

[45]Todos Santos [Santa Rosa] was founded in 1733 by Sigismundo Taraval on the site of the old Santiago Mission near the Bay of Palmas. For a detailed account of its history see **Taraval's Journal of the Indian Uprising in Lower California**, edited by Marguerite Eyer Wilbur (Los Angeles, 1931).

[46]San José [Saint Joseph] was founded in 1730 by Nicolás Tamaral.

[47]The noted astronomer, Chappé d'Auteroche (1728-1769) reached San José on May 19, where he contracted a malady that had already swept away one-third of the inhabitants, and soon cost him his own life. In his brief narrative called **Voyage en Californie** (Paris, 1772), this ill-fated journey is recounted.

[48]A wide variety of opinion as to the classification of the peninsula Indians exists. The usual division, however, places the Edués, or Pericúes between 24º n. lat. and Cape San Lucas, and the Cochimiés, of Yuman stock, in the northern part of the Peninsula. The Coras were a sub-tribe of the Pericúes. See H. H. Bancroft, **Native Races** (5 vols., San Francisco, 1883), I, 556-570; Venegas, **Noticia, op. cit., passim**; and Hodge, **op. cit., passim**.

Missions of the Northwest.
From north to south—

Missions of the Northeast.
From north to south—

	Inhabitants		Inhabitants
San Miguel	430	San Francisco de Borja	71
Santa Catalina	48	Santa Gertrudis	53
Santo Tomás	233	San Ignacio	19
San Vicente	261	Santa Magdalena	35
Santo Domingo	159	Nuestra Señora de Guadalupe	240
Nuestra Señora del Rosario	75	Santa Rosalía de Mulégé	74
San Fernando de Vellicatá	45	San José de Comondú	81
La Purísima (destroyed)		Nuestra Señora de Loreto	
San Luís (destroyed)		(former capital)	200
Todos los Santos [Santa Rosa]	260	San Francisco Xavier	55
Real de San Antonio		San José del Cabo	320
(Actual capital)	717	The port of La Paz	390
Total	2,228	Total	3,766

These missions are in charge of the Mendicant Order of Dominican Fathers of the convent of Santiago de Predicadores of Mexico. The Franciscans control only the missions of Upper California.

*A description of the east coast of Lower California has already been given, and the west coast, an arid land where only a few good moorings are found, offers little of exceptional interest. At Cape San Lucas[49] anchorage is safe only from November to May, the period when northwesterly and westerly winds prevail. This is an important reconnoitering point for ships bound for San Blas, Mazatlán, and Guaymas, whether en route from Europe, Asia, the Sandwich Islands, or Upper California.

How English corsairs often hid in this vicinity preparatory to apprehending Spanish galleons was discussed in the Introduction to this volume. The southern tip of San Lucas is defined by a group of rocks called Los Frailes (the priests). Ships are able to sail close to these rocks and find moorings, but the bed does not offer firm anchorage. Owing

---

*The remainder of this chapter is not contained in the original Mémoire, which continues with a discussion of the interest of various foreign powers in acquiring California, the need for French commercial houses, and De Mofras' itinerary. See Amérique Vol. 43, Mémoire II, folios 108 to 113.

[49]Cape San Lucas: 22° 52' 28" n. lat.; 112° 10' 38" w. long. Declination, 7° 53' N.E. (D. de M.).

to the depth, small ships experience considerable difficulty hauling in their anchors.

Five firms have quarters at the settlement, three being owned by Englishmen or Americans. Within a few leagues lie several small farms or ranchos where corn and sugar cane are raised. Whalers often put in at Cape San Lucas to take on meat, for good beef sells at the port for 8 piasters. An abundance of wood, cheese, and some fresh garden produce may also be procured. Along the shore a few vegetable gardens have been planted, and wells have been sunk in the sand.

After rounding the cape and following the coast about a league northwest of the point, the mission of Todos los Santos,[50] that still shelters a few Indians, comes into view. Here anchorage may be found near a small stream. Nearby water and supplies are available.

Along the twenty-fourth parallel the mountains form a promontory surmounted by three peaks whose flattened summits resemble plateaus. Because of this feature they are called the Tables, or Mesas de Narvaez. From this point the coast extends directly west to a point where the large island of Santa Margarita defines the southern entrance of the vast harbor of Magdalena Bay. This entrance, marked by a lofty hillock called Morro Redondo, exceeds 2 miles in width and has a depth near the center of the channel averaging 40 or 50 meters. Along the shore this decreases to 15 or 20 meters. The roadstead is so extensive that it could readily hold several fleets.

However, no supplies are available, the missions of San Luís de Gonzaga[51] and San Francisco Xavier being now in ruins. Moreover, the port, although teeming with fish, affords neither wood nor good water. When north winds blow, anchor should be dropped at the mouth of the peninsula formed by Point Delgada, at whose tip lies the cape and mountain of San Lázaro that rises to a height of 400 meters. When approaching from afar, this cape appears to be an island.

Several years ago an English whaler ran aground off Point Delgada which is so low that in foul weather the sea breaks over the land. When an easterly or a southerly wind prevails, it is far safer to anchor in the Bay of Las Almejas[52] on the eastern side of Santa Margarita. This island is frequented by two species of tortoises. One of these provides excellent meat, but the shell has no value. Although the flesh of the other is

---

[50]Mission Todos Santos: 23° 26′ n. lat.; 112° 37′ 3″ w. long. (D. de M.).

[51]Mission San Luís de Gonzaga was erected in 1740 by Francisco Wagner, but was abandoned in 1769 when the Fathers moved to Todos Santos.

[52]Almojar in the French text.

unpalatable, yet the shell has a commercial value. American whalers frequently come into Magdalena Bay[53] searching for whale oil.

Beyond Mt. San Lázaro[54] the coast runs directly eastward, affording at all points a level floor in 30 or 40 meters close to shore, as far north as the tiny shelter formed at the twenty-sixth parallel by Point Santo Domingo. The coast now bends northwestward for 20 leagues or more, then stretches 10 leagues toward the southeast until Point Abreojos,[55] surrounded at its tip by dangerous reefs, is reached. Nearby, toward the northwest, rise the two small islands of Asunción and San Roque. For the next 8 miles the coast toward the north is comparatively safe. In the harbor of San Bartolomé,[56] discovered by General Don Sebastián Vizcaíno, anchorage is available.

Ships sailing near the coast should keep well off Point San Eugenio which, together with Natividad Island situated at its western extremity, appears to form a single promontory with Natividad Island. Here, as at Cape San Lázaro, whalers have run aground when attempting to pass between the island and the mainland at night, and have been carried up on the point, which is quite low. The channel between the island and this point is 7 or 8 miles broad, and has a depth of 30 or 40 meters. If the traveler arrives from the south, a fair-sized mountain toward the east, called Morro Hermoso, will serve to indicate the existence of this point. If the approach is from the north, the islands of Cerros and San Benito provide adequate landmarks. East of Point San Eugenio the coast recedes to a considerable extent for a distance of one degree in latitude, forming the great Bay of Sebastián.[57] Within lies the anchorage of Pescado Blanco, formed by a point 5 or 6 miles long, that curves back toward the south. Thirty miles northwest of this point the lofty, white-capped promontory of Santa María is visible, and 10 leagues farther north, the point and anchorage of De las Canoas.

Near the mooring stretches the San Francisco Bay of Lower California that affords adequate shelter in all weather. Ships bound for this port should set their course for a point southwest of the bay, where the opening faces south. Two miles off the southern end the course should

[53]Magdalena Bay: 24° 36′ n. lat.; 114° 25′ w. long. Declination: 8° 15′ N.E. (D. de M.).

[54]Mt. San Lazaro lies in 24° 27′ n. lat. (D. de M.).

[55]Point Abreojos, at the summit of one of its most westerly peaks: 26° 59′ 30″ n. lat.; 116° 7′ 3″ w. long.

[56]Point San Bartolomé, north of the bay, 27° 40′ n. lat.; 117° 11′ 40″ w. long.; declination, 10° 46′ N. E. (D. de M.).

[57]The Bay of Sebastián Viscaíno is in 28° 56′ n. lat. Paris time. (D. de M.).

be set north-northeast, until the point is first sighted off west-northwest, then north-northwest. However, if the wind is offstern, short tacks must be made, care being taken not to approach the eastern shore closer than where soundings show 5 fathoms, for beyond this depth the bottom grows suddenly shallower.

Upon nearing land it is possible to approach within a cable's length offshore, and after the point appears on the west, anchor should be dropped at a depth of 6 to 14 meters, where a sandy bed affords a good holding-ground. Off the end of the point, toward the southwest, a shoal extends south-southwest; this has less than 3 feet of water at low tide. In San Francisco Bay[58] the tide rises 3 meters when conditions are normal, and 4 meters during the equinox. This harbor provides excellent shelter, but wood and water are difficult to procure. The bay has a depth that varies from 15 to 25 meters, except near shore where the average is 6 or 7 meters. The northern entrance is protected by a high point called Las Virgines that juts out toward the west. The mission of Nuesta Señora del Rosario[59] lies about 3 leagues northeast of the anchorage. A fair road leads to the settlement, where cattle, sheep, and some fresh supplies are obtainable.

Approximately 10 miles northward the port of San Quentín, defined by a cape of the same name which is also called Cape Colnett, affords a safe harbor. At the mission of Santo Domingo,[60] a few leagues away, mariners can always find fresh meat. In this port, as in that of San Francisco, extensive salt deposits, as yet unexploited, exist. The Hudson's Bay Company has investigated these two places with the idea of extracting some of this salt. American vessels outbound from Boston have also dropped anchor nearby with this same end in view. However, since labor was difficult to procure, they preferred to bring out from the United States what salt was required to cure the hides collected along the coast of the two Californias.

The coast now runs due north as far as 32° north latitude. At this point the cape appears to terminate in a group of islands; of these the most remote, which is the largest, extends westward. Cape Grajero, or Todos los Santos, forms the southern entrance of the bay of that name,

---

[58]Port of San Francisco in Lower California, at the tip of the northern entrance; 30° 22' n. long.; 118° 16' 57" w. long., variation of the magnetic needle, 12° N. E. (D. de M.).

[59]Nuestra Señora del Rosario was founded in 1774 by the Dominicans.

[60]Mission Santo Domingo was begun a year later by Fathers Manuel García and Miguel Hidalgo.

whose northern end is formed by Point San Rafael which offers excellent shelter except from westerly winds. There are also several lagoons nearby that yield, in the dry season, large quantities of crystallized salt.

The Missions of Santo Tomás[61] and San Miguel[62] two or three leagues away supply provisions and live stock to vessels. Eight leagues south lies Nuestra Señora de Guadalupe, recently founded by the Reverend Father Cavallero, president of the Dominican Order.

From Todos los Santos as far as the port of San Diego, the coast affords no more harbors. Inland the dividing line between Upper and Lower California appears to be defined by two high mountains terminating in broad plateaus known as the Tables, or Mesas de Juan Gómez. After leaving the Bay of San Francisco in Lower California, the land appears less arid toward the north. Certain portions are even suitable for agriculture, especially those adjoining the missions of Rosario, San Vicente,[63] Guadalupe, San Miguel, and Santo Tomás.

The Indian population, however, is small. The Missions of San Miguel and Guadalupe[64] have only about 300 and Santo Tomás 200 Indians. Most of the other missions have been entirely abandoned. San Francisco de Borja houses six Indians; San Ignacio, four Spanish families; Mission Jesús María has not even a solitary occupant. Here and there a few isolated farms owned by white colonists appear.

Near Mission San Vicente a little settlement has sprung up; this is the only mission in Lower California where troops are stationed. A company of 20 native soldiers is retained here to keep the Yuman Indians from the right bank of the Colorado, and to repel any uprisings. The customhouse at Monterey assists this garrison by providing clothes and money. The soldiers, most of whom are farmers, support themselves by raising corn and cattle.

Since the destruction of the missions, an overland journey in Lower California presents inconceivable difficulties. In certain sections travelers must carry sufficient water for two days. The few that attempt this trip sail from Mazatlán or Guaymas to the presidio of Nuestra Señora de Loreto. Then after Mission San José de Comondú is passed twelve days are required for the trip of 80 leagues to Mission San Ignacio. An-

---

[61]Mission Santo Tomás dates from 1791, when it was founded by Miguel Hidalgo and Joaquin Valero.

[62]San Miguel Fronteriza was founded in 1784 by Miguel Hidalgo and Joaquin Valero.

[63]San Vicente Ferrer was founded in 1780 by Miguel Hidalgo and and Joaquin Valero.

[64]Probably Nuestra Señora de Guadalupe. See **supra**, I, 113, **note** 28.

other eight days must be allowed for the next journey of 80 leagues
from San Francisco de Borja to the coast. The remaining 160 leagues
to San Diego can be traveled in seventeen days. This trip of 336 leagues,
which is now extremely dangerous, was formerly made without the
slightest peril. The 170 leagues south from Loreto as far as Cape San
Lucas were also made without difficulty. The chain of missions and
presidios in Lower California extends for more than 500 leagues.

This country has excellent harbors, as well as untapped mineral
resources waiting to be developed. The silver mines near Real de San
Antonio employ a few laborers; but no work is being done on the gold
mines and the rock-crystal deposits near Mission Santa Rosalía. Sulphur,
ochre, mineral salt, and nitrate of potash are abundant in these countries. Carmen Island in the Vermilion Sea has some excellent salt deposits. Not far from Mission San Ignacio extensive salt mines have also
been discovered.

The Pericúes, Cochimíe, Coras, and Monqui[65] Indians who originally
comprised the population of Lower California, are now scattered and
no longer form distinct tribes. Only a few, moreover, have survived. This
country has no rivers and is so arid that even small brooks are scarce.
In certain localities, however, live stock can be raised, and sugar cane
and certain grains cultivated. The climate of Lower California is extremely warm, the air is dry, and the atmosphere remarkably clear. The
thermometer registers as high as 38° centigrade.

Summer is the rainy season and a time of cloudbursts, tempests, and
high winds. Cold is not felt, nor is snow found on the summit of the
ranges until the thirtieth parallel is reached. The mountains appear to
be the product of a series of primeval unheavals, several being composed
of shale and calcareous material. On the contrary, others appear to be
volcanic in origin, for they contain primarily lava, pumice stone, nitrous
salt, minerals, and sulphur. Near Mission San Gertrudis[66] large flakes
of rock crystals in hexagonal prisms are found. Plaster or sulphate of
lime exists near Mulégé in stratified and translucent slabs 4 or 5 feet long,
18 inches wide, and 3 or 4 inches thick. The Fathers used these slabs in
place of window glass. Excellent stone for construction is also available,
and rumors of marble deposits are prevalent.[67]

A small amount of blue lead, or sulphate of copper, in small crystals

---

[65]The Monqui, a branch of the Pericúe, lived in the vicinity of Mission Loreto.

[66]Santa Gertrudis Mission was established in 1751 by Father Fernando Consag; its buildings were planned by a native, Andrés Sestiago.

[67][Francisco] Clavijero, *Storia della California*, p. 38, Venice, 1789. (D. de M.).

is found in damp soil near Mission Guadalupe. In the mountains near Mulégé reddish-colored silver, believed to contain gold, has been discovered, as well as some veins of yellow ochre, and a kind of ceruse, or native white lead, protoxide of lead, which is used to whitewash houses. Near Mt. Rosario and in several other localities salt nitrate or nitrate of potash, and salts of soda, called by the Mexican Indians *tequesquite,* quasi-carbonate of soda, are in a state of efflorescence on the surface of the ground like the pure sulphur found near the extinct volcano of Las Virgenes.

Vegetation in a country as arid as Lower California provides little sustenance. Shrubs and cacti abound. Some of these, especially the cacti, supply the Indians with excellent fruit. One type of gooseberry bush and the berberry bush provide succulent berries; the nopal[68] and the anaba[69] produce savory figs. The berries of several large trees belonging to the Leguminosae family, a group resembling the acacias, the *medesa,*[70] the *dipuá,*[71] the *agisandú,*[27] and the *huizache,*[73] can be eaten in place of beans while others bear oily seeds. From the *jojoba*[74] an oil similar to olive oil that makes an excellent dressing for wounds, is extracted. Herbs and common plants spring up after the rainy season. From the ears of the *teda* grains resembling aniseed are extracted. The *tedegua*[75] is like nettle and contact with it produces the same disastrous results that are experienced with its European cousin. Its seeds, however, are used for food. One variety of thistle which, like the giant cactus,[76] attains a height of 40 feet, supplies nourishing seeds and refreshing juices.

All the fruit trees grown in Europe, as well as oleraceous plants and Leguminosae, prosper wherever planted. This is also true of grains, although wheat does not succeed as well as corn. Where the soil is rich, wheat yields sixty times its weight, whereas corn returns more

---

[68]The nopal: any cactus of the genus **Nopalae,** or prickly pear, many specie of which flourish on the peninsula.

[69]**Anaba** is an Indian term for the **zabate,** a fruit resembling a small fig.

[70]The **medesa** is a large tree producing fruit enclosed in pods, like beans. This the Indians toast, and bake into cakes.

[71]The **dipuá** is another name for the same tree.

[72]The **asigandú** also bears pods used in making cakes.

[73]The **huizache** is a bush with spiny leaves belonging to the bean family. Although unpalatable, animals use it for food.

[74]The **jojoba,** which grows in the arid foothills, bears a fruit encased in an oblong berry resembling the almond, and is highly prized for its medicinal properties.

[75]The **tedegua** is a plant similar to that of the pepper.

[76]The so-called organ cactus, known to the Spanish conquerors as **cordon.** Its curative properties were known to the Fathers, who used the juice for healing wounds and sores.

than three hundred times its original planting. Sugar cane, manioc, tobacco, indigo, the castor oil plant, a kind of reed with a heavy saccharine content, and tinctorial plants, grow wild on the banks of streams. Poisonous plants, especially the *yedra*,[77] where contact even with the air in its vicinity causes a general poisoning of the body, grows in equally large numbers. The *palo de la flecha*,[78] whose poisonous juices make the Indian arrows so deadly, also merits mention. The palms produce excellent dates. Wild grapevines are common; but the stock imported from Europe produces superior wine. A tree like the *garroubier*[79] gives forth pods which the Indians eat and feed to their animals. Black and white ebony, the sumac tree, the tar tree, oak, ilex, and corkwood, different kinds of pines, ironwood, and brazilwood cover the mountains. Unfortunately most of these varieties that might be used for building are found only in places that are virtually inaccessible.

A large number of animals indigenous to Lower California have been observed. These include scorpions, tarantulas, locusts and ants that often devour harvests, centipedes, grasshoppers, wasps, swarms of mosquitoes and other insects. Bees, oddly enough, are absent; wasps, however, give honey. Frogs and toads appear during the rainy season. Land and water tortoises are numerous along the shore. Lizards and adders are not poisonous, but the bite of the rattlesnake, known to the Spanish as the *cascabel,* is often fatal.

Both coasts of the peninsula abound in whale of various kinds, sharks, swordfish, bonito, dolphin, and goldfish. Up and down the shores are found shells of brilliant colors, the oyster pearl, octopus, and murex that supply purple coloring—madrepore and zoöphyte.

Birds that are prevalent are the eagle, falcon, vulture, hawk, crow, owl, buzzard, white pelican, wild duck, gull, mudhen, weaver, humming bird, and mocking bird. The wildcat, bear, coyote, maneless American lion, wild goat, deer, polecat, ground squirrel, beaver, and fresh-water otter are the principal quadrupeds of Old California. What horses, cattle, sheep, pigs, mules, and fowl were introduced by the Fathers have multiplied amazingly.

Off the coast of Lower California are several islands of interest to navigators and whaling ships. In fact, the Tres Marías, south of Cape San Lucas, have already attracted the attention of the Spanish govern-

---

[77]Yedra: poison-ivy.

[78]Palo de la flecha is a vegetable from which poisonous juices were extracted by warring Indians for use on their arrows.

[79]Also spelled garuga: an East Indian tree bearing edible berries.

ment and by a royal decree of Ferdinand VI, dated November 13, 1744, the settlement of these islands was ordered. Toward the end of 1747, this edict was again given a hearing at the court at Madrid, but apparently it was not executed in conformity with the colonization plan of the Spanish government, for these islands are still uninhabited.[80]

Farther out at sea the islands of Revillagigedo—named in honor of the viceroy of New Spain who dreamed of founding a settlement on the group—include several islands, between the eighteenth and twentieth parallels. Their discovery dates from the beginning of the sixteenth century. In 1523 Hernando de Grijalva sighted the largest of these islands which he named Santo Tomás and which is now known as Socorro.[81] This island is about 12 leagues long from east to west, its highest peak being visible 20 leagues away. On the south are two excellent harbors.

North and slightly east of Socorro rises the tiny island of San Benedicto. In 1542, Ruy López de Villalobos discovered and named this land Nublada. To the English it is known as Clouds. This island, which has a circumference of 8 miles, is steep on the north side where the ocean is deep. The southwest coast has one or two sandy beaches where it is possible to disembark on the rocks and where the anchorage is on sand. Nearby is a small fresh-water lake. In place of trees, underbrush will be found. These islands afford a rendezvous for seals and a species of tortoise known as "hawk's bill," whose shell is especially suitable for making combs.

On several Spanish maps the name Nublada is often erroneously applied to an island lying 20 leagues west of Socorro. Santa Rosa is also referred to at times as the Island of Roca Partida.[82] This is the most westerly of the group and when seen from the northwest resembles two ships under full canvas. If seen at sunset this error might cause a serious accident to ships sailing at night.

This same observation applies to a group of rocks called Los Alijos (the Lighters). These were discovered in 1791 by Captain Marquina en route from the Philippines. Four main rocks that extend on a line north and south for three-fifths of a mile comprise this small group. The most easterly of these islands is only 17 meters high. The loftiest

---

[80]Father Burriel, Vol. II, 520 (D. de M.). See also **supra**, p. 103.

[81]Socorro Island, culminating point: 18° 48' n. lat.; 112° 30' 37" w. long. (D. de M.).

[82]Island of Roca Partida: 18° 37' n. lat.; 116° 25' 7" w. long. (D. de M.).

lies toward the west and has an elevation of 30 meters above sea level.[83] The ocean has a depth of several hundred fathoms around these rocks, which incidentally are the only reefs that are passed during the voyage north from Mexico to California.[84]

Several English maps place two or three small islands called Seaotter, Shovel, or Shelvoes,[85] south and east of Cape San Lucas, but these localities have not been verified. Paralleling the Revillagigedo Islands between 116° and 117° west longitude lie other small islands. One of these, scarcely two leagues wide, also bears the name of Nublada.

Near the Californian coast rises the large island of Santa Margarita which forms the southern end of Magdalena Bay. The islands of Natividad, San Benito, and Cerros, north and east of Point San Eugenio, afford several good anchorages. That of Cerros, or Cedros, discovered in 1539 by Ulloa, has a circumference of some 6 leagues, is somewhat lofty, and is of volcanic origin. This lies only 4 miles offshore. The intermediate passage is not dangerous, provided caution is exercised in avoiding a chain of rocks that extend north-northwest off the tip of the peninsula for a distance of half a mile.

English and American whalers come to Cedros to hunt sea elephants and seals, and in 1839 an American ship anchored there for two months, collecting 300 skins of sea otter. The species, as a result, is now virtually extinct. Seals alone are fairly numerous. The small island of San Gerónimo, lying a short distance south of the harbor of San Francisco, the island of San Martín in the north, the islands of Solitarios and those of Todos los Santos, together with the Coronados which rise 15 miles south of the entrance of San Diego Harbor, are also inhabited by these amphibians.

Eighty leagues off the coast rises Guadalupe Island, whose position should be carefully observed, since it serves as a reconnoitering point and landing place for ships bound from Manila to San Blas or Mazatlán.[86] Guadalupe is extremely high, the summit being 1,040 meters above sea level. On the extreme south two small islands about two miles apart are visible. On clear days the island may be sighted for a

---

[83]Rear admiral Dupetit Thouars, op. cit., I, 149. (D. de M.).

[84]Highest point of Alijos: 24° 57′ 30″ n. lat.; 118° 5′ 50″ w. long. (D. de M.).

[85]Known as the Shelvoke Islands. The general map published in 1843 by Captain Belcher in his Narrative of a Voyage Round the World (2 vols., London, 1843), shows them due west, not east, of Cape San Lucas.

[86]Guadalupe Island, the culminating point, as reported by M. de Tessau: 27° 7′ 25″ n. lat.; 130° 42′ 45″ w. long., declination, 11° 30′ N. E. (D. de M.).

distance of 15 leagues. A quarter of a mile offshore the coast is entirely safe with fairly deep water.

The island, which is of volcanic origin and 7 leagues in circumference, is uninhabited. Although somewhat barren toward the south, the northern area has several fertile valleys and mountains covered with vegetation. Ships can procure wood and water near a small creek on the northeastern side of the island. Wild goats, that are found in large numbers, are easily killed. The only safe anchorage is that used by the whaling ships that come to hunt sea otter with extra-heavy coats. This is situated in a cove on the south side of the island, and is sheltered by several small islands stretching in the same direction. Near land anchorage is likewise available in 14 fathoms, with protection from all winds, except those from the southeast or northwest, which rarely blow in these regions.

CHAPTER VII*

Divisions of the American Continent west of the Rocky Mountains. Founding of the missions, pueblos, and presidios of New, or Upper, California.

Having completed in the preceding chapter the description of the western provinces of Mexico and those of Old, or Lower California, it seems advisable, before passing on to describe the new land and the countries adjoining it, to indicate in a few words the major divisions of the American continent west of the Rocky Mountains.

The vast territory that lies between the western slopes of the Rocky Mountains and the northern part of the Pacific Ocean has four distinct divisions. From Bering Strait to the fifty-fourth parallel extends Russian America; from there down to the Strait of Juan de Fuca, New Caledonia, owned by England; from the forty-ninth to the forty-second parallels, Oregon Territory, claimed both by the United States and Great Britain; and, finally, toward the south, Upper, or New California. Inasmuch as these four regions differ in climate, products, and characteristics, a detailed description of each area will be given.

Upon leaving the arid mountains of the peninsula and entering New California, the fertility of the soil and the abundance of pasture land is obvious. Three parallel chains of mountains, forming two vast intermediate valleys, bisect New California.[1] The most easterly of these stretches north and south and is bounded by the Sierra Nevada and a central chain known as the Californian Mountains. The loftiest of these ranges ,which are covered with vast forests, are 1,000 or 1,200 meters in height. Through this valley from south to north flows the San Joaquin River which unites with the Sacramento River before emptying into the Bay of San Francisco. The latter rises in Lake Masqué,[2] at the base of the Sierra Nevada, and flows down toward the sea from

---

*Mémoire No. IV commences at this point. See **Amérique** Vol. 43, folios 150 to 196. Except for a variation in the first two pages there are only minor changes in the printed volume.

[1]The eastern boundary of California at that time was not defined.

[2]Possibly Lower Klamath Lake. Much of western America was unexplored at this early period.

northeast to southwest. Several fresh-water lakes, called the Tulares, from a kind of reed called tule which the Indians use to roof their huts, are also found in the valley. Fish and beaver abound in these lagoons; and the adjacent lands are extraordinary fertile. Several Indian tribes, forming in all a population of some 20,000, are the sole inhabitants of this country. Captain Sutter, however, has founded on the left bank of the Sacramento River a highly interesting colony,[3] which will be discussed in a future chapter.

The third chain of mountains, which does not attain a height of more than 600 or 800 meters, skirts the coast. From north to south this forms the Ross, Santa Cruz, Santa Lucía, Buchón, San Inés, San Fernando, and San Gabriel Mountains that abound in excellent timber suitable for building. In the valley formed by these two chains and on several low areas along the coast lie the regions inhabited by white colonists and the chain of missions. From San Diego as far north as Ross, this zone is approximately 200 leagues long and 10 wide. The most easterly valley is 25 or 30 leagues in width.

At many points this chain is crossed by small streams that usually empty into the ocean. In summer, most of these small rivers are dry. The only navigable waterway in the settled area is the Sacramento; this is open to flat-bottom boats and small steamers for some 50 leagues. The San Joaquin, on the contrary, becomes shallow 3 or 4 leagues above its mouth and so is usually unnavigable throughout the year. Such rivers as the Klamath and the Umpqua, near Cape Mendocino, will be discussed in another chapter.

Through the reports of many maritime expeditions whose history has already been given, the attention of the viceroys of New Spain was directed to the importance of Upper California with her splendid harbors. These officials, as a result, decided to send several military expeditions overland into this virgin territory. The explorers were accompanied by missionaries whose task was to establish colonies.

On June 25, 1767, by order of Charles III, the Marquis de Croix, viceroy of Mexico, and Don José de Gálvez, inspector-general, or *visitador* of this colony,[4] abolished the Company of Jesus and entrusted the administration of the missions, which for many years the Jesuits alone had directed with such wisdom and success, to the Franciscan Order of

---

[3]For Sutter's colony see **infra**, I, 241, 243, **note 152**; 244, 245.

[4]As inspector-general José Gálvez, who was independent of the viceroy, held supreme control over the destinies of New Spain.

the College of San Fernando in Mexico City. At this time various donations and properties forming the Pious Fund of California (*Fondo piadoso de California*) passed into the control of the Franciscans.[5]

Sixteen of these Fathers led by their apostolic prefect, the Reverend Father Junípero Serra, landed in April, 1768, at Loreto in Lower California. Serra was followed on July 16 of that same year by the inspector-general of New Spain, who carried a royal order for the founding of a colony either at the port of Monterey or at San Diego.

After visiting the missions of Lower California, Don José de Gálvez and Father Junípero decided to found the presidios and missions of San Carlos de Monterey and San Diego in Upper California at the two extremities of the province, thus protecting the entire country, and to establish a third, Mission San Buenaventura, at an intermediate location.

Two sloops provided with the equipment necessary to establish these new colonies were now sent to California. In addition to her crew, the *San Carlos*[6] carried two missionaries, the engineer, Costansó, a French surgeon, Prat, and a company of volunteer soldiers from Catalonia in command of Captain Vila and Lieutenant Fages. During his sojourn at the presidio at Loreto, Don José de Gálvez founded a navy training school for Indians, to prepare them to handle ships plying up and down the Vermilion Sea and along the shores of New Galicia, Sinaloa, and Sonora.

Shortly after the departure of these vessels, the overland train in two divisions led by Don Gaspar de Portolá, captain of dragoons and first governor of California, began its journey.[7] Don Fernando Rivera, captain of a company of leather-jackets, marched on ahead to map the route; his orders were to assemble all available animals from the missions. Having found, 40 leagues north of Mission San Francisco de Borja— at that time the most northerly post in California—a place called Vellicatá which seemed suitable for a meeting place, he went on ahead with the Father Prefect, while Governor Portolá followed with the second division composed of a company of muleteers and a large number of

---

[5]Control passed to the Franciscans on June 25, 1767.

[6]The **San Carlos** set sail on January 9, 1769, from La Paz. She carried only one Father, Hernando Parron, 25 Catalonians, and a crew of sailors and minor officers. The second ship was the **San Antonio**. This carried Fathers Viscaíno and Gómez, and was in command of Don Juan Pérez. The **San José** carrying supplies, followed. See Herbert E. Bolton, **Historical Mémoir of New California** (4 vols., Berkeley, 1926), II, 1-18.

[7]Portolá's train followed from the royal presidio at Loreto on March 9. **Ibid** II, 25-30.

Indian converts. The Reverend Father Crespi and a hydrographer, who had charge of taking observations and keeping a journal,[8] completed the party which joined the first expedition after a safe journey on May 14, 1769, at the port of San Diego.

On the site where this expedition camped Father Junípero founded the mission of San Fernando de Vellicatá,[9] which soon numbered 300 Indian converts. In accordance with his royal orders the Father President then founded a mission at San Diego. In the meanwhile the governor of California, Don Gaspar Portolá, with an expedition of 70 men, marched north to found the presidio at Monterey.[10] The inaccuracy of the descriptions left by navigators, however, prevented him from locating this port. Nevertheless, he explored as far north as the Bay of San Francisco, returning, after six months of unbelievable hardships, on January 24, 1770, to San Diego.

On April 16 of that same year the sloop *San José*[11] set sail for Monterey. At the same time a new overland party, after searching for thirty-eight days, discovered the elusive harbor.[12] The number of animals brought into California by these expeditions amounted to 300 or more, among them being 200 cattle. These animals, which multiplied rapidly, formed the basis of the future wealth of the missions subsequently established. Father Junípero, with the coöperation of the governor, then ordered the workmen of the expedition to erect a chapel and presidio which formed the nucleus of Mission San Carlos de Monterey. Later, when its founders realized that the shores of the bay did not afford an adequate water supply for working what little land could be quickly put under cultivation, Mission San Carlos, which was now renamed Mission del Carmelo, was moved a league and a half south, to the edge of a small cove into which emptied a river.

When word was received that the ports of San Diego and Monterey had been occupied, there was universal rejoicing in Mexico. At the request of Father Junípero, the viceroy, the Marquis de Croix, now sent

---

[8]For the diary of this overland journey see **ibid**, II, 109-260.

[9]Vellicatá was founded on May 14, 1769, a day dedicated to the Feast of Espíritu Santo. **Ibid.** II, 30-31.

[10]Monterey was rediscovered on May 24 by Portolá, Miguel Costansó, and Sergeant Ortega. See **infra**, I, 206, also **note 16**.

[11]The **San José** left Cape San Lucas not in April but on June 16, 1770, carrying corn, beans, supplies, and church ornaments for the colonists at San Diego.

[12]**Extracto de noticias del puerto de Monterey**, etc. Mexico, August 16, 1770. Imprenta del Superior Gobierno, with the permission of His Excellency, the viceroy. **Continuación y suplemento del viaje de Don Pedro Fages**, etc. Manuscript in the possession of M. Ternaux Compans. (D. de M.).

out thirty more Franciscans, who departed on January 2, [20] 1771, from San Blas. The plan as proposed by the apostolic prefect was to establish five missions in the territory lying between San Fernando de Vellicatá and the port of San Diego, and ten more between there and Monterey. In the letters of this venerable prelate he calls himself "leader of a seraphic and apostolic band" charged with conquering the souls of poor Indians. In the task of civilizing those barbarous tribes among whom his enthusiasm carried him, he revealed courage of a rare order. His fellow workers followed loyally in his footsteps. During one of his absences, after the Indians had killed Father Luís Jayme[13] who was attempting to placate them, Father Vicente Fuster took refuge in a small cabin with two Spaniards who opened fire on the Indians from this shelter. The latter, aware that their arrows could not reach the white men, hurled some burning brands on the thatched roof of the cabin. Father Vicente in the meanwhile sat down on the dirt floor, which he had covered with his cloak, calmly disregarding the fact that a single spark could destroy them. By this courageous act the Spanish soldiers could more readily continue to fire until their comrades were able to come to their rescue.

In 1771, the Marquis de Croix, who had completed his term of office, was replaced by Bucareli. About this time the Dominicans of Mexico secured a royal decree from the King of Spain, in which the Franciscans were ordered to relinquish to them one or two missions. The Father in charge of the College of San Fernando observed, with justice, that the province of Lower California could not be divided, that its natural boundaries were clearly defined, and that serious inconveniences would arise if these two orders were laboring in the same territory. He accordingly offered, should the Dominicans prefer to take exclusive charge of the entire province from Cape San Lucas as far as San Diego, to turn this territory over to them, together with all the missions originally administered by the Jesuits, that of San Fernando de Vellicatá, and the plans for the additional five missions that were yet to be founded.

The viceroy presented the matter to his council and, on April 30, 1772, a decree was handed down that embodied the agreement concluded by the two prelates.[14] However, it was not until May of the

---

[13]For the deaths of these Fathers at San Diego see Engelhardt, **San Diego,** pp. 26-31.

[14]This edict is discussed in Engelhardt, **Missions and Missionaries of California** (4 vols., San Francisco, 1908), I, 468.

following year that the Dominicans took possession of Lower California. At that time the Franciscans withdrew into their new territory where, by concentrating their efforts on a country less extensive and more fertile, they soon achieved amazing results. At the time of his death in 1784, fourteen years later, Father Junípero had already founded fifteen Indian missions and settlements of Spanish colonists.

While the Fathers were thus building misions to civilize the Indians, the governors were establishing military posts, called presidios, and pueblos or villages composed of married soldiers and white settlers who had been brought up from Sonora, Sinaloa, and Lower California. Since these three types of establishments, missions, presidios, and pueblos, are somewhat similar, a description of one will indicate in a general way their main characteristics. By way of illustration, the mission dedicated to St. Louis, King of France, one of the finest and architecturally the most symmetrical, will be chosen.

Mission San Luís Rey de Francia is built in the form of a quadrangle, 150 meters in width, with a chapel occupying one of the wings.[15] Along the façade extends an ornamental cloister. The building, which is one story high, is raised a few feet above the ground. The interior, in the form of a court, is adorned with fountains and planted with trees. Off the surrounding cloister open doors lead into rooms occupied by priests, majordomos, and travelers, as well as the main rooms, schools, and shops. Infirmaries for men and women are placed in a secluded corner of the mission. Nearby the school is situated. Young Indian women live in what is known as the monastery, *el monjerío,*[16] and are called nuns or *monjas,* for the Fathers are forced to lock them up to protect them from the brutality of the Indians. Placed under the surveillance of faithful Indian matrons, these young women are taught to weave wool, cotton, and flax, and do not leave the monastery until old enough to marry. Indian children are educated in the schools together with the children of the white colonists. A limited number, selected from pupils who display the most intelligence, study music—elementary singing, the violin, flute, horn, violincello, and other instruments. Those who show ability as carpenters, blacksmiths, or farmers are called alcaldes, or chiefs, and are given charge of a group of workers.

In the days before civil authority was substituted for the paternalism of the Fathers, the personnel of each mission consisted of two priests. The

---

[15]See illustration.
[16]Probably la monjería, or convent.

elder took charge of administration and religious instruction, the younger of agricultural development. Although the Franciscans wisely mastered several Indian dialects, yet they were often forced to resort to interpreters, because of the variety of idioms in Upper California, an inexplicable phenomenon encountered, moreover, throughout America. The Fathers employed only what white men were strictly necessary to keep order and discipline in the missions, for they realized how the latter corrupted the natives and how contact with them only developed in the Indians habits of gambling and drunkenness for which, unfortunately, they had a natural taste.

To encourage the Indians to work, the Fathers often labored with them. Only a few years ago Father Caballero, head of the Dominican Order, died at the plow, where he was working among his neophytes at the Mission of Nuestra Señora de Guadalupe. Necessity forced them to be industrious; and it is astonishing to see with what scanty resources they have achieved amazing results. Frequently without the aid of European workmen and with the assistance merely of unintelligent and often hostile natives, they have found time, in addition to their cultural achievements, to construct buildings of considerable architectural merit, and devices requiring mechanical knowledge such as windmills, machines, weavers' looms, bridges, roads, and irrigation ditches. To construct the majority of the missions it has been necessary to carry stone or timber that was cut up in the mountains for 8 or 10 leagues to the site selected and to teach the Indians to make lime, cut stone, and lay adobes.

Surrounding the mission are the workshops, the huts of the neophytes, and the houses of a few white settlers. In addition to the main buildings, 15 or 20 subsidiary farms and some auxiliary chapels lie within a radius of 30 or 40 square leagues. Across from the mission are the quarters of the priests' bodyguard, an escort consisting of four cavalrymen and a sergeant. This guard is also used to relay messages and dispatches from mission to mission, and to repulse Indian raids which, in the early days of the conquest, threatened the settlements.

A uniform régime was followed in each community. For convenience the Indians were divided into working units. At sunrise, as the bells tolled the angelus, all assembled at the church. After mass came breakfast; then the daily tasks began. Luncheon was served at eleven. A period of rest lasting for two hours followed, then work was resumed until the evening angelus, an hour before sunset. After prayers and the rosary, the Indians dined, danced, and played games. Food consisted of fresh beef or mutton and wheat or corn cakes, as well as stews called *atóle*[17] and *pinóle*.[18] The natives also received peas and beans to the amount of an almud, or one-twelfth of a fanega each week; that is, approximately one hectoliter a month. Clothing consisted of a linen shirt, trousers, and a woolen blanket; however, the alcaldes and best workers wore the Spanish costume. Once a year the women received two chemises, a dress, and a wrap.

Whenever hides, tallow, cereals, wine, and oil were sold at a profit to foreign ships, the Fathers distributed handkerchiefs, clothes, tobacco, rosaries, and glass beads to the Indians, reserving the surplus to embellish the churches by the purchase of musical instruments, tablets, and sacerdotal ornaments. Part of the harvest, however, was always stored in the granaries to be used during years when the crops were poor.

Especially notable in the organization of these missions is the fact that no assistance was received from the government. In the original establishments of Lower California the viceroys, on the other hand, supplied some assistance. In the early years of his reign, Philip V granted the missions the sum of 30,000 piasters. But by 1735, the Jesuits, who had received a considerable number of donations which they had managed successfully, were able not only to support their own missions but also to branch out into new territory. In 1767 a resident of Guadalajara, Doña Joseta de Miranda, left to the college of the Company in her city a legacy exceeding 100,000 piasters in currency, which the Jesuits, already embroiled in European scandals, had the delicacy to refuse.[19]

At the present day the properties owned by the Pious Fund of California, with their subsequent increases, are: The lands or haciendas of San Pedro, Torreón, Rincón, and Las Golondrinas, as well as several mines, freight boats, immense herds, and lands that include more than 500 square leagues, all situated in the new principality of León, or the province of Tamaulipas. These properties were donated to the Company on June 8, 1735, by the Marquis de Villa Puente,[20] grand chancellor of New Spain, and by his wife ,the Marquise de las Torres. Other legacies

---

[17]Atóle: boiled or dry maize, an ancient Aztec food.

[18]Pinóle: ground maize that had been toasted. By reason of its highly nutritious properties it was often indispensable to travelers, as it could be carried in small compass. Sometimes it was mixed with meat stew.

[19]Clavijero II, 170, **op. cit.** (D. de M.).

[20]Don José de la Puente, Marquis de Villa Puente, whose generous donations won him the sobriquet of benefactor of California. The early peninsula missions were founded by funds thus supplied.

that have materially enriched the properties of the Society of Jesus are situated near San Luís de Potosí, Guanajuato, and Guadalajara.[21]

The estate known as the Hacienda de la Ciénaga del Pastor, which lies near the latter village, still brings in annually, despite its dilapidated condition and poor management, more than 24,000 piasters. Another property owned by the company, the Hacienda de Chalco, belongs to the Pious Fund which also possesses a large number of houses and other buildings situated in the cities, especially Mexico City.

In 1827 the government confiscated the sum of 78,000 piasters in specie that had been deposited in the bank at the capital, which represented the profits from the sale of Arroyo Zarco, a property of the Company. The Pious Fund also had extensive lands confiscated by the Congress of Jalisco and, as has already been said, President Santa Anna sold the entire Pious Fund to the firms of Barrio and Rubio frères.

During the Spanish régime revenues amounted approximately to 50,000 piasters. These were adequate to pay the stipend or *sinodo,* made to the Fathers—15 Dominicans at 600 piasters and 40 Franciscans at 400 piasters. After subtracting this total of 25,000 piasters, the balance was used to purchase materials, machinery, tools, and sacred ornaments for the faith. The government in turn reimbursed the procurator of the missions in Mexico for various kinds of furniture made by the missions for the companies at the presidios. The procurator then converted this money into merchandise which he shipped at his own expense overland to the port of San Blas. From there frigates transported this twice a year gratuitously to the various ports of California.

During the prosperous reign of Charles III the port and arsenal of San Blas achieved considerable importance. At the instigation of the Spanish government, an intelligent agent came out to show the Fathers how to handle hemp; and, since the land belonging to the missions offered conditions favorable to its cultivation, the priests raised crops with such success that they were able to send out large shipments annually to the boatswain's warehouse at San Blas. An amount equal to the value of these products was then paid from the royal treasury to the procurator of missions in Mexico City. For the last twenty years this valuable industry has been inactive and at all the ports along the west coast of Mexico ships can procure rope made only in Europe or the United States at exorbitant prices.

---

[21]Archives of the royal notary, Don Pedro del Valle, in Mexico, now in the possession of D. Ramon Villalobos. (D. de M.).

From 1811 to 1818, and from 1823 to January 1831, the missionaries, owing to the political troubles which at this time were rife in Spain and Mexico, failed to receive their regular salaries. Thus, by adding the amounts due Franciscans in Upper California alone, and increasing by 192,000 piasters, the 78,000 taken forcibly from the Order, there remain 270,000 piasters which the missions of Upper California should recover for furniture made at the presidios. This, together with the revenues derived from the Pious Fund properties for a period of ten years or more, makes a total in excess of 1,000,000 piasters which the Mexican government has confiscated from the various missions in open defiance of the wishes of the donors.

On May 25, 1832, the Mexican Congress handed down a decree whereby the executors were ordered to consolidate the properties held by the Pious Fund for seven years and impound its revenue in the national treasury.[22] A second decree of Congress, enacted September 19, 1836, ordered the Pious Fund to be placed once more at the disposal of the new bishop of California and his successors. This was to enable the prelates, to whom its administration had been entrusted, to use this revenue to develop missions or similar enterprises in conformity with the wishes of its founders.

On February 8, 1842, General Santa Anna, acting president, by virtue of his discretional power received from the bishop of California, in the face of his protests, the administration of the Pious Fund.[23] By a decree of the 21st of that same month, this was entrusted to General Valencia, commander-in-chief of the army. To those familiar with this country, the true significance of the term administrator is obvious. This was the last blow before the final sale, directed against an organization built by the Jesuits. In all fairness, however, the fact should be mentioned that up to the present time the few Franciscans remaining in California have received an annual subsidy of 400 piasters, but in merchandise quoted at exorbitant prices.

So long as the Fathers retained complete control both of temporal and spiritual matters at the missions, an annual report was made of the births, marriages, and deaths of the Indians, the amount of grain planted, harvests, and the increase in live stock. The Fathers were not compelled, however, to give a minute account of their products, for they were

---

[22]Memorial presented to Congress in February, 1831, by D. Lucas Alamán, Minister of Foreign Relations. (D. de M.).

[23]See **Diario del Gobierno de la República Mexicana**, of February 8 and 21, 1842. (D. de M.).

known to be devoted to the interests of their neophytes who were as dear to them as if they had been their own children. These reports, sent to the apostolic prefect, were dispatched to the governor of the province who transmitted them to the viceroy of Mexico and the king of Spain, and, later, to the Mexican Government. A copy of these documents was also sent to the Royal College of San Fernando and through this channel finally reached Madrid and the Commissioner for the Indies, who was head of the Franciscans in America. From there these reports were sent to the general of the Order at Rome.

While the Mexican Government was thus absorbing the Pious Fund and removing from the Fathers the temporal administration of the missions, their agents were working diligently to pillage these same establishments and destroy their live stock which was worth a fortune. Already by 1822, the fatal year of separation from Spain, a few partisans of the new régime were advocating the idea of secularization.

Notwithstanding, until 1830 the Spanish missionaries were able to retain control. But in 1831, the Reverend Father President Sánchez, who had courageously opposed the advent of civil control, had died of grief and the majority of the Fathers who had been harshly treated decided to leave the country. And so these men who had consecrated thirty or forty years of their lives to enlightening and civilizing the Indians, who had succeeded by their efforts in turning them from their heathen ways, who had acquired agricultural properties and live stock of considerable value, who had administered immense sums, amounting at one time to more than 500,000 francs, these venerable Fathers departed from a land they had civilized by their own labors and apostolic teachings, carrying with them as their entire capital only a few coarse woolen garments!

A fundamental principle in the establishment of the Spanish mission system was that the fruit of their labors and the soil itself belonged to the Indians, the Fathers being merely administrators and directors. The sacred precept, *Pater est tutor ad bona Indiorum*,[24] was carefully followed, and the prelates watched to see that the priests took from the revenues only what was needed for food and clothing. Furthermore, the Franciscans observed the vow of poverty, and could own no personal property.

During the Spanish régime, the priests were under the control of a

---

[24]**Pater est tutor ad bona Indiorum:** The Father is the guardian of the Indians' welfare.

president or apostolic prefect, a member like themselves of the Royal College of San Fernando in Mexico City. In Lower California the Dominicans also had their local president.

In 1833 the ranks of the Spanish Franciscans were materially reduced by the departure, or death, of several of their members, and as the College at Mexico City could not replace them, the government appealed to the College of Nuestra Señora de Guadalupe, at Zacatecas, which sent ten of its members to New California. The Mexican clergy soon met opposition from the older Spanish Fathers who by their exemplary conduct and austere morals formed a striking contrast to the lax habits of the creoles. To avoid difficulties the two Orders separated; and as a milder climate proved more suitable to the aged Franciscans, they withdrew to the southern missions, while Mexican priests took charge of administrating those in the northern territory.

Prior to that time the popes, by a series of bulls,[25] had accorded the apostolic prefect various ecclesiastical powers. Finally, on April 27, 1840, Gregory XVI established the bishopric of the Californias and appointed to this seat the Reverend Father Francisco García Diego, a Franciscan from Mexico, who had served many years as a missionary, designating San Diego, the most central point in these two provinces, as his place of residence. In the meanwhile the bishop for various reasons failed to reach California before January, 1842. Since the mission at San Diego is extremely poor, and since he was receiving only a small subsidy from the government, he decided to take up his residence at the mission that afforded the most resources, and so located temporarily at the pueblo of Santa Bárbara.

The influence of the bishop, under these circumstances, will not be widespread; his advanced age and his Mexican education will not permit him to take part in any spiritual conquests, nor augment the imposing foundations that are the glory of the Spanish Fathers. To erect new establishments, or to rehabilitate those now in ruins, requires men who are young, ardent, and of pure morals, men who are imbued with high ideals and undaunted by hardship or danger. Only by their religious proselytising did the early Fathers succeed in winning over the Indians, for the latter seldom understood Spanish and the Fathers did not always know the local dialects. In this task of conversion, even though religion was their aim, material considerations proved the

---

[25]Bull of Léo X, dated April 25, 1521; of Adrian VI, May 9, 1522; of Clement XIV, June 16, 1774. Archives of Carmel Mission. (D. de M.).

means to this goal. The Fathers also solved the important problem of how to make work attractive. They also led the Indians to believe that by living near the missions they would be sheltered from the attacks of hostile tribes, and could more readily find a livelihood by taking part in the simple and varied tasks at the mission rather than by seeking it in the dangerous and uncertain manner afforded by hunting and plunder.

At certain seasons when agricultural work was suspended, many neophytes returned to their own tribes. The tales they invariably told of the kind treatment received at the missions encouraged their friends to visit the nearest settlements where they were regally received by the Fathers, who showered them with gifts. From time to time the latter also went out on scouting trips of exploration among the native tribes, where they succeeded, both by persuasion as well as by the distribution of trinkets, in winning over Indian converts. That they ever used force to attain this end is entirely false.

For foreign writers to slander the Spanish clergy from whom they have received the most generous hospitality is indeed deplorable. With typical English coldness, Captain Beechey and Mr. Forbes,[26] men imbued with the intolerance of Protestantism, are inclined to ridicule and cast insinuations on the activities of the Fathers. Facts, however, clearly disprove their contentions.

What has become, moreover, of the population of the Tahitian Islands under the tutelage of the Methodists, Anabaptists, and other sects? They now number scarcely 6,000 inhabitants! And what has happened in the Sandwich Islands, where Captain Cook found 400,000 natives, and where at the present there are fewer than 100,000? When the English colonists settled along the New England coast and in Pennsylvania, these lands were occupied by large and powerful Indian tribes. Yet, with the exception of the unfortunate Seminoles[27] whom the government at Washington has already spent over $6,000,000 in an attempt to exterminate, not a single Indian is found along the coast of the United States. In the Spanish possessions, on the other hand—Mexico, New Granada, Chile, Buenos Ayres, and even in the Philippines, all lands where Catholicism has extended its benign influence—there exist en-

---

[26]Beechey, **Narrative of a Voyage to the Pacific Ocean**, (2 vols., London, 1831). Forbes **A History of Upper and Lower California**, (London, 1839) (D. de M.).

[27]Originally a branch of the Creoles who settled in Florida after the native tribes had been destroyed by the whites. In 1843, after a war lasting seven years, the majority were removed to Indian territory.

tire tribes of Indians who have retained their own manners, customs, and traditions under the paternal care of the Fathers. Travelers are invariably impressed to discover near Indian villages where the lands are carefully cultivated and where irrigation is highly developed, colonies of white settlers living in abject misery, who rank as freemen under so-called republics.[28]

While the inferior intelligence of the Indians did not permit them fully to understand the mysteries of the faith, yet the Fathers, with the aid of the sign language, usually succeeded in making them understand its main truths. They attempted especially to develop in them moral instincts and sound habits. Their relationship with the Indians was primarily paternal, being not unlike that of father and son. When a Father met an Indian, he greeted him with the words, "Love God, my son!" "Love God, Father," was the reply.

Although instances are not unknown where Indians, instigated by the medicine men and sorcerers of their tribes who were jealous of the influence of the Fathers have massacred the latter, yet they usually revered them as supernatural beings. This was especially pronounced after they watched the Californian missions which had been erected by their own hands, and the cattle which had been raised with infinite care by their own efforts, being destroyed and confiscated by Mexican agents. For after they themselves were forced to submit to harsh treatment, they thought with regret of the ways of these charitable men who knew how to temper rigid justice with kindliness, men to whom they could always turn for help in times of need and for consolation in times of sorrow.

Presidios were invariably built in the following uniform manner: After a suitable place had been chosen, a trench about 4 meters broad and 2 deep was then excavated. What earth was removed was used for an outer embankment. The presidio was then enclosed by a quadrangle that measured approximately 200 meters on each side. The rampart, or wall, constructed of adobes, was 4 or 5 meters high and a meter thick, with small bastions at each corner. The presidio had only two gates. These fortifications were never protected by more than eight bronze cannon, usually of 8, 12, or 16 pounds. Although incapable of resisting a serious attack by warships, these fortifications were adequate to repulse Indian raids. Not far from the presidios, at a point selected to conform with

---

[28]Duflot de Mofras' statement is hardly true, for during the Mission period the Indians of the southern half of California were almost decimated.

the local topography, stood the outpost batteries, inappropriately designated as the *castillo,* or fort. Within the presidio, the church, barracks for officers and soldiers, the houses of a few settlers, and the
stores, shops, stables, wells, and cisterns were provided. Outside stood
more groups of houses. A short distance beyond lay the king's ranch,
called *el rancho del rey,* used to pasture the horses and pack mules of the
garrison.

Four coastal batteries and four presidios, situated at San Diego,
Monterey, San Francisco, and Santa Bárbara, provided the defense for
Upper California. The first was founded in 1769, the second a year later,
the third in 1776, and the fourth in 1780 [1782]. After 1770, the infantry
was replaced at all garrisons by cavalry known as leather-jacket soldiers.
These soldiers, who formed the presidial garrisons throughout Upper
California, wore in addition to the usual cloth uniform, a kind of deer-
skin garment not unlike a coat of mail, which was impervious to arrows
and which hung down as far as the feet. This uniform was worn only
when fighting in the open. The head was covered at such times by a
helmet having a double visor. A leather shield, worn over the left arm,
was used to ward off arrows or thrusts from a lance in hand-to-hand
fighting, for when these soldiers were defending themselves with the
saber or lance, they could not use their pistols or muskets. The horses,
furthermore, like those of the ancient knights, were covered with leather
armor.

During the first days of the conquest the troops and colonists came
either by land from San Blas, or crossed from Sonora to Loreto and
traveled overland by way of the peninsula of Lower California. During
a journey the Reverend Father Junípero Serra[29] made to Mexico City
in 1773, he clearly pointed out to Bucareli, who was then viceroy, the
length and difficulties of the journey. As a result, in August the latter
ordered Don Juan de Anza, captain of the presidio of Tubac in Upper
Sonora,[30] to march to Monterey with colonists and soldiers by way of
the Gila and Colorado rivers, following the route mapped in 1770 by
the Reverend Father Garcés, a Franciscan and the only man who had
explored these regions. The expedition, which left Sonora in September,
arrived safely at Monterey. From there in May, 1774, Captain Anza
set out for the return trip over the same route to Mexico City, where

---

[29]Vida del Junípero Serra, 201, **op. cit.** (D. de M.).
[30]Now southern Arizona. The ruins of Old Tubac lie a few miles north of
the Mexican border on the Nogales-Tucson highway.

he was to furnish to the viceroy a complete account of his journey.[31] The latter was so impressed with the success of this undertaking that he ordered Captain Anza to prepare a second expedition backed by the royal treasury.

On September 29, 1775, Anza, accompanied by more than one hundred colonists and a large train of pack-animals, left San Miguel de Horcasitas in the province of Sonora. On January 4, 1776, Mission San Gabriel was safely reached. Owing to stops which had to be made to rest the horses as well as the cattle, the trip lasted three months.[32] Several expeditions followed in 1777.

At this time the Spanish monarch created the office of captain general of the internal provinces which was independent of the viceroyalty in Mexico City, and which included New Mexico, Sonora, and the Californias. To this office, Teodoro de Croix was appointed. De Croix,[33] while en route to his port, stopped on August 15 at Querétaro, where he gave orders for the Franciscans of the local Santa Cruz College to found two missions on the banks of the Colorado River.[34] These were needed to facilitate the trip from Sonora to California, by affording a place of rest and a means of protection to trains coming overland.

Unfortunately, these two missions were established under a new system. They had no presidios for their support, although each had a guard of eight soldiers in charge of an ensign for its defense. Eight colonists and their families who had charge of the live stock lived near the mission. The Fathers, four in number, had charge only of the spiritual life of the community. The Indians continued to live among their own tribesmen beyond the jurisdiction of the Fathers, instead of being grouped around the missions as they were in Upper California. The two missions were established on the right bank of the Colorado above its mouth. The first was dedicated to San Pedro y San Pablo; the second,

---

[31]De Mofras' dates are not correct. Captain Juan Bautista de Anza left Sonora on January 8, reaching Monterey, a journey of 384 leagues, on April 18, 1774. He departed on April 22 and reached Tubac on May 27. See Herbert E. Bolton *Anza's California Expeditions* (5 vols., Berkeley, 1930), II, 1-243.

[32]For the diary of Anza's second expedition see ibid, III, 1-153.

[33]On March 20, 1780, orders were issued by De Croix to found two mission-pueblos on the Colorado. Each was to have ten soldiers, ten settlers, and six laborers. In the autumn the colonists reached their new homes. In charge of La Purísima Concepción were Fathers Garcés and Barreneche, and of San Pedro y San Pablo de Bicuner, Fathers Díaz and Matias Moreno. On July 17 of the year following the colonists were massacred by the hostile Yumas.

[34]*Crónica Apostólica del Colegio de la Santa Crúz de Querétaro, Mexico,* 1780, 1 vol. (D. de M.).

established three leagues farther south, was called Purísima Concepción. These lay about 60 leagues east of the port of San Diego, and approximately 80 from Mission San Gabriel.

Later, in 1781, De Croix sent Captain Don Fernando Rivera, in command of a company of 75 cavalrymen, with approximately 100 colonists and their families and 2,000 animals, to found the presidio, pueblo, and three missions planned along the Santa Bárbara channel, as well as the pueblo of Nuestra Señora de los Angeles on the tiny Porciúncula River. Having reached the Colorado, Captain Rivera sent his train on toward Monterey, then stopped with seven soldiers on the banks of this river to give his animals time to rest. The Yuman Indians, who lived nearby, had been watching the founding of new colonies with some displeasure, for the colonists seized what little fertile land lay along the river banks and prevented the Indians from planting their usual crop of corn, beans, melons, and gourds. Their live stock also destroyed the pastures where the Indians formerly found abundant game, as well as several kinds of barley and wild oats whose kernels when boiled afforded an agreeable diet. To these grievances the Spanish soldiers added further insults by abusing several Indians and their wives. As the missionaries, stripped of temporal authority, were unable to restrain them, the tribes began to hate the white settlers, and resolved to exterminate them. The Fathers, aware of this situation, tried to persuade the soldiers to be more moderate and prudent, but the latter paid no heed to their sage counsel.

Vengeance came swiftly. One Sunday in July several thousand Indians attacked the two missions simultaneously after Mass, set them on fire, killed Captain Rivera, his soldiers, most of the colonists, and the four Franciscan Fathers who, as soon as the massacre commenced, began to exercise their saintly calling. The Indians then pillaged the houses, carried off all the animals, and took prisoners all whom they could find. A lone soldier, stationed on the left bank of the Colorado River, escaped and carried this sad news to the nearest presidio in Sonora. Almost simultaneously an ensign and a few soldiers who arrived from Lower California where they had met some frontier Indians, communicated the news to the Governor of California, Don Felipe de Neve, who at the time was at Mission San Gabriel. The governor immediately sent an ensign and nine veterans down to the missions that had been destroyed. Upon arriving at the scene of the massacre they found the buildings in ashes and the bodies unburied.

Attacked shortly after by the Yumas, who killed two men, they were obliged to withdraw in haste to San Gabriel. Informed of this calamity, the captain general of the internal provinces then ordered Colonel Don Pedro Fages to march down with a detachment of Catalonian dragoons and leather-jacket soldiers to avenge their countrymen. These troops crossed the Colorado, reached the scene of the disaster, collected the bodies of their Fathers, and succeeded in rescuing all those taken captive. They were unable, however, to punish the Indians, who cautiously carried on all transactions from a safe distance by signals, and kept well beyond the range of firearms.

This tragic experience revealed to the Marquis de Croix that the original plan adopted for the foundation of the missions, which placed in the hands of the Fathers full spiritual and temporal control, alone could succeed. As a result he now directed his attention solely to the founding of pueblos and the organization of presidios. This led to the development of the triple system which has proved so admirable a phase of the Spanish colonization policy: religious control for the missions; civil control for the pueblos; and military control for the presidios.

Under the Spanish régime the garrison of Upper California was controlled in the following manner: The governor usually held the rank of lieutenant colonel, while each of the four presidios was in charge of a lieutenant, an ensign, and a presidial guard numbering around 70 soldiers. From these companies, four or five men with a sergeant were detached at each mission and pueblo to protect the Fathers and carry arms to timidate the Indians.

The salaries, uniforms, arms, and rations of these troops represented an annual expenditure of around 55,000 piasters. Of this amount the governor received 4,000, lieutenants 550, health officers 450, ensigns 400, sergeants 265, corporals 225, and soldiers 217 piasters. In addition, annual gratuities of 10 piasters paid out of a common fund were given each man. A carpenter and two blacksmiths, with annual salary of 180 piasters, were supplied to each presidio. Every soldier had seven horses and one mule which were cared for by a muleteer at the king's ranch belonging to the presidio. An adequate number of artillerymen were also supplied by the naval department at San Blas. How the missions sold a large proportion of their supplies to the presidios, for which they were reimbursed in specie at Mexico City, has already been mentioned.[35]

---

[35]See **Real reglamento de la provincia de Californias**, Mexico, 1784; also Governmental Archives at Monterey.

Spanish pueblos resemble to a certain extent the villages and towns of Europe, being a conglomeration of houses, gardens, and cultivated lands clustering around a church. Colonization laws, which are of interest, have the following salient features.[36] Lands were first selected by the governor, preference being given to locations that were well wooded, supplied with water, and readily accessible. Each colonist, or *poblador,* received four sections of fertile land called a *sitio,* or *suerte,* which was equivalent to four hectares, and a building site for a house with the proviso that this be built facing the street or the square.[37] These lands had to be planted out by the owner with ten fruit trees to each hectare, and were not transferable; neither could they be hypothecated or sold, and were transmitted only by inheritance. These conditions have recently been abolished by a decree that allows foreigners to own land in Mexico.[38]

In addition to the lands set aside for the new colonists, other parcels were reserved for the crown, for common pasturage, and for public timber for each municipality. Colonists received rations as well as 120 piasters annually for the first two years, and 60 piasters for the next three years. During these five years they were exempt from assessments and taxes of every character. Upon arrival they were also supplied with a pair of oxen, two mares, two cows with their calves, two sheep, two goats, pigs, chickens, a pack mule, two saddle horses, a lance, a shield, leather armor, a gun with ammunition, plows, spades, hoes, together with other agricultural implements, hatchets and miscellaneous supplies such as are used by carpenters. The colonists were forbidden to kill any animals before owning 15 cows, a bull, 15 mares, a stallion, 12 sheep, a ram, 10 goats, and a buck. At the end of this period the colonist was required to render an accounting to the agent of the royal treasury of what he had received.

After the families had taken out of the harvest an amount adequate for their own use and for planting the next crop, they were allowed to sell what remained at the presidios to the treasury, after reserving a bushel or almud of corn each for community planting. A stud farm and community forge were also established at each village. The head

---

[36]See the cédula of Emperor Charles V of Sept. 9, 1531, to further colonization in America in the **Colección de documentos inéditos para la Historia de España,** by Navarette, Salvá, and Baranda, Madrid, 1843, and above all the admirable **Leyes de Indias.** (D. de M.).

[37]A square measuring 200 Spanish vares on each side; one vare is 84 centimeters. (D. de M.).

[38]Decree of President Santa Anna of March 11, 1842, officially published in the **Diario del Gobierno.** (D. de M.).

of every family was required to maintain two horses fully equipped for two cavalrymen, which might be requisitioned on short notice by the government. Thus the citizens prepared for war. Young men, recruited from civilian ranks, were selected to replace the soldiers of the presidial companies who either returned to Spain, or married and became settlers, or *pobladores*. Philip II by his wise regulation materially promoted colonial expansion in America. Not satisfied with making laws to protect the Indians, in 1575 he ordered the viceroy, Don Martín de Almanza, to compile the history of the conquest of Mexico, and to assemble the necessary documents for the purpose. At this time he also sent his cosmographer, Domínguez, and his personal physician, the learned Hernandez, on a scientific expedition to New Spain.

The commissioner of the royal treasury kept a record of the lands granted and land titles consigned in the name of the king. This agent also kept a supply of tools and live stock to distribute on behalf of the government, for the Californian missions were so improverished that the first eight were founded with only eighteen head of live stock each. For police duty and the administration of justice the governor appointed for the first two years, the alcaldes and members of the city council, or ayuntamiento. Later the citizens themselves selected these officials, submitting the names of those whom they nominated for the approval of the governor of the province.

A squad of four soldiers under a sergeant had charge of maintaining order in each pueblo, keeping the Indians tranquil, and acting as messengers. One of the two Fathers from the nearest mission was required to fulfill the office of chaplain at the pueblo or presidio. In addition, the governor gave the sum of 1,000 piasters for the founding of each new mission.

This plan of creating presidios, missions, and pueblos was established and put into execution by means of royal cédulas dating from 1769 down to the time when New Spain separated from the mother country. To the observance of these wise rules the twenty-one missions of Upper California owe their foundation and prosperity.

In 1822 the revolt of Mexico was announced in California by the canon, Don Fernando de San Vicente. The Spanish governor, Don Pablo de Sola,[39] faithful to his oath, refused to serve under the new

---

[39]Pablo Vicente Sola served as governor from November 15, 1815, to November 22, 1822, when he was appointed delegate to the Mexican Congress. See Theodore H. Hittell, **History of California** (4 vols. San Francisco, 1898), I, 633-667; II, 43-50, and Bancroft, **California, passim.**

government and left Monterey with several royalist soldiers. Captain Don Luís Argüello,[40] a Californian by birth, was then appointed provisional governor. California was now declared a territory, a provincial assembly was established locally, and the captain of the presidio at Santa Barbara, Don José Noriega,[41] was sent as delegate to the general congress in Mexico. Although his reputation was above reproach and he was thoroughly in touch with the new organization and the needs of his country, he was not admitted because of his Spanish blood.

The first governor and political leader sent up from Mexico was Lieutenant Colonel Don José María Echeandía.[42] Echeandía arrived in 1824, and was at first warmly received by the inhabitants. After appointing administrators and alcaldes at the missions, he then sought to remove from the Franciscans all temporal authority.

In 1830 the director of finances, Don Vicente Herrera,[43] chose a time when the governor was in San Diego to incite the troops at Monterey to revolt on the grounds that they had not been paid. The presence of Echeandía sufficed to restore order; he removed Father Martínez, a Franciscan, and abused the president of the missions, the Reverend Father Sánchez, a Spaniard, who had refused to swear allegiance to the constitution.

The complaints of pillaging that were soon brought against Echeandía forced the government to replace him toward the end of 1830, by Lieutenant Colonel Don Manuel Victoria.[44] The latter suppressed the civil administrators and gave back to the Fathers full charge of the missions. Yet this able man failed to please the Californians who, after 1822, cast envious eyes at the rich prizes afforded by the religious establishments. Finally, as the result of a conspiracy hatched between the inhabitants of San Diego and those of Los Angeles, he was forced to leave their country. Before departing, however, he was wounded in a clash with the insurgents.

In 1831 two French missionaries, Fathers Bachelot and Short,[45] were

---

[40]Argüello became provisional governor in November, 1822. See Hittell, op. cit., II, 51-81.

[41]For Noriega, see infra, I, 194, also note 153.

[42]Echeandía was appointed governor of the Californias not in 1824, but in January, 1825. See Bancroft, California, III, passim.

[43] José María Herrera, as he is usually known, became involved in a dispute with the governor that led to his return to Mexico. He returned to California, however, in 1834, but was again exiled for failure to support the Alvarado government.

[44]Victoria held office from January 31 to December 9, 1831.

[45]See infra, I, 195.

received by the Spanish Fathers as brothers after they had been in-
humanely abandoned without food on the coast of California. Their
plight was caused by the Methodist ministers of the Sandwich Islands,
who, in defiance of all treaties, had expelled them ruthlessly from these
islands. The two missionaries passed several years in California, and
the manner in which they fulfilled their apostolic duties inspired universal confidence.

The captains at the presidios enjoyed almost autocratic powers until
November, 1831, when Brigadier General Don José Figueroa[46] arrived
to take command. During the régime of this leader, seven Spanish
Fathers were forced to depart. For the next three years the welfare of
the missions was constantly in jeopardy. Finally, in August, 1834, a
decree issued by the provincial junta and sanctioned by General Figueroa
removed from these Fathers all jurisdiction over their properties, and
although they were promised payment amounting to 1,000 or 1,500
piasters, with another 500 for ecclesiastical purposes, yet up to the
present time they have received no compensation.

That same year, under the direction of the president, a company
with the imposing name of Compañía Cosmopolitana was organized in
Mexico City with the object of colonizing California. Under the leadership of Don José Hijar,[47] the president of Mexico, Gómez Farías, now
sent out an expedition of 200 Mexicans, consisting of musicians, gold-
smiths, dancers, and plotters and adventurers of every character. With
this group came only one farmer. Among them, however, were several
printers who took along a small press—the first press to be brought into
California. To supply funds for this expedition and purchase the three-
master, the *Natalia,* which was to carry them up to California, lands
belonging to the Pious Fund were sold. Actually the aim and plan of
those who organized this party was to appropriate the missions for their
own use. While the ship was at sea, General Santa Anna recalled Gómez
Farías and sent a courier by way of Sonora who carried a message warning General Figueroa not to receive the Hijar colonists. Upon their
arrival, the latter were sent on to the headwaters of San Francisco Bay,
and from there about 15 leagues inland to a locality north of Mission San
Francisco Solano and only a few leagues from the Russian farms. These
poor colonists, who had believed they were about to find unlimited
wealth, were as a result soon plunged into the depths of despair. The
majority had no alternative but to return to Mexico.

---

[46]For Figueroa see Hittell, **op. cit.,** II, 219-294.
[47]For the Hijar and Padrés colony see **infra,** I, 214, **note 35.**

Not long after an attempt was made to colonize Santa Cruz Island,[48] lying a short distance from the mainland, with a group of 40 galley slaves sent up from San Blas, who were equipped with live stock, agricultural implements, and seeds for planting. These men, however, when left to their own resources, first ate the grain and cattle, then built crude boats with reeds and planks. In these they now traveled over to the shore near Santa Bárbara and San Buenaventura, where the officials allowed them to scatter throughout the interior and mix with the population.

In the process of secularizing the missions General Figueroa had reserved the major portion of the live stock and lands for what he termed governmental use. He then made a pretense of distributing land and a few head of cattle among the Indians. The latter, however, soon lost, gambled, or sold what was given them. The rancheros who did not lose their animals killed them themselves, selling the hides to foreign vessels to procure liquor.

While these events were taking place, a large number of English sailors and many American trappers were coming into California over the Rocky Mountains from the United States. The sole wealth of these adventurers who lived by the hunt was in their rifles. Establishing themselves in California, they soon participated in the local revolutions.

On September 29, 1835, General Figueroa died at Santa Bárbara. He was replaced by Captain—later Lieutenant Colonel-Nicolas Gutiérrez, a Spaniard, who in turn was succeeded by Lieutenant Colonel Don Mariano Chico.[49] After a few months, however, the former succeeded in unseating his rival and regaining his former post.

From that time on the intentions of the citizens of the United States were clearly revealed. In October, 1836, the Californians, incited by the promises of these foreigners, attempted to break away from Mexico. The customs administrator, Don Angel Ramírez, and the provincial assessor, Don Cosme Peña, although Mexicans, were the ringleaders who instigated this insurrection with the expectation that by this rupture they would rise to hold important offices. Don Juan Bautista Alvarado, a Californian employed at the customs for whose arrest Gutiérrez had issued orders, now placed himself openly at the head of the movement. At Mission San Juan Baustista, about 40 leagues from Monterey, he

---

[48]See **infra**, I, 191.
[49]Chico served as governor from May to September, 1836; Gutiérrez, his successor, until November, 1836.

soon assembled 30 sharpshooters, or American trappers, led by a man called Graham. To this group were added 60 rancheros, also able riflemen, all on mounts. During the night of November 2 Alvarado arrived at Monterey and seized the barbette battery which overlooked the harbor and protected the village and presidio. In the meanwhile Governor Gutiérrez continued to hold the presidio with 70 men, in the belief that Alvarado had no ammunition. However, three American ships then at anchor in the harbor, the *Don Quixote,* Captain Hinckley, the *Europa,* Captain French,[50] and the *Caroline,* Captain Stech,[51] supplied him with powder. Adequate funds for this purpose were supplied by two Americans, Jones, former consul to the Sandwich Islands, and Larkin, a local merchant. On the fourth, Gutiérrez, deserted by his soldiers, was forced to capitulate. A cannon ball fired from the fort which flew over and demolished a wall of the presidio, decided the victory in Alvarado's favor. Despite their agreements, the officers, Mexican employés, and some of the members of Hijar's colony were deported without delay on the brig *Clementine,* which landed them in the bay near Cape San Lucas in Lower California.

The United States warship *Peacock,* Captain Kennedy, had anchored several weeks before this revolution broke out in Monterey Harbor, and its presence, according to rumor, merely hastened the revolt. In the meanwhile the Americans, hoping to persuade the Californians to declare their independence from Mexico and to secure admission to the Union, thus placing themselves under the protection of the United States, had prepared a flag somewhat like that of their Union, with a single star. The warship *Peacock,* it was said, might return shortly to back such a movement. Alvarado, with his supporters, took possession of the presidio and fort. But the Mexicans, Peña, Ramírez, and a few foreigners, including an English merchant, David Spence, the Spaniards, Amesti and Munraz, and a Frenchman, Oliver Deleissèques, captain of a trading vessel, succeeded in persuading the Californians not to support the United States.

Alvarado, who had directed the movement, was then proclaimed governor by the provincial deputation, Lieutenant Don Mariano Guadalupe Vallejo was made commander-in-chief of the military forces, and Don José Castro, a military leader, was appointed prefect of Monterey. California was now proclaimed a free and sovereign state—*El estado*

---

[50]Hinckley and French were supercargoes, not masters of these ships.
[51]This was the **Sarah and Caroline**, Captain Joseph Steel, not Stech.

libre y soberano de la Alta California. However, complete separation
from Mexico was only conditional, and the state of California was to
enter the Mexican confederation only after the central government of
Mexico was overthrown and the federal constitution had been adopted
by all the states. With the termination of the revolution at Monterey,
envoys were sent to Santa Bárbara and Los Angeles, where the citizens
refused to recognize Alvarado as governor. With his troops he then advanced on Santa Bárbara, where he encountered superior forces under
the command of Castillero. Instead of fighting, the two leaders pledged
themselves to abide by the following arrangement: Alvarado, who
agreed to recognize the central constitution of Mexico, was proclaimed
the political head ad interim; while Castillero guaranteed to return
to Mexico, arrange matters with the government, and serve as delegate
to congress, at a salary of 3,000 piasters. He left as agreed for Mexico
City, and from his reports of the wealth still existing at the mission, congress was induced to pass the law of August 17, 1837, which deprived the
clergy of all temporal power and gave it into the absolute control of
the governor.

On November 1, 1837, while the frigate, *Vénus,* commanded by
Dupetit Thouars, lay off Monterey, a courier from Mexico brought word
of the nomination of Don Carlos Carrillo,[52] a former deputy to Congress, to the governorship. Alvarado, however, was opposed to his
policies and, accompanied by 25 or 30 American trappers who were
always ready to serve for a stipend, and 30 rancheros, marched on Santa
Bárbara. Carrillo's following, although more numerous than that of
Alvarado, dreaded the accurate aim and seasoned guns of the trappers.
The result was that no serious encounter ensued, only one man was
killed by accident, and Alvarado's power was now recognized throughout the land.

The constant revolutions in California are reflected in the numerous
and absurd *pronunciamientos* or edicts of Mexico. The Mexican government, upon learning of events in California, unwisely confirmed
the nomination of Vallejo as commander of the military forces, and that
of Alvarado as constitutional governor, without taking into consideration the fact that these two men not only were opposed by the two
legal governors appointed by the central government, but had even

---

[52]Carrillo, although appointed governor, never assumed control, but in 1837
and 1838 he waged a series of campaigns against Alvarado. See Bancroft, **California, III, passim.**

declared the independence of California, intending to hand it over to a foreign nation. These facts, inexplicable as they seem, do not astonish those who are aware of the deplorable condition of internal affairs in Mexico. This nation, in fact, does not maintain either soldiers or navy along the Pacific, and has done nothing for California except to send out officials to occupy positions which the inhabitants themselves could have filled in a far more able manner.

Alvarado's supporters received generous compensation. The American and English trappers were given money and live stock; Captain Graham took for his share a ranch and 200 mules. Alvarado, moreover, appropriated part of the live stock owned by Carmel Mission, and also sold at a profit the vineyards and buildings of Mission Nuestra Señora de la Soledad, where the venerable Father Sarría set the noble example of preferring death through misery and starvation to deserting the small band of Indians living at the mission. The *comandante general,* Lieutenant Vallejo, who was now raised to the rank of captain, seized all the goods and animals at Mission San Rafael and Mission Solano, while the lieutenant of military forces, Don José Castro, who had been appointed prefect, appropriated all the furniture and fixtures at Mission San Juan Bautista. The administration of these missions now passed into the hands of the leaders of the revolt.

In August, 1839, the frigate *Artémise,* commanded by M. La Place, put in at Monterey and, like the *Vénus,* was hospitably received by Alvarado and the local citizens. No important events occurred while these ships were in port.

The decrees issued by the governor, under date of January 17, 1839,[53] and March 1, 1840, purporting to establish what was called the organization of the country, merely hastened the downfall of the missions. The Mexican government, wearied by the demands of the clergy, through the medium of Don José Marin, Minister of the Interior, issued an order dated November 17, 1840, in which the governor of California was enjoined to return to the Fathers the complete temporal control of the missions which they had held prior to the law of August 17, 1837. This decree, it is needless to add, was never executed in California.

In April, 1840, the American and English trappers, convinced that Alvarado's government had failed to advance their interests, plotted to overthrow it and proclaim the independence of California, prepara-

---

[53]Alvarado's important decree of January 17, 1839, is quoted in Engelhardt, **Missions,** IV, 142-145; that of March 1, 1840, in **ibid,** 163-169.

tory to its admission into the Union. These adventurers, under the leadership as usual of an American, Isaac Graham,[54] were 46 in all. Of this number 25 were Englishmen, primarily sailors, who had deserted their vessels, and 21 Americans, for the greater part hunters, who had come overland from the United States. Just when this plot was about to be executed a man named Garner,[55] won over by the hope of compensation, deserted his confederates and exposed the scheme to Alvarado. The latter immediately summoned some soldiers and loyal rancheros. On the night of April 7, 1840, a band commanded by José Castro surrounded a log cabin a few leagues from Monterey, where the principal leaders of the expedition were sleeping. Castro, aware that the foreigners were armed to a man with long carbines, did not dare wage an open fight, and ordered his men to fire on the cabin. Graham and his comrades were wounded where they slept. One man attempted to escape, but was knocked down by a blow from a saber. At the time Castro was committing this atrocious act, two envoys from Alvarado persuaded Graham's remaining comrades to appeal to Alvarado, who, when they appeared, had them arrested and made prisoners.

Three or four Frenchmen, who had not taken part in the conspiracy, were arrested by mistake and at once dismissed. The rancheros, passing the houses where our countrymen were staying, merely called out, "There are no foreigners inside, only Frenchmen," reserving the term foreigner primarily to designate Englishmen and Americans.

Alvarado placed his prisoners in the custody of Castro, aboard the three-master *Guipuzcoana,* owned by a Spaniard named Aguirre.[56] The ship left Monterey April 24, and after touching at Santa Bárbara to take on a few Americans, reached San Blas on May 8. The prisoners, maltreated by Mexican officers and soldiers, were then marched to Tepic.

The sloop, *Danaïde,* in command of M. de Rosamel, put in at Monterey toward the end of May, where she was greeted by the citizens and officials with the same enthusiasm shown the *Vénus* and *Artémise.* Simultaneously a United States warship, the *St. Louis,* anchored off Monterey. Her captain, Mr. Forrest, put ashore an officer, Mr. Estabrook, to serve as consular agent, then sailed on down toward Mazatlán.

Upon the arrival at Tepic of the prisoners sent by Alvarado, the consuls of the United States and England, and an American called

---

[54]See **infra**, I, 217, also **note** 52.
[55]William Robert Garner, an Englishman who had deserted from a whaler. He was one of Graham's lieutenants. See Bancroft, **California**, VI, **passim**.
[56]Aguirre: see **infra**, I, 191, also **note** 143.

Mr. Farnham,[57] rendered them assistance. At the same time the British and American legations in Mexico City dispatched forceful protests to President Bustamante. However, a decision was reached that all prisoners who wished to return to California would be transported at the expense of the Mexican government, that they would receive an indemnity of three piasters a day for time lost, and, in addition, be reimbursed in full for valuables or merchandise which had been seized. An English warship was sent up to Monterey to supervise this latter indemnity, as well as to protect British subjects. The prisoners had been sent to Tepic without legal instructions, the government had no written proof of their guilt nor affidavits from witnesses, no attempt had been made at executions, and although a kind of moral conviction of guilt prevailed, yet the only charge actually brought against those deported was the deposition of Garner, who had received from Alvarado, as the price of treason, a farm and some live stock.

On May 25, 1841, the United States warship, *St. Louis,* with 22 cannon, returned to Monterey, took on the officer who had been left there, and ascertained that the Americans residing at the port were not being oppressed by Alvarado. The liberated prisoners reached Monterey from Tepic on July 27, on a ship leased by the Mexican government. They were proud of their success, and full of plans for vengeance against Alvarado and Castro by whom they had been unjustly treated. These are the men who intend to make another Texas out of New California, whenever they can recruit adequate numbers, and are fully assured of United States support.

On August 16 the American ship *Vincennes* dropped anchor at San Francisco. She was soon followed by gunboats from that same country the *Porpoise,* the *Oregon,* and the sloop *Flying Fish.* The warship, *Peacock,* which was part of this expedition, was lost in July at the mouth of the Columbia River. All these ships were stationed there until October. On November 13 another United States gunboat, the *Yorktown,* carrying 16 cannon, came into Monterey. Her commander[58] protested that he had no other aim than to protect his countrymen and that another ship was coming out later to adjust the allotment of indemnities.

On the 15th of the same month an English boat of 28 cannon, the

---

[57]Thomas J. Farnham, an American lawyer who reached Monterey in April. His **Life, Adventures and Travels in California** (New York, 1852), discusses this episode at considerable length.

[58]J. H. Aulick.

Curaçoa, carrying Captain Jones, who had come out to arbitrate between Alvarado and the interested English parties as to the amount of indemnity to be collected, reached Monterey. The affair was adjusted in the following manner:

Indemnity to an Englishman called Carmichael, owner of a small shop _____4,500 piasters

Indemnity to 15 Englishmen for time lost for fifteen months at 78 piasters a month; each man to receive 1,170 piasters _____17,550 piasters

Indemnity for belongings lost or stolen_____2,000 piasters

Total _____24,050 piasters[59]

Four Englishmen died in prison, or as a direct result of their imprisonment, but the claims thus arising have not been included in the above estimate. The only indemnity inserted is compensation for time lost; claims for arbitrary imprisonment, bad treatment, and violation of the fundamental rights of man, will be fought out between the English and Mexican governments. Albert Morris, an Englishman who has accepted indemnity of 1,170 piasters, originally claimed £15,000 although when he was captured he had been in California less than two months, was in rags, and had no resources!

American claims have only recently been adjusted. The amount asked by the leader of the trappers, Isaac Graham, for loss of time, properties, and live stock stolen during his absence and imprisonment was 109,000 piasters. William Chard, who had a small business, claimed 5,000 piasters. Thirteen Americans asked 3 piasters for each day's work for a period of fifteen months, amounting monthly to 78 piasters. For fifteen months this totalled 1,170 piasters each, or 15,210 piasters for 13 men. Total claims reached 129,210 piasters. Two Americans died at Mexico; the claims put in by their families are not, however, included in the above amount. Thus of the 46 prisoners, 6 died, 9 did not return to California, and 31 went back, among whom were 15 Americans and 16 Englishmen.

In this matter of claims the cabinet at Washington moved with its usual caution and slowness with unfortunate Mexico. She allowed England to put in her claims promptly, but dragged out at considerable

[59]Bancroft, **California**, IV, 37-41, **notes**, questions the accuracy of these figures.

length those of her own citizens, thus piling up a large number of grievances which were not difficult to ascertain in the case of Mexico, and for whose redress more will be exacted in the future than mere pecuniary indemnity.

Alvarado has remained head of the government. Nothing has disturbed his tranquil rule except a revolt that broke out in January, 1842, at Mission Todos Santos in Lower California.[60] Here Father Gabriel, a Spanish Dominican, aided by several rancheros, had attempted to check the wholesale pillaging of the mission, which the political chief intended to carry out for his own benefit. But after the Father was made prisoner and sent to Mexico, peace was restored.[61]

In October, 1841, about a hundred Americans arrived by the overland route from New Mexico.[62] Alvarado, fearing a new revolution, however, demanded troops from President Santa Anna, and by a decree of February 21, 1842, the latter ordered 300 convicts to start for Upper California. These convicts were taken from the Mexican jails and were promised pardons for good conduct, as well as lands, live stock, and farm implements. To replace Alvarado as governor and commander general, Santa Anna also sent out Brigadier General Micheltorena,[63] who set sail from Mazatlán July 25, 1842, for San Diego. He was accompanied by 450 men, including 300 convicts, many professional men, and a number of Mexican employés of every sort and description, to replace the Californians. Alvarado was then appointed head of the departmental junta, with a salary of 1,500 piasters. Vallejo and Castro were now raised to the post of lieutenant colonel.

General Micheltorena landed at San Diego about August 20,[64] and after a short visit continued slowly on his journey, reaching Los Angeles early in October. There he learned that an American squadron had recently seized Monterey. In fact, Commodore Catesby Jones,[65] in command of the United States naval forces in the Pacific, acting on

---

[60]See the **Diario del Gobierno de Mexico**, No. 2, 455. (D. de M.).

[61]See **ibid**, of this date. (D. de M.).

[62]One of these was Benjamin Davis Wilson whose "Observations on Early Days in California and New Mexico" appears in **Annual Publications of the Historical Society of Southern California** (Los Angeles, 1934), pp. 74-150.

[63]Manuel Micheltorena, who was appointed governor on January 22, 1842, and reached San Diego on August 25. En route to Monterey he learned that an American fleet was demanding the surrender of his capital.

[64]On August 25.

[65]Thomas Ap Catesby Jones, with five ships and 116 guns, demanded the surrender of Monterey on October 19, but was forced to make amends for his rash conduct.

a rumor that war had been declared between the United States and Mexico, had assumed the task of taking possession of the capital of California. Monterey, moreover, was unprepared to resist any assault. The commodore, however, assured that peace between the two governments had not been disrupted, immediately reinstated the governor, who had not even defended Monterey, but had, on the contrary, ordered all the citizens to withdraw into the interior, taking their live stock, with the idle hope of starving out the American squadron.*

The authority of General Micheltorena seems as yet scarcely consolidated; in the course of time he will probably meet the fate of his Mexican predecessors.[66] Influential Californians frequently remark that since they receive nothing from Mexico they merely pretend to use the revenues of the country to pay their soldiers in California. They also add that even if, at any time, a small troop of soldiers were maintained, it would be only on condition that danger of attack on the part of convicts, who are allowed their freedom—since the presidios are in ruins, and no preparations have been made to place them in confinement— is eliminated. Signs indicate, furthermore, that General Micheltorena will soon meet the fate of governors Victoria, Herrera, Chico, Gutiérrez, and Carrillo.

Undoubtedly the American commodore acted unwisely in seizing Monterey, but once this step had been taken, he should have been able to retain his hold and even capture the port of San Francisco. No nation in the world would have dared dispute the United States, with the possible exception of England, who, jealous of being forestalled, might have protested. No one, however, can ignore the fact that this great power, although haughty with those who fear her, knows how to make concessions when she meets adversaries who do not allow themselves to be intimidated.

---

*This paragraph varies somewhat from the original **Mémoire**.

[66]Micheltorena's political career terminated when his army was defeated by Alvarado and Castro's forces in February, 1845, near Los Angeles.

SAN LUIS REY MISSION IN 184-

CHAPTER VIII*

Upper or New California. Its political, administrative, and military organization. White population. Foreigners. Mission topography, pueblos, and presidios of the southern part of the province. Environs and port of San Diego and Santa Bárbara. Coastal islands.

In the preceding chapter a general survey of the colonization and revolutions of California has been given; what now remain to be presented are a concise description of its organization and a detailed account of each mission, pueblo, and presidio.

Geographically speaking, this superb province extends from 32° to 42° north latitude. On the north it is bordered by Oregon Territory, on the south by Old California, on the east by the Rocky Mountains, and on the west by the Pacific Ocean.

From a political standpoint, the two Californias form a single department of the Mexican government known as the *Departamento de Californias*. This department is represented in the Mexican Congress by the deputy Castillero,[1] who receives an annual salary of 3,000 piasters. Before the recent arrival of a superior military officer, the constitutional governor, or *gobernador constitucional*, residing at Monterey, was invested with supreme authority. However, owing to the distance and the difficulty of communication, Lower California is now administered by a political chief, or *jefe politico,* who lives at La Paz and who is in direct communication with the *comandante general* of the province of Sonora, residing at Mazatlán. Thus, the power of the civil governor extends in reality only over Upper California. His annual compensation has been raised to what General Micheltorena now receives—4,000 piasters. He also carries the title and rank of colonel of the civil militia which, as a matter of fact, is not organized.

The department is divided into four districts. Monterey and San Diego have each a prefect who receives a salary of 2,000 piasters. The

---

*This is Mémoire No. V of Amérique Vol. 43, folios 196 to 249. The differences between manuscript and chapter as published are negligible.
[1]Castillero, see infra, I, 191, note 142.

prefect of Monterey, Don José Estrada,[2] is the brother-in-law of Alvarado. The prefect of the district of San Diego, Don Santiago Argüello,[3] formerly captain of the presidio, lives in El Pueblo de Los Angeles. The districts of Santa Bárbara and San Francisco are administered by two sub-prefects from the district of San Francisco, who receive one piaster a day. The sub-prefect of the district of San Francisco resides in the town of San José de Guadalupe, to which Alvarado has vainly tried to give his name. This sub-prefect is a Spaniard called Don Antonio Suñol,[4] who has served in the French army and is devoted to the French people.

Analytical Table of the white population and of the political and military divisions of Upper California by districts and presidios, from south to north.

District and presidio of San Diego founded in 1769		
	Port, pueblo, presidio, and mission of San Diego	100
	Mission San Luís Rey de Francia	
	Mission San Juan Capistrano	
	Mission San Gabriel Arcángel	
	Mission San Fernando, Rey de España	
	Port of San Pedro	
	Pueblo de Nuestra Señora de la Reyna de Los Angeles	1,200
	Total	1,300

District and presidio of Santa Bárbara founded in 1780 [1782]		
	Port, pueblo, presidio, and mission of Santa Bárbara	800
	Mission San Buenaventura	
	Mission Purísima Concepción	
	Mission Santa Inés	
	Mission San Luís Obispo de Tolosa	
	Total	800

---

[2]José Ramon Estrada, a former alcalde at Monterey, held the post of prefect from 1841 to 1843, and later that of administrator of Mission Santa Clara. His wife was María Castro. Alvarado was his step-father, not brother-in-law.

[3]Santiago Argüello served for a time as alcalde of San Diego, and as administrator of Mission San Juan Capistrano. From 1840 to 1843 he was prefect of Los Angeles.

[4]Antonio Suñol, see **infra,** I, 219, also **note** 63.

District and Port, presidio, and capital of San Carlos de
presidio of   Monterey _____600
Monterey   Mission San Miguel Arcángel_____
Capital of   Mission San Antonio de Pádua_____
Upper   Mission Nuestra Señora de la Soledad_____
California   Mission del Carmelo (Mt. Carmel)_____
founded in Pueblo and Mission of San Juan Bautista____100
1770   Mission de la Santa Cruz_____
           Pueblo or village of Branciforte_____300
             Total _____1,000

District and Port and presidio of San Francisco de Assisi,
presidio of   Mission de los Dolores de San Francisco,
San Francisco village of Yerba Buena on San Francisco
founded in   Bay _____100
1776   Pueblo of San José de Guadalupe_____550
           Mission Santa Clara_____
           Mission San José_____
           Mission San Rafael_____
           Mission San Francisco Solano, pueblo of
             Sonoma, belonging to the mission_____150
           Captain Sutter's colony of New Helvetia on
             the Sacramento River_____100
             Total   _____800

           Remainder of population at missions or iso-
             lated ranches_____ 1,100
                                              5,000

This makes a total of five thousand inhabitants scattered over some
2000 square leagues in Upper California.

Division by nationality of the white population of Upper California.
Californians of Spanish descent_____4,000
Americans from the United States_____ 360
English, Scotch, Irish_____ 300
Spanish Europeans_____ 80
French, including a few Canadians_____ 80
Germans, Italians, Portuguese, Sandwich Islanders, and others_ 90
Mexican colonists from Mexico_____ 90

Total white population_____5,000

Americans are especially numerous at the Pueblo of Los Angeles and the village of Branciforte, the English at Monterey and Santa Bárbara, the Spanish at Santa Bárbara and Monterey, and the French at Los Angeles and Monterey.

Throughout California the whites are called *gente de razón*[5] to distinguish them from the natives who are usually termed Indians, or neophytes, if connected with the missions. The 300 convicts and the few soldiers who came up with General Micheltorena[6] constitute a foreign element; and it is doubtful whether the inhabitants will allow them to remain much longer. (A special section will be subsequently devoted to the Indians.)

Comparative Table of the Missions of Upper California under Religious Administration in 1834 and under Civil Administration in 1842.

Names of Missions from South to North	Date of founding	Distance from preceding (leagues)	Number of Indians male & female		Number of cattle		Number of horses		Number of sheep, goats and pigs	Harvests of wheat, corn, beans, barley (fanegas)	
			1834	1842	1834	1842	1834	1842	1834	1842	1834
San Diego	June 16, 1769	17	2,500	500	12,000	20	1,800	100	17,000	200	13,000
San Luís Rey	June 13, 1798	14	3,500	650	80,000	2,000	10,000	400	100,000	4,000	14,000
San Juan Capistrano	Nov. 1, 1776	13	1,700	100	70,000	500	1,900	150	10,000	200	10,000
San Gabriel	Sept. 8, 1771	18	2,700	500	105,000	700	20,000	500	40,000	3,500	20,000
San Fernando	Sept. 8, 1797	9	1,500	400	14,000	1,500	5,000	400	7,000	2,000	8,000
San Buenaventura	March 31, 1782	18	1,100	300	4,000	200	1,000	40	6,000	400	2,500
Santa Bárbara	Dec. 4, 1786	12	1,200	400	5,000	1,800	1,200	160	5,000	400	3,000
Santa Inés	Sept. 17, 1804	12	1,300	250	14,000	10,000	1,200	500	12,000	4,000	3,500
Purísima Concepción	Dec. 8, 1787	8	900	60	15,000	8,000	2,000	300	14,000	3,500	6,000
San Luís Obispo	Sept. 1, 1771	18	1,250	80	9,000	300	4,000	200	7,000	800	4,000
San Miguel	July 25, 1797	13	1,200	30	4,000	40	2,500	50	10,000	400	2,500
San Antonio	July 14, 1771	13	1,400	150	12,000	800	2,000	500	14,000	2,000	3,000
N. S. de la Soledad	Oct. 9, 1791	11	700	20	6,000	800	1,200	500	7,000	2,000	2,500
Carmelo	June 3, 1770	15	500	40	3,000	800	700	500	7,000	2,000	1,500
San Juan Bautista	June 24, 1799	14	1,450	80	9,000	800	1,200	500	9,000	2,000	3,500
Santa Cruz	Aug. 28, 1791	17	600	50	8,000	800	800	500	10,000	2,000	2,500
Santa Clara	Jan. 18, 1777	11	1,800	300	13,000	1,500	1,200	250	15,000	3,000	6,000
San José	June 18, 1797	7	2,300	400	24,000	8,000	1,100	200	19,000	7,000	10,000
Dolores de S. Francisco	Oct. 9, 1776	18	500	50	5,000	60	1,600	50	4,000	200	2,500
San Rafael	Dec. 18, 1817	8	1,250	20	3,000	60	500	50	4,500	200	1,500
San Francisco Solano	Aug. 25, 1823	13	1,300	70	8,000	60	700	50	4,000	200	3,000
21 Missions	On a line of	262 leagues	30,650	4,450	424,000	28,220	62,500	3,800	321,500	31,600	122,500 or 70,000 hectares

---

[5]Gente de razón: the intelligentsia, or intelligent white class.

[6]On January 19, 1842, José Manuel Micheltorena was named **comandante general** of the Californias, and charged to check the growing wave of American emigration. Having released from Mexican prisons some 350 criminals, with this company of ragged, unfit men, he reached California the following summer.

[7]For correct dates of founding of missions see Engelhardt, **Missions, passim.**

Wheat comprises three-fifths of all grain raised. Several missions also produce considerable cotton, oil, hemp, and wine. From official reports published by the inspector-general of the missions, live stock belonging to the missions early in 1840 numbered 57,000; since that time, however, pillage has been on the increase. Unfortunately the Californians were not materially benefited by the secularization of the missions. The majority, instead of breeding live stock, killed their animals, selling the meat and hides to foreign vessels. They also failed to cultivate their lands since Indian laborers were no longer available.

	Résumé Under religious administration in 1834	Under civil administration 1842
Indians	30,650	4,450
Cattle	424,000	28,220
Horses	62,500	3,800
Sheep, goats, and pigs	321,500	31,600
Grain harvested	70,000 hectares	4,000 hectares

These estimates, compiled from the most authentic sources, speak more eloquently than any comments.

Each pueblo has an alcalde,[8] or justice of the peace, who serves without salary. The mission administrators fulfill a similar function, although in addition to their enormous perquisites, they receive a distribution that varies from 300 to 600 piasters. An inspector-general, or *visitador-general,* who draws a salary of 3,000 piasters, has full charge of these establishments. All employés are appointed by the governor. The Mexican law does not allow a municipal council, or ayuntamiento, in any village with a population of less than 6,000 inhabitants. Thus neither the capital, Monterey, nor the other pueblos, come under this regulation. Affairs pertaining to the province are regulated by a departmental council, or *deputación departamental,* composed of six members, who receive salaries of 1,500 piasters.

The administration of justice is vested in the hands of a superior tribunal, or *tribunal superior,* consisting of five members. Each receives a salary of 3,000 piasters. This tribunal, however, is not as yet functioning,

---

[8]Alcalde: a word derived from the Turkish term **cadi.** In Spain and Portugal, an alcande was a sheriff, or justice of the peace; in early California, however, his functions were often broader, including that of mayor and judge.

for the members have not been appointed, inasmuch as citizens with the qualifications necessary to fill these offices have not been found. Those now in control are rancheros, or farmers, who have grown rich by plundering the missions and who, under the Franciscan régime, served as majordomos, cowboys, and servants to the Fathers. Some idea of the humiliation suffered by the Franciscans when they found these new-comers absolute masters of their property can only be surmised. The junta,[9] or departmental body, exists in name only; the whims of the governor comprise the law. Some idea of how justice is administered is revealed by the fact that in 1841 the justice at Monterey was an illiterate peasant.[10]

Officials of this character afford slight protection to foreigners. In September, 1840, near Mission San Francisco Solano, an Indian shot and killed a French carpenter, Pierre Dubosc,[11] yet General Vallejo, who knew who had committed the crime, made no effort to apprehend the murderer. In August, 1841, a young German[12] who was engaged in business, was assassinated in El Pueblo de Los Angeles. When the authorities paid no attention to this affair, the foreign colony, united by mutual interests, assembled, and under the leadership of some French-men, among them M. Charles Baric, instigated a search for the culprits, whom they soon located. The Spanish Father at San Gabriel, Tomás Esténega, was able to inspire in the guilty men so keen a desire to re-pent that they even asked pardon in public for their crime and further confessed that, if they had not been apprehended, they had intended to assassinate and rob several foreigners reputed to be extremely rich. The latter, convinced of the necessity of making an example of these men, sent word to the governor that they personally would see that the culprits were put to death if he did not order their execution. Al-varado immediately dispatched from Santa Bárbara a dozen soldiers and an officer, who shot the condemned men.

While sojourning in September of that same year at San José for a few days, two Englishmen were murdered.[13] The sub-prefect of San

---

[9]Junta: a deliberative or administrative council or committee.

[10]Possibly Simeon Castro, who held office until November, 1841, when he was succeeded by José Amesti.

[11]See appendix A.

[12]In January, 1841, a German merchant named Nicholas Fink was murdered in Los Angeles. His murderers were tried and sentenced to death, but no local authorities had the power to execute the sentence.

[13]Contemporary records indicate the murder of one, not two, Englishmen. The victim was Anthony Campbell, who lived near Santa Clara, for whose murder Manuel González was executed in July, 1842, at Monterey.

José, who had neither soldiers nor resources, could not set out in pursuit. At Monterey, after pressure had been brought by the foreign colony, the judge finally imprisoned a young Mexican, but without bringing charges against him. A few weeks later the man was released.

The new *comandante general* of the department, who has charge of Micheltorena's forces, resides at Los Angeles;[14] the former *comandante,* Don Mariano Vallejo, who was head of the infantry at the presidio of San Francisco, lives north of the bay, at the pueblo of Sonoma near Mission San Francisco Solano, which he has pillaged even to the point of demolishing the church in order to build a house out of the materials. The troops are divided in the following manner: the company of San Francisco has 20 men, 2 lieutenants, and an ensign, or *alféres, at* Sonoma; 10 soldiers with an officer of the same rank are stationed at the presidio in San Francisco, which is in ruins. At the latter fort, which has been abandoned, only four bronze cannon remain, two eight-pounders having been transported to Sonoma.

The garrison at Monterey consists of the local *comandante,* who is general of the unorganized militia, three captains and second lieutenants, who are Californians, about 40 soldiers, and more than a dozen artillerymen under an artillery officer.

The presidio has been demolished; the fort, which is nothing more than a battery, has only three bronze cannon mounted on gun-carriages that are in working order. These cannon, which were cast at Manila or Lima in the seventeenth century, differ in caliber from eight, twelve, and sixteen-pounders.

At Santa Bárbara, the garrison at the presidio, which is now in ruins, includes a dozen soldiers in command of four officers. Four bronze pieces lie buried in the sand. At San Diego the fort and presidio are inhabited; on one side of the fort under the crumbling walls a few pieces of bronze cannon lie partially buried. At the pueblo a few soldiers in charge of an officer reside.

Not a single soldier is stationed at the missions, while the garrisons throughout Upper California total only 160 armed men. Most of these troops are without mounts and are poorly equipped, being armed with antiquated sabres and muskets. Their equipment lacks uniformity; the 40 soldiers at Monterey are the only men outfitted with the same type

----

14This was Rafael Tellez, or Telles, who remained in California from 1842 to 1844 in command of Micheltorena's forces. His attempts to inject discipline into the troops proved his downfall. See Hittell, op. cit., II, 335-336.

of arms and uniforms. In California, as in Mexico, there are nearly as many officers as soldiers, the former numbering approximately 100.

Some forty years ago ex-governor Alvarado purchased for the government an 86-ton schooner, the *California,* and this represents the entire naval strength of California. This small vessel is commanded by an Englishman, John Cooper,[15] and carries a crew of ten men. The ship, which is unarmed, is used primarily to make occasional trips to Mexico or over to the Sandwich Islands for commercial purposes in behalf of the governor or in the interests of foreign merchants to whom it is often leased. However, a lieutenant of a Mexican ship who acts as captain of the port is stationed at Monterey.

The entire revenue of the country is derived from the customs tax paid by foreign ships at Monterey, the only port open to foreign commerce.[16] The officals at the customhouse are eight in number; an administrator who draws a salary of 2,000 piasters, a controller, a checker, a head-officer of customs at 1 500 piasters, and four guards, each at an annual stipend of 800 piasters.[17] Obviously the staff materially exceeds the needs of the organization. The customs receipts are handled by a commissioner of finances called *comisario de hacienda,* who has charge of their distribution.

On an average the annual receipts from this source do not exceed 70,000 or 80,000 piasters; yet expenses total at least 120,000 piasters. This annual deficit of 40,000 or 50,000 piasters adequately explains why officials of all classes resort to pillaging the missions.

Following this detailed account of the settled communities, the topography of the country, and its various products, at this point imports and exports, as well as what business opportunities might be open to French merchants interested in commercial expeditions to this country, will be analyzed.

The most important shipping point in this portion of the country is the harbor of San Diego,[18] which was discovered in 1542 by Cabrillo,[19] who first named it San Miguel. Later, in 1602, General Vizcaíno gave it the name it now has. This is the first port of call in Upper California. If a line

---

[15] John Cooper: see **infra,** I, 210, **note** 25.

[16] Officially foreign ships were taxed 25 per cent on goods imported, but actually taxes amounted at times to 100 per cent. Approximately $200,000 was raised annually by these methods.

[17] Salaries were not so high as De Mofras indicates. The administrator received only 1,000 piasters annually, and his subordinates much less.

[18] The port of San Diego lies in 32° 39′ 30″ lat., and 119° 37′ 13″ w. long., Paris time; variation, 11° E.; establishment of the port 10 h; rise of tide 1m 40′. (D. de M.).

[19] For Cabrillo at San Diego see **supra,** I, 51, also **note** 18.

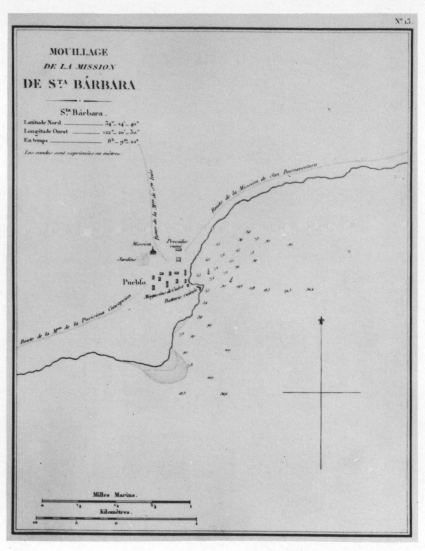

Courtesy of the Henry E. Huntington Library

PORT OF SANTA BÁRBARA

were drawn due east, the mouth of the Colorado River would be reached, and this line would mark the boundry between Old and New California.

From the sea the landmarks defining the port of San Diego are as follows: Eight leagues south of the port, on the coast, a high mountain terminating in an extensive flat plateau known as Las Mesas de Juan Gómez; 20 miles south and directly in line with the hill or *loma* of San Diego, a small group of rocks, the Coronados, which may be seen 10 leagues away. The Coronados lie 4 leagues offshore; the passage between them is safe for ships and has a uniform depth of 20 or 30 meters.

To one approaching from the north, a slight error in latitude would be serious for 8 miles north of the point which marks the entrance to the main harbor lies another opening, unnavigable because of its bars and surf, which leads into False Harbor (Puerto Falso). This mistake, moreover, is readily made for, when passing False Harbor, the white limestone buildings of the presidio and the houses in the pueblo are visible; on the other hand, when approaching by way of the other harbor no buildings are in evidence; only when the shore is approached are the ruins of the fort and the wooden shacks used for storing hides apparent. Yet marked differences exist between the two entrances; for instance, False Harbor is situated farther from the Coronados; the hill which in the latter instance is situated south of the entrance, lies north of the true harbor. False Harbor is also dotted with islands that are not found in the other port; south of the former the shore curves slightly toward the west, whereas south of the main harbor it bends considerably toward the east; and, finally, the mouth of False Harbor is obstructed by a circular line of breakers about a mile in length, while the opening of the main port, on the contrary, is free from all dangers.

When doubling Point Loma of San Diego, which is an abrupt promontory, ships should keep a quarter of a mile offshore, in order to avoid certain rocks which extend out in a southwesterly direction. After the point has been rounded, a course should be set north quarter-north-west bearing directly for the fort, until close to land. The bay is extremely deep at this point; 100 meters offshore the depth ranges from 6 to 15 meters. By following these directions one avoids the bank of Zuñiga, conspicuous by its foaming breakers, which has barely 3 feet of water and which lies a mile to the east. Near Point Guijarro,[20] a small

---

[20]Point Guijarro, or Guijarros, is a small anchorage one mile from the promontory of Point Loma where Cabrillo originally landed. It is also known as Ballast or Cobblestone Point. The site was once used for a fort and in 1800 barracks and guns were erected nearby.

spit of land on which rise the ruins of an old fort, soundings taken a few fathoms offshore vary between 16 and 20 meters. After this point has been passed, an excellent harbor well sheltered from winds will be found off toward the west. Here ships may anchor directly opposite the houses, in 8 to 15 meters of water, on a base of mud and sand, which affords excellent anchorage.

In the outer bay, the floor of the sea invariably consists of sand. The ebb and flow of the tide is about a mile; the currents, generally speaking, follow the shoreline from north to south. Only ships of 400 tons, drawing less than 20 feet of water, are allowed to enter the port of San Diego. Certain areas are shallow, and some parts are so covered with sandbanks that ships can easily run aground on the silt that the tiny San Diego River brings down from the mountains in the rainy season. The Spanish Fathers checked this peril by changing the river's course and forcing it over into False Bay, but within the last few years the river, through the negligence of the inhabitants, has reverted to its former channel, and now empties into the waters of San Diego Harbor. The fort and neighboring buildings are deserted and in ruins; fragments of six or eight bronze cannon may be seen embedded in the sands.

An inspection of the general plan will reveal how easily the mouth of the harbor might be fortified. This could be accomplished by setting a battery on the hill which would command the entire bay, rebuilding the fort, and locating a few guns on the opposite spit of land, so that shots would focus on the neck of the harbor which could be captured by fire from a battery erected south of the little point where the warehouses are now situated.

A dozen English and American sailors off ships that trade along the coast transporting hides comprise the population at the port. Wood is difficult to obtain, and water has to be brought from the villages in carts; each hogshead costs one piaster. By sinking wells, good water might perhaps be obtained; there is no water supply, however, near the anchorage. Five large wooden sheds—each capable of holding 15,000 or 20,000 hides—which were brought down from Monterey, serve for warehouses.[21] In these some Indians, and occasionally Kanakas from

---

[21]This flourishing trade that centered at San Diego has been aptly described by Dana. The hide warehouses, known as Hide Park, stood at La Playa, over on Point Loma, and along the bay. The most complete account of these old buildings is found in Winifred Davidson, **Where California Began** (San Diego, 1929), pp. 86-96. See also William E. Smythe, **The History of San Diego** (2 vols., San Diego, 1908), I, 101-104.

the Sandwich Islands, live together with the white sailors. The road leading to the village is in good condition; and can be reached on horseback in less than an hour.

The village, which is situated near a stream, consists of 20 houses.[22] Of these the most pretentious belong to several prominent English and American merchants, who control all commerce. The white population is in excess of 100 inhabitants who own the majority of the small ranchos in the surrounding country. The presidio, founded in 1769,[23] is built on a small hill a few hundred meters from the village and is in ruins; two bronze cannon are in evidence, while a third is half buried in the center of the village.

The pueblo is under the direct control of an alcalde, or justice of the peace, who fulfills the dual function of captain of the port and auditor of customs. There are no Frenchmen at San Diego. Among important residents are the English Captains Snook[24] and Stokes,[25] and Captain Fitch,[26] an American, all of whom are merchants. The king's rancho, known as the Rancho del Rey,[27] that belonged to the presidio, has been acquired by a private individual. Near the coast several salt mines of some importance have been found, but have not as yet been worked. The large rancheria of Choyas[28] Indians, who lived originally on the shores of the bay, is no longer in existence. The bay abounds in fish and is often visited by whales.

The mission of San Diego,[29] which lies two leagues or more from the pueblo, was founded on June 16, 1769, by the Reverend Father

---

[22]The San Diego of this period has been fully described by the following travelers: Richard H. Dana, Two Years before the Mast (New York, 1841), pp. 144-147, 177-208, and passim; Edward Belcher, op. cit, I, 327 ff. Alfred Robinson, Life in California (New York, 1846), passim; William H. Davis, op. cit.

[23]This historic settlement, founded on July 16, marks the beginning of California. See Bolton, Palóu's New California, II, passim.

[24]Joseph Francisco Snook [or Snooks] was an English merchant who came to California on the Ayacucho. At San Diego he married María Antonia Alvarado. Snook spent considerable time at sea, merely making his headquarters at San Diego between voyages.

[25]Edward Stokes, an English sailor who came to California probably in 1840, where he married Refugio Ortega.

[26]Captain Henry D. Fitch came to California in 1826 as master of the brig María Ester. In 1833, after marrying Josefa Carrillo, he became a naturalized citizen. Opening a store in Old Town, he soon became rich from trade. Later he held many important offices.

[27]Rancho del Rey, also known as Rancho de la Nación, a property of 6 leagues lying south of the presidio, had been acquired by John Forster.

[28]Las Choyas, or San Antonio Indians; a small colony living near San Diego. See Zephyrin Engelhardt, San Diego Mission (San Francisco, 1920), p. 349.

[29]A full account of this mission is found in ibid, and its founding in Bolton's Palóu, II, 265-274.

Junípero Serra, although San Diego Harbor had been discovered at a much earlier period. This, together with the presidio, was the first Spanish settlement in New California. The mission, known to the Franciscans as the mother mission, lies 17 leagues north of San Miguel, the last mission in Old California, and 40 leagues from that of San Luís Rey de Francia, its nearest neighbor. It is situated on the banks of the San Diego River, in a long, narrow valley formed by two parallel chains of hills. Today the buildings and church are in ruins. Except for some few differences in proportions, its architecture is identical with that of the mission whose plan has already been given.

In front of the buildings stands a superb grove of olives; nearby stretch flourishing vineyards that are capable of furnishing the best wine in California. What cotton is produced is of a superior quality; but a shortage of labor has retarded its cultivation. The neighboring country, or prairie, is virtually devoid of trees. Seven or 8 leagues toward the east tower forests, while up in the mountains grow pine, oak, and other wood suitable for construction. Because of its favorable climate, at San Diego all European fruit trees, even palms and oranges, attain extraordinary size. In January, 1842, the thermometer at noon averaged 15° to 18° centigrade above zero. Notwithstanding, off in the east appeared the distant snow-capped peaks of the Sierra Nevada. All oleraceous plants and cereals, such as wheat, corn, buckwheat, barley, oats, and beans flourish, especially during years of heavy rainfall.

In its prime this mission supported 2,500 Indians, 14,000 cattle, 1,500 horses, and 32,000 sheep. Neophytes and live stock lived on the ranchos of Santa Mónica,[30] El Cajón de Santa Isabél,[31] San José,[32] San Bernardo,[33] San Dieguito,[34] San Pasqual,[35] San Alejo[36] and La Soledad.[37] These ranchos now belong to private individuals who have appropriated them, and even all cattle owned by the mission have disappeared. The

---

[30]Santa Mónica, or El Cajón, of 11 leagues, belonged to Miguel Pedrorena and family.

[31]El Cajón de Santa Isabél, 17,000 acres, was now in the possession of José Ortega and Edward Stokes.

[32]San José del Valle had been granted in 1836 to Silvestre de la Portilla.

[33]Cañada de San Bernardo, 4 leagues in extent, had been acquired by Joseph Snook.

[34]San Dieguito, a rancho of 2 leagues, had passed to Juan M. Osuna.

[35]San Pasqual may have been one of the properties of Mission San Diego.

[36]San Alejo, or La Joya, one of the mission ranchos.

[37]La Soledad, on which a portion of the town stood, had been granted in 1838 to Francisco Alvarado.

See Bancroft, **California**, I, 650, for map showing locations; and Engelhardt, **San Diego**, pp. 221, 223, 229.

mission buildings are now occupied by a few Indians, a white family, and the Reverend Father Vicente Oliva,[38] a Spaniard from Aragon who is already well-advanced in years. This Father was able to save from pillage only the rancho called Santa Isabel that lies 10 [17] leagues toward the mountains, and here 500 Indians have congregated under the direction of their alcaldes and a majordomo. These poor wretches own a few pair of work oxen, and harvest barely enough grain for their own support. At San Isidro, 14 leagues east of San Diego, gold and silver mines were discovered and exploited fifteen years ago by a man from Guanajuato.

The country that extends for some 60 leagues as far as the western bank of the Colorado River is not only extremely picturesque, but also abounds in wood and pasturage. However, the Yuman Indians who inhabit this territory frequently raid the lands occupied by the white men. Recently, in 1839, a band of these Indians unexpectedly apppeared at Jamúl,[39] a rancho lying 8 leagues from San Diego, owned by the family of Sergeant Pico. Here the savages massacred four white men and carried off two white girls, whom they mistreated. These miserable girls, however, inspired keen jealousy among the Indian women. Finally, selecting a time when the men of their tribe were off hunting, these natives hung the captives to trees, and then stoned them to death.

The natural inference would be that when the relatives and friends of these victims learned of their hideous death, they would have united and demanded vengeance. Yet they did nothing; and as the authorities were powerless to move, the crime remained unpunished. Under Spanish rule, at the first news of such an outbreak the company from the presidio at San Diego, aided by armed men from the ranchos, would have gone in pursuit, undoubtedly apprehended the assassins, and made them fully atone for their hideous crime.

In the days when there was considerable travel between Sonora and California, the ruined missions of San Pedro y San Pablo at Santa Isabel were passed on the trail leading to San Diego. Frequently, however, to facilitate the crossing of the Colorado River, a route 30 leagues farther north was taken. Caravans would then reach their destination at El Pueblo de Los Angeles by the following route:

---

[38]Vicente Pasqual Oliva y Martin went to San Diego in 1820. In 1818 a chapel, or mission station, had been erected at Santa Isabel or Elcuanan. By 1822 this also had a granary, several houses, and a large Indian colony.

[39]The French traveler seems to refer to the murder of Ybarra, his two daughters, and two employés, that occurred in 1837 at Rancho San Isidro. See Smythe, op. cit., I, 182-186; and Davis, op. cit., pp. 169-170.

From Pitic, the capital of Sonora, or Hermosillo, to the presidio of
  Altar _____60 leagues
From the presidio to Quitobaca_____40   ” .
From Quitobaca to Santo Domigo_____16   ”
From Santo Domingo to Agua Salada _____ 4   ”
From Agua Salada to Tule_____25   ”
From Tule to Tinaja Alta_____ 7   ”
From Tinaja Alta to the Algodones River_____18   ”
From the Algodones River to Pozo del Alamo_____18   ”
From Pozo del Alamo to Pozo Hondo_____ 7   ”
From Pozo Hondo to Carricito_____13   ”
From Carricito to Los Vallecitos_____ 5   ”
From Los Vallecitos to San Felipe_____ 3   ”
From San Felipe to San José_____ 7   ”
From San José to Temécula_____15   ”
From Temécula to Temascal_____10   ”
From Temascal to Santa Ana_____ 8   ”
From Santa Ana to Los Angeles_____11   ”
Total _____267 leagues

All these points are Indian villages, most of which were frequently
visited by the Spanish Fathers. Several travelers who have made this
dangerous journey have been interviewed and the trip is one which
should be undertaken only with guides on whose loyalty absolute
reliance can be placed. The Yuman Indians and, farther northwest along
the Colorado River the Amagaguas,[40] own large numbers of horses and
cattle, cultivate the soil, and harvest various cereals and oleraceous
plants. They also plant cotton which they spin and weave into fine cloth,
and hunt buffalo and beaver, selling the skins to American trappers
from the United States, or to Canadians sent down by the Hudson's
Bay Company from the Columbia River as far south as the mouth of
the Colorado River.

At one time Mission San Diego produced 6,000 fanegas of wheat
and the same amount of corn, but the present crop does not exceed
1,800.[41] Where 30 barrels each of wine and brandy were once made, now
the vineyards are for the most part abandoned, not more than 15 or 20

---

[40]Amagaguas: From **hamok**, three; **avi**, mountains, referring to the peak
known as "The Needles—the Mohave name for themselves.

[41]This mission disintegrated rapidly. Sir Edward Belcher, a visitor in 1839,
wrote, "The mission is in decay and ruin; not more than twenty four-footed
animals remain." Belcher, **op. cit.**, I, 327.

barrels of wine being produced. In addition to what was harvested at Santa Isabel, the Indians lived on seeds from indigenous plants, nuts, and the flesh of wild deer and goats, which are numerous. At the mission plain woolen and cotton cloth was woven, as well as some strong materials made from hemp. The climate here is too dry, however, for sugar cane. This mission also operated a tannery, and even manufactured soap from soda extracted by burning seaweed gathered along the shores of the bay. In the hands of any other power, the port of San Diego would soon acquire importance, and by affording a link between Sonora and the two Californias should become the center of a large population and a vast commerce.

To reach Mission San Luís Rey de Francia the shore should be followed, when the tide is low, as far as Mission San Juan Capistrano. The usual route, however, lies one or two leagues inland. There is comparatively little variation in scenery; on all sides stretch vast, verdant prairies, dotted with a few scattered clumps of trees and, here and there, isolated ranchos. Those of San Dieguito, or Osuna,[42] and El Agua Hedionada[43] lie near the road. Not far from a lagoon is the small Indian settlement of Los Ojitos. In the lowlands where this village is situated, a large quantity of hemp was raised at one time by Mission San Luís Rey for the use of the royal Spanish navy at the arsenal of San Blas.

The mission of San Luís Rey de Francia, founded June 13, 1798,[44] by the Reverend Father Antonio Peyri,[45] a Spanish Franciscan from Catalonia, is situated on a superb stretch of open country on the banks of the tiny San Luís River, about 6 kilometers in from the Pacific Ocean. The distance from San Diego to San Luís is 14 leagues; 13 leagues beyond, toward the northwest, lies Mission San Juan Capistrano. Architecturally, San Luís Rey de Francia is the most beautiful, the most

---

[42]Rancho San Dieguito, or Osuna, was claimed in 1836 by Juan M. Osuna, but the grant was not confirmed before 1845. Osuna, a soldier from San Diego, was an important local figure, having held the offices of alcalde, **juez de paz**, and majordomo and administrator of Mission San Diego.

[43]Rancho Agua Hedionada, a grant of 6 leagues, was acquired in 1842 by Juan María Marron. Marron was administrator of San Luís Rey.

[44]Mission San Luís Rey, named for St. Louis, King of France, often called King of the Missions, is fully described by Fr. Zephyrin Engelhardt in **San Luís Rey Mission** (San Francisco, 1921). The majority of early narratives also describe this noted colony.

[45]Antonio Peyri (1769-1835) reached California in 1796. After spending two years at San Luís Obispo, he founded San Luís Rey, and its branch, San Antonio de Pala. A true Spaniard, he failed to become reconciled to Mexican rule and in 1832 left California. This was the Father whom the Indians revered as a holy man. See **infra**, I, 178.

symmetrical, and the most substantial mission in California; the details of its interior arrangement, as shown by the accompanying plan, will give a fair indication of its importance.

Three extensive orchards and vegetable gardens that were once intensively cultivated by the Fathers adjoin the main buildings. This mission once supported approximately 3,500 Indians, who lived at twenty ranchos scattered over more than 100 square leagues. Several of the most important of these ranchos, such as San Antonio de Pala[46] and Las Flores, formed veritable villages,[47] each with its own chapel where one of the Fathers from the mission often remained in residence. Rancho de San Antonio,[48] lying 8 leagues east toward the mountains, is noted especially for its pasture lands and fine building timber. Rancho del Agua Caliente,[49] on the other hand, has a spring of sulphur water.

In 1834 San Luís Rey ran 80,000 cattle, more than 10,000 horses, and 100,000 sheep. Harvests included 14,000 fanegas of grains, 200 barrels of a fine grade of wine, and an equal amount of brandy. Now scarcely 600 Indians, 2,000 cattle, 400 horses, and 4,000 sheep remain. Many of the fine vineyards have been recently abandoned.[50] In its prime this mission was in the habit of sending its products by *carreta*[51] over a good road to the port of San Diego, since the nearest anchorage, that of Las Flores, in the Bahía de Los Temblores, is extremely dangerous. On the outlying ranchos, forges, tanneries, soap factories, distilleries, large carpenter shops, and looms for weaving linen, cotton, and hemp, were in operation. Saline deposits, containing salt of sparkling whiteness, may be seen a league from the mission.

---

[46]The mission station of San Antonio de Pala lay 7 leagues or more northeast of San Luís. Established about 1810, soon a church, dwellings, and granaries were built, and vineyards and orchards planted. The old chapel is still intact, and used for services. See Engelhardt, San Luís, passim.

[47]Las Flores, or San Pedro, situated near the coast, was originally one of fourteen Indian settlements in that vicinity that spoke the same [Luiseño] dialect. By 1823 houses, including a chapel and granary, had been built. Hides were often stored here to await shipment. The buildings are still visible. See plan in Engelhardt, San Luís, p. 106, also passim.

[48]Rancho de San Antonio [Abad] was occupied by Santiago E. Argüello, a ranchero.

[49]Rancho del Agua Caliente, now known as Warner's Hot Springs, was granted in 1840 to José A. Pico, but subsequently came into the hands of J. J. Warner. See Joseph J. Hill, The History of Warner's Ranch and its Environs, (Los Angeles, 1927).

[50]The visit of Duflot de Mofras to San Luís took place between January 18 and 27, 1842. The historian, Father Engelhardt, fails to agree with his estimates of mission wealth.

[51]Carreta: a two-wheel wooden cart used in early California and the Southwest.

The topography from San Diego as far as San Luís Rey, San Juan Capistrano, and even up to Santa Bárbara, shows slight variation. The main range of mountains rises 8, 10, and 12 leagues in from the sea, the coast being broken up by small, sparsely-wooded hills. The neighboring valleys, watered by brooks, are remarkably fertile.

The parish of San Luís Rey is in the charge of the Reverend Father Francisco González de Ibarra,[52] a Spaniard no longer in his prime, who was able to save something from the wreckage of the mission and assemble 400 Indians at Rancho Las Flores where they live with a white family. The Fathers at Mission San Luís are daily subjected to the most humiliating situations. Father González, for example, is obliged to sit at the administrator's table and to listen to the insults of the same cowboys and majordomos who, a few years ago, would have deemed it an honor to serve the Fathers in the capacity of servants.

The leading ranchos of this mission are: Las Flores, San Antonio de Pala,[53] San Jacinto,[54] Santa Margarita,[55] Agua Caliente,[56] San Onofrio,[57] San José,[58] and Temécula,[59] nearly all of which have been plundered.

Two leagues north of San Luís lies Rancho Santa Margarita, now in the hands of a private owner who raises extraordinarily fine grapes. Two leagues beyond Margarita is the large rancho and chapel called Las Flores. Rising on a slight eminence a few hundred meters in from the shore, this settlement presents a most pleasing picture. On the day of our visit, an opportunity was afforded to witness the extraordinary hold the Fathers still retain over their neophytes. As a result of the religious persecutions inflicted on him by the Mexican authorities,

---

[52]Francisco González de Ibarra succeeded Father Fortuny at San Luís Rey, remaining there from 1837 to 1842. He reached California in 1820 from Spain, and was stationed at San Fernando. For his difficulties with Pío Pico see Engelhardt, San Luís Rey, pp. 107-117, and passim.

[53]San Antonio de Pala was one of the outpost stations of Mission San Luís Rey.

[54]San Jacinto, 4 leagues, had passed to José A. Estudillo, for a time administrator of San Luís Rey.

[55]Santa Margarita, together with Las Flores, was granted in 1841 to Pío and Andrés Pico.

[56]Agua Caliente, or Valle de José, 6 square leagues, was granted in 1840 to Antonio M. Pico.

[57]San Onofrio, or Onofre, was one of the mission properties.

[58]See supra, I, 172, note 32.

[59]Temécula, an important Luiseño Indian village in the valley of the same name in Riverside County. About 1875 the inhabitants were compelled to vacate their lands and to move to Pachango Cañon. For the location of these ranchos see Engelhardt, San Luís Rey p. 257.

Father Antonio Peyri, founder of San Luís Rey, left California in 1832 as poor as when he had entered, yet his mission was left in a flourishing condition. The Indians who had always retained for this saintly man a respect bordering on adoration, saw him depart with despair, aware that in losing their Father they had also lost their protector.

A few hours after our arrival at Las Flores, the Indians, headed by two chieftains carrying batons as a mark of leadership, advanced to meet me, accompanied by their families. After all the men, in accordance with their custom, had touched my hand, the following conversation took place between their principal chieftain and myself:

"Captain, we understand that you have just come from Spain. Have you seen the king?"[60]

"Yes."

"And Father Antonio?"

"No, but I know he is at Barcelona."

"We have heard," added the other leader, "that he is dead."

My first interrogator turned toward his colleague with a look of consternation.

"No, Monsieur, this Father cannot die." (*No Señor, este Padre no muere!*), he replied.

At San Luís Rey a tablet was seen that represented Father Peyri surrounded by several Indian children. When the Indians stop before this portrait, they offer up the same prayers that are said before the images of saints that adorn the church. They have not abandoned hope of having the good Father return to this mission.

The alcaldes first question seeking news of the King of Spain evoked my interest, and during my conversations with him and several other Indians who spoke Spanish fluently and with a strong Castilian accent, I could readily understand the meaning of the colloquial phrase *muy castellanos*[61] so frequently used in California, and came to realize that Father Antonio had instilled in his neophytes some idea of politics, and of the fact that the Catholic king was their rightful sovereign. The natives also explained what unjust treatment they had received from the white men, how their live stock had been driven off,

---

[60]The Indians, who are in the habit of communicating with the captains of ships, call all strangers who appear to have a military or political character, captain. I did not consider it necessary, upon replying, to inform the chief that King Ferdinand was dead, and that a queen now governed Spain. (D. de M.).

[61]Muy castellanos: one who speaks the pure Castillian Spanish as distinguished from that of Mexico.

and how their private lands which they planned to cultivate had been taken over by the same race to graze cattle.

"You can see, captain," they remarked, "how miserable we now are; the Fathers cannot protect us, and those in power rob us. To stand by and watch these men take over the missions we have built, the herds we have tended, and to be exposed incessantly, together with our families, to the worst possible treatment and even death itself, is a tragedy! Would we be blamed if we defended ourselves, and returned to our tribes in the Tulares, taking with us all the live stock that could be led away?"

I advised the Indians to be patient and forced myself to inspire in them what was in reality false hope; yet at the bottom of my heart I could not fail to recognize that retaliation on the part of the Indians would be only just reparation for the cruel and arbitrary conduct of the white men.

When the missions were under the sole jurisdiction of the Fathers, the so-called *gente de razón* were restrained from mistreating the Indians. Only when their authority began to be usurped by civil power, did evidence of brutality toward the natives appear. The neophytes remember one of Father Peyri's sermons, in which the following passages occur:

"In this country there are two distinct races, the barbarians, and the semi-barbarians; the semi-barbarians are our poor Indians, the barbarians are the so-called *gente de razón,* who seem devoid of all reason." In fact these Indians displayed both docility and a willingness to work, whereas the white men spent their time gambling, drinking, and dissipating.

The Indian idea of vengeance is, moreover, excellent. They begin by stealing horses from the rancheros, aware that a Californian without a horse is unable to follow in pursuit, and as a result cattle can then be easily stolen and even white women carried away.

Mission San Juan Capistrano,[62] founded November 1, 1776, by the apostolic prefect, Father Junípero Serra, rises on a magnificent plain a league in from the sea on the bank of a small river that is never dry. Fairly good anchorage offshore from the winds that blow from east

---

[62]Named for St. John Capistran, born in 1385 at Sulmona, Italy. Bolton's **Palóu's New California** IV, 55-60, describes its foundation and gives the date as October 30. The fine stone church was begun in 1797 and completed in 1806. In 1812 this was severely damaged by an earthquake. For its history see Engelhardt, **San Juan Capistrano Mission** (Los Angeles, 1922).

to west is available.[63] The distance from there to San Luís Rey is 13 leagues, and to San Gabriel, 10 leagues toward the north. The road connecting these two missions is in good condition.

Mission San Juan Capistrano is now in ruins, despite the resistance made to its devastation by the Spanish Father, the Reverend José María de Zalvidea, a Biscayan.[64] In its prime this mission controlled some 2,000 Indians, 70,000 cattle, 2,000 horses, and more than 10,000 sheep. Harvest included 10,000 fanegas of grain, some olive oil, and 500 barrels of wine and brandy. Today only 100 Indians, 500 cattle, 150 horses, and not a single sheep remain. Harvests, too, have dwindled to 300 fanegas of grain, and 50 or 60 barrels of wine. Rancho del Agua Caliente,[65] lying 4 leagues east-northeast, is notable primarily for its spring of nitrate water. The extensive ranchos of Trabuco,[66] Ciénaga,[67] and San Mateo[68] have passed into private ownership. This mission, too, had its tanneries, and manufactured soap by using carbonate of potash, that rises to the surface of the ground. A Frenchman called Jenssens lives at the mission and conducts a small business.

Not far from the buildings stretch excellent grazing lands, but in certain low areas horses have been known to die if pastured there in the rainy season, a situation attesting to the presence of certain poisonous plants destroyed no doubt by drought.

Nine leagues north-northeast, on the road leading toward San Gabriel, a vast rancho resembling a miniature village is passed. This belongs to a Californian called Yorba, and was originally the Rancho de Santa Ana[69] owned by Mission San Gabriel. The vast property, im-

---

[63]Anchorage at San Juan Capistrano, California: 33° 27′ n. lat., 120° 1′ 24″ w. long. (D. de M.).

[64]Duflot de Mofras visited the mission in January 1842 and found it at the abyss of disintegration. José María Zalvidea, who came there from San Gabriel in 1826, was now a chronic invalid, lacking the necessities of life. See Engelhardt, San Juan p. 103, ff. and pp. 151-154.

[65]Rancho del Agua Caliente probably refers to the area in the vicinity of San Juan Capistrano Hot Springs.

[66]Trabuco was used by Santiago Argüello as a cattle run.

[67]Ciénaga de las Ranas had been similarly appropriated by José Sepúlveda.

[68]San Mateo, 3 leagues southeast of the mission, had been occupied by Agustín Jenssens, or Jansens, on behalf of Argüello, who hoped to acquire this holding. In February, 1841, the latter had been appointed majordomo of the mission.

[69]Rancho Santiago de Santa Ana had been granted in 1810 to the soldier Antonio Yorba and his nephew Juan Pablo Peralta. In 1825 the grant passed to his heirs, represented by Bernardo Yorba, under whom it became one of the richest properties in the state. See Terry Stevenson, Caminos Viejos (Santa Ana) 1930, p. 29ff., and the Orange County History Series, Vol. 2, 1932, passim, where a rare picture of the old ranch is reproduced as the frontispiece.

portant because of its fertility and the number of its live stock, lies along
the Santa Ana River that flows down into the sea. Rancho Santa Ana,
which is 7 leagues in from the sea, ships its products from the anchorage
at San Juan. On its lands graze 10,000 cattle, 1,500 horses, and 3,000
sheep. Approximately 300 persons, white men and Indians, comprise its
population. Four leagues before reaching San Gabriel, on the river
bearing the same name, a large rich rancho, El Coyote,[70] owned by the
Nieto family, is reached.

Mission San Gabriel Arcángel,[71] founded on September 8, 1771,[72]
by the Reverend Father Junípero Serra, is situated 18 leagues north of
San Juan Capistrano, 9 leagues east-southeast of San Fernando, 10
leagues in from the sea, 12 leagues from the port of San Pedro, and 4
leagues from El Pueblo de Nuestra Señora de Los Angeles. This mission, the largest and richest in the two Californias, lies at the foot of a
rugged, wooded mountain, in the center of a plain of vast extent on
the site of rancherías belonging to the Juyubit, Caguillas, and Sibapot
Indians.[73] The surrounding lands are noted for their fertility. The herds
at one time were so numerous that they were frequently forced to kill
off horses to conserve the pasturage for the cattle. In 1834, San Gabriel
then in its prime had 3,000 Indian neophytes and owned 150,000 cattle,
20,000 horses, and more than 40,000 sheep; while 20,000 fanegas of
grain, 500 barrels of wine and the same quantity of brandy were in
storage. Now only 500 Indians, 700 cattle, 500 horses, and 3,500 sheep
survive.[74]

---

[70]El Coyote, or Los Coyotes, 10 leagues in extent, was a portion of the large
grant made to Manuel Nieto in 1784, to which, in 1834, Juan José Nieto fell
heir. See **Pioneer Notes from the Diaries of Judge Benjamin Hayes,** edited by
Marjorie Tisdale Wolcott (Los Angeles, 1929), p. 110. See infra, I, 187, **note 111.**

[71]For its history see Zephyrin Engelhardt, **San Gabriel Mission** (San Gabriel,
1927). For the Indians assembled at San Gabriel and San Juan Capistrano see
Gerónimo Boscana, **Chinigchinich,** edited by Phil Townsend Hanna (Santa Ana,
1933).

[72]The first chapel at San Gabriel was built about 5 miles southeast of the
site of the present edifice. Bolton's **Palóu,** II, 321-328, describes its humble origin.
San Gabriel subsequently became the hub of the South and the rendezvous for
emigrants from Mexico and the United States. Its holdings stretched from the
mountains to the sea, affording vast cattle ranges and rich fields for agricultural
purposes.

[73]These obscure Indian settlements have various names. Juyubit appears
also as Jupibit, or Juiubit; Caguillas, according to Hodge, is Cahuilla; Sibapot
appears as Sibapet, or Toyipet. For their history see Hugo Reid, **The Indians of
Los Angeles County** (Los Angeles, 1926), and the notes by J. P. Harrington in
Boscana, **Chinigchinich.**

[74]Mission statistics disclose that prosperity reached its peak between 1828
and 1832. In the latter year, the last recorded in Engelhardt, San Gabriel had

To the Reverend Father Zalvidea, who has already been mentioned, San Gabriel owes the introduction of the grapevine. Originally 70,000 cuttings,[75] were set out and this won for him in this region the sobriquet of "Father of the seventy thousand vines"—*el padre de las setenta mil cepas*.

Near the mission are some fine groups of palms and, adjoining them, three extensive vineyards covering nearly 200,000 cuttings, four thriving orchards and vegetable gardens, an extensive grove of olive trees and another with 400 orange trees. The vineyards, gardens, and orchards are enclosed by impenetrable fences or hedges of opuntia,[76] or the barberry fig tree. The Reverend Father Zalvidea[77] at one time negotiated with an American firm[78] for some iron fencing to enclose his vines, and was about to place an order when secularization took place. This Father was famous for his initiative; once a year he sent a shipload of oil, hemp, and flax to San Blas; at other times he prepared cargoes of soap or tallow for shipment to Lima. The number of hides furnished annually by this mission varied between 30,000 and 35,000. Near this mission a stream, the San Gabriel River, that flows down into the sea and a lake large enough to be valuable for irrigation, may be seen. Two gristmills, a mechanical sawmill, large shops, wine presses, stills, spinning mills, looms suitable for weaving wool, cotton, hemp, and flax fabrics, tanneries, and soap works were at one time in operation at the mission.

The mission owned a total of seventeen ranchos for raising large animals such as cattle and horses, and fifteen ranchos for smaller animals such as sheep, goats, and pigs. Twelve hundred yoke of oxen were used

---

16,500 cattle, 1,200 horses, and 8,500 sheep. Neophytes were 1,320 in number. Crops fell as low as 500 fanegas. Of Duflot de Mofras, Engelhardt writes, "Although his figures on the wealth of other missions are extravagant enough, concerning mission San Gabriel, he surpassed himself in exaggerating the situation in the district which included San Gabriel and Los Angeles at the time of the confiscation. For this latter description he had, of course, to rely upon the veracity of the territorial officials. These endeavored to paint the missions as large plantations where agriculture and live stock raising were carried on under the management of priests for whom the Indians had to labor without receiving anything more than food and clothing."—**San Gabriel,** p. 197.

---

[75]To San Gabriel are attributed 3,000 rather than 70,000 vines. One was called the Vina Madre, or mother-vine of California. A portion of this old vine may be seen today at San Gabriel.

[76]Opuntia: One of the genus of cactaceous plants usually known as the prickly pear whose fruits are edible.

[77]For Zalvieda see **supra,** I, 180.

[78]Probably through a member of the Ashley party.

for plowing. On the great Rancho San Bernardino,[79] which lies 16 leagues
east toward the mountains, there were originally a church, a priest, and
200 Indians. The mountains supply juniper, oak, walnut, and superb
pine, as well as hot sulphur springs and other mineral waters. San Bernardino is now privately owned and runs 2,000 cattle and 300 horses.
The most important ranchos are: Mission Vieja[80] and La Puente[81] in
the south; Santa Anita[82] in the north; Azusa,[83] La Brea,[84] San Antonio[85]
in the northeast; San José,[86] El Chino,[87] Cucamonga,[88] Jurupa,[89] Agua
Caliente,[90] Jesapita,[91] and San Bernardino in the east; and, 26 leagues
further east, San Gorgonio.[92]

Surrounded by such prosperity the Indians were naturally happy,
well fed, and well clad. In one of the reception rooms at the mission
were two enormous chests that contained, only a few years ago, more
than 100,000 piasters[93] in currency. Frequently the Fathers kept 200,000

---

[79]San Bernardino was a cattle rancho 8 square leagues in extent. On it
buildings, however, were erected for the majordomo and his family; these stood
between the modern town of Redlands and Redlands Junction. While never an
asistencia, or auxiliary church, Mass was often held here by a visiting Father. In
1842 this property passed to José del Carmen Lugo and his son, remaining in this
family until sold in 1851 to the Mormons.

[80]Mission Viejo, or Merced, of one league, owned by F. P. E. Temple and
Juan Matias Sánchez.

[81]Puente, the property of John Rowland and Julian Workman. This contained over 48,000 acres.

[82]Santa Anita, a grant of 3 leagues, was owned by Hugo Reid, although
claimed by Henry Dalton.

[83]Apparently the 6,500 acre grant of Andrés Duarte, although a second Rancho
Azusa was held by Henry Dalton in what is now San Bernardino County.

[84]Rincon de la Brea, owned by Gil Ibarra, under grant of February 23, 1841,
by Juan B. Alvarado. It contained 4,452 acres.

[85]This was now the property of Antonio Lugo, but was granted in 1810 to
the Lugo family by Governor Argüello. It contained 29,514 acres, and was one
of the great ranchos of the South.

[86]San José, 2 square leagues in extent, was held by Ignacio Palomares, to
whom it had been granted in 1837 by Governor Alvarado.

[87]Santa Ana del Chino, 5 square leagues, was owned by Antonio María
Lugo. A second grant of the same name, of 3 leagues, adjoining the former,
was held by Isaac Williams.

[88]This grant of 3 square leagues was made in 1839 by Governor Alvarado to
Tiburcio Tapia.

[89]Jurupa, 7 square leagues in extent, granted in 1838 to Juan Bandini.

[90]Alamos y Agua Caliente, 6 square leagues, was held by Agustín Olvera,
and claimed subsequently by Francisco López.

[91]Possibly an old Indian settlement. Ogden Hoffman, **Report of Land Cases**,
(San Francisco, 1862), does not mention this ranch.

[92]Usually known as San Jacinto y San Gorgonio, claimed by Louis Roubidoux.
The town of Beaumont now occupies a portion of this grant.

[93]The amount of currency on hand appears to be considerably exaggerated.
Engelhardt, **San Gabriel**, p. 199, **note**, says that there was not that much money
in all California. Hides were the common medium of exchange, not silver.

francs' worth of European merchandise in their storerooms. All this was confiscated by the civil administrators; lands within a few feet of the mission have been given away, and on these several Englishmen and Americans have already erected houses.[94] Only two ranchos still belong to the mission. What little protection is now afforded the Indians results from the efforts of the youngest and most active of the Spanish Franciscans, Father Tomás Esténega,[95] of Viscaye (Spain).

Upon visiting him one day, I found him out in the fields working at a large table; his robe was turned inside out, his sleeves were rolled up, and he was kneading clay, teaching the neophytes who flocked about how to make bricks. As soon as he saw me in the distance, he waved his hand and called out: *"Amigo! con este familia, Consilio Manuque!"*[96]

By order of the governor of California, Don Felipe de Neve, El Pueblo de Nuestra Señora de la Reyna de los Angeles (city of Our Lady of the Angels)[97] was founded in the latter part of December, 1781, by Spanish colonists sent up from Sonora. The village is situated on the bank of the Porciúncula, or Los Angeles River, on a vast plain covered with trees, olive groves, orchards, and extensive vineyards, and lies some 4 leagues southwest of Mission San Gabriel, 9 southeast of that of San Fernando, and 10 leagues from the port of San Pedro. With a population of 1,200, this is the most thickly settled area in California. Americans are in the majority; among them Juan Temple and especially Abel Stearns, who is extremely rich, are the leading citizens. Several Frenchmen have married, settled here, and become successful vineyardists, notably Mm. Bouchet,[98] Giraudeau,[99] Saint-Sevain,[100] and M. Vignes[101]

---

[94]In November, 1841, a group of immigrants from New Mexico, led by Rowland and Workman reached San Gabriel; several of them acquired lands near the mission.

[95]Father Tomás Eleuterio Esténega came to America from Spain in 1810. After studying at the College of San Fernando, in 1820 he was sent to Monterey. Having served at San Miguel, San Francisco, and San Rafael, he came to San Gabriel in 1833, where he remained almost unassisted until 1846, the year of his death.

[96]"My friend, with such a family, wisdom and strength [are needed]."

[97]The date of the foundation of Our Lady, Queen of the Angels, has not been clearly established, although September 4, 1781, is generally accepted as her natal day. See **Publications of Historical Society of Southern California Vol. XV,** (1931), **passim.** For contemporary accounts see the records of Simpson, **op. cit.,** I, 402.

[98]Louis Bouchet, also known as Bauchett, or Bouchette was a French cooper who came to Monterey in 1828, later settling at Los Angeles, where he owned a large vineyard.

[99]The name of Giraudeau does not appear in contemporary records of this

of Bordelaise.[102] The latter, on behalf of the French colony, sent a barrel of Californian wine to us to deliver to the king, while the Reverend Father Tomás donated another for M. le Maréchal, the Duke of Dalmatia, who had protected his monastery during the Spanish war. These two gifts, after traveling safely from California to Mazatlán and from there to Hamburg, where they were to be put aboard a ship for France, were destroyed by fire in the docks at Hamburg, while in storage in the warehouse.

During his exile from the Sandwich Islands, Father Bachelot served as a priest at El Pueblo, where he formed many pleasant associations.

Caravans travel once a year from New Mexico to Los Angeles. These consist of 200 men on horseback, accompanied by mules laden with fabrics and large woolen covers called *serapes*, *jerzas*, and *cobertones*, which are valued at 3 to 5 piasters each. This merchandise is exchanged for horses and mules, on a basis, usually, of two blankets for one animal. Caravans leave Santa Fe, New Mexico, in October, before the snows set in, travel west, cut through the Sierra Nevada, descend south of the Navajo River, pass the missions destroyed by the Moqui, Apache, and Yuman Indians, cross the Colorado River near the thirty-fourth parallel, travel across the Sierra Nevada, the Tulare Valley, and the Californian Mountains, and finally reach the outlying ranchos of California from where the trail leads into El Pueblo de los Angeles. This trip consumes two and one-half months. Returning caravans leave California in April in order to cross the rivers before the snow melts, taking with them about 2,000 horses.

The expedition that reached El Pueblo[103] in November, 1841, included

---

period and may possibly refer to Raumereau, a local French resident.

[100]Pierre Saint-Sevain or Sainsevain was the nephew of Vignes and came to California in 1839 to assist his uncle with his vineyards. In 1855 he purchased some of these same holdings.

[101]Louis Vignes (1771-1862) came to California from Honolulu, probably in 1831, on the **Louisa,** and in 1832 settled in Los Angeles where he became a pioneer wine merchant and owner of the largest vineyard in California. His house stood on Aliso Street near Alameda. Vignes was among the most prominent of the early settlers. Levy, **Les Premiers Français en California** (San Francisco, 1884), p. 64, and **An Illustrated History of Los Angeles County** (Chicago, 1887), p. 130.

---

[102]Many other Frenchmen were already in the south.

The census of 1836 lists the following Frenchmen in Los Angeles: Victor Prudhomme, Charles Baric, Jean Mayen, Joseph Feviru, Louis Tolmayes, or Tolmayr, Jean L. Braun, Pierre Raumereau. See **Le Guide Français,** edited by Fernand Loyer and Charles Beaudreau (Los Angeles, 1932), p. 20.

[103]Los Angeles was usually termed "El Pueblo."

in addition to some 200 New Mexicans, 60 or more North Americans.[104] About the same time 40 of these adventurers who had left the main train reached the village of San José de Guadalupe in the north. In January, 1842, several more of these same trappers appeared, with the announcement that in the near future a large number of emigrants would follow. This latest indication of invasion merits the closest consideration.

The pueblo of Los Angeles is extremely rich, for the spoils from the neighboring missions have fallen into the hands of the local inhabitants; and within an area of 15 or 20 square leagues, local residents own over 80,000 cattle, 25,000 horses, and 10,000 sheep. Vineyards yield 600 barrels of wine, and an equal amount of brandy; grains, however, contribute less than 3,000 fanegas. This light harvest arises from the lazy habits of the settlers, who are disinclined to work. All labor in El Pueblo is done by Indians recruited from a small ranchería on the banks of the river on the outskirts of the village. These poor wretches are often mistreated, and do not always receive in full their daily pay, which is fixed at one real in money and one real in merchandise, in other words, one-fourth piaster. El Pueblo has in addition sixty *huertas,* or gardens, planted out to vines that cover an area roughly estimated at 100 hectares. Some soap, too, is manufactured locally, and a tannery is in operation. All commerce is carried on by foreigners.

One of our countrymen, M Charles Baric,[105] a man who, because of his intelligence and knowledge of this country was able to render us invaluable services, has been a trader throughout the country, but has of late been exploiting a mine of virgin gold ore which he discovered at Rancho San Francisquito, 6 leagues toward the mountains beyond Mission San Fernando and 15 leagues from Los Angeles. This vein extends 6 leagues, following the direction of the ravine in which it is located. The ore is found close to the surface of the ground, and some few specimens weigh from two to three ounces. These are valued, out in this country, at 14 piasters an ounce, payable in species, or 16 piasters in merchandise. At Rancho Cahuenga, 2 leagues northwest of

---

[104]This was the Workman and Rowland party—whose numbers are exaggerated—the advance-guard of the American overland movement. The group that reached San José was known as the Bartleson party. See Bancroft, **California,** IV, 276-278. See also **infra,** I, 184, **note** 94.

[105]Charles Baric came to California in 1834 with the Padrés and Hijar colony, and resided for ten years at Los Angeles. Gold was discovered locally, however, long before his day, and since 1834 placers had been worked by Francisco López. See W. W. Jenkins, "History of the Development of Placer Mining in California," in **Annual Publications of the Historical Society of Southern California.** Vol. VII (1906-7-8), p. 71.

El Pueblo, a mineral deposit of silver ore exists, but this has not been exploited for lack of mercury and capable miners. The Indians often bring bits of native copper, fragments of opals, and specimens of sulphureted lead down from the mountains.

Two leagues toward the southeast, on a vast prairie, four large deposits of asphalt[106] have been located that spread over the surface of the ground. Among these areas are interspersed pools of cold water that lower the temperature of the bitumen. Although this water has a distinct mineral flavor, yet this does not prevent its use by animals. At sunrise these springs are coated with heavy deposits of asphalt, often a meter high, resembling great soap bubbles. As the air grows warm, the gas in these balls expands and the bubbles finally burst with a loud report. The inhabitants collect the solidified asphalt and use it to plaster the roofs of their houses which are made of reeds or planks. Ships also transport bitumen to various points in the country. The substance, however, is readily melted in the sun and, collecting under the roof, finally drips down through the ceiling. Houses thus roofed demand constant attention, but this is not costly, for the springs are used by each individual as the need arises.

The names of the leading ranchos around Los Angeles are: Los Alamitos,[107] Los Cerritos,[108] Los Domínguez,[109] San Pedro,[110] Los Coyotes,[111] La Bolsa Grande, La Bolsa Chiquita,[112] Palos Verdes,[113] Javonería,[114] Los Cuervos,[115] La Laguna,[116] Serrano,[117] Verdugo,[118] Feliz,[119] La

---

[106]These deposits from which many skeletons of prehistoric monsters have since been taken, are still visible near La Brea and Wilshire Boulevards, Los Angeles.

[107]Los Alamitos, originally owned by the Nieto family, had been sold in 1835 to Governor Alvarado.

[108]Los Cerritos of 27,000 acres, granted to Manuel Nieto, was claimed by Juan Temple.

[109]Los Domínguez was granted in 1784 to Juan José Domínguez and still held by the family.

[110]San Pedro was the name subsequently given to the Domínguez Ranch.

[111]Los Coyotes, 56,000 acres, was held by Juan José Nieto, but claimed by José Pico.

[112]La Bolsa grande y chiquita, of 7 leagues, was now occupied by the Ruíz family.

[113]Palos Verdes, 31,000 acres, was owned by José Sepúlveda.

[114]La Javonería probably refers to the central portion of Rancho San Antonio, owned by Antonio María Lugo.

[115]Los Cuervos, or Tajuata, belonged to Anastasio Ávila.

[116]La Laguna, apparently the upper portion of Lugo's San Antonio.

[117]Serrano was Cañada de los Alisos, a grant of 2 square leagues owned by José Serrano.

[118]El Verdugo, granted in 1784 to Don José María Verdugo, was 8 square leagues.

[119]Los Feliz was owned by María Ignacio Verdugo.

Bayona,[120] San Vicente,[121] Rodeo de las Aguas,[122] Sauzal Redondo,[123] Arroyo Hondo,[124] and La Rosa de Castilla,[125] 2 leagues from Los Angeles, where a mill belonging to two Americans is situated. M. Saint Sevain has also erected a fine mill, and a mechanical sawmill on a small stream of water.

El Pueblo supports a church, where a Father from San Gabriel holds services, and a small private school which is in charge of a woman. Local government is limited to a prefect and two justices of the peace, or alcaldes. In the plaza stands a decrepit iron cannon that has been abandoned, but is often used for public celebrations. Until the recent arrival of General Micheltorena, who has made this his temporary residence, the village had neither militia nor soldiers.

The citizens of Los Angeles, envious of the supremacy of Monterey, have made several attempts to change the capital to El Pueblo, and during all the revolutions that have swept the country have played leading rôles. Many foreigners, especially Americans, reside in Los Angeles.[126] Frenchmen and their families, however, do not exceed in all 40 persons; they make model citizens, however, being held in high esteem by the community.

The Mission of San Fernando Rey de España, founded September 8, 1797,[127] lies 9 leagues west quarter-northwest of San Gabriel, 7 leagues from El Pueblo, and 14 leagues from the port of San Pedro. At one time 1,500 Indians were connected with the mission, which controlled, in 1838, 14,000 cattle, 5,000 horses, and 7,000 sheep. A harvest of 8,000 fanegas of grain, and 200 barrels of wines and brandies, was put in the warehouses. Now only 400 Indians, 1,500 cattle, 400 horses, and 2,000 sheep remain. Through the untiring efforts of its Spanish missionary,

---

[120]Bayona [Ballona], 13,919 acres, had been granted in 1839 to Agustín Machado.

[121]San Vicente y Santa Monica, 30,259 acres, was granted in 1839 to Francisco Sepúlveda.

[122]Rodeo de las Aguas, of 4,449 acres, was held by M. R. Váldez.

[123]Sausal Redondo, 5 square leagues, had been granted in 1837 to Antonio Ignacio Ávila.

[124]Arroyo Hondo may be the north part of the Cerritos.

[125]La Rosa de Castilla, a small ranch north of the pueblo grant of Los Angeles, granted in 1831 to Juan Ballesteros.

[126]"El Pueblo de Nuestra Señora," according to a contemporary traveler, "has a population of 1,500 souls and is the noted abode of the lowest drunkards and gamblers in the country." George Simpson, op. cit., I, 402.

[127]The first buildings were completed in 1798, and subsequently enlarged to the present fine structure. The Indian village lay west of the mission. De Mofras' estimate of mission wealth is again too high. For its history see Zephyrin Engelhardt, San Fernando Rey (Chicago, 1927).

Father Blas Ordáz[128] of Castile, this establishment has been fairly well preserved. The mission, which stands at the foot of the Sierra, controls rich pasture lands and timber suitable for construction. Among its most extensive ranchos are Las Virgenes,[129] La Amarga,[130] Cahuenga,[131] and San Francisquito,[132] on which gold and silver, as already indicated, were discovered.

Near San Fernando a spacious gorge cuts through the Sierra, forming an entrance into a vast plain that reaches as far north as the San Joaquin and Sacramento rivers. The plain, which is broken only by a few gentle undulations, extends from north to south and is about 150 leagues long, and 10, 15, and, in places, 20 leagues wide. This valley is inhabited by barbarous tribes and a few Indians who have deserted the missions. The soil, watered by many streams and heavily wooded, is of extraordinary fertility. Specimens brought in by the Indians indicate that the mountains are rich in several kinds of mineral ore. Innumerable bear, deer, elk, and wild horses roam freely over these broad prairies.

The port of San Pedro is situated 14 leagues from Mission San Fernando, 12 from that of San Gabriel, and 10 from El Pueblo de los Angeles. This anchorage should not be termed a port, for it is merely a large bay with a mouth that measures about 15 miles from point to point. Only one store, or hide warehouse belonging to Mr. Stearns, has been erected at the port. The Lugo Rancho lies half a league away.[133] The anchorage is good only in the summer season, for the bay is open to the prevailing northwesterly winds. However, if the sea is rough, anchor must be cast a mile or two offshore. One-half mile off the coast the depth varies from 4 to 5 fathoms, and affords a sandy bottom and firm anchorage, with Point San Pedro on the northwest, a small island on the east, and the center of Santa Catalina Island on the south. At the head of the bay a large lagoon stretching inland is visible and

---

[128]Blas Ordáz was a Spaniard who came to California in 1820. After serving at several missions, from 1833 to 1838 he resided at Buenaventura. He died in 1850 at San Gabriel.

[129]Las Virgenes, granted in 1837 to J. M. Domínguez and Antonio Machado.

[130]La Amarga, apparently one of the ranches of Mission San Fernando.

[131]The Cahuenga, of 6 leagues, was in control of J. Y. Limantour.

[132]A portion of the vast ranch of 22 square leagues granted in 1819 to Antonio del Valle, who sold a part of it to Jacob Feliz.

[133]The Lugo property, known as Rancho San Antonio, contained nearly 30,000 acres and stretched from San Pedro to the San Bernardino Mountains. See supra, I, 183, note 85.

might be navigable by vessels drawing 8 feet of water, if the entrance now obstructed by a small sandbank were excavated.

Commercially San Pedro is of considerable importance.[134] Through its harbor arrive and depart not only all merchandise destined for Los Angeles, the missions, the ranchos of San Fernando and San Gabriel, but also what they export. Three thousand hides are shipped annually. In 1834, from 100,000 to 120,000 hides and 2,500 quintals of tallow were exported. In addition, ships usually take on cargoes of soap. Wine, at El Pueblo, sells for 20 piasters and brandy for 50 piasters for a barrel containing 90 bottles; and soap for 2½ piasters an arroba, or 10 piasters a hundredweight.

Off the coast of San Pedro, 20 miles toward the south, lies Santa Catalina, an island 6 miles in length from east to west and 3 in width. This land is so lofty and has so deep a depression in the center that from afar the appearance is that of two separate islands. Twenty miles south of Santa Catalina is a second island, Clemente, discovered in 1542 by Cabrillo.[135] The latter is somewhat loftier and larger than the former island and extends in a northerly and southerly direction. Ten leagues farther west, on the same parallel as Santa Catalina, rises the small island of Santa Bárbara. Off in the same direction and approximately the same distance west is San Niscolás, where, in 1602, Vizcaíno landed.[136] Both are 16 leagues distant from Point Conversion[137] over on the mainland. A few miles northwest of San Nicolás towers an isolated rock; the passage, however, is open between the two islands.

The Santa Bárbara channel is formed by the shoreline stretching from Point Concepción to Point Conversion, and the four islands of Santo Tomás or Anacapa, Santa Cruz, San Miguel, or Santa Rosa, and San Bernardo,[138] where Rodríguez Cabrillo is buried.[139] It was this fearless navigator who, in 1542, discovered all these islands and a large part of the coast. Eight miles west of San Bernardo appears a small group of rocks known as El Farallon de Lobos.[140] A route between these islands is open and safe on all sides. The majority have good anchorages, with

---

[134]Port San Pedro: 33° 43′ n. lat.; 120° 34′ w. long. (D. de M.).

[135]Cabrillo reached the islands on October 7, 1542, naming them Victoria and San Salvador for his vessels. See **supra**, I, 51-52.

[136]Probably named by Vizcaíno's expedition on December 6, 1602. See Wagner, **Spanish Voyages**, pp. 240, 403.

[137]What the Spaniards called Punta de la Conversion is now Point Mugu.

[138]San Bernardo: San Miguel Island.

[139]Cabrillo's grave is believed to be at Cuyler's Harbor on the northeast end of the island of San Miguel, originally known as San Bernardo.

[140]El Farallon de Lobos: Now called Richardson Rock.

wood and water. Of these the best are at Santa Catalina, especially on the west side near the center of the depression where ships from Boston frequently come to salt down their hides, on the northwest side of San Miguel, and on the east at San Clemente. At one time Indians inhabited these islands, but within the last few years they have withdrawn to the mainland to avoid abuse at the hands of American sailors and other foreigners who came over to hunt sea otter and fur seals. A few Indians, however, go to San Clemente, and bring back bits of kaolin or sulphate of iron.

Santa Cruz Island, the largest of this group, is not more than 10 miles from the moorings at Santa Bárbara. This island, which has an area of 20 leagues, has a good harbor and a small river on its west side. An unsuccessful attempt made by the government at Monterey to colonize Santa Cruz[141] has already been mentioned. This island[142] has recently come into the possession of a Spanish merchant, Don Antonio Aguirre,[143] of Santa Bárbara, who intends to breed live stock, since the pasturage is excellent. Trading vessels carry on an extensive contraband trade with these islands, which are often used as places of trans-shipment.

Along the Santa Bárbara Channel the current comes down from the north and skirts the coast. Asphalt deposits emptying into the sea spread over the surface of the water a black oily covering which is visible from afar and gives off a bituminous odor from a distance of several leagues. With the exception of the Farallon Islands, which are situated opposite the entrance to the Bay of San Francisco, and which will be described in conjunction with that magnificent port, there are no other islands along the coast.

Mission San Buenaventura, which was founded on March 31, 1772 [1782][144] by the Reverend Father Junípero Serra, is situated 10 leagues

---

[141]See supra I, 151.

[142]Santa Cruz Island was owned not by Aguirre, but by Andrés Castillero, to whom, on May 22, 1839, its 60,000 acres has been granted by Juan B. Alvarado. Castillero was a Mexican captain, a prominent politician, and a friend of Governor Chico. He was also the discoverer of the Almadén mine. See Ogden Hoffman, **Report of Land Cases**, Appendix, p. 25.

[143]José Antonio Aguirre was one of the most prominent merchants of that day, carrying on trade with Manila, Canton, and Mexico. At this time Aguirre, who had married a member of the Estudillo family, owned the finest residence in Santa Bárbara. Long a landmark on Carrillo Street, it is now demolished.

[144]De Mofras is in error regarding the date of its foundation, which was March 31, 1782. By 1800 granaries and a church had been constructed. In 1809 the new church was completed and a chapel called Santa Gertrudis established at Casitas. The present building is in excellent condition, being used regularly for services. See Engelhardt, **San Buenaventura** (Santa Barbara, 1930).

west of San Fernando,[145] 10 leagues southeast of Santa Bárbara, and a
mile back from the shore. Here, in 1834, lived 1,100 neophytes. At this
time, 4,000 cattle, 1,000 horses, and 6,000 sheep roamed their lands,
while the harvest yielded 2,500 fanegas of grain.[146] Now only 300 Indians
and about 1,000 head of live stock, large and small, remain. There is no
longer a missionary in residence. The last Spanish Father, Ventura
Fortuny,[147] has just died and church services are held from time to time
by one of two Franciscan Fathers from Mission Santa Bárbara. San
Buenaventura is pleasantly situated near a small stream bearing the
same name, and its vast fields are still watered by the Santa Clara River
that enters the sea several miles south, near Point Conversion. When
the weather is fair ships can anchor in a small cove 2 miles from the
mission in 5 to 8 fathoms of water. The ranchos of Simi[148] and Conejo[149]
have been given away. The gardens and orchards which are usually fertile, are filled with bananas, oranges, and palms; but in the absence of
a Father no benefits are derived from these fine properties. The mission
buildings are in a deplorable condition, for the rancheros have even
removed portions of these structures.

En route from San Fernando to San Buenaventura the San Fernando mountains with their picturesque rocks and wooded areas are
crossed. At the foot of the eastern slope of this miniature chain of mountains that requires three hours to pass, a green plain extends for a distance of 15 leagues. On this plain several ranchos, including the rich
property of Simi, are situated.

The San Buenaventura Indians are renowned throughout California
for their skill at basketry.[150] Their products, made from rushes and
brilliant feathers, are finely woven and also water-tight. However, these
are now difficult to procure, for the majority of the more dexterous
Indians have returned to their own tribes. From San Buenaventura to

---

[145]Mission San Fernando was approximately 23 leagues from San Buenaventura.

[146]Mission statistics for 1834 disclose 4,500 cattle, 2,800 sheep, and 340 horses,
and a total harvest of 1,950 fanegas.

[147]Buenaventura Fortuny, as he is usually known, came to California from
Spain in 1806, serving at the northern missions until 1837. He died on December
16, 1840, at Santa Bárbara.

[148]Simi, or San José de Gracia, a property of 92,000 acres, was granted in
1795 to Patricio Javier and Manuel Pico by Governor Borica and later to de la
Guerra.

[149]The Conejo which was granted to Captain José de la Guerra y Noriega of
Santa Bárbara, in 1822, contained 48,000 acres.

[150]An excellent exhibit of local Indian basketry is now housed in the Santa
Bárbara Museum of Natural History. For the history of these Indians see David
B. Rogers, **Prehistoric Man of the Santa Bárbara Coast** (Santa Bárbara, 1929).

Santa Bárbara, the trip of 10 leagues can be made by *carreta* along the coast. In certain localities the cliffs are worn off perpendicularly, exposing strata of brilliant slate in various tints of yellow.

By the sea approach the anchorage at Santa Bárbara is not difficult to recognize.[151] The crest of the chain of mountains paralleling the sea flattens out as it comes down from the north, then drops abruptly, forming a large gap for some 4 miles, which rises sharply toward the south and forms several rugged peaks. The central anchorage resembles that of Santa Cruz Island. By the land approach the façade and two belfries of the mission, situated a league from the shore, are visible. The large sheds used for hides guide ships to anchorage. Anchorage is safe within a mile of the shore, where the depth varies from 7 to 8 fathoms. Here the bed of the sea, which is of hard sand and covered with large masses of seaweed, affords firm anchorage.

The small point on which was once situated the ancient Spanish battery, which is now razed, protects ships on the northwest end, but when passing around this point, which terminates in hidden rocks over which the sea breaks, ships should keep at a safe distance. Frequently the landing at Santa Bárbara proves dangerous; at times the canoes capsize, for at this port there is usually a heavy surf. Provisions may be procured, but wood and water are scarce.

Near the shore only a few wooden shacks have been erected. The presidio and neighboring village are situated a mile back from the sea on a plain that slopes almost imperceptibly toward the mountains. From careful observations the fact has been established, however, that the ground around the presidio is a few feet below sea level, a condition which might entail grave inconveniences should this locality experience a severe earthquake. Near the mission, which stands a league back from the shore, the land rises gently, the chapel being four meters above sea level.

The presidio, which was founded in 1780, [1782],[152] is in ruins. Only a few sections of adobe walls are now standing; the jails, too, have

---

[151]Port of Santa Bárbara: 34° 24′ 40″ n. lat.; 122° 30′ 30″ w. long.; Time: 8h 9m 22s. (D. de M.).

[152]The founding of the presidio of Santa Bárbara was celebrated by Mass on April 29, 1782. Local Indians who received food and gifts aided Spanish soldiers to construct a small palisade which stood on a slight knoll bounded by Figueroa, Cañon Perdido, Garden and Anacapa streets. By 1790 a substantial structure of adobes, 330 feet square, was constructed. One or two of the original presidio buildings are still standing. The name Santa Bárbara is that of a virgin and martyr of Asia Minor, believed to have been the daughter of a pagan, Dioscoro, who tortured her for her adherence to Christianity. She is the patron saint of artillerymen in the Spanish army.

crumbled, and the chapel alone has escaped destruction. The Rancho del Rey, or royal rancho, belonging to the presidio, has been given to Captain Noriega,[153] in recognition of his long years of service.

There are, however, several fairly substantial houses in the village. The white population numbers 800,[154] the majority of these citizens being rancheros. Trade is conducted wholly by foreigners. Englishmen, however, are more numerous than Americans. Of the two Frenchmen who reside here only one is an agriculturalist, and the other, M. Ardisson,[155] a merchant. Authority at Santa Bárbara is vested solely in a sub-prefect, and an alcalde, or justice of the peace. At the presidio remain one four-pounder and two bronze eight-pounders, while a garrison of 15 soldiers and 5 officers, most of whom are native Californians, have been retained. This settlement, because of its geographical situation, plays an important part in the internal affairs of the land. By holding the balance of control between Los Angeles and Monterey, this pueblo has always been a decisive factor in revolutions. Even today Santa Bárbara still retains many traces of the firm precepts of religion and order that have descended from the days of royal Spanish rule. This may be attributed to the presence here of three Spaniards who exert a profound influence throughout California, the Reverend Father Narciso Duran,[156] president and apostolic prefect of the southern missions; Don José Noriega, former captain of the presidio, and Don Antonio Aguirre, the most prosperous merchant in the country, a man with whom nearly all the local residents have mutual interests. These three leading citizens, who are united by a close friendship, are the leaders of the so-called Spanish party, which has already been mentioned in its bearing on Mexico.

The mission of Santa Bárbara, founded December 4, 1786,[157] is situated a league from the sea and 2 kilometers from the village at the foot of a chain of arid mountains that protect it against northerly

---

[153]José de la Guerra y Noriega was a Spanish captain who came to Santa Bárbara about 1800 as **comandante**. He acquired immense wealth, including Las Positas, Callegua, El Cajon, San Julián, and Simi ranchos, estimated at 200,000 acres. See Bancroft, **California**, III, 650-651.

[154]The contemporary traveler, Sir George Simpson, places the population at 900, and refers to the fine residences, erected at a cost of $6,000 and their luxurious furnishings op. cit., I, 379-401.

[155]Estéban Ardisson, who came to Santa Bárbara about 1840.

[156]Duran: See infra, I, 222, note 72.

[157]The formal founding of the mission, which is still used for services, took place on December 16, 1786, although the fourth, the fête-day of Saint Bárbara, is usually celebrated as its birthday. Father Engelhardt resided for many years at this mission. See his **Mission Santa Bárbara** (San Francisco, 1923), pp. 52-53.

and easterly breezes. The edifice is constructed in a symmetrical manner; the cloister which is formed by arcades, and the church which has two fine towers, are built of shaped stone. The gardens and orchards are extensive and have an ample supply of water. On the mission grounds is a large fountain whose waters, brought down from the mountains, are used to turn a staunch mill. Up in the mountains are calcareous shell deposits which are used for building. This mission, confined as it is between the mountains and the sea, owns only a small amount of land suitable for agriculture, and so has never developed to any considerable extent. In 1834 this mission had 1,200 Indian neophytes, 5,000 cattle, 1,200 horses, 5,000 sheep, and harvested 3,000 fanegas of grain. Now only 400 Indians, 1,800 cattle, 160 horses, and 400 sheep remain.[158] Mission Santa Bárbara is the residence of the apostolic prefect, Father Narciso Duran, and Father Antonio Ximénez,[159] a Mexican from the College of San Fernando. This Father, who is still young, holds services at the missions of San Buenaventura and La Purísima Concepción, which are without resident priests.

The following incident, which should be cited at this time, will reveal the widespread power of the French Catholics. Upon their arrival, Fathers Bachelot and Short were welcomed like brothers; and to the former, because of his ecclesiastical record—Father Duran had always kept in touch with our missionaries in the Sandwich Islands—was entrusted the parish of Los Angeles. The successive expeditions of the *Vénus,* the *Artémise,* and the *Danaïde* gave the Franciscans and the inhabitants of California a high opinion of France for sending out three frigates to protect one member of its clergy.

Father Duran learned from us of the arrival at the Sandwich Islands of Monseigneur, Bishop of Nilopolis, and of the active part he was taking in the efforts made by the Association for the Propagation of the Faith to sustain remote missions. The president delivered a sermon in Santa Bárbara which he sent in the form of a pastoral letter to be read in the churches urging the faithful to assist in this work by making an annual contribution of one piaster. Within a short time in Santa Bárbara alone he had actually collected 300 piasters, and early last year the same amount was sent by Don Antonio Aguirre, through his correspondent at Lima, to the treasurer of the Association at Lyon. Thus

---

[158]Mission statistics of 1834 should read: 556 neophytes, 3,400 cattle, 340 horses, 2,614 sheep, and 2,473 fanegas of grain.

[159]Not Ximénez but Antonio Jimeno who came to California in 1828, reaching Santa Bárbara a year later. Here he remained until 1858.

within twelve months the village of Santa Bárbara, which is not even known in Europe, has remitted to France the sum of 6,000 francs to carry on the work of the faith. This small settlement has fewer than 800 inhabitants, and yet how many towns in France with a population in excess of 8,000 makes the same yearly contributions! There is something profoundly moving in the fact that the Spanish Fathers, while watching the missions they had so carefully constructed crumbling away, yet take pride in sending their own mite to distant France to aid in erecting new churches.

The circular letter of the apostolic prefect, after explaining the general plan of the Association, ends as follows:

"My dear brothers: Who would believe that the same France which 50 years ago in the turmoil of an ungodly and revolutionary fever repudiated all creeds, now deserves to be chosen by Providence as the medium to extend the holy Catholic faith among all nations? It is indeed this nineteenth century France who in her admirable wisdom and her divine sympathy is the one destined to carry the true faith to those tribes scattered among the islands and along the shores of the Pacific Ocean!

"I desire God to bless this work, which is entirely his own and which will magnify his glory and honor, as well as the spiritual and temporal prosperity of France and their Very Christian Majesties who so worthily bear this title, the finest in their crown, in lands so remote from the center of their own empire."[160]

A league and a half up the coast, north of Santa Bárbara, stretches Rancho La Brea. Nearby several pools of bitumen empty into the sea, and along the shores and at several other localities bitumen deposits are also found. Seven leagues from the sea, 26 leagues from Los Angeles, and directly east of Santa Bárbara, at Las Pozas Rancho,[161] a volcano has been found from whose crater fumes occasionally pour. The lands near this volcano are thickly impregnated with sulphur. For a league around the mission, springs of sulphur water with a temperature close to boiling are encountered. There is no native wood suitable for building close to Santa Bárbara. Since it would be too troublesome and costly to bring wood down from the mountains 7 or 8 leagues away, timber is shipped in via Monterey from the sawmills belonging to Mission Santa Cruz.

---

[160]The original letter is in our possession. (D. de M.).
[161]Las Pozas belonged to José de la Guerra y Noriega.

Further up the coast, the rancho and anchorage known as El Refugio are passed.[162] This is situated 7 leagues north of Santa Bárbara, and is readily recognized from a distance by its white house covered with red tiles which stands near the shore. From El Refugio to Point Conception the coast runs directly west. South of the point is the anchorage of El Cojo,[163] so-called in honor of a lame chieftain of the tribe living on these shores. This mooring and that of El Refugio have a depth of from 5 to 10 fathoms close to shore, but are exposed to the prevailing winds in summer. The ranchos of Las Pozas, Mescaltitán,[164] El Refugio, Los dos Pueblos,[165] and San Julián[166] which belonged to Mission Santa Bárbara, have passed to private ownership.

Mission La Purísima Concepción[167] which was founded on December 8, 1787, lies 17 leagues west-northwest of Mission Santa Inés. It is situated on the banks of a little river, 4 miles in from the sea between Point Conception and Point Argüello, and is now almost wholly demolished. About 60 Indians who have no Father live nearby. Live stock consists of not more than 800 cattle, 3,500 sheep, and 300 horses; but in 1834 the mission had 900 neophytes, 15,000 cattle, 2,000 horses, 14,000 sheep, and harvested 6,000 fanegas of grain.

The eighteen leagues that separate Mission de la Concepción from that of San Luís Obispo consist primarily of an extensive plain called La Larga. This land, watered by the San Geraldo[168] River, is noted for its fine grazing. Toward the center, 4 leagues from the sea and near the Rancho Guadalupe,[169] lies a small crater which emits sulphur fumes at rare intervals. This plain is also of remarkable fertility.

---

[162]In 1834 Nuestra Señora del Refugio, a property of 25,000 acres, came into the possession of Captain Antonio María Ortega, of the presidio at Santa Bárbara. Trading ships often stopped at the anchorage. See Davis, op. cit., p. 203.

[163]Rancho El Cojo, of 90,000 acres, was owned by the Murphy family. El Cojo, or Sisolopa, was originally a fishing village of the Mission Purísima branch of the Chumash Indians at Cañada del Cojo, named for a lame chieftain who befriended early Spanish travelers. Father Palóu calls it Santa Teresa.

[164]Mescaltitán, also known as Sagspileel, or San Miguel, was originally one of the wheat ranches of the mission. In 1841 it passed to Raimundo Carrillo.

[165]Dos Pueblos, also called San Pedro and San Pablo, passed in 1842 to Nicholas A. Den, an Irish physician, who subsequently leased the Santa Bárbara mission. Den later acquired large holdings near Santa Bárbara, including the valuable San Marcos.

[166]San Julián, a wheat rancho, was granted in 1837 to George Rock, who was agent for José de la Guerra y Noriega, to whom it soon passed.

[167]This mission at the town Lompoc is now in ruins. Purísima was also a small, unimportant mission, and even at its peak had far less live stock than De Mofras' estimate.

[168]San Geraldo: The Santa María River.

[169]Rancho Guadalupe, a grant of 30,000 acres, was acquired in 1840 by Diego Olivera and Teodoro Arellanes.

Mission Santa Inés,[170] founded September 17, 1804, is situated 12 leagues northwest of Mission Santa Bárbara, 8 leagues from La Purisíma Concepción, and 15 leagues south of San Luís Obispo. On the road leading from Santa Bárbara to Santa Inés is a long hilly region called La Cuesta de Santa Inés.[171] Several hours of hard traveling over a difficult route are required to cross these hills. This accomplished, the mission, which two parallel mountain ranges protect from the winds off the sea, as well as those from the northeast, appears at the foot of the eastern slope surrounded by extensive plains. These lowlands are well watered and unusually fertile, while the hills are crowned by superb forests.

Because of this favorable situation, the mission was able to amass extraordinary wealth less than thirty years after its foundation. Thus, in 1834 Santa Inés had 1,300 Indian neophytes, 14,000 cattle, 1,200 horses, 12,000 sheep, and a harvest of 3,500 fanegas of grain.[172] At the present, through the efforts of the Spanish Father Antonio Moreno[173] and his colleague the Reverend Father José Ximénez, 10,000 cattle, 500 horses, and 4,000 sheep have been saved. Not more than 250 Indians, however, remain in the neighborhood. This mission is now the richest in live stock in California; but there is grave danger that the government and its agents will soon dissipate this last source of wealth. From Santa Inés to San Luís Obispo the route continues on up the valley in a westerly direction, leading past lands well adapted to cultivation.

The Mission of San Luís Obispo de Tolosa de Francia,[174] founded on September 1, 1771 by the Reverend Prefect Junípero Serra, lies eighteen leagues north of Purísima Concepción, 15 leagues northwest of Santa

[170]Because of the fertility of its lands, Santa Inés, named for Saint Agnes or Inés, a young girl martyred at Rome in the fourth century, was one of the rich missions. The earthquake of 1812 seriously damaged the buildings, which were rebuilt. After 1816, however, the mission declined. Today Santa Inés is in a fair state of preservation and is used for services. A fine collection of priests' robes and early Indian relics are among its treasures. See Engelhardt, **Mission Santa Inés** (Santa Bárbara, 1932).

[171]San Marcos Pass.

[172]Mission property at its peak never attained by half the total given by De Mofras.

[173]Antonio,or Juan Moreno, was a Spanish Franciscan who came to California in 1825. He served at Santa Bárbara, Santa Cruz, and San Juan Baustista before his term, 1842-1845, at Santa Inés. José Joaquin Jimeno, the brother of Antonio Jimeno, served at Santa Inés from 1833 to 1850.

[174]One of the oldest churches in California, Mission San Luís Obispo is still holding services. The town of the same name has now grown up around its walls. By 1810 its buildings and properties were extensive, and a small chapel had also been erected at San Miguelito. For its founding and history see Bolton, **Palóu's New California**, II, 359-365, and **Engelhardt, Mission San Luís Obispo** (Santa Bárbara, 1933).

Inés, and 13 leagues south of San Miguel. This was one of the most flourishing missions, having in 1834 nearly 1,300 neophytes, 9,000 cattle, 4,000 horses, 7,000 sheep, and harvests amounting to 4,000 fanegas of grain. A large part of its revenue was derived from the olive oil produced from an extensive olive orchard which rivals in size the finest in Andalusia. The mission lies on a slight elevation 3 leagues inland, in a pleasant valley sheltered by a wooded mountain. In front of the buildings flows the San Luís River[175] which propels a sturdy windmill, thus irrigating the gardens, the vineyards, and the extensive orchards. Today the Indians are scattered far and wide; fewer than 100 now remain. All the lands, including two extensive ranchos, the Santa Margarita,[176] and the Asunción,[177] have passed into private ownership. The mission has retained only 300 cattle, 200 horses, and 800 sheep. In September, 1840, a band of Shawnee Indians, together with some American trappers who were hunting in the Tulares, raided the mission during the night, and, after breaking down the wooded enclosure, stole 1,200 animals. This robbery went unpunished, as the government had no troops to pursue the culprits.

Under the able management of the Reverend Father Martínez,[178] a Spanish Franciscan who was brutally exiled from the country in 1832 [1830] by the Mexican governor, the neophytes of San Luís Obispo made remarkable industrial progress. The Father imported or had built some modern looms, then taught the Indians to spin and weave ordinary cloth, and even very fine cotton fabrics. Many women, in fact, are still using these *rebozos,* or silk shawls, made by the Indians under the direction of Father Martínez.

Within the building, now in a dilapidated condition, was found living, in the most abject poverty, the oldest Spanish Franciscan in all California, the Reverend Father Ramón Abella,[179] of Aragon, who in 1787 knew

---

[175]The San Luís Obispo River.

[176]The Santa Margarita, of 4 leagues, or 17,000 acres, had passed into the ownership of Joaquin Estrada.

[177]Asunción, a grant of 10 leagues, was owned by Pedro Estrada, a soldier.

[178]Luís Antonio Martínez was a Spanish friar who in 1798 arrived in California, subsequently residing for thirty-two years at San Luís Obispo, where in 1830 he was arrested and banished from the country. Martínez excelled as a business manager, and his ability contributed largely to the success of the mission.

[179]Ramón Abella was a Spanish Franciscan who served forty-four years in the missions of California. His term at San Luís Obispo extended from 1833 to 1842. His declining years were spent in abject poverty at San Luís, although in 1842 he was removed to Purísima, and finally to Santa Inés, where, on May 24, 1842, he was buried.

the illustrious La Pérouse.[180] The mission has been so neglected that this poor Franciscan sleeps on a hide, drinks from a horn, and eats only meager strips of jerked beef. The venerable Father distributes what little is sent him among the few Indian children who still live with their families in the ruins near the mission. Several charitable persons, including Father Duran, have offered shelter and rest to Father Abella; but he always refuses, saying he prefers to die at his post. This estimable man, who has established several missions in the northern part of the country, has been a priest for some sixty years; he still talks of going out to make conquests (*ir á la conquista*) and even at his advanced age endures without complaint the humiliations and privations to which he is subjected by his poverty.

The anchorage of San Luís is 3 miles from the mission; by the sea approach the leading landmark is the mountain of El Buchón, so-called because the chief of the tribe that lives along this shore has an enormous goitre. This mountain is cone-shaped, and stands out sharply from the chain that parallels the coast. Mooring may be had inside a large bay, 8 miles broad, which is bounded on the south by Point Sal and on the north by Point San Luís, where El Buchón looms. At the far end of this point, 2 miles offshore, lies a small island; given favorable winds, ships may pass on the east. Although the passage is safe, yet the navigator should steer cautiously; and whenever possible the western channel should be used.

The mountain rises perpendicularly from the sea, then descends gently toward the south for 3 miles, terminating in a white cliff 40 meters high, at whose base flows the tiny San Luís River. Anchorage is opposite this cliff, about a mile offshore, in 5 to 8 fathoms with a firm base, and here ships are exposed only to northwesterly and easterly breezes. Drinking water is not only excellent, but also ample; but, to prevent water from being brackish, it should be removed at low tide from the holes worn in the river bed 200 feet above the mouth where it is shaded by bushes. Wood and fresh meat are also available, while fresh produce may be procured at a small rancho, formerly owned by the mission, that is situated on the main road 2 kilometers from the beach. In a large cliff near the shore there is a natural grotto of considerable beauty and here ships sometimes store hides procured from San Luís.

On the coast, approximately 10 leagues north of Point San Luís Obispo, the peninsula and bay known as Los Esteros, defined by a small

---

[180]See **infra**, I, 207, also **note** 17.

island near shore, are situated. At rare intervals ships anchor in this bay. On the shore lie excellent salt deposits, but the land is unoccupied. Sheltered by a slight eminence, 8 leagues above Los Esteros and 7 from San Miguel Mission, lies the mooring place known as San Simeón. This is open to the northwesterly trade winds, and has 5 or 6 fathoms of water close to shore. Not far from the beach stands a rancho. From here on up as far north as Monterey the coast is marked by several promontories or small capes at the foot of the Santa Lucía Mountains that assume protection from the prevailing summer breezes. This anchorage should prove quite valuable at some future date when the thick woods that dot the mountains acquire commercial value.

Mission San Miguel Arcángel[181] founded July 25, 1797, is situated 13 leagues north of San Luís Obispo, and 13 leagues southeast of San Antonio. The buildings at San Miguel, though partially demolished, are superb. Having arrived at this mission, we found it to be uninhabited. Of the 1,200 Indians living here as late as 1834, only 30 remain; of the 4,000 cattle, 2,500 horses, and 10,000 sheep, there are now only 80 large animals and 400 sheep. This mission also owned at one time some fertile agricultural lands which produced 2,500 fanegas. Today these lands are no longer under cultivation, all the mission holdings and live stock having passed to the rancheros.

San Miguel lies on a magnificent plain into which open toward the east several parallel gorges which afford ready access to the broad Tulare Valley, mentioned when describing Mission San Fernando. Some 3 leagues east of San Miguel, at a locality called Telamé,[182] the Spanish Fathers planned at one time to found a presidio and several missions which would have formed from San Luís Rey up to San José, a second mission chain paralleling that near the sea and which, by penetrating the heart of the Tulare country, would have afforded a barrier against Indian invasions. As early as 1817, Father Mariano Payeras, apostolic prefect, proposed this plan to the King of Spain, but unfortunately this was never executed. The lands of the Tulares are bordered on the east

---

[181]Mission San Miguel, a few miles north of Paso Robles, was erected at what was known as Las Pozas. The Indians called the place **Vahca**. The buildings are now being restored and preserved. San Miguel was always a small and relatively unimportant mission. De Mofras' report of mission wealth is inaccurate; no report was issued in 1834, but in 1832, property included 3,700 cattle, 8,200 sheep, and 700 horses! The Indians brought into San Miguel belonged chiefly to the Salinan stock. See Engelhardt, **San Miguel Arcángel** (Santa Bárbara, 1929).

[182]Telamé: one of the neighboring rancherías, or Indian settlements. The inhabitants are identified as the Telamni, a division of the Yokuts.

by the Sierra Nevada and on the west by the Californian Mountains. Watered by the San Joaquin and Sacramento rivers, this appears to be the most fertile portion of California. The Indian population in this valley has gradually declined within the last few years; a mysterious malady has destroyed whole tribes, and as a result the white colonists have had no difficulty settling in this country. In this same Tulare Valley Governor Alvarado wisely proposed to give land to 500 French families with the hope that, by establishing a population closely in sympathly with the Spanish colonists, the encroachment of the Anglo-Americans would be retarded.

CHAPTER IX*

A topographical description of the Mission, Pueblos, and Presidios in the northern part of New California. Settlements and Ports of Monterey and San Francisco.

The two districts that form the northern part of New California are of major importance. Their harbors are the finest and most frequented throughout the province; the mountain ranges paralleling the sea, notably the Santa Lucía and Santa Cruz, are thickly wooded, accessible for exploitation, and rich in waterfalls and streams suitable for mechanical sawmills and manufacturing purposes. A route that passes San Miguel Mission leads into the Tulare [Valley] where the soil is far more adapted for agricultural development than lands farther south.

The Santa Lucía range, which begins at Mt. Buchón and terminates at the southern extremity of Monterey Bay at Point Pinos, is covered with pine, ash, oak, juniper and plane trees of extraordinary size. These forests are still in their virgin state. The range is nearly 40 leagues long and 10 or 12 leagues wide. In certain areas where the forest is impenetrable, the settlers hesitate to explore its depths because of the many bears that roam at large.

The country between Missions San Miguel and San Antonio takes the form of an immense valley called El Cañon,[1] that extends as far as the eastern shore of San Francisco Bay. The valley, which is bordered on the east by a range that separates it from that of the Tulare and on the west by the Santa Lucía Mountains, is fed by innumerable streams. The slopes of the mountains are covered by rich pastures, while through the floor of the valley, which is level, wanders a pleasant route shaded by trees. Near San Miguel several important ranchos, among them the San Bartolomé[2] and San Antonio,[3] are situated.

---

*This is Mémoire VI, in Amérique Vol. 43, folios 219 to 314. With the exception of two pages of the Mémoire which have been omitted, this follows the manuscript copy.

[1] El Cañon: the Salinas Valley.

[2] San Bartolomé was a sheep ranch, midway between San Miguel and San Antonio.

[3] San Antonio was probably San Antonio de los Ojitos, usually known as Los Ojitos, which lay 3 leagues south of Mission San Antonio. In 1810 it was con-

The Mission of San Antonio de Pádua,[4] or Los Robles, the oaks, founded July 14, 1771, by the Reverend Father Junípero Serra, stands surrounded by great oaks on the immense plain just described, 13 leagues northwest of San Miguel, and 11 leagues south of Mission Soledad. From an architectural standpoint this mission is comparable to San Luís Rey. The buildings, which are extensive and extremely beautiful, are in a perfect state of preservation. As late as 1834, this establishment with its 1,400 Indians owned 12,000 cattle, 2,000 horses, 14,000 sheep, and harvested 3,000 fanegas of grain. Today fewer than 150 neophytes, 800 cattle, 500 horses, and 2,000 sheep remain under its control.[5] A brook and several fountains used for watering the orchards, vineyards, and gardens, trickle in front of the buildings.[6]

From the standpoint of climate, San Antonio lies on the boundary line between northern and southern California; the orange and palm trees that adorn the mission gardens are the last found toward the north. Not long ago this church owned several large properties which have been seized recently by agents of the government. Among them was the vast Rancho San Benito,[7] 6 leagues west of the mission that supported no fewer than 4,000 cattle. Inasmuch as San Antonio is situated between three mountain ranges, it is so warm during the summer season that

---

verted into a cattle ranch for the latter mission. In 1823 an adobe house containing two rooms was erected for the use of neophytes who had charge of the cattle.

---

[4]San Antonio de Pádua, named for Saint Anthony of Padua, known as the Wonderworker, who was born at Lisbon, Portugal, in 1195 and died in 1231.

[5]Soon after the missions were secularized in 1834, José Ramírez became administrator of this mission. He abused the Indians and wasted their patrimony. Undoubtedly De Mofras overestimates the wealth of the mission, for on June 1, 1842, Father Gutiérrez, a paralytic and ill, writes of conditions as follows: "There are no more cattle, nor sheep, nor wool to make habit cloth, nor any one to weave it; nor is there tallow nor manteca, nor are there any neophytes to serve, nor anything to give them, or to pay the expenses of the church. The worst of it is that all relief is far away, and the pagans are becoming insolent, the Christians rebellious and fleeing." Engelhardt, **Mission San Antonio** (Santa Bárbara, 1929), p. 76. The mission church is still standing in a fair state of preservation on the Hearst ranch.

[6]At San Antonio De Mofras fell into disgrace, according to Spanish accounts, because of his harsh treatment of Indian guides who acted as his servants, and was put in the local jail from which the kindly Father aided him to escape. Rumors were afloat that the Frenchman was the bastard son of the King of France and that he regarded all Spaniards as no better than Indians. See Mariano Vallejo, **Recuerdos Históricos y Personales**, Vol. IV, (1839-1845), pp. 244-245. MS. Bancroft Library.

[7]In 1820 the San Benito, 6 leagues east of the mission on the river, was converted into a cattle ranch to provide meat for Mission San Antonio. This as well as most of the adjacent ranches, is now in the hands of the Hearst family.

cotton and other plants of a tropical nature can be cultivated. The horses belonging to this mission are of a breed noted for their swiftness and sure-footedness. Reared with complete freedom on the ranges, where they are often pursued by bear that come down off the mountains, these animals have developed amazing agility.

The only Father who still resides at San Antonio is the Reverend Gutiérrez, who extended us a cordial welcome. However, to our indignation an old servant, who has been made administrator of the mission, appeared to be taking advantage of the paralytic condition of this venerable Father, placing him on short rations and depriving him even of the bare necessaries of life.

Five leagues north of San Antonio, after crossing over a chain of low mountains, the traveler approaches the plains of Soledad. These terminate on their western end at the Bay of Monterey and extend east as far as the missions of San Juan Bautista and San José.

Mission Nuestra Señora de la Soledad,[8] founded on October 9, 1791, lies 11 leagues north of San Antonio and 15 leagues southeast of Carmel Mission and the village of Monterey in the broad valley of El Cañon.[9] As late as 1834 the mission had 700 neophytes, 6,000 cattle, 1,200 horses, 7,000 sheep, and an annual crop of 2,500 fanegas.[10] But at the present neither Indians nor live stock remain. The place is in ruins; vines are rotting, gardens are overgrown with weeds, and orchards are decaying from lack of care.

In 1838, a Spaniard, the Reverend Father Sarría,[11] died of poverty and starvation at Soledad Mission which he was unwilling to abandon, together with the few wretched Indians who were still living in his parish. One Sunday in August, though weakened by suffering and malnutrition, he had called his neophytes together in his chapel and was about to celebrate Mass when his strength failed and he fell at the foot of the altar, dying in the arms of the Indians to whom for thirty years or more he had given protection and instruction.

---

[8]Our Lady of Solitude.

[9]The original site of Soledad Mission lies at the foot of the mountains west of the town of Soledad. The buildings are now in ruins.

[10]De Mofras again overestimates the wealth of this mission; for the Hartnell report of 1839 lists only 78 neophytes, 45 cattle, 865 sheep, 25 horses, and 2 mules. The property passed from mission control into the hands of Tiburcio Castro. See Engelhardt, **Mission Soledad** (Santa Bárbara, 1929).

[11]More authentic than De Mofras' report are the records of the Catholic historian, Engelhardt, who observes that Father Vicente Francisco de Sarría died May 24, 1835, aged sixty-eight. Sarría was born in 1767 in Spain, and reached California in 1809. He served at San Carlos and later at Soledad. He was a scholarly, dignified, and able Franciscan.

In May, 1841, Governor Alvarado, after leading away what few animals had escaped former confiscation and carrying off all iron and even tile from La Soledad to roof one of his own houses, finally gave what remained of the buildings and land to one of his friends, Soberanes,[12] in exchange for a ranch situated near Monterey.

Along the road leading from Soledad to Monterey several ranchos are passed; of these the Zanjones[13] and the Buena Vista[14] appear to be the most prosperous. Two leagues before reaching Monterey at a point where the sand dunes that surround Monterey Bay are first encountered, it is possible, by following a road that forks to the right, to detour to Carmel Mission, now in ruins.

The Mission of Nuestra Señora del Carmelo[15] was the second mission founded in California (San Diego had been the first) by the venerable Father Junípero Serra. First erected in 1769 on the shores of Monterey Bay, the shortage of water and grazing lands brought to the attention of the Fathers the necessity of removing it to a more suitable locality. One June 3, 1770,[16] the Father President laid the cornerstone of the new mission on the banks of a stream a short distance from the shore on the little Bay of Carmel, 4 miles from the presidio at Monterey. Carmel Mission, which lies on the northern tip of the Santa Lucía Mountains, is hemmed in by ranges and has never enjoyed extraordinary prosperity.

---

[12]Although Feliciano Soberanes may have occupied the mission at an earlier date, it was formally sold to him on June 4, 1846, for $800. For a time Mariano Soberanes had charge of the mission.

[13]By Zanjones De Mofras probably refers to Rinconado del Zanjon, a ranch of a league and a half beyond San Antonio, granted in 1839 to Gabriel de la Torre.

[14]Buena Vista, on the Salinas River, was originally used by Anza as a camp-site. In 1822 it was granted to Santiago and José M. Estrada, remaining for a long period in the hands of this family.

[15]Our Lady of Carmel.

[16]This was the day on which formal possession was taken of the port of Monterey, on the site where, in 1603, Sebastián Vizcaíno had celebrated Mass, and on the site of the mission baptized by Father Junípero Serra. Not until later, in August, 1771, however, was the church removed to a site near Carmel Bay. The most reliable record of these events is Bolton, Palóu's New California, II, 290-322. The stone church, replacing the first structure, was begun in 1793 and completed in 1797, and was probably the most notable edifice of its kind in California. The home for many years of Serra and Palóu, many noted travelers enjoyed its hospitality. In contrast to De Mofras' lavish estimate of mission resources, official reports for 1834 reveal 312 cattle, 491 horses, and 9 mules. By 1840 little remained but the ruined buildings. A prominent resident of Monterey, Manuel Crespo, subsequently took possession of the property. In 1884 restoration was begun and the fine church is now in an excellent state of preservation. The tomb of Father Junípero Serra is in the side chapel. Sir George Simpson, who visited here in 1842, reported that only a caretaker and his wife were in charge of the mission, which had been badly damaged by an earthquake.

Under its control, however, in 1834 were 500 neophytes; and, in addition, 3,000 cattle, 700 horses, and 7,000 sheep, while harvests totaled 1,500 fanegas. Today all this has disappeared. Under the pretext of starting a village nearby the mission has been allowed to crumble into ruins, while the Indian population is composed, at the outside, of 30 individuals. Since this establishment, like that of Soledad, was closer to the seat of government, it was one of the first to be plundered. The Father from Carmel now resides at Monterey.

In September, 1787 [1786], the noted La Pérouse,[17] with his ships *l'Astrolabe and La Boussole,* anchored off Monterey and paid an official visit to Carmel Mission. There the Reverend Father Francisco Palóu,[18] garbed in his apostolic vestments and assisted by two Fathers, received him with the utmost ceremony at the door of his church, honoring him as captain general. One of the officers of the *l' Astrolabe* made a sketch depicting this ceremony, and this momento, now so priceless, was hung in the vestry of the mission. In 1827, an Englishman, Captain Beechey,[19] offered to purchase the sketch, but Father Abella[20] refused to part with it. Later, when the *Vénus*[21] and *Artémise*[22] put in at Monterey, their commanders expressed a desire to own this picture. A thorough search was made, but the treasure had disappeared. I made every effort possible to locate this personally, even offering a reward of 1000 piasters, but these attempts proved futile. Local residents are of the belief that sometime when the mission was pillaged, some one coveting the gilt

[17]This was Count Jean François Galaup de la Pérouse, who with the ships **Boússole** and **Astrolabe** visited Monterey not in 1787 but in September, 1786. See his **Voyage autour du monde** (4 vols. and atlas, Paris, 1797), II, 247-292, for a full account of early Monterey. La Pérouse, who was a popular visitor at the Monterey presidio and Carmel mission because of his scholarly attainments, polished manners, and generosity, left many gifts to the mission, including the potato, brought up from Chile, and heretofore unknown in California.

[18]Francisco Palóu, or Paloú, a native of Mallorca, came to California with Junípero Serra, whom he aided in establishing the missions in this new land. His labors as an historian are notable; his **Vida del V. P. Junípero Serra** and his **Noticias de la Nueva California** are monumental works of information. The former has been edited by G. W. James (Pasadena, 1913), the latter, by Dr. H. E. Bolton with the title **Palóu's New California.** See supra I, 57, **note** 48.

[19]This was Captain Frederick William Beechey, in H. M. S. **Blossom,** who visited Monterey in January, 1827, and again in October and November of that year. See Beechey, **op. cit.,** II, 85-87, 319-321, 428-429. An excellent general description of California is found in II, 1-88.

[20]Father Ramón Abella, who was in charge of San Carlos until 1833. See **supra, p. 199, also note 179.**

[21]The **Vénus,** carrying Abel Dupetit Thouars and 300 men, anchored at Monterey on October 18, 1837.

[22]The **Artémise,** with Cyrille La Place aboard, came to Monterey in August, 1839. She carried 50 guns and 450 men.

frame, might possibly have destroyed the sketch and replaced it with the image of a saint.

At Carmel I found two old Indians who clearly remembered La Pérouse, as well as the handmill and seeds he presented to the Fathers, and the pieces of red cloth given the neophytes. By way of appreciation, while the frigates were in port, every morning the friars sent down carts laden with vegetables, milk, and fresh meat in sufficient quantity to feed all the crew, for which they declined to accept any remuneration.

The miniature Bay of Carmel on which the mission is situated has an opening 5 miles wide; on the north this is defined by Cypress Point and on the south by Point Lobos or Carmel. The center of this harbor is extremely dangerous, for it is studded with submerged rocks. At night, or in foggy weather, ships enter at their peril, and several vessels have already been wrecked. A slight error in latitude of 5 miles is adequate to confuse Cypress Point with Point Pinos which marks the southern entrance of Monterey Harbor. Distinguishing landmarks, on the other hand, are fairly numerous: the mouth of Monterey Bay between Point Pinos and Point Santa Cruz is more than 20 miles wide; the Carmel anchorage has a width of only 5 miles; Point Pinos is low and broad; and Cypress Point is high and round, resembling a large island disconnected from the mainland. The tiny island of Lobos, just off Point Carmel, is nothing more than an arid, barren rock, whereas the small islands north of Cypress Point are thickly covered with trees. Furthermore, in passing between Carmel and Cypress points, the mission buildings are seen in the distance; on the contrary, it is only after Point Pinos has been completely rounded and the ship is close to anchorage that the tower on the church at the Monterey presidio is visible.

The islands and shores of the port of Monterey[23] are alive with fur seals and sea otter which are easily killed with clubs; but the seals, formerly so numerous, have been almost wholly exterminated. The road leading from the mission to Monterey meanders through magnificent rolling hills, covered with superb pines and abounding in game, that slope down to the sea.

In clear weather from the anchorage of Monterey it is possible to see, at a distance of 15 or 20 leagues, the lofty mountains surrounding

---

[23]De Mofras, who had left Mazatlán on April 13, 1841, on the **Ninfa**, reached Monterey early in May, probably the 6th. For the next five months he visited the surrounding country, finally departing from San Francisco on October 18 aboard the **Cowlitz**, bound for Fort Vancouver. See Bancroft, **California**, IV, 249, **note 43**.

PORT OF MONTEREY
Upper California

ISBA
Type of house built by the Russian colonists in America

the harbor. The summit of the range culminating in the peaks Año Nuevo and Santa Cruz that mark the northern side of the entrance, is approximately 21 miles from Point Pinos.[24] During foggy weather the course should be set for the latitude of Point Pinos, and reckonings made accordingly; but when in doubt, vessels should signal with guns until the port and ships at anchor reply. Several rocks protrude around the point. Notwithstanding, the waters are so deep that with a stiff breeze ships can sail within a quarter of a mile of shore; under light winds it is advisable, on the other hand, to keep well off the breakers, for the currents run in that direction, and the waters are too deep to cast anchor with safety. After Point Pinos has been passed, a second promontory which, because of its dangerous reefs must be skirted at a safe distance, is visible. Then, finally, the belfry and houses come into view. After sailing on a short distance, anchorage in 12 or 18 meters is reached one-sixth of a mile from shore. The fort lies off toward west-southwest. A bank hidden in the southeastern corner of the bay, and soon found by means of the large amount of seaweed covering the water, should be avoided, since its shallowest point has only about 4 or 5 fathoms, and the deepest 7 or 8.

Heavy seas, swept in by the northwesterly winds, often pile into the bay. These, however, are not dangerous, being partially checked by the Santa Cruz Mountains, while Point Año Nuevo tempers the force of the swell. The two extremities of the shore are quite safe and have considerable depth; even large ships can drop anchor at all points. Here, in 1827, the Spanish ship the *Asia,* of 74 [tons], rode for some time at anchor.

Since the mouth of Monterey Bay is unusually wide, the bay might appear unsafe; however, in summer during northwesters, and in winter during southeasters, ships of all kinds seek shelter here, and accidents are unknown. The wreck near the mooring is that of an American whaling ship, deliberately destroyed in 1837 by her captain. When the sea is rough, ships should be fastened by two anchors, for although there are relatively few currents in the harbor, yet squalls often blow in offshore.

Two small rivers, the Monterey and the Pajaro, empty into the east side of the bay. They are not navigable, however, for in summer they run almost dry. Six miles north of the Pajaro, behind a small point in-

---

[24]The northern side of the entrance to Monterey Bay lies in 36º 37' 15" north latitude. (D. de M.).

dicated on the accompanying map, is the anchorage of Otay. Nearby an ample supply of excellent wood may be loaded aboard ship. There are also two more anchorages safe in fair weather where timber is taken to be cut into boards at the sawmills. The first of these landing places is situated opposite the village of Branciforte, east of the island; the other lies in a small cove into which empties the stream that passes Mission Santa Clara.

Among the grave inconveniences at Monterey Harbor is the lack of adequate water to supply ships on long journeys. Two miles away several good springs are found; but since the women use these for washing clothes, the water is usually mixed with soap. Transportation by cart from the wells to the landing, furthermore, costs one piaster a barrel.

To send longboats to the Monterey and Pajaro rivers—15 or 20 miles away from anchorage—is both dangerous and slow. Santa Cruz is still more remote, and there it is also necessary to go some little distance up the river to find water that is not brackish. Some deep wells could be easily sunk near Monterey, for those already put down by the local residents are shallow and almost invariably dry in the summer season. With slight expense water from brooks and little falls above the village, that come down off the east slope of the chain of hills terminating in Point Pinos, could be utilized and brought down to port. On the other hand, wood for fuel and masts is abundant; the pines, which are only a few rods from shore, are available for use by paying a small municipal tax of one real for small trees, up to one piaster for the largest specimens.

Monterey is a port of call frequented by whalers[25] who come there to lay in fresh supplies, especially meat, which is sold locally as well as throughout California at a moderate price. Beef on the hoof costs 4 or 5 piasters and yields approximately 250 kilograms of excellent meat. At the present it is both difficult and often impossible to procure wheat or flour; the cultivation of grains has been largely abandoned and during the entire year spent in the country bread was found only

----

[25]Whaling vessels first began trading with California in 1823 when four ships reached San Francisco. Although local ports were officially closed, yet John R. Cooper landed at Monterey with a cargo of merchandise and persuaded Governor Argüello to allow him to trade after paying taxes. This opened the way for American trade and Monterey soon became the center of the whaling industry. An old whaling station on Decatur Street now owned by Franklin Baldwin that was originally built in the '30's, and subsequently enlarged, is still an object of interest to local visitors.

in about a dozen houses. Vegetables, eggs, poultry, and milk are scarce and expensive at Monterey; chickens cost half a piaster, and probably could not be purchased in quantities. The local inhabitants have ample supplies of beef and mutton, as well as corn-cakes called tortillas. Vegetables can be procured only after waiting several days for the ranchos, situated several leagues inland, to make delivery.

Those having at their disposal a large ship's boat should send it to Mission Santa Clara for supplies, for there the well-irrigated lands and kitchen gardens indicate the possibility of finding more vegetables than at Monterey, which is extremely arid. When fruits are ripe, Mission San Juan Bautista can supply several cartloads of raisins, apricots, apples, peaches, and pears of a delicious flavor. Such grains as wheat, beans, peas, and kidney beans should be purchased at San Francisco. The local wine at Monterey sells for 20 and 30 piasters, and brandy for 60 piasters a barrel, which holds about 80 bottles. Monterey is the only place to secure such supplies as sailcloth, rigging, chains, cables, anchors, painters, and cordage; but even these are found only in small quantities and at prohibitive prices.

In September and October the English, and particularly the American whalers reach Monterey in large numbers. We ourselves saw eight of the latter nation riding at anchor. At this season whales are so abundant along the coast and in the bays that the *Saphir* of Boston, while at anchor in September, 1841, harpooned three whales in one day from its small boats near its mooring.

The presidio of Monterey, at one time the most important fort in the province, is now entirely demolished, few traces of the foundations remaining.[26] Although strategically situated with guns commanding all ships entering the port, yet it was built of such inferior materials and was so poorly equipped that it would have been unable to resist any serious attack. In 1819 [1818] a pirate,[27] flying the colors of insurgents

---

[26] In the early '40's the town of Monterey was a small settlement. Sir George Simpson, a contemporary visitor (**op. cit.**, I, 343), calls it "this horrible port of Monterey," and describes the cheerless aspect of the dark, windowless adobes, erected at random throughout the town, its four public buildings, the decaying church and shabby castillo, the mud hut used as a guardhouse, and the uncompleted customhouse. De Mofras, however, enjoyed its social life to the full, and many amusing tales center around his sojourn at the venerable Spanish capital. He spent some time at the neighboring Hartnell ranch, east of Salinas, and its mistress, Señora Teresa de la Guerra Hartnell, writes somewhat bitterly of this visit. See her **Narrativa de una Matrona de California**, MS. Bancroft Library.

[27] De Mofras refers to two Chilean privateers in command of a Frenchman,

from Buenos Ayres, fired on the presidio and, going shore, seized some cattle needed aboard his vessel. During the wave of revolutions that swept over Monterey, the presidio was pillaged by inhabitants who used the material for building houses. Plans, however, have been made to reconstruct the church, which, although in a weakened condition, is still standing. The edifice on the whole is devoid of interesting features.

A small barbette battery known as El Castillo,[28] stands on the west side of the anchorage, a few miles offshore. On the sea approach, its sole support is a small earthen embankment, 4 feet high. In the vicinity are a crumbling building inhabited by 5 soldiers and a small shack used as a powder magazine. The battery has neither moat nor counter-guard, and can be readily approached on all sides since it is on a level with the surrounding land. In conjunction with the presidio its situation is strategic, for El Castillo properly built and equipped could sweep with its guns any ship that approached moorings.

The ancient gun carriages, the two or three hundred copper cannon balls, the trucks, the ammunition chests of old Spanish material, all lie abandoned on the ground. The defense consists of 2 useless brass pieces, a brass falconet, 2 twelve-pounders, a sixteen-pound gun mounted on half-rotten gun carriages, and 2 pieces of eight, mounted on cart wheels. During public celebrations the latter, drawn by oxen, are used to fire off volleys and salute warships. Years ago these pieces, as well as those at San Diego and Santa Bárbara, were cast in bronze in Peru or Manila, and bear the insignia of Spain with the inscription *Real Audiencia de Lima ó de Filipinas.*[29] Opposite the battery stands the flagstaff, visible to ships entering the harbor. Obviously this so-called castle is incapable of withstanding attacks and its sole function is to reply to cannon fired during fogs by ships searching for anchorage. As a matter of fact the Spaniards were wise enough to establish a small battery near Point Pinos, but few traces of this now remain.

The old presidio of San Carlos de Monterey, founded in 1770,[30] and originally inhabited by officers and their families who lived within the

---

Hippolyte Bouchard, who appeared off Monterey on November 20, 1818. Opening fire on the port the following morning, after inflicting considerable damage the buccaneers pillaged the town.

---

[28]El Castillo was a small structure surrounded by a low adobe wall, garrisoned by 5 soldiers, who had charge of 8 or 10 rusty guns.

[29]Royal Audiencia of Lima or the Philippines. (D. de M.).

[30]For its history see Zephyrin Engelhardt, **Mission San Carlos Borromeo** (Santa Bárbara, 1934); and Bolton's **Palóu, passim.**

walls of the fortifications, has always been the seat of the government of the province. Not until 1827 did this settlement, which is known by the somewhat pretentious title of capital, begin to take on the aspect of a village. The first house was built by an English merchant called Hartnell.[31] The village at the present time consists of two parallel streets and several groups of houses scattered over the flats. The majority of the houses are constructed of sun-dried bricks, or adobes, and have wooden roofs, floors, and partitions. Many of them are fairly attractive. Inasmuch as all the dwellings have gardens and large courts, the village spreads over a wide area and from afar has the appearance of a large city. The inhabitants, most of whom are foreigners, number fewer than 600.[32] The main façade of the houses invariably faces southeast, thus avoiding the strong northwesterly winds that blow six months of the year. Viewed from the sea, Monterey presents a sightly appearance. In fact, no site could be more picturesque and more suitable for a large city.[33]

Toward the east appears a panoramic view of the summits of the Californian mountains; from the southeast to west extends a wooded range which takes the form of an amphitheatre terminating in a semi-circle of hills crowned by tall pines. Between the shore and the foothills extends a rugged plain 4 or 5 miles in width. The country lying between the harbor and Point Pinos, however, seems more suitable for future expansion. This arm of land measures 5 miles at its widest point, and has a length of 2 leagues that diminishes as it approaches Point Pinos. The shore adjoining the bay is entirely flat and does not rise above sea level. The coast affords stone for building, while the slopes farther inland not only provide timber suitable for construction, but also have majestic forests and green pastures. Although the coast exposed to the open sea is rocky on the eastern side, yet this is protected by the peninsula from gales off the ocean. Fortunately this intervening area is broken up into

----

[31]This was William E. P. Hartnell (1798-1854), who came to California in June, 1822, in the capacity of agent for an English shipping firm which handled mission produce. In 1825 he married María Teresa de la Guerra. Hartnell was a leading citizen of Monterey and held many public offices. The Hartnell adobe stood on the site now occupied by the Monterey Hospital on Hartnell Street. On his ranch "Alisal" near Salinas Hartnell conducted the first boys' college in California. Two of these old buildings are still standing.

[32]This estimate of the population of Monterey in 1841 was probably low. The official census of 1836 gives a total of 694 inhabitants.

[33]See map. The ranchos del Rey, Amesti, Rodríguez, etc., as far as the village of Branciforte, are located accurately only as to latitude; however, they are situated 6 miles farther east. (D. de M.).

small coves and rocky gorges suitable for quays, dockyards, and shelter for small ships.

Monterey has no important buildings; the government owns only the customhouse and a kind of barracks that house the officers, the soldiers of the garrison, and a school established only two years ago by a Frenchman called Cambuston.[34] Since the arrival of this young man, with the assistance of several foreign residents the interest of Governor Alvarado has been aroused and he has supplied a location, furniture, and the necessary equipment, as well as 100 piasters a month to Mr. Cambuston who, after a few weeks, had nearly 60 pupils receiving elementary instruction without charge. The small press belonging to the Compañía Cosmopolitana[35] was used to prepare some primers, and is still employed occasionally to print a few ordinances, administrative regulations, and proclamations.

The leading merchants of Monterey are: a Scotchman, David Spence,[36] a reputable citizen, who is extremely friendly toward France; James Watson,[37] an Englishman; Larkin,[38] an American; and Deleissèques,[39] a Frenchman and formerly captain of a trading vessel. With the customhouse at Monterey, this port[40] is the logical center for commerce and a place where most ships call. This, however, will be discussed in another chapter.

---

[34]Henri Cambuston was a Frenchman who came to California from Mexico in 1841, opened a school, and married Gabriela Soberanes.

[35]The Compañía Cosmopolitana was organized in Mexico in 1833 by José Padrés and José Hijar, to bring colonists to California. Mariano Vallejo and Agustín Zamorano attempted to aid these colonists in founding a settlement in the Santa Rosa Valley. The project, however, was not favored by Governor Figueroa, and subsequently abandoned. See Bancroft, California III, 270-300; George L. Harding, Don Agustín V. Zamorano (Los Angeles, 1934); and supra, I, 150.

[36]David Spence was a Scotchman who came to Monterey in 1824. In 1829 he married Adelaide Estrada, subsequently becoming an active merchant and politician. The Spence house stood on Alvarado Street above Bonifacio. Dupetit Thouars, II, 78-79, mentions his aid to sick Frenchmen.

[37]James (or David) Watson was an English sailor who became a trader at Monterey and rose to the rank of a leading citizen.

[38]Thomas Oliver Larkin (1802-1858), was a Yankee who came to California in 1832 and opened a store at Monterey. His major rôle was that of confidential agent for the United States government, and his activity aided that power to secure control of California. From 1844 to 1846 he served as U. S. consul at Monterey. The Larkin house, on the corner of Main and Jefferson Streets, the scene of so many historic incidents, is still standing. Larkin is mentioned by Davis, op. cit., passim., and the majority of writers of his day. Many manuscripts dealing with California from the period of Larkin are housed in the Bancroft Library at Berkeley.

[39]Olivier Deleissèques was a Frenchman who lived for a time at Monterey and later at San Juan Bautista.

[40]See Simpson's account, supra, I, 211, note 26.

The country around Monterey, especially south and northeast following the curve of the bay, is sandy for several leagues and devoid of pasture. This land is valuable primarily for its salt deposits, its rich soil, and the vast plain that extends from Mission Soledad to San José and begins approximately 8 miles inland.

On the route leading from Monterey to Mission San Juan Bautista lies the Rancho del Rey, or King's Rancho,[41] now owned by Don José Estrada, brother-in-law of Governor Alvarado; and the property called Los Pilarcitos,[42] on the banks of the Monterey River. Near the right side of the road on the rancho that Alvarado[43] took in exchange for Mission Soledad, a sulphur and galena mine has been found. In the absence of chemical tests, or the equivalent, it would be comparatively easy, by applying heat and treating the ore with potash, to establish evidence of the physical presence of lead and silver.

Mission San Juan Bautista,[44] established on June 24, 1799, lies 14 leagues from Monterey, 16 from Santa Cruz, and 18 from Santa Clara, and is situated on a plateau with the Pajaro River below. Today these vast buildings are owned by rancheros. At the time it was wrested from the hands of Father Anzar in 1834,[45] the mission had under its control 1,400 Indians, and owned 7,000 cattle, 1,200 horses, and 9,000 sheep. Wine was produced and 3,500 fanegas of grain harvested. This was taken over in its entirety by José Castro's family,[46] who were among Alvarado's sup-

---

[41]Rancho del Rey, originally the lands on which the cattle and horses belonging to the Monterey presidio were pastured, is now the site of Salinas. José Antonio Estrada, its owner at that time, was a military man and a leading citizen of Monterey.

[42]Arroyo de los Pilarcitos, of 4,424 acres, had been granted by Governor Alvarado to C. Miramontes.

[43]Juan B. Alvarado (1809-1882), eleventh Mexican governor of California, 1836-1840, was one of the notable leaders of California, who acquired several large ranchos in California. His gubernatorial residence is still standing on Dutra Street, Monterey. His summer capital, now in ruins, lay about 4 miles beyond Salinas, near Hartnell's College. For his life and activities see Bancroft, **California**, III, IV, **passim**; and Hittell, **op. cit.**, II, 236-314. Alvarado has left a voluminous manuscript called **A History of California**, now housed in the Bancroft Library.

[44]St. John the Baptist.

[45]Mission wealth in 1835 was considerably under this estimate. See Engelhardt, **Mission San Juan Bautista** (Santa Bárbara, 1931), pp. 57-58. For Father José Anzar's portrait see **ibid.**, p. 53. His pathetic letter to Governor Figueroa, written in January, 1835, at San Juan Bautista, discloses conditions after secularization. See **ibid.**, pp. 53-56.

[46]For a time José Tiburcio Castro, one of the military leaders of California, was majordomo and adminstrator of San Juan Bautista, and was one of the noted politicians and military leaders of that day. Castro and Pió Pico mortgaged the mission to pay war debts, subsequently selling the property. Later, American

porters, and who aspired to found a village bearing their own name. The Castros built houses and had the village made the seat of the prefecture, which has since been established at Monterey. Now the buildings are distintegrating, the neophytes have scattered and what few remain approximately 100—are reduced to the direst poverty. San Juan Bautista is noted throughout the land for the superior grade of European fruit grown. The situation is suitable for the founding of a village.

Because of innumerable marsh lands and river openings it is impossible to reach the village of Branciforte and the Santa Cruz Mission by following the coast. The traveler is obliged to go by way of the Rancho del Rey as far as Rancho Natividad[47] on the banks of the Monterey River, thus leaving the arid and tiresome region of sand dunes, paralleling the shore line of the bay, some 5 or 6 leagues inland. The plain is extremely beautiful, pine and juniper cloak the hills, and the valleys afford abundant pasturage. The rich ranchos of Vallejo,[48] Rodríguez,[49] and Amesti[50] lie nearby. A few leagues before reaching the Pajaro River, an area measuring a few hundred meters where the ground trembles under the horses feet, although the earth is hard and covered with turf, is encountered. This place, known as La Tembladera, is probably formed by a solid crust superimposed on a vast miry base.

On the shore a short distance northwest of the Amesti Rancho several piles of pinewood are passed near the anchorage of Otay. Then, after crossing several brooks, the plateau on which Branciforte and Santa Cruz Mission are situated, is reached.

The village, or settlement, known as Branciforte Village,[51] was founded in 1796 [1797] and was named in honor of Don Miguel de Lagrua, Marquis de Branciforte, who was then viceroy of New Spain.

---

soldiers used the buildings for corrals and barracks. The old José Castro adobe, one of the first examples of the architecture of that period, is still standing on the plaza near the church. The mission itself has been restored, and contains many fine relics, including a quaint hand-organ, whose old-fashioned waltzes and polkas once delighted the neophytes.

---

[47]The Natividad, a property of 2 leagues, was owned by Manuel Butron and Nicolas Alviso.

[48]Cayetano, of 2 leagues, was owned by Ignacio Vallejo.

[49]Either Bolsa del Pájaro, a property of 2 leagues owned by Sebastián Rodríguez, or Arroyo del Rodeo, a small ranch owned by Francisco Rodríguez.

[50]José Amesti, a Spanish-Basque merchant of Monterey, owned Corralitos.

[51]The pueblo of Branciforte was one of the settlements of Spanish colonists established July 24, 1797, by order of the Spanish government. See Hittell, op. cit., I, 576 ff. More authentic than De Mofras is the padron, a census of 1842 listing 127 Spanish Californians, 23 foreigners, and 46 Indians. Sir George Simpson, op. cit., I, 364, places the population at 150.

Today this small village has 300 white residents. Of these the majority are North Americans who have married the feminine descendants of the Spanish colonists. Although some are engaged in commerce and agriculture, the majority live by cutting wood or working in the saw-mills. The Americans are reputed to be trouble-makers; after aiding Alvarado to become governor, they were subsequently made prisoners at his order, and now, flushed by their recent successes in California, they are prepared to undertake new ventures.

The trip can be made from Branciforte to Monterey on horseback in eight or ten hours, and by sea in two or three hours. If the need arises, James Graham,[52] whose rancho lies near the village, can instantly rally to his support 100 riflemen and American trappers, armed with long carbines. The fact should be clearly recognized that Monterey could be seized by them at any time as easily as their fellow-countrymen in the south could become masters of El Pueblo de Los Angeles.

The village of Branciforte lies one mile east of the mission at Santa Cruz. These two settlements, which are pleasantly situated one kilometer from shore, face southward and command a sweeping view of Monterey Bay. The houses are scattered over a vast area covered with vegetation and shaded by groups of pines. Seven brooks pouring down from the Santa Cruz Mountains serve to propel mechanical sawmills, water the pastures, and enrich the fields ripe for cultivation.

Santa Cruz Mission,[53] founded August 28, 1791, lies a mile from shore, 6 leagues from Mission San Juan Bautista, and 17 leagues from Santa Clara. The buildings are commodious and in a good state of preservation. All furniture, however, has been stolen, the ranchos have been given away, and the live stock divided among the governor's friends. The mission no longer owns any property. In place of the 600 Indians that once gathered at her gates, fewer than one-sixtieth remain. In 1834,[54] 2,500 fanegas were harvested, and the community possessed 8,000 cattle, 800 horses, and 10,000 sheep. The lands surrounding Santa Cruz are especially adapted to raising vegetables such as beans, peas, and

---

[52]This was a lawless Kentucky trapper, Isaac Graham, who reached California in 1833. After many adventures, including a plot against the government, he bought Rancho Sayante near Branciforte and erected a sawmill.

[53]Mission of the Holy Cross.

[54]Mission statistics of 1835 list among the holdings of Santa Cruz 2,900 sheep, 500 horses, and 3,700 cattle; and, in 1837, 36 cattle, 127 horses, and 1,026 sheep. See Engelhardt, Franciscans in California (Harbor Springs, Mich., 1897), p. 379. For a complete history of this mission see H. A. Van Coenen Torchiana, Story of the Mission Santa Cruz, (San Francisco, 1933).

kidney beans; local corn, however, grows better than wheat. The fact
that ample water is available for irrigation contributes materially to the
successful cultivation of kitchen gardens. For this reason many whaling
ships anchor here at Santa Cruz to take on vegetables which are so
difficult to procure at Monterey. In the area extending between the mission and the village of Branciforte, several new houses have been built
and all signs indicate that in time this settlement will grow into an
important village.

The range extending from Santa Cruz to Point Lobos, the southern
extremity of San Francisco Harbor, is covered with extensive forests that
extend down to the shore. This coast is entirely safe; near shore the
depth is in the neighborhood of 25 fathoms, and two shelters are available
from northwesters in the lee of Point Año Neuvo and that of San Pedro.

The route from Santa Cruz to Santa Clara, or rather to the pueblo
of San José, leads over the mountains for a distance of 8 leagues through
superb forests notable primarily for a particular species of tall oak, with
straight trunks, called Encina de la Sierra,[55] which is highly prized in
this land. In the tiny valleys near the waterfalls cattle ranchos and sawmills are situated, while ranchos are also scattered along the coast as far
as San Francisco. Like the Santa Inés range, that of Santa Cruz abounds
in many kinds of bear, buck, and deer.

Santa Cruz Mission is situated on a detour west from the main route
that leads to the other settlements. Thus, in order to continue a description of the country from south to north, the narrative must be continued
from San Juan Bautista. An immense plain, quite level, that measures
16 leagues long by 6 or 8 wide, separates San Juan from the pueblo of
San José. This country is almost uninhabited, only four small ranchos
being found along the route. These are: La Brea,[56] a league from the
mission, near which is a deposit of solidified bitumen; Los Germanos,[57]
a mile beyond; and, on the left a mile from the latter, Rancho Castro.[58]
A league east lies the vast rancho of Las Ortegas,[59] owned by a Scotch-

---

[55]Mountain oak.

[56]La Brea was probably the old sheep ranch lying north-northeast of one
owned by the mission that contained deposits of pitch and sulphur.

[57]Los Germanos was a grant of a league, called Juristac, made in 1835
to A. and F. German.

[58]Numerous ranchos were held by the Castro family: Mariano Castro owned
Rancho de las Animas, or Sitio de la Brea, by grant of August 17, 1802; in 1834,
6 square leagues called Las Llagas had been awarded to Carlos Castro.

[59]In 1833, a league grant, La Polka, went to Isabel Ortega, and another
league, San Ysidro, to Quintín Ortega; the latter had originally been held by
Ignacio Ortega.

man, MacRoy.[60] This has about 100 occupants and a large amount of live stock and seems destined to become an important center with its abundance of water, plains, and excellent farming lands. Several Englishmen have already come here to reside; a Frenchman, Desforges,[61] also has a shop and does a good business.

The pueblo or village of San José[62] was founded under the protection of Our Lady of Guadalupe early in November, 1777, by Felipe de Neve, governor of California, acting under orders issued by the able viceroy of New Spain, Don Antonio Bucareli. The village proper lies on a broad plain near the tip of the banks of the Guadalupe River that empties into San Francisco Bay, some 3 leagues away. On the Santa Cruz range are several large forests, which, by protecting the village from winds off the ocean, assure a mild climate. Enclosed on the east and west by two parallel mountain ranges, the valley is well watered and adequately wooded. The country produces fine grain, cheese, and fruit. Vineyards are also proving successful, although their cultivation has been neglected by the colonists. The population at San José is made up of 500 white inhabitants and a few hundred Indians who are employed in the fields. Among the white settlers, Englishmen and Americans predominate. Control is vested in a sub-prefect and an alcalde. There is no garrison.

The sub-prefect, Don Antonio Suñol,[63] originally of Barcelona, has served in the French navy and was on board the *Epérvier* at Rochefort in 1815 when the emperor left that ship to board the *Bellérophon*. M. Suñol speaks French fluently and seems friendly towards France. Since he owns two ranchos and considerable live stock, and has charge of a

---

[60]The MacRoy referred to by De Mofras is undoubtedly John Cameron of Inverness, who reached Monterey in 1813, where, having deserted his ship, he assumed his mother's name of Gilroy. In 1821 he married the daughter of Ignacio Ortega, subsequently inheriting part of his ranch. The town of Gilroy now bears his name. Fraser's **History of Santa Clara County** (San Francisco, 1881), pp. 271-274.

[61]Auguste Desforges was a Frenchman who in 1834 came to California with the Híjar and Padrés colonists.

[62]Named for Saint Joseph, the settlement, a farming community, was founded on November 29 on the east bank of the Guadalupe River, a mile or so north of the present city, by 14 men and their families. In 1841, official estimates place the population at 934 inhabitants—considerably above De Mofras' figure. For its history see Frederick Hall, **History of San José** (San Francisco, 1871); also James and McMurray, **History of San José** (San José, 1933).

[63]Antonio María Suñol had come to California in 1817 as a sailor on the **Bordelaise**. He was sub-prefect from 1841 to 1844. His property, El Valle de San José, contained more than 50,000 acres. Edwin Bryant, **What I Saw in California** (Santa Ana, 1936), p. 296 describes his visit to Suñol at San José.

business that assures him high standing in the community, his assistance would be invaluable to French vessels arriving at Monterey or San Francisco.

The citizens of the pueblo, grown rich through despoiling the missions nearby, own between them some 50,000 cattle. At the present writing they no longer own horses, for the latter have been carried off in daily raids by the Indians who were turned out of the missions and have since taken refuge in the Tulare [Valley]. Governor Alvarado aspired to bestow his own name on the village, but the old appelation has remained. San José is also known in local circles as El Pueblo de Arriba, or Upper Village, to distinguish it from El Pueblo de los Angeles, or Lower Village, El Pueblo de Abajo.

Santa Clara Mission[64] is situated on the same plain as El Pueblo de San José, and about a league beyond the settlement. The connecting road leads past green meadows and is shaded by magnificent trees that form a charming promenade. The mission is 19 leagues beyond that of San Juan Bautista, 11 from Santa Cruz, and 6 from San José. Founded on January 18, 1777, by the first apostolic prefect, the Reverend Father Junípero Serra, it is one of the oldest in the country. The buildings, of sturdy construction, are in excellent condition. This mission is surrounded by extensive orchards and kitchen gardens, and its wine is superb. As late as 1834, 1,800 Indians were living near the mission, which harvested 6,000 fanegas, and owned 13,000 cattle, 1,200 horses, and 15,000 sheep. But now fewer than 300 neophytes, 1,500 cattle, 250 horses, and 3,000 sheep remain.

The ranchos of San Francisquito,[65] Las Pulgas,[66] and San Mateo[67]

---

[64]Mission Santa Clara de Asis, which is still standing, was founded, according to Father Palóu, on January 12. See Bolton's **Palóu**, IV, 159-161. A contemporary visitor, Charles Wilkes, **Narrative of the U. S. Exploring Expedition during the years 1838, 1839, 1840, 1841, 1842** (5 vols. and atlas, Philadelphia, 1845), V, 203 ff., describes it as follows: "The church and mission house have a dilapidated look; their title roofs and whitewashed walls require extensive repairs, as well as all the woodwork of the doors, posts, etc. The church flanks the mission house on the north, and is about 150 feet long by 40 wide, and about 50 high. It is surmounted by a small steeple. The mission house is of only one story, with a corridor extending the whole length." Santa Clara was the last mission to be confiscated. Finally, on December 28, 1836, José Ramón Estrada took posession. Ten years later, in 1846, Governor Pío Pico sold the mission to Andrés Pico and Juan B. Alvarado for $12,000. In 1841, Ignacio Alviso was administrator.

[65]Rinconada del Arroyo de San Francisquito had passed to Doña Soledad Ortega, and in 1839 to Antonio Buelna.

[66]Las Pulgas, 4 leagues, in San Mateo County, had been acquired in 1836 by Luís Argüello.

[67]For San Mateo see infra, I, 225, note 86.

have been given away. Two leagues northeast, near the Santa Clara River, at the foot of the Bay of San Francisco, an excellent landing is available for small boats handling produce. As the population of the pueblo increases, undoubtedly the land lying between there and Santa Clara will be built up with houses, since the situation is extremely favorable for the growth of a large city. A party of 40 Americans who had come overland from the United States early in 1842 arrived at the pueblo with the intention of locating there, while 24 of their comrades, who had crossed the Sierra Nevada, went down to Los Angeles with the idea of becoming settlers.

Santa Clara has always been one of the leading missions. The ideal situation and the mildness of the climate attracted the natives, and the Spanish Fathers gave so much thought to their education and instruction in the mechanical arts that they became skilled carpenters, blacksmiths, and even masons.

Music was also taught with marked success, and their neophyte orchestra was known throughout the land. One of the Fathers purchased from a French whaler thirty complete uniforms and organized a band of musicians. Our party was privileged to attend some of their performances when at Santa Cruz on September 14, 1841, the fête day consecrated to the exaltation of the Holy Cross, and it was not without keen surprise that we heard musicians, brought over from Santa Clara, sing the *Marseillaise,* as the congregation rose, and escort the procession singing *Vive Henri IV*. After mass, upon asking one of the Fathers how these Indians happened to know these airs, I was informed that one of his predecessors had brought a small hand organ from France and that the Indians, after hearing the airs, had instinctively arranged the songs for use by the various instruments.

Several times at Santa Clara our party received the most cordial hospitality at the hands of the Reverend Father José del Mercado.[68] Without the horses he was kind enough to lend us, it would have been impossible to have continued our explorations. Two leagues from Santa Clara and one from the pueblo of San José, an English concern, the Hudson's Bay Company, has stationed an intelligent agent, Don Diego

---

[68]Jesús María Vásquez del Mercado—as he is correctly known—came to California from Zacatecas, Mexico, in 1833. Of him Bancroft, (California, IV, 682, note) says: "Although a man of good abilities and education, of fine presence and engaging manners, he was an intriguer, arbitrary in his acts, and always ready to quarrel with anyone who would not accept his views." He left Santa Clara in 1844.

Forbes,[69] the son of an Englishman, although born in Spanish America. Forbes is an active and energetic young man, and an ideal type to further the ambitious plans of the company, as will be later disclosed. Married to a Californian, he now owns a vast rancho southeast of San Francisco Bay, as well as an excellent wharf, thus enabling the company to transport goods by water from the main warehouse situated near the moorings of Yerba Buena, and facilitate the handling of grain, hides, wools, and silks from the many ranchos in the vicinity of Missions San José and Santa Clara, and El Pueblo de San José de Guadalupe.

Mission San José,[70] founded June 18, 1797, by the Reverend Father Francisco de Lasuen, is situated about 10 leagues from the pueblo of Santa Clara, and 17 from Mission Dolores. This is the last church east and south of San Francisco Harbor. The buildings stand near a chain of hills whose eastern slope is watered by the San Joaquin River.[71] Because of the proximity of the Tulare [Valley] this mission has been able to gather under its roof hordes of natives. The Reverend Father Narciso Durán,[72] apostolic prefect, who has now retired to Santa Bárbara, left at San José, in 1834, 2,300 neophytes, 24,000 cattle, 1,100 horses, 19,000 sheep, and supplies to the amount of 60 barrels of wine and 10,000 fanegas of grain.[73] Of the latter commodity 2,000 fanegas were sold to the Russians who came down once a year from their colony of New Archangel on the island of Sitka.

Father Duran's successor, the Reverend Father José González,

---

[69]Otherwise known as James Alexander Forbes, of Scotland, who went to San Francisco on one of the early whaling vessesl. For a time he served as assistant to Father Viador at Santa Clara. In July, 1834, he married Ana María Galindo. Later he became local agent for the Hudson's Bay Company at San José and in 1842 became British vice-consul at Monterey, although much of his time was spent in San Francisco. He was not, as so often believed, the Alexander Forbes whose volume on California was so widely circulated. Because of his official position, he was widely known throughout northern California. His rancho was the Potrero de Santa Clara.

[70]This mission was formally consecrated on June 11, 1797, by Father Lasuen, on the site of land known to the Indians as Oroyson, as La Misión del Gloriosísimo Patriarca Señor San José. Because of its proximity to the land of the hostile Tulare Indians, the mission was subject to attack. In 1808 the adobe church was completed. On May 5, 1846, the mission was sold by Governor Pío Pico to Andrés Pico and Juan Alvarado for $12,000.

[71]For Mission San José see Edwin Bryant, op. cit., p. 288 ff.

[72]The Spaniard, Narciso Durán, came to California in 1806 and was stationed at San José. For several years he served as the superior of the California missions. For his life see Engelhardt, Missions, II, III, IV, passim.

[73]A report made made by Father González in 1835 lists mission wealth as follows: 18,000 cattle, 15,000 sheep, 1,100 horses, and property valued at $20,000. Neophytes probably numbered 1,500. San José was a wheat producing mission, possibly the richest in the state.

acting president[74] of the northern missions as late as 1837, turned over to the agents of the government 17,000 cattle, after spending 6,000 piasters for supplies for the colony. Today 8,000 cattle, 200 horses, and 9,000 sheep remain. Father González has been able to retain about 400 Indians who are enjoying the spoils of the former mission wealth and appear extremely well fed and dressed. In fact, chiefs or alcaldes were seen fully garbed in woolen garments, with cloaks, trousers, blue vests, waistcoats, red sashes, shirts of white linen, shoes, stockings, broad felt hats, and cravats of black silk.

This mission, together with San Gabriel and San Luís Rey, offers the most favorable opportunity to study the remarkable system introduced by the Spanish Fathers, of which the Jesuits have the honor of being the founders. The buildings and church are extensive and well preserved. At the rear of the edifice are some fine vines, a grove of olives, and an extensive orchard filled with fruit trees imported from Europe. A school in which were assembled 60 Indian children who showed amazing facility in learning Spanish, reading, writing, and especially arithmetic, was inspected with considerable interest. Unfortunately, only two or three white children were attending the school, although more than 50 were living in the mission. However, most of the rancheros, who spend their time in gambling and debauchery, pay slight attention to their families.

Mission San José has been victimized by the relatives[75] of the *comandante general,* Don Mariano Vallejo,[76] who have grown rich from the spoils. Some have carried off the animals; others have taken land and have even built houses opposite the mission with Indian labor and

---

[74]In 1833 Father Durán was succeeded by Father José María de Jesús González Rubio, who remained until 1842.

[75]José de Jesús Vallejo, brother of Mariano, was administrator of the missions. Live stock had been taken from the mission by Mariano Vallejo, Antonio Buelna, Mariano Guillermo Castro, Juan Alvires, and Rafael and Santiago Estrada.

[76]Mariano Guadalupe Vallejo was born in 1808 at Monterey, where he attended school and entered military service. In 1831 he took charge of the presidio in San Francisco. In 1832 Vallejo married Francisca Carrillo of San Diego. Two years later he acquired Rancho Petaluma, north of San Francisco, and the following year founded the town of Sonoma. As comandante Vallejo soon rose to be the most powerful leader in California and the military dictator of the north. Although in sympathy with the movement of the Americans in California, yet he experienced humiliating treatment at their hands when, in 1846, the Bear Flag was raised at Sonoma. See Bancroft, **California, passim**; also Davis, **op. cit., passim.** Like Sutter, Vallejo is mentioned in the majority of contemporary records and has left many manuscripts, now housed in the Bancroft Library.

the use of mission material. All the ranchos belonging to the community
have been confiscated until scarcely a square league of vacant ground
remains around the mission. Notwithstanding, to complete its despolia-
tion and separate the neophytes from their old haunt, an Indian settlement is soon to be formed some distance from the mission, and the
natives supplied with live stock which will soon be confiscated or dis-
sipated by their owners.

At San José the spectacle of a Father put on rations by the administrator was again witnessed. Each time this building was visited, it was
always from Father González that hospitality was sought. This poor
monk was then obliged to see the majordomo in order to secure two
portions of food, his own rations being sufficient only for one person.
And although the administrator was living well and eating wheat
bread, he sent the president a plain piece of beef and some inferior corn
cakes. Father González endured these humiliations without complaint,
only raising his voice to defend his neophytes against plunder and
cruel treatment at the hands of the white men.

About two leagues from San José, either at Point Potrero or one of
the many openings at the mouth of the Calaveras River, small boats
often land. Following the coast that forms the southeastern area of the
Bay of San Francisco lie several ranchos rich in cattle and of extreme
fertility. These are known as San Leandro,[77] Estudillo, Martinez,[78] San
Antonio,[79] Peralta, and Castro.[80] The latter lies at the tip of Point San
Pablo which forms the southern entrance to the strait and bay of that
name. A range of hills, 2 or 3 leagues inland from the shore, parallels
the coast, ending at Point San Pablo. Some of its peaks are nearly 600
meters in height, and are crowned by magnificent red pines, *palos
colorados*. Two French carpenters, Mm. Sicard[81] and Leroy,[82] are exploit-

[77]At this point De Mofras has confused names of properties with names of
owners. San Leandro was owned by José Joaquin Estudillo, who raised sheep,
cattle, and a few horses.

[78]Don Ignacio Martínez owned Rancho Pinóle on the south side of Carquinez
Strait, where he raised thousands of head of cattle.

[79]San Antonio, on which Oakland and Alameda now stand, was owned at
this time by Don Luís Peralta.

[80]West of Rancho Pinóle was the Joaquin Castro property of San Pablo, also
used to raise cattle and fine horses. Another Castro rancho was that of Don
Guillermo, the San Lorenzo.

[81]Pierre Theodore Sicard was a sailor and carpenter who reached California
in 1833, subsequently working on various ranches and later as a miner on the
Yuba River.

[82]Joseph Leroy was a young Frenchman who came to the coast in 1836.
Little is known of his life in California.

ing these woods to good profit. The various streams that descend from the mountains are navigable by small boats that take on loads of planks and timber; most of this lumber is sent over to the opposite coast to the small village of Yerba Buena, which has no wood for building purposes.

On the eastern slope of the mountain range a few ranchos still exist, among them that of Amador[83] near the Bay of Carquinez; another belonging to an American, who calls himself Dr. Marsh,[84] lies on the left bank of the San Joaquin River at the foot of Mt. Diablo, the highest peak in the Californian range, whose actual height is 1,149 meters. The end of this chain is designated locally as Sierra de los Bolbones. The location of Mt. Diablo is important to navigators; being visible from afar it marks the entrance to San Francisco Harbor.

The route from Santa Clara Mission leading to that of San Francisco traverses a long plain dotted with clumps of oaks where numerous herds graze. Soon the small streams of San Francisco and San Mateo are crossed, near which grow laurels of regal proportions and extraordinary height. The road winds in and out among the majestic trees leading past the ranchos of San Francisquito,[85] San Mateo,[86] Los Juanes,[87] Buri-Buri,[89] and Sánchez.

On the right, on the edge of the plain, mountains crowned with red pines stand out conspicuously; in the foreground the waters of the bay frequently approach the road where areas encrusted with salt deposits appear, which from a distance sparkle in the sun like vast fields of snow. On the left towers the San Bruno range, terminating in that of Santa Cruz, with its lofty peaks of 400 or 500 meters. The range is dominated by Mt. Santa Clara, visible for more than 10 leagues out

---

[83]Don José María Amador, and his partner, Don Dolores Pacheco, owned a great ranch east of Castro's San Lorenzo.

[84]Dr. John Marsh, whom De Mofras calls March, was a Yankee who first came to Los Angeles in 1836, after spending several years in the Southwest. Acquiring a large land grant, Los Medanos, near Mt. Diablo, he established a residence and subsequently amassed a large fortune. His eccentric ways made him unpopular, and he lived the life of a recluse. After Sutter he was probably the best-known foreigner in California, being mentioned in the majority of early diaries and records. The romantic tale of his life and adventures has been ably told by Dr. George D. Lyman in **John Marsh, Pioneer** (New York, 1930).

[85]San Francisquito had been granted in 1839 to Antonio Buelna. There was also San Francisquito de las Llagas of 6 leagues owned by Carlos Castro.

[86]San Mateo, of 2 leagues, was the property of José Sánchez.

[87]Possibly Los Juanes was Las Pulgas, owned by the Argüello family, a large rancho adjoining Buri-buri on the way to San Francisco.

[88]Buri-buri Rancho was owned by José Sánchez. It lay above the towns of Belmont and Redwood City.

at sea. Having reached the tip of San Bruno, the land becomes arid, being sandy near the mission. Near the coast, however, on the western slope of the San Bruno range, vegetation appears on the lowlands. Here lie the prosperous ranchos of Vásquez,[89] Sánchez,[90] and Guerrero.[91]

Mission Los Dolores de San Francisco de Asis,[92] founded October 9, 1776,[93] by the Reverend Father Serra, the first apostolic prefect, stands at the head of the peninsula that forms the southern entrance to the Bay of San Francisco, and is the last one southwest of this port. The mission is 14 leagues from Santa Clara, 2 leagues from the presidio and anchorage of Yerba Buena, and half a mile from the shore. Although this mission owns good pasturage, its holdings for the greater part are not adapted to cultivation, and are not extensive. The northwest winds make this locality somewhat disagreeable, and the port, as a result, has never shown marked development. All cultivation was carried on on the other side of the bay at Point San Pablo, occupied today by the San Castro Rancho, which was capable of yielding 2,500 fanegas. In 1834 more than 400 Indians, 5,000 cattle, 600 horses, and 4,000 sheep belonged to the mission. The inmates have been stripped of all they possess, and now control fewer than 60 cattle, 50 horses, and 200 sheep. Approximately 50 Indians still live in huts near the mission, where they work small tracts of land, sheltered from the winds that extend between Points Alvisadera and San Quentin at what is known as Las Cámaras del Padre Ramón.[94] The buildings are extensive but dilapidated; there is no missionary in residence, and the church is in charge of the Reverend Father Mercado of Santa Clara.

[89]Tiburcio Vásquez owned Corral de Tierra in San Mateo County, a grant of a league made in 1839. In 1841 Vásquez became administrator for Mission Dolores.

[90]In 1841 José de la Cruz Sánchez had been granted 2 leagues called Rancho San Mateo.

Sánchez held many political offices in San Francisco, including a term as administrator of the mission.

[91]Don Francisco Guerrero y Palomares, alcalde and justice of the peace, was a prominent resident of San Francisco who resided for a time at the mission. In 1839 he acquired Rancho Corral de Tierra below San Francisco near Half Moon Bay.

[92]The Sorrows of St. Francis of Assisi.

[93]Mass was held on the site of the mission on June 29, 1776, a date generally accepted as that of its foundation. See Engelhardt, Mission San Francisco Dolores (Chicago, 1924), p. 47; also Bolton, Palóu, IV, 132. Owing to its commanding situation near the bay, Dolores was visited by the majority of all foreigners who came to California. Sir George Simpson, op. cit., gives an excellent description of the buildings and statues of the mission in 1840. Hartnell's report of 1839 lists 750 cattle, 950 horses, 1,275 sheep, and 40 mules. In 1842 Tiburcio Vásquez acted as administrator.

[94]Las Cámaras del Padre Ramón: The granaries of Father Ramón. This was Father Ramón Abella who served at Dolores from 1797 to 1817.

The small village of Yerba Buena,[95] the village of mint, is situated on the shore of the anchorage that bears the same name. Founded only a few years ago,[96] it has at the outside not more than twenty houses,[97] which belong exclusively to foreigners and are used merely as places to store goods coming in by ship. This locality is, however, of considerable importance, all commerce in the Bay of San Francisco being now concentrated at this port, and the Hudson's Bay Company considers this point in so favorable a light that in September, 1841, they purchased the largest and finest house[98] near the shore. Here they established a trading post which is in the charge of Mr. William Rae, the son-in-law of Dr. McLoughlin,[99] chief factor and head of their posts on the Columbia River. With the exception of this English house, the principal dwelling is one occupied by two Americans, Mr. Spear[100] and Captain Hinckley.[101] In a large factory these men have established an ingenious mechanism which by means of four mules caused a wheat mill, a complete system for sifting flour, and a sawmill which cuts wood into any desired length,

[95]El Paraje de Yerba Buena (place of mint) was a small cove less than a mile wide. The Island of Yerba Buena lay beyond its mouth.

[96]The first house was built near the cove by Jacob Leese, a trader, in July, 1836, on what is now the south side of Clay Street, just west of Dupont. See John S. Hittell, A History of San Francisco (San Francisco, 1878), and Zoeth S. Eldredge, The Beginnings of San Francisco (2 vols., San Francisco, 1912), for the history of this city.

[97]Of Yerba Buena, Lieutenant Wilkes, an astute visitor of 1842, comments: "Its buildings may be counted, and consist of a large frame building, occupied by the agent of the Hudson's Bay Company, a store, kept by Mr. Spear, an American; a billiard-room and bar; a poop cabin of a ship, occupied as a dwelling of Captain Hinckley; a blacksmith's shop and some out-buildings."

[98]This store had been built and used by Jacob Leese, who sold it, together with four lots. It stood on the west side of Montgomery, between Clay and Sacramento Streets. Rae, now in charge, was a handsome Scotchman and a heavy drinker, who committeed suicide five years later. At this time the store was stocked with goods valued at $10,000. In September McLoughlin, his daughter, Eloise (Rae's wife), and De Mofras reached San Francisco aboard the Cowlitz.

[99]See the interesting story of this great pioneer by Eva Emery Dye, McLoughlin and Old Oregon (Chicago, 1900).

[100]William Heath Davis, op. cit., p. 98, writes: "Wilkes on being informed that De Mofras had been a guest of Spear while stopping at Yerba Buena was greatly interested, and inquired carefully and particularly about De Mofras' visit to California, asking Spear for all the details of his movements here and his conversations. He was particularly anxious to know if De Mofras ever divulged that the French government had any designs or intentions in regard to the Bay of San Francisco."

[101]In 1838 William Sturgis Hinckley and Nathan Spear opened a business in San Francisco. Their store, completed in 1840, stood on Montgomery Street, near Clay. From William Heath Davis, Spear's nephew, we know that De Mofras was a guest of Spear. Davis tells many amusing anecdotes of this visit. See op. cit., pp. 52-54.

to operate simultaneously. The firm makes a specialty of turning out shingles or planks for roofing. A Swiss captain, M. Vioget,[102] owns a well-built house and a shop. M. Prudon also possesses a house built by another Frenchman called Mathurin.[103] The former may prove quite useful, for he is thoroughly familiar with the topography of the bay and is an excellent pilot. At Yerba Buena it is impossible to procure anything in the way of supplies except fresh meat; water is not available and wood is inaccessible and difficult to obtain. The only person of authority at Yerba Buena is a man named Guerrero,[104] who resides at the mission and fulfills the duties of an alcalde, customs officer, and port captain for the southern end of the Bay of San Francisco.[105]

The presidio of San Francisco is now falling into decay,[106] is entirely dismantled, and is inhabited only by a sub-lieutenant and 5 soldier rancheros with their families. The building stands 2 leagues north of the mission and Yerba Buena, and 2 kilometers from the fort; the adjacent land consists of sand dunes, covered with brush. The Fort of San Francisco lies at the northern extremity of the peninsula which forms the southwestern part of the Bay of San Francisco and marks the exact opening of the entrance.

The fort[107] is situated on a small point some hundred meters long

---

[102]John J. Vioget, who made the first survey of San Francisco in 1839, was a Swiss surveyor who came to California in 1837. In 1840 he was granted two lots on which he erected a store. This stood near that of the Hudson's Bay Company and was used as a public bar where captains and merchants congregated. Ibid., pp. 258-259.

[103]Louis Mathurin, who built and perhaps occupied Prudon's home for a time.

[104]Francisco Guerrero y Palomares, one of the founders of San Francisco, was alcalde at the time De Mofras visited the village. He was kind-hearted, intelligent, and affable. Simpson, op. cit., who knew Guerrero, did not regard him with high favor.

[105]Port of San Francisco: 37° 48' 30" n. lat.; 124° 48' 26" w. long.; time 8h 19m 14s; inclination 62° 25', declination, 15° 30' n. e. (Jan. 1842); establishment of the port at Yerba Buena, 10h 34m; at Sausalito, 12h; height of tide, 2m 5. (D. de M.)

[106]The presidio was founded on September 17, 1776, on the left side of the entrance to the bay on land now held as a U. S. military reservation. Buildings under construction until 1800 were surrounded by an adobe wall 14 feet high and 5 feet thick. In the early days all soldiers and colonists made their homes within these walls. For many years the presidio was in charge of Mariano Vallejo, who subsequently made his military headquarters at Sonoma. Between 1840 and 1842, Mesa, a sergeant, and 12 soldiers were stationed at the presidio which was now falling into ruins. The story of its founding is told in Bolton's Anza, passim.

[107]Castillo de San Joaquin, also known as Fort Blanco, stood on what was known as Punta del Cantil Blanco, a large promontory rising 100 feet out of the water on the left side of the mouth of the bay. The fort, built in 1794 of adobe, was shaped like a horseshoe, and had fourteen apertures for cannon. Barracks for the soldiers lay within the edifice.

which juts out into the sea and is made up of a simple adobe battery shaped like a horseshoe. This has 16 openings and is equipped with 3 obsolete guns, a cannon, and 2 good bronze pieces of 16 calibre, cast in Manila. These pieces are mounted on wooden gun-carriages which date from 1812 and are partially decayed. In the center of the horseshoe, the barracks, used originally to house soldiers, have fallen into ruins, and no one is living near the battery. On the land approach there is neither ditch nor outside protection; in fact all the fortifications are in range of a small hill a gunshot away, which thus commands the fort whose loop-holes face only toward the sea. The fort does not respond to guns fired at random, but there are always ships at anchor which will reply to signals, which it is advisable to give, especially in foggy weather.

The fort has been so completely abandoned that a ship could easily send its small boats over to the shores below and without attracting the attention of the presidio carry off the cannons that could be easily rolled down the cliff. This point, furthermore, is too high to permit accurate firing on ships that pass below, for vessels come within range only at the neck of the bay, and batteries to be effective would have to be erected at a lower level.

Before describing the immense Bay of San Francisco, a group of rocks known as the Farallon Islands should be mentioned, for these,[108] in a general way, indicate the entrance. At night, or in foggy weather, the islands are extremely dangerous owing to the submerged rocks surrounding them. They are divided into two small groups;[109] those toward the south, where the highest island can be seen 8 or 9 leagues away extending south, 3° east some 18 miles from Point Reyes. The northern group extends toward the northwest, where the surf continues in that direction for a considerable distance. Around the Farallons soundings disclose 50 to 60 meters, with a floor of hard clay.

The largest island, 2 miles in circumference, is oblong in shape and lies east-northeast and west-southwest. Each tip terminates in a mountain about 100 feet high which, descending gradually toward the center of the island, forms a small valley giving the appearance of a saddle when seen

---

[108]Southern Farallons, at the highest point; 37° 41′ 55″ n. lat., 125° 18′ 52″ w. lat. (D. de M.)

[109]The Farallons, a group of seven small, rocky islands devoid of vegetation, lie about 30 miles beyond the Golden Gate. Otter and fur seals, prized by Russian traders, lured hunters to these islands in the early nineteenth century. By 1812 the Farallons were the southern outpost of Fort Ross and annually housed from 6 to 30 Aleut workers and a few Russians. So successful were their operations that 8,000 seals were killed in one year.

either from the north or the south. The entire group is of volcanic origin. Apparently the rocks have been in a state of fusion, for in the lowlands innumerable pumice stones are found. There is neither water nor vegetation on these islands, but multitudes of sea birds come here to nest. On these islands in 1825, Russians from the port of Bodega established a trading post, composed of several Russian soldiers and 30 Kodiak Indians, to hunt seals, leopards,[110] and sea elephants which, at this time, swarmed over the rocks. So cruel was the war they waged against them that these species have been virtually exterminated.

When approaching by sea the traveller may recognize the entrance to the Port of San Francisco by the Farallons that lie on the same parallel, or toward the north, by Point Reyes and the Table Mountain, a peak nearly 800 meters high, and on the south by the Santa Clara Mountains and another peak of the San Bruno range, that from afar resembles two islands.

About 8¼ miles from the port the entrance to the harbor is blocked by a sand bar that extends in a southeasterly direction across the entrance of the bay. The soundings, as the bar is approached, decrease gradually to 6, and finally, to 4 fathoms at low tide. At high tide deep water increases regularly on the far side of the bar until bottom can no longer be found by sounding. When crossing the bar it is advisable to run at a safe distance south of the northern entrance, and to keep the small white island of Alcatraz on a direct line with the fort. In this way a depth of 12 to 14 meters will be assured. However, if a ship follows the northern shore line near Point Boneta and keeps the rock south of this point and the island of Yerba Buena in direct line, only a fathom and a quarter will be found, which is insufficient even for small ships owing to the heavy seas pounding over the bar which break with terrific force. On the northern end of the bar the water is shallower than toward the south.

Upon approaching the entrance it is advisable to remain near the center of the channel, where the depth is 40 or 50 fathoms, and keep in sight directly on the east a group of enormous pines that grow opposite the straits on a mountain some 600 meters high. Behind this mountain appears Mt. Diablo, the culminating point of the Bolbones chain which is 1,200 meters high. On the south all the dangers are exposed. If unavoidable, it is possible to pass south or to the lee of the rock that lies one-half mile offshore opposite Point Lobos. However, it is safer to avoid this on account of the treacherous currents. A dangerous surf extends

---

[110]Obviously an error; there were no leopards on the islands.

southwest of Point Boneta and a ship should not approach farther than necessary to come in line with the fort and the island of Yerba Buena. This line forms the extreme northern end of the entrance.

When passing through the mouth special attention must be paid to reefing in sail because of the eddies, tides, and squalls from offshore. Small boats should be kept ready to be lowered into the water for the entrance is narrow and the current adequately strong to pull the ship up on shore. Moreover, the depth is too great to cast anchor, and the wind is apt to subside just when most needed. Once Point Boneta is passed, the water is again deep, with a current along the northern shore that has tremendous force. If the ship is forced by the currents into the small sandy bay situated west of the port and guarded by the fort and Point Lobos, a good mooring in 10 or 15 fathoms will be found, and here it is possible to wait until the ebbing of the sea subsides. There is no danger just below the fort and an approach can be made to within 50 fathoms.

The entire northern shore of these narrow straits is more rugged and steeper than its southern area. Two little knolls command the fort which could be reached by guns of reasonable size. The width of the channel at this point does not exceed 1,600 meters. The fact is also generally known that cannon of large calibre hurl their projectiles for a distance of some 3 kilometers, while mortars, charged with 10 pounds of powder, can project their bomb for more than 2,600 meters.

Upon entering the harbor, three islands are visible—Yerba Buena, Alcatraz, and Angel Island. Two white rocks protrude from the water, one west and the other northwest of Alcatraz Island, both being at a distance of three-quarters of a mile. There is also a third and extremely dangerous rock, Blossom, named for the ship commanded by Captain Beechey by whom, in 1827, it was discovered. This rock is always submerged and has only a fathom of water at low tide. It lies on a direct line between the southwestern tip of the islands of Yerba Buena and Alcatraz, and is a mile and two-thirds from the southeastern extremity of Yerba Buena Island, seven-eighths of a mile from the southern point of Alcatraz, and a mile due north from the nearest point on the coast. Surrounding the rock the depth varies from 2 to 5 fathoms; but at a distance of two cable lengths there is from 18 to 20 meters of water. This rock presents the only hidden danger in the entire bay.

San Francisco Bay is divided into two arms; that of Santa Clara, extending south-southeast for exactly 30 miles, stretches between two chains of parallel mountains. One of these, the Santa Clara and San

Bruno range, follows the coast as far down as Monterey; the other, starting from San Pablo Bay, passes behind San José Mission and terminates in Mission San Juan Bautista. This arm of the sea ends in a group of lagoons and small channels that lead to the neighboring missions. The other arm extends in a northerly direction, passing between the points of San Pedro and San Pablo. Its entrance is marked by the tiny island of Molate[111] and other small islands. This forms San Pablo Bay, which is almost circular and approximately 15 miles in diameter. The missions of San Rafael and San Francisco Solano, and the village of Sonoma, are situated on the northern shore of this bay. On the east, through the Strait of Carquinez, San Pablo Bay joins that of Carquinez. The latter is equally extensive. Into its lower end flows the San Joaquin River, which unites, after flowing in from the south, with the Sacramento coming down from the north-northeast. The Jesús María River[112] is another fork of the Sacramento which, as it joins the main stream, forms an island 10 miles in length.

Generally speaking, the water in San Francisco Bay is deepest where the current is strongest and in addition to the current some difficulties invariably arise when disembarking at low tide. All the small creeks have comparatively little water and are frequently dry at low tide. The northeast coast, from Point San Pablo as far as San José, is so shallow that only light craft can navigate for a mile and a half offshore, the water being frequently only a fathom deep. The north shore presents the same characteristics.

After passing the fort, a ship can find shelter toward the north in the Bay of Sausalito, where moorings are available, or head south and cast anchor within sight of the pueblo of Yerba Buena. The moorings at Yerba Buena are available either directly in front of the houses or preferably a short distance north, one-half mile offshore. Here the water is 9 to 15 fathoms, with a mud bed and good anchorage. This locality is entirely safe, although at times exposed to gusts of wind and such strong seas that frequently for a period of eight or ten days vessels are unable to send skiffs ashore. For a quarter of a mile the water is so shallow that

---

[111]Mare Island.

[112]The Jesús María and the Sacramento rivers appear to be the same; the Jesús María, represented by explorers as running in a northerly direction and passing behind Bodega and Cape Mendocino, has never been identified. Many earlier travelers, however, referred to them as separate rivers; Gabriel Moraga called the Feather River the Sacramento and the Sacramento the Jesús María. De Mofras' description of the stream coincides in a general way with the Feather River. See map in Bancroft, California, IV, 244.

at low tide small boats cannot approach close to the houses. They must then come alongside the tip of a small point north of the anchorage, where a few flat rocks afford a good landing place.

The anchorage at Sausalito, or Whaler's Harbor, does not present any obstacles. Opposite the watering place, for a quarter of a mile, the depth is not less than 14 to 16 meters, with as much as 12 meters a cable's length off the point at Sausalito. Near shore the water is deep, ships being able to anchor at all times. Wood is available near by in large quantities. Table Mountain shelters this small bay from the violent northwest winds that make a sojourn at Yerba Buena cold and disagreeable, even in midsummer. Although these two places are not more than 5 miles apart—a distance that can be covered in less than one hour—the thermometer frequently registers 12 to 15 degrees higher at Sausalito than at Yerba Buena. Thus, when it is possible to bathe in the sea at Sausalito, at Yerba Buena a fire is needed. Behind the promontory at Sausalito, a few steps from the shore, looms a small rancho owned by an Englishman, Captain Richardson,[113] who holds the local rank of captain of this port. His house, however, is only a wooden shack. This man, who married a Californian and has several children, is an excellent pilot. Here horses, cattle, and a certain amount of fresh vegetables can be procured.

When navigating inside the bay accurate information about the tides should be secured. The two arms of the bay, oddly enough, lie approximately at right angles. In the center of the harbor where these unite, the tides change. Here eddies and cross currents extremely hazardous to shipping are formed. The tide starts to ebb in the arm of Santa Clara an hour before the flow reaches Yerba Buena and Angel Islands. High tide comes in by way of the same estuary of Santa Clara and the south shore, driving the waters that came down from the north arm of the bay toward Yerba Buena Island. The surge first strikes the calcareous rocks at the southern point of the Plaza de los Caballos, dividing as it strikes Alcatraz Island, where one division moves toward the arm of Santa Clara, and the other, after passing over the submerged rock Blossom, passes behind the tip of Angel Island. There it unites with a

---

[113]This was William A. Richardson, an English mate on the whaler **Orion** who reached San Francisco in 1822. In 1825 he married a local belle, María Antonia, daughter of Ignacio Martínez, commandant of the presidio. His boat that plied up and down the bay was often used to pilot vessels. In 1835 he became the first resident of San Francisco, living in a tent, then in a wooden shack, and finally an adobe on Dupont Street near Clay. In 1835 he moved to Sausalito where he secured a ranch. Davis, **op. cit., passim,** often refers to Richardson.

rapid current that proceeds from the narrow channel formed by the broad side of the island, and travels rapidly in a northerly direction between the two points in the Bay of San Pablo. The two white rocks and Alcatraz Island thus lie where the current reaches its peak.

When leaving San Francisco the direction of the wind should be observed. If this comes off the southwest, many difficulties will arise. East winds, on the contrary, are frequently only light breezes. These often prove deceptive, exposing ships to the danger of being becalmed off the bar, where it is perilous to cast anchor because of swells and shallow water. Winds off the north are undoubtedly the most favorable and are the prevailing winds along the coast. Upon departure ships are advised to head southwest in order to cross the bar in 7 fathoms. Given stiff breezes, this course is also desirable for entering port. In any event the small sandy bay south of Point Lobos, and especially the shore northwest of Point Boneta, should not be approached.

The bay contains three main islands and several small islands. Of these Angel Island is the largest and most important, being almost circular in shape and one mile and a quarter in diameter. On its eastern side the island has a watering place and excellent anchorage where ships can be overhauled. This island has wood and pasturage, and is now used to graze cattle belonging to a Californian, Don Antonio Osio.[114] The island is quite mountainous and has several peaks, the highest, in the center, being some 226 meters above sea level. From a military standpoint Angel Island is important, for this island to some extent commands the entrance to the port. Guns at the anchorage at Sausalito and shots fired at random could, however, cover most of the moorings and important points in the bay.

The Island of Yerba Buena lies about a mile and a half offshore opposite the anchorage bearing the same name. Except for the eastern shore, which is semicircular and offers anchorage in 4 or 5 fathoms, it is quadrilateral in shape. The southern part of the island is the most rugged and appears to be 300 meters high with a circumference approximately of 3 miles. This has a few brooks and some timber, but no herds.

Alcatraz Island,[115] so-named from the immense flocks of pelicans who nest here in the crevices of the rocks, is less than a mile and a half in circumference and 10 to 15 meters high. It is glistening white and

---

[114]Ocio in the French text. Antonio M. Osio was a native Californian who held many political offices and acquired large land holdings. Los Angeles, now Angel Island, was granted in 1838 to Osio, but was never occupied.

[115]Alcatraz was also known as Des Pelicans, or Pelican Island. (D. de M.)

devoid of all vegetation. Off its northeastern side this small island has 13 fathoms of water, but on the west, at the foot of the rocks, this is only 3 to 4 fathoms. A cable's length away, however, 9 to 12 fathoms prevail.

The two small rocks that lie a mile northwest of Alcatraz Island are a few meters long and 2 broad. Here, on the extreme south, soundings show a depth of 5 or 7 fathoms, and on the opposite side from 3 to 4 fathoms. Viewed from afar, both resemble ships in full sail. Various kinds of seals often lounge on these rocks.

The tiny island of Molate, the smallest in the harbor, is little more than a large mass of rocks, a mile in circumference, rising 15 or 20 meters out of the water and barren of all growth. It lies in the northern end of the bay, a mile from shore and a league south of Point San Pablo. On all sides of the island the depth is 8 to 15 fathoms, and ships can approach in safety. In the vast expanse of San Francisco Bay near the shore other small islands rise, but since they may be approached safely, their description would be superfluous.

The entrance to San Pablo Bay, a mile and a half wide, is formed on the north by Point San Pablo and on the south by Point San Pablo. The trip across the strait materially shortens the journey for those traveling overland by way of the Russian ranchos and the Missions of San Rafael and San Solano down the eastern side of the San Francisco Bay to San José and Monterey. The Straits and Bay of San Pablo are sufficiently deep for large merchant vessels, the minimum depth being at least 8 or 9 fathoms. In navigating across the bay, ships are warned to keep near the south shore, for on the north there is only a fathom, and sometimes less, a league offshore. A lagoon, situated at the head of the bay, reaches within 3 kilometers of Mission San Francisco Solano and the village of Sonoma. San Pablo Bay is virtually circular in shape, its diameter at its widest point from north to south is 3½ leagues, and from east to west, 5 leagues.

Toward the east, the Bay of San Pablo terminates in Carquinez Strait. This forms the etrance to the bay of the same name, and in extent, shape, and location is similar to those leading into San Pablo Bay. Into the tip of Carquinez empty, after being united, the only three rivers of any importance in California, the San Joaquin, Jesús María, and especially the Sacramento. These will be subsequently described in considerable detail. Smaller streams like the San José, Guadalupe, Santa Clara, San Mateo, and others which are unnavigable have already been discussed. At this point the settled areas north of San Francisco Bay will be described.

At the foot of the large cove of Sausalito, north of the spit of land that juts out and two leagues east of Richardson, the rancho of the Irishman, Read,[116] a pilot who has since died, is situated. Near the house where the ground is low, there stands a fine grove of pines, whose trunks, cut in huge pieces, are brought down to the sawmills at Yerba Buena. The land in this vicinity has remarkably fine pasturage. Ships requiring a large supply of salt meat should apply to Read's Rancho rather than that of Richardson. The herds of the former are in excellent condition and his widow owns 4,000 cattle.

When visiting the country north of the bay for the first time, I reached Read's Rancho at sunset. There in the wilderness, to my surprise, the distant sound of a horn was heard. Approaching at a gallop I soon recognized the national Irish air, Robin Adair. Almost simultaneously upon a small hillock, a man on horseback appeared playing the bugle. This man proved to be Read, who had trained his herds to come every night at the sound of this horn.

Beyond the ranchos of Richardson and Read, stretching north and west toward the sea for a distance of 8 to 12 leagues, lie the small ranchos of Las Gallinas,[117] Berry,[118] García,[119] Osio,[120] and, near Point Reyes, adjoining the port of Bodega, one owned by Bòhorques,[121] More remote in the northeasterly direction are Ortega,[122] Martin,[123] Petaluma,[124] Los Vallejos,[125] Dawson,[126] and McIntosh:[127] The latter is the northern

[116]This was John Read, or Reed, an Irish sailor, who came to California about 1826. For a time Read served as majordomo of San Rafael Mission, and later operated a ferry on the bay.

[117]Las Gallinas was the property of an Irishman, Timothy Murphy, who had been granted 3 leagues of land at Points San Pedro, Santa Margarita, and Las Gallinas, near the town of San Rafael. Murphy was a sportsman and philanthropist who served from 1837 to 1842 as administrator of San Rafael Mission.

[118]James Richard Berry was an Irishman who in 1836 became grantee of Rancho Punta Reyes.

[119]That same year Rafael García acquired 2 leagues called Tamales y Baulinas in Marin County, where he built a large adobe.

[120]Antonio Osio was the owner of Punta de los Reyes in Marin County. See supra, I, 234, also note 114.

[121]Bartolomé Bohorques, whom De Mofras calls Bojorquez, a soldier, held Rancho Laguna de San Antonio.

[122]Antonio Ortega, grantee of the Arroyo de San Antonio in Marin County.

[123]John Martin, a Scotch sailor, lived on the Corte de Madera de Novato rancho in what is now Marin County.

[124]The vast Petaluma ranch (Pitaluma in the French text), on the site of Sonoma, had been granted in 1823 to Mariano Vallejo.

[125]Los Vallejos probably refers to the three great ranchos of Petaluma, Temblec, and Suscol near Sonoma, owned by Mariano Vallejo.

[126]Dorson in the French text. This pioneer settled on the Estéro Americano Rancho near Bodega, and, later, on the Pogoloni property.

[127]MacKintosh in the French text. Edward McIntosh settled on the Estéro Americano with Dawson, and subsequently acquired the property.

outpost in Mexican territory and lies only a league away from Vasili Khliebnikov's farm, the first of the extensive Russian holdings situated eighteen leagues from San Francisco Bay.

Five miles north of Read's Rancho, a short distance inland from the shore, rises San Rafael Mission,[128] now in ruins. This was founded December 18, 1817, by the Reverend Father Fortuny. At one time San Rafael controlled 200 neophytes, 3,000 cattle, 500 horses, and 4,500 sheep, while its harvests yielded 1,500 fanegas. The mission served as a convalescence home for neophytes from Mission Dolores, who were unable to withstand the harsh climate of San Francisco. Now, among its ruins only 20 Indians and an Irishman named Murphy reside. The mission lands are rich and fertile, and tobacco plants raised by a man named Ortega appear to thrive. Two thousand feet of vines have been removed at the order of Comandante Vallejo and planted on his ranch at Petaluma originally owned by San Solano Mission. Live stock from San Rafael have been confiscated in a similar manner by this same individual.

After leaving San Rafael and passing the extensive salt marshes and Rancho del Indio, a farm run by a few liberated Indians, San Francisco Solano, 13 leagues from the preceding mission is reached.

Mission San Francisco Solano, founded August 25, 1823, by the Reverend Father Amorós,[129] a Spanish Franciscan, is the last and most northerly of these religious establishments that so richly deserve to have been preserved. San Solano is delightfully situated, and the vast fields surrounding it are extremely fertile. The mission lies only a few miles from the end of San Pablo Bay and at least 12 leagues from the Russian settlements. Two chains of parallel hills shelter the mission from stiff ocean winds as well as those from the north. So rapid was the expansion of this mission that in less than ten years Solano had attracted 1,300 neophytes and owned 8,000 cattle, 700 horses, 4,000 sheep, and harvested 3,000 fanegas. Today none of this wealth remains. The buildings, except

---

[128]San Rafael was originally an asistencia, or branch of Mission Dolores. Engelhardt, in his **Franciscans in California**, p. 440, gives the date of its foundation as October 14. The branch mission prospered as a sheep raising community, reaching its peak before 1830. The maximum number of Indians was 1,150; and live stock never reached De Mofras' estimates. In 1846 the property was sold to Antonio Suñol and Antonio María Pico for $8,000.

[129]Father Juan Amorós was one of the saintly characters of that era. Originally priest to the garrison at Monterey, he came to San Rafael in 1819, remaining there until his death in 1832. He was an able business manager and mechanic, as well as a spiritual leader. Apparently De Mofras has confused him with Father José Altimira, the actual founder of Solano. At its peak, in 1833, this mission had 4,800 cattle, 1,100 horses, 7,000 sheep, and produced 13,450 fanegas of grain. In 1835 the mission formed the nucleus of the pueblo of Sonoma.

for one chapel and a small sleeping-room for the priest, have been destroyed, the materials having been used by Don Mariano Vallejo to erect a fine house. Vallejo also confiscated live stock, vines, and gardens, taking into his employ as servants the 50 Indians who remained at San Francisco Solano.

Around a large square near the mission, Comandante Vallejo founded a pueblo which he named Sonoma de Vallejo.[130] This first word is the name bestowed by the Indians on this locality. In time this settlement will undoubtedly expand. In fact, recently the population has increased 150 persons, among whom are 20 foreigners. San Solano is the main residence of an intelligent Frenchman, M. Victor Prudon,[131] who has established a local school and also supervises a small rancho. At one time M. Prudon hoped to locate at Monterey as secretary to the governor, an office he has already filled.

In 1827, the Reverend Father Amorós had already laid the foundations for a new mission and constructed the chapel of Santa Rosa[132] 6 leagues northwest of San Solano and the same distance from the Russian farm owned by Vasili Khliebnikov. The lands near this chapel are extraordinarily fertile, and especially adapted to raising wheat. The valleys have ample water, and the hills are covered with timber. Within a few years the Fathers had gathered around them large numbers of Indians, while the live stock multiplied and flourished. Santa Rosa had been selected as the home of the colonists who came up from Mexico in 1834; but, as will be subsequently indicated, the enterprise failed miserably. Today the ranchos of Santa Rosa have been considerably enlarged and have become the property of the Vallejo family, who shared in the spoils of several missions.

---

[130]The old town of Sonoma is one of the few settlements in California that still retains its old Mexican character, having changed but slightly in the last seventy-five years.

[131]Victor Prudon, an educated and affable Frenchmen, came to California in 1834 with the Hijar and Padrés party. His adobe, built in 1839, stood at the corner of Montgomery and Pacific Streets. In 1843 he settled at Sonoma, procuring several grants near by. He assisted Vallejo in favoring the United States cause.

[132]The following incident is told by Salvador Vallejo, who describes the traveler as "a crazy Frenchman." "While in Sonoma," he writes, "Señor de Mofras annoyed me greatly with his many idle questions and arrogant demeanor, so I decided to play a joke on him. After a while he asked me if I would procure a few pounds of vanilla beans for his collection of herbs (vanilla was unknown at this time in California). I told him any amount could be gathered at Mission Santa Rosa. The French writer immediately made a note of the existence of a mission at Santa Rosa, and later stated he had visited the mission." Vallejo, **Notas Historicas sobre California**, pp. 128-129. MS. Bancroft Library.

Along the shore of San Francisco Harbor, a wide variation in temperature between north, south, east, and west prevails. The southwestern section is the coldest area, notably during the summer, when the wind blows steadily from the northwest. In winter the prevailing wind is off the southeast, and at Yerba Buena the average temperature at noon during November and December is always 11° or 12° centigrade above zero, while the barometer fluctuates almost imperceptibly, averaging about 778 millimeters. The temperature at Monterey is identical within a degree, while at these two settlements the surface of the sea is always a few degrees warmer than the atmosphere.

Into the foot of Carquinez Bay the mouths of three rivers, called by the Canadians the Three Forks, open. These are formed on the right and east by the San Joaquin, on the center and north side by the Sacramento, and on the left and northwest by the Jesús María River. For a considerable period the belief prevailed that this latter river was an independent stream, but further explorations proved that the Jesús María was a branch of the Sacramento which, 7 leagues before emptying, forks, and forms a large island bearing the same name. This low narrow island is covered with reeds and high grasses; during the rainy season this area is generally inundated. In this vicinity large trees are quite rare, but a group was observed on the southern tip of the island at a place known as Hunters' Retreat. The island is inhabited by deer, buck, and beaver, as well as a few rattlesnakes. The Indians frequently visit this island in their balsas, a kind of reed skiff, to hunt freshwater otter. After pitching camp and exploring the island, our party felt assured, upon departure, that the Jesús María River is a myth.

Throughout the following record Spanish or English terms will be used in instances where discoverers happened to be Spaniards, Englishmen or Americans; French names given to localities discovered by French Canadians, however, will be accorded particular notice.

The origin of the San Joaquin River, or river of Saint Joachim, cannot be definitely ascertained. The stream flows from southeast to northwest through the immense plain of Tulare and is fed by a thousand minor streams that descend from lakes in the main valley or flow down the eastern flank of the Californian Mountains and the western slopes of the Sierra Nevada. The San Joaquin proper rises at the point that is on the same parallel as Mission San Fernando. However, not until the country behind Mission San José, at the foot of the Bolbones Mountains, is reached, does it commence to widen. Nevertheless, the stream may be

forded in summer within a few leagues of its mouth. This river and the
Tulare Valley were thoroughly explored in October, 1811, by the Spanish-
Franciscan Fathers, Fortuny and Abella,[133] who were accompanied by a
military expedition,[134] but their boat, although of light draught, could
not ascend beyond the latitude of San José. The rivers and freshwater
lagoons, so numerous in the valley, abound in fish, especially enormous
salmon and otter. Fathers from San Fernando, San Miguel, and San
Antonio have made further explorations and established the fact that the
San Joaquin is navigable only with canoes and that in deep water the
course is exceedingly dangerous owing to the trunks of trees that lie
submerged in the water. During the rainy season the river becomes a
raging torrent, with a rise of 8 or 9 feet, and frequently overflows its
banks, inundating an area several leagues in extent. These banks, however, are comparatively low. Many magnificent trees such as oaks,
pines, and sycamores, dot the valley.

The Sacramento River—the river of the Holy Sacrament—is fed
by two branches that unite almost opposite the mouth of the San Joaquin
River. The western fork, inappropriately named the River of Jesús
María, travels north-northwest, then bends toward the east 20 miles,
ultimately joining the main stream. Although the river describes a
thousand curves, yet the general direction is north, a quarter-northeast,
and northwest. The average width of this stream is 300 meters, with a
depth varying from 3 to 4 fathoms during the summer. The tides rise
to a considerable height in this river. Fifty miles east of the Sacramento
is the small river Dubreuil[135] that empties into the San Joaquin; 8 miles
beyond, in the same direction, lies the river Sans Nom.[136] Above the fork
of the river, at the point where it forms a large island, the Martine
River[137] comes in from the west, and on the east, a few leagues beyond,
the American Fork, 30 meters wide, which is about 30 leagues from the
mouth.

---

[133]Father Ramón Abella of Dolores and Father Buenaventura Fortuny of
Mission San José, accompanied by a sergeant and troops, left San Francisco
and explored the east or main branch of the San Joaquin River, which they
called the San Juan Capistrano. They returned via the Sacramento, calling it
the San Francisco.

[134]The manuscript journal of this interesting exploration is in our possession.
(D. de M.)

[135]Because of the inaccuracy of their locations on the De Mofras map these
tributaries of the Sacramento are difficult to identify. This, however, appears to
be the Mokelumne.

[136]Probably the Cosumne.

[137]This appears to be Cache Creek.

Captain Sutter's New Helvetia is situated in the angle formed by the Sacramento and its fork [The American Fork]. The Canadians, oddly enough, apply the general name of fork to any river that empties into another stream. The Young River[138] flows on the west bank above the American Fork, and on the opposite side, 8 miles beyond, is the fork known as Feather River, some 40 meters broad, that comes in directly from the east. Six miles away, on the opposite shore, the Beaulieu[139] joins the stream, and 8 miles east, the Three Buttes which rise like the American Fork at the foot of three remarkable peaks that stand off from the flank of the Sierra Nevada and appear to be a thousand meters high. Above, for a distance of 30 miles or more, the Sacramento flows directly north, being joined on the west by the Avoine[140] and the Liard,[141] and on the east by the Champagne,[142] the Three Forks,[143] and the Trou River.[144] The latter, of considerable size, is formed by the Chevaux Fork[145] and the Malheur River,[146] both of which have their source in the foothills of the Sierra Nevada. As far as the Trou River, that is, for a distance estimated at 50 leagues, the Sacramento is navigable and free of falls and portages.[147] The term portage is used by Canadians to designate a point where, because of obstacles, a canoe must be carried for a time and then replaced in the stream. As far as where the Trou River joins the Sacramento the depth is 9 or 10 meters. The only danger to which navigation is exposed comes from the submerged trees which must be avoided with the utmost care, for they can stave in small vessels, causing them to sink rapidly. Until these dangers are rectified, vessels should avoid navigating at night. Above the junction of the Trou, the river, growing shallower, has a depth of 5 or 6 feet. Stockades of piles that impede the flow of the river also exist. These are dams constructed by the Indians to catch salmon. However, they can be readily lifted and flat-bottom boats are able to navigate for another dozen leagues past a great bend, described by the Sacramento toward the west. From this point the river flows north once more, and then east as far as Lake Masqué.

---

[138]The Trough, or backwater of the Sacramento.
[139]Willows Creek.
[140]Grindstone Creek.
[141]Thomas Creek.
[142]Deer Creek.
[143]North fork of the Pit.
[144]South fork of the Pit.
[145] [146]The identity of these rivers is not clear.
[147]Point where the Sacramento ceases to be nagivable by boats of moderate tonnage: 38° 46′ 47″ n. lat.; 124° 00′ 54″ w. long. Distance from the anchorage at Yerba Buena, 156 miles; breadth of the river, 30 meters. (D. de M.)

The lake, as the name indicates, is hidden in the lowlands and covered with thick reeds. The lake is formed by waters descending from the Shasta Mountains, the western chain of the Sierra Nevada, which extend toward the sea between the forty-first and forty-second parallels, and appear to form the natural boundary between California and the country watered by the tributaries of the Columbia and Willamette rivers. For some time it was believed that the Sacramento arose in Salt Lake, or Youta[148] as it was known to the Indians. To our knowledge no map gives the position of Lake Masqué. On old maps Salt Lake is called Timpanagos, and Teguayo, and usually two lakes are portrayed in place of one. This confusion should be rectified, since Lake Utah lies definitely at the foot of the Rocky Mountains. No river empties into it, and Lake Masqué and the Sacramento are more than a hundred leagues west, being separated from the former by the Sierra Nevada. Twenty leagues away, southeast of Lake Masqué, lies Trout Lake,[149] which abounds in beaver.

The Sacramento River traverses a plain of rare grandeur. Toward the north the view is dominated by mountains that stretch from the east to the sea, affording shelter from cold winds; on the east towers the Sierra Nevada capped with eternal snows. On the west rises the Californian chain, crowned with forests; on the south this river and the San Joaquin, with their flock of tributaries, wind. When the snows melt, the waters overflow three meters, as the débris clinging to the trunks of the trees clearly reveals, but after these have receded a new life is infused in the vegetation. Oak, willow, laurel, pine, sycamore, bindweed, native shrubs, bands of wild horses, immense herds of cattle, deer, and antelope also enliven the landscape. The Indians live in hovels hollowed out of the ground and covered with branches. Although primarily fishermen, they own cattle and horses. Some who have escaped from the missions even cultivate the soil. The only dangerous animal that roams these vast plains is the grizzly bear (*Ursus terriblis*) which is often found up in the oak trees, throwing acorns to his cubs. Few rivers are more suitable for navigation by steamer than the Sacramento; for even close to the water an abundance of wood is available. Undoubtedly this stream, traversing virgin land and emptying into one of the finest ports in the world, will become extremely important at the time—and the day is not remote—when California changes masters.

---

[148]Now Utah, after the Ute Indian tribe.
[149]Apparently Lower Lake.

The country west of the Sacramento in the vicinity of Mission San Solano, Santa Rosa chapel, and the Russian holdings as far as the sea, is equally fertile. From San José down to San Fernando the valley, which is 200 leagues in length and varies in width between 20 and 40 leagues, has the same general character. And so the venerable Fathers and the old Spanish soldiers were justified in telling travelers who admired their missions situated near the coast that the beauty of their lands was negligible in comparison with those in the interior of the province.

Three years ago the Hudson's Bay Company obtained from Governor Alvarado a land grant of 11 square leagues lying along the Sacramento River above the San Joaquin as a favor to one of its agents called Desportes MacKay,[150] a relative of Dr. McLoughlin, head of their concessions along the Columbia River. As yet this land has not been occupied; however, should the company send out colonists, they would be French Canadians in their employ.

An American named Marsh[151] owns a farm on the south bank of the San Joaquin, at the foot of Mt. Diablo, where he resides with three or four sailors, fellow-countrymen and deserters from United States vessels.

Captain Sutter[152] of New Helvetia is a Swiss who formerly served

---

[150]Desportes MacKay, also known as Jean Baptiste Desportes McKay, came to California in 1825 with the Hudson's Bay Co. trappers to purchase cattle. Although rumors of a grant having been made to MacKay were current, there is no evidence of such a concession. See Bancroft, California, IV, 212-214.

[151]Marsh, see supra, I, 225, also note 84.

[152]Johann August Suter, or Sutter, was born in February, 1803, at Kandern near the Swiss border in Germany. At Burgdorf, Switzerland, Sutter became a grocer's clerk, and there in 1826 married a young Swiss girl, Annette Dübeld. The small merchandise store in which he next engaged in business is still standing on the main street of the village at Burgdorf. Sutter, faced with bankruptcy, loaded his shelves with goods stuffed with paper to appease his pressing creditors, abandoned his wife and four young children, and hastily left town, in 1834, escaping to America. After many adventures he reached San Francisco on July 1, 1839. In August he ascended the Sacramento into the wilderness and established the nucleus of a small settlement patterned after the Hudson's Bay Company posts he had visited en route to California. The fort was begun in 1841 on the site of the modern Sacramento and called Sutter's Fort, or New Helvetia, and was not completed when seen by De Mofras. Ultimately the settlement was a rectangular structure 500 by 150 feet, surrounded by 18-foot adobe walls. For a time Sutter's fortune seemed assured, but litigation and misfortune wrecked his life, health, and career. He died on June 17, 1880 at Washington, D. C. See Bancroft, California, passim; Julian Dana, Sutter of California (New York, 1935); Heinrich Lienhard, Californien, unmittelbar vor und nach der entdeckung des Goldes(Zurich, 1898); Das Burgdorfer Yahrbuch 1935 (Burgdorf, 1935), pp. 59-74. In addition to these secondary sources are the accounts of travelers of that period, all of whom visited the fort and knew Sutter. The Huntington Library at San Marino, and the Bancroft Library at Berkeley, California, also contain a large amount of manuscript material that bears directly or indirectly on Sutter.

twelve years in our royal guard. Shortly after 1830 he migrated to the United States where for several years he managed a farm on the shores of the Missouri. Accompanied by three Germans, in 1836 Sutter joined a party of Americans who were traveling overland to the Columbia River. Crossing the Rocky Mountains he arrived safely at Fort Vancouver, the main post of the Hudson's Bay Company. From there, after a brief sojourn, he crossed over to the Sandwich Islands, subsequently engaging in commercial enterprises at New Archangel, capital of the Russian colonies. In 1839 he reached California. In accordance with the provisions of Spanish law, Governor Alvarado, who was then at Monterey, made a grant of 11 *sitios*[153] or cattle pasturage; in other words, 11 square leagues.[154] The situation of this land was to be selected by Sutter.

In order to avoid near neighbors, Sutter selected land[155] on the left bank of the Sacramento River between the Sans Nom and Feather rivers. Between these two rivers flows the American Fork, watering the adjoining prairies. These streams are bordered by woods and supply salmon and beaver. Invaluable services were rendered Sutter in founding New Helvetia by a Frenchman, M. Octave Custot.[156]

Sutter's settlement is situated two miles east of the river and a mile south of the American Fork. Upon leaving the landing place, a vast plain, shaded by enormous oaks, is first crossed.[157] Houses cannot be built close to the banks of the Sacramento River, however, owing to spring floods. On the north, the fort of New Helvetia adjoins a small

---

[153]Sitio: literally, a country place.

[154]Each square league is called a **caballeriza**. In the pueblos strangers are given a **solar**, or a **cuadra**; in other words a plot or square from 60 to 100 vares on each side (50 to 85 meters) at an average price of one fourth a piaster per vara, or from 15 of 25 piasters for 5 to 9 acres. In outlying regions land was given gratuitously. (D. de M.).

[155]Land was not granted until Sutter had pacified the local Indians and proved his worth as a pioneer. The grant formally made by Governor Alvarado on June 18, 1841, recognized the fact that Sutter "had sufficiently accredited his laboriousness, good conduct, and other qualifications required in such cases, and has already in advance manifested his great efforts, constant firmness, and truly patriotic zeal in favor of our institutions, by reducing to civilization a large number of savage Indians, natives of these frontiers." Bancroft, **California**, IV, 231.

[156]Octave Custot reached California in 1837, where he introduced the manufacture of beet sugar on Vallejo's ranch at Petaluma. In 1839 he became superintendent for Sutter at New Helvetia.

[157]Contemporary manuscripts indicate that De Mofras reached Sutter's Fort on September 1, 1841, long before its completion. Sutter, always convivial with strangers, apparently took the French traveler into his confidence. Many plans, as outlined, finally matured, and his fort became the finest edifice of its kind on the coast. See letter of Sutter to Suñol, New Helvetia, September 1, 1841. Sutter-Suñol correspondence, MS., Bancroft Library.

stream whose steep sides form a natural defense. The property is also surrounded by a wall 5 feet thick, built of sun-dried bricks, strengthened by heavy timbers, each side of the quadrangle being protected for a distance of 100 meters. The corners are flanked by square bastions two stories high, whose four surfaces are pierced with openings, while an outside gallery tops the entire wall.

Equipment consists of 16 or 18 small cannon, carronades of various sizes purchased from ships, and two fine bronze fieldpieces procured by M. Sutter from the Russians. Sutter possesses in addition to these pieces enough guns and rifles to arm 60 or 80 men, without counting pistols and sidearms. Their ammunition is also good and abundant. Active watches, including guards and night patrol, have been organized, for during the first years of this establishment the Indians upon several occasions attempted to assassinate M. Sutter, who invariably managed to keep them under his control.[158]

M. Sutter, who has finally succeeded in keeping peace with the Indians, now has 100 natives in his employ. They receive their food and a daily wage of two reals in merchandise, such as glass beads, necklaces, handkerchiefs, goods, and other articles. New Helvetia houses at the present time 30 white men, including Germans, Swiss, Canadians, Americans, Frenchmen, and Englishmen. The majority are engaged in cutting wood, operating forges, or in carpentry. A few have formed groups and scour the valleys and rivers for beaver.

In New France and the colder regions of North America where lakes and rivers freeze, beaver are forced to congregate to build winter quarters. Their dams and bars are built in rivers which are in danger of overflowing, and provide a way to catch fish. In the warmer countries, lying south and west of the Rocky Mountains, however, these amphibians do not need to erect these remarkable hydraulic works that are found in the lakes of Canada. As the rivers here do not freeze and the ground is never covered with snow, as a result beaver live in isolated spots, feeding principally on roots and bark. Usually they make their homes in holes dug along waterways or in lagoons. When floods occur, they withdraw to dry localities where new dwellings are then erected.

Naturally, their nomadic habits make these animals more difficult to hunt. However, since one man can watch a number of traps, they are rapidly caught. Traps are of iron, like those used for obnoxious animals in France. Bait, called medicine, is placed in the center. The trap,

---

[158]See Davis, op. cit., p. 20.

attached to an iron chain, is held down by two small weights of the same metal, for if wood and hemp were used, by means of his teeth the beaver would soon regain his liberty. Frequently hunters hide, and, without setting traps, shoot the creatures. Their skins are so heavy that one man cannot carry more than ten or twelve. Each trapper is invariably accompanied by an Indian or a horse to transport his skins.

Beavers caught in traps usually have a nose or a paw broken, and are at once dispatched with a knife. The skin, stretched on a board, is then hung in the sun. When hunting, beaver meat is used for food. This invariably has a marshy flavor, although by western trappers the tail is considered as much a delicacy as the bison's hump by hunters along the Upper Missouri.

In 1830 Jean Baptiste Desportes MacKay, a well-known trapper of the Hudson's Bay Company, caught within six months near Carquinez Bay more than 4,000 beaver. This is an enormous number, inasmuch as skins sell for 2 piasters a pound in California and a pound sterling in New York and London.

From the start M. Sutter devoted his time to purchasing and raising live stock. He now owns in excess of 4,000 cattle, 1,500 horses and mules, and 2,000 sheep. He has 200 cows which supply milk as well, and hopes to export butter and cheese in large quantities. What grain and vegetables have been raised have proved a financial success, and M. Sutter also anticipates substantial profits from his many cotton plantations. Probably the lowlands could be converted into rice and indigo plantations. Lands protected from floods could be planted to vines, olives, and European fruit trees, which, according to all indications, should thrive in this country.

The Sacramento and its branches yield enormous salmon of superior type that come in from the sea to spawn. The natives erect barricades across the small streams and kill the fish as they come up with stones or pointed spears. These salmon can also be caught with hooks or by means of staunch nets stretched across the river. The fish, after being salted, is consumed to a large extent in the Sandwich Islands where it is exported in large quantities by the Columbia River Company. Ships also come out from New York expressly to load on salmon. M. Sutter confidently believes that the exportation of this product should return large profits. No branch of business, in fact, is overlooked by this pioneer, who must pay off within a short time the amount he owes the Russians for the purchase of their live stock and farms.

What European goods he requires are so costly in California that he has attempted to establish direct relations with the largest trading posts in the Sandwich Islands. To complete these arrangements, on August 18, 1841, one of his English colonists, M. Sinclair,[159] was sent out to Honolulu to obtain goods on consignment and establish business connections. At the time our party was leaving California, M. Sutter felt confident that the firm of M. French,[160] an English merchant, and his associate, M. Greenway,[161] an American, would supply him not only with merchandise and credit,[162] but would also send over a few white colonists, or Kanakas, from the islands.

In the center of his fort, M. Sutter has constructed a few houses. The largest, which is extremely well built, is planned to accommodate his family whom he intends to bring out from Basle, together with some additional Swiss colonists. Two miles from New Helvetia, on the banks of the American Fork, Sutter has granted a portion of his land to two Englishmen named Morris[163] and Sinclair,[164] who have erected buildings and begun to cultivate their land.

M. Sutter intends to give free of rent a few plots of land to emigrants who will come out and locate near his colony. In the meanwhile, his white laborers receive, over and above food, two or three piasters daily which are paid partly in money and partly in merchandise. All these men live with Indian or Californian women and the colony totals no fewer than 200 souls. Governor Alvarado has appointed M. Sutter alcalde and judge with jurisdiction over the territory east of the Sacramento River. Comandante Vallejo who makes a pretense of governing the country lying on the right bank of the river under his control, has

---

[159]Sainclair in the French text.

[160]Probably William French, an American trader from Honolulu, who touched frequently at Monterey.

[161]His partner, Greenway, does not appear in Bancroft's Pioneer Register.

[162]One factor contributing to Sutter's success was his ability to acquire goods on credit. His engaging personality invariably inspired confidence, which was too often abused. One of his achievements was the purchase—largely on credit—of Fort Ross, its lands, live stock, and equipment, on December 13, 1841. See Clarence Du Four, "The Russian Withdrawal from California" in the **Quarterly of the California Historical Society**, Vol. XII, No. 3 (September, 1933), pp. 240-276.

[163]Albert F. Morris was a British sailor who came to California and joined Graham's forces. In 1842 with Captain Phelps he went up the Sacramento where De Mofras met him.

[164]John S. Sinclair was a Scotchman who had been an employé of the Hudson's Bay Company in Oregon, editor of a newspaper in Honolulu, and then agent for Sutter in California. In 1842 he was employed on the El Paso Rancho near New Helvetia, and later joined Sutter in his military activities. He was a popular and well-known character around Sutter's Fort.

watched with a certain amount of jealousy the growth of New Helvetia and has attempted to check M. Sutter's activities. In November, 1841, the latter wrote Vallejo that if he continued to make trouble he would hoist the French colors over his fort, leave for Sonoma, and force the issue.

During September, 1840, a Bordelaise named Dubosc[165] was killed by an Indian on a ranch adjoining San Solano. Vallejo overlooked the affair and allowed the assassin, whom he knew, to escape.[166] Upon learning of this crime, M. Sutter and M. Custot immediately sent several squads to the scene, scoured the valley, and apprehended an Indian from one of the tribes whom they suspected of being the murderer. After the native had established his innocence, however, he was released, and the search continued for the true culprit.

The importance M. Sutter's colony acquired by the purchase from the Russians of live stock and considerable property near the port of Bodega can be readily understood by taking into consideration the fact that it is possible to go from New Helvetia to the sea either by following the Sacramento or by crossing the stream and taking a westerly route leading behind Mission San Francisco Solano and the chapel of Santa Rosa. Since Russian farmhouses, being of wood,[167] are easily taken apart, M. Sutter has been able to build up a business free of customs duties and the Mexican authorities and he can receive people and goods either overland from the port of Bodega or by sending his boat to meet them at this same port.

M. Sutter, who has served in the French army, is classed as a Frenchman in California although residing in a country that nominally belongs to Mexico; yet he is surrounded by, and makes an effort to attract, Canadians and Frenchmen. Within a few years New Helvetia is destined to be a settlement of considerable importance,[168] being the point through which trains coming overland from Canada, the Columbia River, and the United States will pass, and M. Sutter has frequently

---

[165]Pierre Dubosc was a Frenchman who was killed by an Indian at the rancho of McIntosh.

[166]On July 20, 1841, while at Monterey, De Mofras wrote to Alvarado offering to defray the costs of locating the Indian who killed Dubosc. **Departmental State Papers**, V, 117. MS. Bancroft Library. On July 27, the latter replied, promising assistance. See his letter in **Archives of California, Departmental Records**, XII, 41, MS. Bancroft Library.

[167]See picture of an isba, or Russian house. (D. de M.).

[168]This prediction was soon realized. From 1846 when overland immigration reached its zenith until 1850 when the Gold Rush brought foreigners by the thousands into California, Sutter's Fort was the rendezvous for new settlers, who in the end ruined his lands, stole his cattle, and caused his downfall.

expressed the desire to have a few French missionaries reside at his fort to civilize the neighboring Indians. This plan deserves to be given consideration.

After leaving San Francisco Harbor and heading north, a lofty promontory culminating in a peak called Point Reyes appears. This lies 20¼ miles from the summit of Table Mountain in a northerly direction 79° 36′ west longtitude.[169] South of Point Reyes extends a large bay that opens toward the south; this in 1542 was called Puerto de los Reyes by the Spaniards, by whom it was first discovered. Notwithstanding, the English have attempted to rename this Sir Francis Drake's Harbor, in honor of the celebrated pirate who stopped here in July, 1579,[170] for a brief sojourn.

This port is tenable only during summer and when northwest winds prevail. Not far from shore the two ranchos of Osio and García are situated. In foggy weather, or in the event of a slight error in latitude, Point Reyes might be mistaken for the entrance to San Francisco Harbor, an error fraught with danger. On the night of September 27, 1841, the brig *Ayacucho* under Captain Limantour,[171] owned by the firm of Bizat and Roussel of Bordeaux but operating under the Mexican flag, ran aground south of the point while en route from Monterey to San Francisco. The captain and crew were able to reach shore and procure help from San Francisco. An American boat was then chartered and part of the cargo salvaged; but the brig could not be floated, and after a few days she was completely demolished by the sea.*

---

[169]Point Reyes: 37° 59′ 40″ n. lat., 125° 19′ 54″ w. long. (D. de M.).

[170]For Drake's voyage see supra, I, 52, also note 21.

[171]Joseph Yves Limantour was supercargo on the **Ayacucho** of 93 tons. Since records show that the ship reached Monterey in October on her way north, the wreck must have occurred later than September. Later Limantour opened a store in San Francisco to dispose of his wares.

*At the conclusion of this chapter two pages, folios 314 and 315, of the **Mémoire,** have been omitted. These deal with the treaty between Spain and the United States whereby the boundaries of the former power in California were defined. De Mofras places the Russian holdings at Fort Ross definitely beyond these limits.

CHAPTER X*

Status of agriculture in California. Live stock. Wood for building purposes. Commerce. Imports. Exports, Shipping. Customs. Whaling vessels. New field for Whalers. Foreign consulates.

Agriculture and the raising of live stock comprise the principal wealth of California. Yet these sources of revenue, because of the revolutions in the country and the removal of the mission Indians, are diminishing day by day. Despite the crudity of the agricultural implements in use, the raising of grain has produced some remarkable results, notably in the northern part of the province on the plains adjoining San Francisco Harbor.

Near Mission San José some land was visited where, in 1839, 10 fanegas of wheat were sown, and the next year the soil, left fallow, produced without cultivation 600 fanegas. The poorest lands available yield from 30 to 40 fanegas annually; but certain localities, among them low and humid lands like those found at Santa Clara and Santa Cruz Missions, are better suited to corn. At the latter, definite instances of surprising but authentic returns may be cited. An almud of wheat, or a dozen fanegas yielded, for example, 137 fanegas, in other words, 1,644 per cent increase. Wheat is planted in December and January, or even later, and harvested in June or July; corn and vegetables are planted in March. Vineyards are pruned in February and the grapes taken in the latter part of September. These lands, and even the vineyards, are on low ground enriched by the rivers. Thus, in dry years the grains and vines frequently lack moisture. Irrigation, however, is not essential; north of San Francisco the Russians harvest excellent wheat without irrigation even on the hills overlooking the sea.

The Californians refer to the former mode of cultivation as *siembras de riego,* or irrigated crops, and the latter as *siembras de temporal,* crops depending on rainfall. Each method has its disadvantages: one

---

*Mémoire VI continues throughout this chapter, with slight variations. See Amérique Vol. 43, folios 315 to 348. At the end of the chapter, however, a section of folios 347 and 348 have been omitted. These recommend a French consul at Monterey to watch the movements of the English, Russians, and Americans.

suffers from too soft soil, if irrigation is followed by heavy rainfall; the other exposes crops, as in Europe, to the hazards of the weather. In California, however, the former method is considered more successful.

The custom of creating artificial fields is unknown in the country. Barley and oats are not often cultivated; among vegetables, however, beans are universally used by the inhabitants. What wine and brandy are produced are inadequate for local consumption, and wine is imported in large quantities. At one time oil was exported to San Blas, but at the present the fine olives planted near the missions are entirely neglected, as is the cultivation of flax, hemp, cotton, and tobacco which give promise of proving highly productive.

The cattle are large, exceedingly strong and agile, and produce excellent meat. Cows raised in green pasturage give an abundant supply of milk rich in quality and suitable for making cheese. They show a fecundity unknown in Europe, bearing calves after the second year. The current price of beef is five piasters when sold in quantities, and seven if sold by the piece.

The horses of this country are worthy of note. They have neither the slight build nor the heavy gait of the horses of the warm provinces of Mexico. In size they are somewhat like the racehorses in England, with long necks, slender frames, and sleek, nervous bodies. They are allowed to roam at liberty on the ranges. Horses are caught either by chasing and throwing them with the lasso, or by enticing them into corrals with breeding mares. With few exceptions these horses are remarkable for their agility and extraordinary endurance. However, not having been taught to trot or to pace, gaits popular in New Spain, they either walk or gallop. When traveling, it is not unusual to see horses gallop steadily twelve or fifteen hours.

To make 40 or 50 leagues a day a rider usually takes four or five horses that are driven before him and that graze on the way. When his horse tires, a slipknot is thrown on another mount. This is done in rotation every two or three hours. Many times my horse has covered 18 or 20 leagues in four or five hours, almost without rest. In pleasant weather, moreover, the roads are firm and smooth.

The Californian horses are so strong and swift that it is extremely difficult for a deer to escape the lasso of a ranchero following in pursuit. The colonists do not shoe their horses, nor cut their manes and tails. By using a powerful bit, in the middle of a swift run a horse is trained to stop short by means of exerting strong pressure with spurs and bridle.

While this manoeuvre makes their mouths extremely tough, yet it is invaluable training, since the riders frequently lasso bulls and bears of prodigious size. When the leg or horn of the bull has been caught by the slipknot, the animal puts forth every effort to break away. If at that moment the rider and horse should move ahead, the strain put on the lasso, fastened to the pommel of the saddle, would throw them. At the time a bull is lassoed, the rider halts his horse and as a counter-check strains heavily on the side opposite the taut lasso.

Often the hurling of the lasso is so rapid that the man has the two phalanxes of his right thumb ground against the bow of his saddle and pulled off. It frequently happens, too, that the bear or bull, once seized, charges the rider; in this event the sole recourse is quickly to sever the lasso with a knife tucked away in the right boot near the knee, and take flight. Californians display rare skill in handling horses. An interesting sight is to watch a rider, after indicating on what part of the body the rope will hit, throw an animal with the lasso while riding at full gallop. The lasso does not have balls like the *bolas* used by the pamperos in Buenos Ayres, but consists merely of a leather thong as thick as a finger, ending in a slipknot. This is about 30 feet in length, and is made up of strands of woven leather which are strong, but extremely pliable.

Not only is it difficult to procure a good lasso, but it also requires skill to learn how to handle it. This is done as follows: If on foot a man holds the end in his right hand, or if on horseback he fastens it to the pommel of his saddle. A knot is then made and the rope arranged in coils five or six feet long, which are held between the fingers and thumb. The lasso is then whirled in circles above the head—a feat which on a galloping horse is not easy—and, at an opportune moment, thrown. Care must be exercised to keep it in the air in such a way that the animal is unexpectedly caught by the descending loop of the rope. The custom of using a lasso is so universal that children, mission Indians, and even women can handle it with equal agility.

Californian horses are prized throughout New Spain, New Mexico, and the United States, some even being exported. Mules and donkeys also appear to come from fine stock. All these animals are hardy, and are rarely sick. After traveling at a furious gallop, when they have called into play all the agility and sure-footedness of desert races, they can be allowed to stand dripping with sweat, out in the cold driving rains, or left several days in a corral without food or water. Like the

Arabs to whom they are remotely related, Spanish settlers consider that a horse should fast before being taken on a long, rapid journey.

Unfortunately the supply of horses is now diminishing in California, for the Indians carry on endless raids, and almost every night hundreds are carried off to the Tulare Valley. Some of these animals are used for food; others, however, are sold to American trappers who take them to the new lands adjoining the headwaters of the Arkansas and Missouri rivers. The value of horses has materially increased since these Indian depredations. At one time horses were sold like cattle; but today even a mule is valued at 10 or 15 piasters. However, if several hundred head are purchased, the cost is approximately 8 piasters each.

Superfine sheep are also bred in California, but since they receive no care, their wool never acquires its maximum fineness. Herds of goats and wild pigs, which are neglected by the inhabitants, are numerous. Sheep are sold from one-half to one piaster, and pigs for 3 or 4 piasters.

Wood suitable for building purposes is abundant in California; the most valuable of this timber belongs to the coniferous family, whose names may be found in the accompanying botanical appendix. White and green oaks, arbutus, royal laurel, ash, fir, maple, sycamore, red, white, and yellow juniper, and various kinds of pine fill the forests. The latter attain majestic proportions. In 1828, an early French traveler, Captain Duhaut Cilly,[1] measured a pine [redwood] near San Francisco which had bark 2 feet thick, and was 20 feet in diameter, the trunk at its thickest point being 30 feet. The tree from the base to tip measured 230 feet, and the limbs which had been cut off must have exceeded 25 feet. In 1831, the scholarly English traveler, Mr. Douglas, measured some pines which had attained a height of 100 meters, and a diameter of 20 feet.

These measurements tally with those made personally. The exploitation of these trees is a simple matter; most of these forests are on hills which border the sea, thus giving the plains of California a majestic and stately aspect. In the northern part of the province a few camphor laurels exist. These, however, grow no higher than bushes. There are few poisonous plants; but the *yedra,* a shrub like our elder, is often found, and contact with it, and even the effluvium, is highly dangerous to some individuals. All that is necessary, in fact, is to pass near the *yedra,* or touch it, to experience almost instantaneously a general swelling of the body which, with children, frequently entails grave complications.

---

[1]Captain Duhaut Cilly, **Voyage autour du Monde II, 225. Mémoires of M. Douglas, in the Companion to the Botanical Magazine, 1836, vol. II, (D. de M.).**

The valleys and woods are inhabited by deer, stag, goat, bear, tiger, beaver, squirrel, rabbit, and antelope. Flocks of tufted partridges, ducks, herons, bussards, humming birds and, near the sea, kingfishers, gulls, superb vultures, and great brown eagles with white heads also abound.

The only dangerous reptile is the rattlesnake, which is small in size, and which glides off instead of attacking human beings. A species resembling a boa-constrictor also exists, but this reptile is never more than 8 or 10 feet long. Scorpions, tarantulas, lizards, the Californian iguana (*Amblyrynchus ater*) are extremely scarce. The European bee (*Apis mellifica*), strangely enough, does not exist in this country.

The sea and ports abound in all kinds of fish, amphibians, and large sea mammifers, among them the spermaceti whale, porpoise, bonito, a variety of cod, salmon, sea-lion, sea-elephant, and schools of sardines. Shells found are murex (a shell that gives purple dye), limpets, helix, and magnificent haliotis (Venus shells), highly esteemed by the natives, which are found only at Monterey and in New Zealand. In the appendix referring to natural history accompanying this volume, local zoological specimens will be listed.

Since California has no industries of any kind, her exports consist exclusively of the natural products of the country. Cattle hides comprise the principal export. When dried these are sold locally for 2 piasters' worth of merchandise, or one and one-half silver piasters. At one time these hides were large and weighed approximately 50 and 60 pounds, only four or five-year-old animals being slaughtered. Until 1838, animal hides exported averaged 200,000. At the present this number has been cut in two. When young animals are killed, their hides do not weigh more than 25 or 30 pounds; these are exported to Valparaiso and the Sandwich Islands where they sell for 2 silver piasters, and also to Boston where the price is 3 piasters, that is, from 11 to 12 cents a pound. These hides are excellent in quality, although they are not dry like those from Buenos Ayres. The ships collect skins from the ranchos and missions along the coast and then land them at the port of San Diego where the salting establishments (*saladeros*) and warehouses are situated. When their cargo has been finally loaded, ships take their departure from the latter port.

The process of salting hides requires considerable time. First, the hides must be softened by being soaked for several days in salt water; they are then stretched out on the ground and weighted down with small stones to dry. Next, any bits of flesh that might decay are care-

fully removed with a knife, care being taken not to injure the skin. When
this operation has been completed, they are placed on racks to dry.
After the inside has become thoroughly saturated with salt, the hides
are folded lengthwise, with the hair on the outside. They are now
placed in a press and flattened out. When finally loaded, jacks are used
for weights, thus enabling a larger number to be stowed away.

For instance, a brig of 160 tons, burden, with 40,000 hides, and an
American three-master of 360 tons carrying 30,000, were seen.[2] Californian hides are in universal demand throughout the United States and at
Valparaiso; but since they require a long tanning process, the price is
lower than those from Buenos Ayres. Despite the rich salt deposits
found in California, ships prefer to bring out their own salt from
Boston. This has proved cheaper than purchasing local salt, for labor
is relatively scarce in this country. The port of San Diego is the only
place where hides are salted, although the Hudson's Bay Company has
established a factory at San Francisco to prepare their own hides. There
is some demand for horses' hides, which sell for one piaster in merchandise or three-quarters of a piaster in silver. Deer hides command
one or one and one-half piasters, according to size.

Beaver skins usually sell for 3 piasters a pound, more than 3,000
pelts being marketed each year. The skins of sea otter formed at one
time an important article, being, until 1790, a monopoly of the Spanish
government. Into the royal treasury poured enormous profits derived
from the hides, for their agents purchased the skins from the Indians
for one or two piasters, or even less, then sold them at Manila for 40
or 45 and, at Canton, for 70 or 80 piasters. In 1812, when the Russians
were living at the port of Bodega, they brought over from the Aleutian
Islands many Kodiak Indians, who proved able fishermen.[3] Against
sea otters and seals there was now waged a war of extermination that
brought lavish profits to the Imperial Russian-American Company
established at St. Petersburg. At that time San Francisco Harbor was
seldom visited, and the lagoons were so thickly inhabited by sea otter
that the Russian hunters killed as many as 800 each month in the bay
alone. The coast and islands were also exploited and entirely depopu-
lated of these creatures. Now scarcely a hundred skins a year, which
sell locally for 35 to 40 piasters, at Mazatlán for 50 or 55, and in Mexico
[City], for 60 or 70 piasters, can with difficulty be procured. Oddly

---

[2]For the traffic in hides see **supra**, I, 170, also **note 21**.
[3]For Russian activities see **infra** II, 1-10, 248-266.

enough as late as 1839, an American ship, coming from the Sandwich Islands killed 300 sea otter on Cedros Island in Lower California in a few weeks. These pelts are no longer exported to China, where the price has declined to 40 or 45 piasters, because of the abundant supply furnished by the Aleutian Islands and the superiority of the northern skins over those from the south. The hides of freshwater otter are not in demand, and have a value of not more than 2 or 3 piasters.

San Clemente Island is the home of innumerable wild goats of extraordinary size whose skins are worth one-fourth of a piaster. The skins of the hair seal have a value of 6 reals, and those of the fur seal from 3 to 4 piasters. At London the latter command from 25 to 30 shillings.

The handsome appearance and black color that characterize bear skins found in Russian America are lacking in California. Other fur-bearing animals, which will probably be exploited when a large white population inhabits this province, are found in California. Fox, American tiger, wildcat, ground squirrel—the small gray type-mountain sheep, badger, rabbit, and hare, will undoubtedly be included among pelts exported.

Next to hides, the most valuable local commodity is tallow. Beef tallow sells for 4 silver piasters a quintal, or 6 piasters if exchanged for merchandise; that of deer commands several reals more. The hard and brittle character of the latter product does not permit it to be used alone; but when mixed with beef tallow, superfine candles can be made. All tallow is exported directly to Lima where it is used for lighting purposes and for machinery at the mines. Stripped of its hide, a fine steer which costs 7 piasters on the hoof, yields 3 quintals of fat and tallow, and from 200 to 250 kilograms of good meat. Since there is no demand for the horns of deer or steer, they have no market value.

The deer common to California is about the height of a large race-horse; the meat is excellent and supplies two quintals of tallow. Deer horns are often two meters high with an equal amount of spread. These animals are found mainly north of San Francisco in herds of 700 or 800; and as they always run with the wind, they are easily killed after the herd has been scattered. The rancheros hunt them in groups of eight or ten, using their best horses and armed with the lasso. They attempt first to break up the herd and then scatter them, in order to follow an isolated deer which, after being caught by the noose, is surrounded by a circle of men and pulled down. One of the hunters then dismounts, cautiously approaches the animal, and with his knife cuts his hamstring, or strikes his throat. After a certain number have been caught, they are loaded on horses and oxcarts and brought in to the ranchos. The does, unincumbered by horns, run more swiftly than the males and are more difficult to catch.

The Spaniards, as a usual thing do not eat deer meat, but discard it. Foreigners, especially Englishmen, Americans, and French Canadians, prepare from it excellent steaks and smoked meat. The hide is reserved for trousers, saddles, harnesses, moccasins, and boots. After being melted, the fat is turned, like that of beef, into large hide sacks and securely sewed to avoid leakage in warm weather. Formerly the missions shipped loads of soap and oil to San Blas and Peru, but today this commercial activity is virtually suspended. Only a few thousand-weight of soap, priced at 2 and 2½ piasters a quintal, is exported.

When the harvesting of grain has been abundant, 2 or 3 fanegas may be purchased for 2 piasters, or even for a silver piaster; the highest grade of flour then brings 8 piasters a quintal. But since the missions have been plundered and agriculture abandoned, it has become increasingly difficult to procure grain of any kind.

The cultivation of cotton, hemp, flax, and tobacco, which was so successful, leads to the belief that in the future these products will have an established place among exports. This should also hold true of wines and brandies, whose price is now unreasonably high. Wine costs 15 and 20 piasters for a barrel holding roughly 80 bottles, and brandy 30 piasters. This is the established price at Los Angeles, but at Monterey, with the added freight and profit, this price doubles. Furthermore, a municipal tax of 18 piasters a barrel is added. At one time several missions shipped annually to the arsenal at San Blas large supplies of hemp for the royal navy of New Spain, but now the cultivation of hemp has been entirely abandoned.

The exportation of horses overland by way of New Mexico has gone on steadily for many years. The Santa Fé train alone uses 2,000 horses, paying 8 or 10 piasters apiece in blankets and heavy woolen cloths. These horses are resold later for 40 or 50 piasters. A limited number of mules and select horses are shipped from time to time to Mexican ports or to the Sandwich Islands. The agents of the English concern, the Hudson's Bay Company, and the Canadians established along the Columbia and the Willamette rivers, also came to California searching for animals. The company has already sent 7,000 or 8,000 sheep by water.

Wool should become an export of considerable importance. This sells for only 6 piasters a quintal in the grease, and for 10 piasters washed. In 1840, the Hudson's Bay Company shipped some wool to London where it brought half a shilling a pound. No country in the world is better adapted to sheep raising than California, not only because of the mildness of the climate, but also because of the richness of pasturage.[4] The example set by the English along the Columbia River who have already imported from Scotland a fine breed of rams to improve the Californian strain, which supply wool of superior quality whose fineness is gradually increasing, should be followed. The down and feathers of wild swans, bustards, various kinds of ducks, and several rare birds, as well as heron aigrettes will undoubtedly, at some future time, enter the field of exports.

Californian wood is exported only to the Sandwich Islands. Planks and joists are primarily in demand and these sell for 50 piasters a thousand feet. Shingles for covering houses (*tajamanil*) retail at 8 piasters a thousand. The price of masts, yards, and rigging is based on their size. Californian wood, especially that used for masts, will be greatly in demand in Europe when communication is established at some future day between the two great oceans by way of Central America, either via the Isthmus of Panamá, or through the Lake of Nicaragua.

As yet no minerals have been found that can be exported from California.[5] The silver and lead mines situated near Monterey are known only from the results of simple assay tests. The various veins of marble, copper, and iron, the traces of coal found near Santa Cruz, the ochre, sulphur, kaolin, and salt deposits, have not been carefully examined. The only mine being worked in the country at the present time is a vein of virgin gold near San Fernando Mission that was exploited by a Frenchman, M. Baric. This yields daily about one ounce of pure gold. All articles exported, irrespective of the nationality of the exporter, are free of export taxes. The total value of annual exports is estimated at 280,000 Spanish piasters.

It is difficult to ascertain what articles have the largest consumption. The principal article currently used, however, is ordinary calico, which is taxed one silver real or one-eighth of a piaster for each Castilian *vare* (85 centimeters), and which sells for one-quarter of a piaster. Ecru

---

[4]By the sixties California was raising large flocks of sheep. Life on these great sheep ranches has been delightfully told by Sarah Bixby Smith in **Adobe Days**, (Los Angeles, 1931).

[5]For early gold discoveries see **supra** I, 186, also **note** 105.

calico is a more popular material than white calico. About 100 pieces of ecru calico should be carried to 40 pieces of white. All European commodities, with the exception of luxuries, can be imported into California for the country produces absolutely no manufactured articles. Everything in daily use, even ordinary brooms, comes from London or Boston. The Mexican tariff imposes an average tax of eighty per cent on listed articles; but in California, where nothing is prohibited, goods of this category are admitted on an average of forty per cent *ad valorem*. Foreign ships pay, in addition, a piaster and a half a ton anchorage tax.

Whalers are admitted with a special tax of 10 piasters when they come merely to take on provisions; however, if they dispose of any merchandise they are compelled to pay the regular taxes. Ships forced to put in at port are not taxed, but only on condition that they sell nothing.

Mexican ships coming from Mexican ports do not pay these taxes, and are not liable for tariff except when coming from a foreign port. Monterey is the only port open to outside commerce, and any ship—unless stopping for repairs—that touches at another port, is under suspicion as a contraband trader and runs the risk of being seized. After the ships have discharged their cargoes at the Monterey customs and paid their taxes, they are allowed to reload and trade along the coast, until they dispose of their entire cargo. That contraband trade flourishes under such regulations can be readily understood.

American and English ships arriving from foreign ports usually unload merchandise at various isolated points along the coast. They prefer, however, to remain at sea or at uninhabited islands, like those in the channel of Santa Bárbara, waiting for ships that have already paid the taxes, on which they reload part of their cargo. In this manner, certain ships have sold two or three times the amount of their original cargo. Legal tender being scarce in California, the captains, supercargoes, and merchants have the privilege of paying a portion of the duties in merchandise or local exchanges. This quota may be varied at the discretion of the customs administration. Two-thirds is usually paid in merchandise and one-third currency. Everything at Monterey is inspected and passes through the hands of Don José Abrego,[6] commissioner of finances (*comisario de hacienda*). The latter holds office

---

[6]José Abrego reached California in 1834 and opened a store in Monterey. He soon acquired considerable influence and held many political offices. The adobe house which he built is still standing on Abrego Street.

as a result of a division of duties between the military and civil employés in the province who are obliged to have an authorized agent at the capital for this purpose.

Commercial houses rich enough to purchase the entire cargo of a ship do not exist in California. Thus, foreign owners in conjunction with large ships have a small boat that travels up and down the coast and is able to land at any point. The Hudson's Bay Company, which has adopted this system, maintains its principal depot at San Francisco; another is close to San José, and a third near Monterey. The company intends to establish additional posts at Santa Bárbara and Los Angeles, and to use light vessels to carry merchandise and take on hides and tallow.

French articles sell readily in California, but only in small quantities. Many of them, however, are more popular than English articles, especially manufactured articles, and shoes. Cotton prints in large designs and bright colors from Mulhouse, for example, bring a piaster and a half a *vare,* whereas pale-colored English prints have a market value of only 4 or 5 reals. Bordeaux wine in cases of twelve bottles that carry one piaster tax, brings 6 piasters, and there is a steady market for brandy, notwithstanding the exorbitant import tax of 21 piasters, as well as the local tax of 18 piasters a barrel. Certain silks, which must compete with those of China, can be imported advantageously, as well as furniture, canned goods, liquors, mild wines, crockery, tools of all kinds, glassware, powder arms, paper, cloth of medium weight, some military equipment, and a small amount of fashionable objects and articles from Paris. In brief, consumption is practically the same as throughout Spanish America.

Notwithstanding, collections are so slow that a shipper is never advised to send all his cargo to this destination. To conduct a business on this coast the custom followed by the English and Americans should without fail be adopted. This consists of establishing at the port for a term of two or three years agents or supercargoes to travel through the country on horseback and secure customers. While an office ashore has many advantages, yet it entails employing at least ten assistants and, in addition, the captain and crew of a small ship. Credit is extended for one year, but if the season is dry and pasturage unavailable, the live stock cannot graze and the rancheros, in the belief that they will not produce much tallow, kill as few as possible.

As a usual thing one-third of the live stock is killed annually, for the cows calve every year. Cattle, horses, and sheep are marked by a special device on the ear, and branded on the flank with the initials of the missions or the owners; and notwithstanding the large numbers, errors in identification are never made in marking. Annually in September and October, owners assemble their live stock in a corral to mark them with hot irons and count the young. With the approach of the dry season, the animals which have been grazing out at pasture through the winter and spring are again collected and a choice is made of those who are to be sacrificed. The first operation is known as *el herradero* (the branding), and the second, *la matanza* (the slaughter). If the year has been poor, the rancheros do not market any of their products and extend the payment of their bills to the following year, continuing in the meanwhile to order goods for current needs. That debts thus accumulate indefinitely and become increasingly difficult to collect, not only on account of the diminished supply of live stock but also because of the increased consumption of merchandise, particularly spirits, whose use, unfortunately, Californians abuse, is quite obvious.

Comparatively few French trading vessels have visited California. The first was that of M. de Roquefeuil who arrived here in 1816.[7] The *Héros* of Havre, Captain Duhaut Cilly,[8] that reached California in January, 1827, made several sales along the coast, and, leaving an agent on shore to make collections, went down to Lower California, Mazatlán, and Lima, returning the following year to Monterey, with the hope of collecting the bulk of his invoices. However, he experienced considerable difficulty in making collections. His shop was stocked by the firm of Martin Laffitte of Havre and Javal frères of Paris. In August, 1827, a ship from Bordeaux, the *Comété,* reached Monterey and transacted some profitable business.[9] Since affairs are not done on a cash basis, it is inadvisable to send out a single expedition, for subsequent business dealings are usually unavoidable.

[7]Camille de Roquefeuil, in command of the **Bordelaise** touched at California en route to China where he hoped to establish commercial relations. His first stop, from August 5 to 14, 1817, was at Yerba Buena; on his second stop, on September 19, 1818, he remained a month, visiting many points and describing at length the population, military strength, settlements, industries, and climate of the coast. See his **Journal d'un voyage autour du monde pendant les années 1816, 1817, 1818, et 1819** (2 vols. Paris, 1823), I, 147-173, II, 231-273.

[8]Among records familiar to De Mofras was that of Auguste Duhaut Cilly [Bernard du Haut Cilly], a sea captain, member of the Academy of Industrial Manufacturers, farmer, and merchant. Duhaut Cilly was master of the **Héros,** a ship of 250 tons, that touched on January 26, 1827, at Yerba Buena, remaining on the west coast until August, 1828. See his **Voyage autour du Monde pendant les années 1826, 1827, 1828, et 1829** (2 vols. Paris, 1834), I, 309 ff.

[9]In August, 1827, the **Comété**, a trading ship of 500 tons, carrying 43 men, in charge of Antoine Placiat, put in at Santa Bárbara, paying duties on goods sold to the amount of 1,048 piasters.

Several of our whalers have landed at ports in Upper California, but often—as with the English and Americans—there are wholesale desertions. For instance, in 1839 the *Joseph* of Bordeaux lost 14 out of 25 members of her crew. Good sailors being difficult to procure out on this coast, obviously such desertions imperil the interests of the owners, and at times even the existence of ships. The local officials, powerless to check these desertions, do not even attempt to rectify conditions. A resident French consul and the presence of our warships might indeed prove effective against future attempts of this nature. On the other hand, in September, 1841, the *Elisa,* a whaler from Havre, whose captain, Malherbe, rejoiced over the fact that he had not lost a single man, though carrying a crew of 35, reached San San Francisco Harbor.

The total value of imports into California has grown 150,000 piasters. One hundred thousand are brought in under foreign flags; the balance under Mexican colors. The following statistics will indicate definitely the movement of foreign ships in the course of a year. This also shows that all Mexican ships belong to foreigners and American vessels, particularly those from Boston, supply half the total tonnage. Nevertheless, with the latter there is grave danger that within a few years ships of the Hudson's Bay Company will prove formidable rivals.

Captains and supercargoes should be careful to avoid having any disagreements with the customs at Monterey, since disputes are not decided in this country, but come up for hearing before the *tribunal de hacienda* (tribunal of finances) that sits at Hermosillo, Sonora. What delays and countless difficulties are apt to arise from this long distance settlement can be readily surmised.

In August, 1837, Comandante Vallejo made a proposal to Governor Alvarado to move the customs office from Monterey to the port of San Francisco, giving as his pretext the fact that the anchorage was better there and contraband easier to prevent. However, in reality he desired to be in a position to appropriate the port taxes paid by vessels. Naturally Alvarado refused, and his attitude was among the major causes of dissention between these two leaders.

In 1840 the government wished to close the coastal trade to foreign ships. Thereupon the latter refused to unload and Alvarado soon realized he would be obliged to lift the ban, since the only revenues in the country came from the customs, and the insignificant sums realized from fines, municipal taxes on shops, the importation of spirits, and logging, were handled by the alcaldes and used for the pueblos' expenses.

Foreign ships are allowed to trade in California; but according to law they must carry a Mexican captain or be in command of a naturalized foreigner. In other instances the ships must stop at San Blas and obtain from the head official of the shipping office for this district naturalization papers signed by the president.

Irrespective of the tonnage of a ship sent out to California, the valuation, represented by the purchase price of the cargo, should not exceed 6,000 to 8,000 piasters, or 10,000 at the most. Such cargoes usually consist of basic commodities and merchandise no longer fashionable in Europe.

Comparatively few ships sail directly to California from England, since the majority touch first at Lima or Valparaiso. Those owned by the Hudson's Bay Company come over from Honolulu, or the Columbia River, whereas most of the American ships sail from Boston, and occasionally from the Sandwich Islands. Many of these ships, furthermore, discharge part of their cargo at Peru or Chile prior to their arrival at California.

Table of Imports in California

	Piasters
Mexican ships	50,000
American ships	70,000
English ships	20,000
Miscellaneous and Whalers	10,000
Total imports	150,000

Table of Exports from California

	Piasters
Hides	210,000
Tallow	55,000
Pelts, wood, and other articles	15,000
Total exports	280,000

Table of Exports based on Nationality

	Piasters
Mexican ships	65,000
American (from Boston 110,000	
(from the Sandwich Islands 40,000	150,000
English	45,000
Miscellaneous	20,000
	———
Total exports	280,000

A discrepancy exists between the profits of Mexican ships and those of other countries, for the former often return empty or with cargoes of unequal value. Mexican ships carrying hides sail to Valparaiso and return with European merchandise. Those laden with tallow, however, are bound for Lima, where, having delivered a cargo, they frequently sail up the east coast to Guayaquil to take on cocoa which is subsequently unloaded at Acapulco. At the latter port, as well as at San Blas and Mazatlán, they take on European merchandise that is no longer in fashion and objects manufactured in Mexico, principally at Puebla, Queretaro, and Guadalajara, such as blankets or woolen serapes, jackets, silk and cotton shirts, hats, trimmings, women's slippers, tanned hides, harnesses, saddles, cigars and cigarettes, white and raw sugar, mescal, and brandy made by distillation from the American agave.

In 1841, a year when a small amount of wheat was planted in Upper California, the harvest, owing to a dry season, proved to be so poor that two small boats were sent down to take on flour at San Blas and Guaymas. In other years, on the contrary, when the weather has been favorable, loads of wheat are shipped from Monterey to Acapulco.

English ships, as a general thing, do not return to England, but sail over to the Sandwich Islands or down to Valparaiso. Those owned by the Hudson's Bay Company also travel to the Sandwich Islands and from there to Fort Vancouver on the Columbia River. Some of the American ships set sail for the Sandwich Islands, while others return directly to Boston. The latter, however, carry nothing but hides. Oddly enough, many of them, either on the trip out or on the return voyage, do not round Cape Horn, but pass through the Strait of Magellan, which has excellent harbors. Moreover, through the excellent hydrographic work of the Spaniards, a work that has been recently continued by England and which has acquired new significance since the Malouine

Islands.[10] have been acquired by that nation and since settlements have been recently established through the foresight of the Chilean government, its coast line is known. In 1839 an American scientific expedition in command of Lieutenant Wilkes[11] explored the Strait of Magellan in some detail in an attempt to establish a foothold, in the interest of United States commerce, by frequenting this passage.

TABLE OF NAVIGATION AND COMMERCE IN CALIFORNIA
Status of 43 ships that entered the port of Monterey and San Francisco in new California from September, 1840, to September, 1841.

Mexican Merchant Vessels Name	From	Tonnage	Crew	American Merchant Vessels Name	From	Tonnage	Crew
Bark *Clarita*	Acapulco	191	12	Brig *Bolivar*	Boston	180	15
Schooner *Ayacucho*	Lima	97	9	Brig *Lama*	Sandwich I.	208	10
Schooner *Ninfa*	Mazatlán	84	11	Brig *Corsair*	Boston & Lima	217	12
Bark *Guipuzcoana*	Lima	210	18	Brig *Perkins*	Sandwich I.	203	16
Brig *Catalina*	Mazatlán	160	16	Brig *Maryland*	Sandwich I.	128	13
Brig-Schooner *Ayacucho*	Lima	125	10	Schooner *Juliana*	Boston	106	10
Schooner *California*	Sandwich I.	86	10	Three-master *Monsoon*	Boston	400	23
Schooner *Colombina*	Mazatlán	55	9	Three-master *Alert*	Boston	360	19
Brig-Schooner *Leonidas*	Lima	160	12	Three-master *Tasso*	Boston	314	19
Brig *Chato*	San Blas	105	11	Three-master *Don Quixote*	Boston, Sandwich & Bodega	276	16
Ten ships		1273	118	Ten ships		2392	153
Whalers				Whalers			
None				Eight in one group. Two under Sandwich Island flag.		3075	240
Warships				Warships		Cannon	Crew
None				3 sloops-of-war Another sloop lost From the Sandwich Islands & Northwest Coast 2 Brigs 1 Schooner		90	800
10 Mexican Ships	Total	Tons 1273	Crew 118	24 American Ships	Total	Tons 5267	Crew 1173
Imports 50,000 piasters		Exports 65,000 piasters		Imports 70,000 piasters (excluding whalers)		Exports 150,000 piasters	

[10] The Falkland Islands.
[11] For Wilkes see supra, I, 200, note 64.

English Merchant Ships				Miscellaneous Merchant Ships				French Merchant Ships			
Name	From	Tons	Crew	Name	From	Tons	Crew	Name From Tons Crew			
Three-master *Index*	England and Valparaiso	203	11	Brig *Cervantes*	Lima	160	13	None			
Three-master *Colombia*	London, S. Is. & Columbia River	356	15	Brig *Juan José* of Ecuador	Guayaquil & Lima	217	14	However the schooner *Colombina* and the brig *Ayacucho* belonging to two Frenchmen, MM. de Hélia and Limancourt, were unfortunately lost, the former with crew and cargo.			
Three-master *Cowlitz* (These two ships belong to the Hudson's Bay Co.)	Id.	356	18	Schooner *Carolina* of New Granada	Union Port	72	12				
Schooner *Fly*	Lima	92	10								
4 ships		1007	54	3 ships		449	39	None			
Whalers				Whalers				Whalers			
None				None						Tons	Crew
								Elisa of Havre took on 900 barrels in nine months.		500	35
Warships		Cannon	Crew	Warships				Warships			
One corvette from San Blas		28	200	None				None			
		Tons	Crew			Tons	Crew			Tons	Crew
5 English ships, total		1007	274	3 Miscellaneous ships, total		449	39	1 French ship		500	35
Imports 20,000 piasters	Exports 45,000 piasters			Imports 10,000 piasters	Exports 20,000 piasters Including Whalers			Imports None	Exports None		

Comparative summary of ships flying the Mexican flag in Upper California on January 1, 1842.

Name	Tons	Crew	Name of owner
Bark *Guipuzcoana*	210	18	D. Antonio Aguirre, a Spaniard of Santa Bárbara
Schooner *Léonidas*	160	12	
Brig *Chato*	105	11	D. José Castaños, a Spaniard of Tepic
Schooner *Ninfa*	84	11	Captain Fitch, an American of San Diego
Schooner *Ayacucho*	97	9	Captain Daze, an American
Schooner *Esmeralda*	80	8	Hugo Reid, a Scotchman of Los Angeles
Schooner *Mosca*	92	10	Captain Wilson, an Englishman of San Francisco

Schooner *Juan Diego*	90	10	Captain Scott, an Englishman of Santa Bárbara
Schooner *California*	86	10	Government of California, at Monterey
Three-master *Clarita*	191	12	M. de Virmond, a merchant of
Brig *Catalina*	160	12	French extraction of Mexico and Acapulco
Total 11 ships	1,355	123	Thus only one small schooner was actually of Mexican ownership

By way of comparison, the following table of commerce in the Sandwich Islands during the same period as that included in the analysis of the commerce of New California should be consulted.

Status of 88 ships entering the ports of the Sandwich Islands from September 1840 to September 1841.

American	Merchantmen	14	Whalers	50	69	
English	"	13	"	3	16	Total, 88 vessels
French	"	00	"	2	2	
Mexican	"	1	"	0	1	

General Imports, 455,000 piasters; General Exports, 98,000 piasters

Imports into California, 150,000 piasters; :exports from California, 280,000 piasters.

From this comparison the commercial status of California appears to be far more satisfactory than that of the Sandwich Islands, although twice the number of ships visited the latter port. Although the population is twenty times as great, yet in California, as a matter of fact, the value of the export trade is twice that of the import trade, whereas in the Sandwich Islands imports are four and one-half times larger than the value of the exports. The enormous deficit that will result at some future date from this vast discrepancy between production and consumption is self-evident. Of 88 ships that visited the Sandwich Islands, 55 were whalers, among them being 50 American and two French whalers.

The latter, however, prefer to operate around Chile, Sydney, and New Zealand, rarely passing north of the Galápagos Islands. But our ships should be urged to explore regions not as yet visited, situated north of the equator and along the coast of Mexico, the Red Sea, the two

Californias, the Northwest Coast, with its many archipelagoes, and the Aleutian Islands, the waters, briefly speaking, between the equinoctial line and 60° north latitude and from 90° to 180° west longitude, Paris time.

Even an approximate estimate of the number of whales in this part of the hemisphere cannot be given. The American whaler, anchored off Monterey, that caught three whales in one day, has already been mentioned. Captain Malherbe of the *Elisa* of Havre, who has returned from the Northwest Coast, claims the distinction of being the first French whaler to go as far as latitude 54°. At this parallel, in less than a month, he took in 900 barrels of oil.[12]

Notwithstanding the dense fogs, the heavy seas, and the northwest winds that blow almost without respite, whaling is conceded to be comparatively simple in these waters during the summer season, especially in the many bays that are sheltered by the thousands of small islands along the coast. The Aleutians, the Kodiaks, and the Indians of Quadra and Vancouver Island are not afraid to venture forth in frail canoes to attack whales, whose flesh and oil are used for food. These waters also afford adequate shelter at the ports of Unalaska, Unimak, l'Ephiphanie on Kodiak Island, Port Mulgrave at the foot of Mt. St. Elias, Port des français, Archangle, Bucareli, Cordova, Nootka, Puget's Bay in the Strait of Juan de Fuca, and the superb harbor of San Francisco.

However, it is only at the latter port or at Monterey that whalers can procure supplies. Those who fish further south might be allowed to take on supplies or at least rest in the harbor of San Diego, and, in Lower California, at La Magdalena, the Mission of Todos los Santos, Mission San José at Cape San Lucas, La Paz near Port Pichilingue, Loreto, Guaymas, Mazatlán, San Blas, Manzanillo, Acapulco, the gulfs of Fonseca and Nicoya, the Bay of Panamá, and finally Otaheite and the Marqueses Islands. Thus, the waters lying between the Tropic of Cancer as far north as 55° appear to be the most important for whalers. These regions, that serve as a refuge for the cetaceans that are incessantly pursued south of the equator, are undoubtedly the least frequented of all fishing grounds.

Irrespective of the time of departure from France, our whalers should arrive in these upper latitudes only at a favorable time of year,

---

[12]See new fishing regions indicated on the map of the Pacific Ocean. (D. de M.).

that is, about the first of May. This will enable them to fish there for five months. Then, in October, the month when the Americans reach Monterey and San Francisco, whalers can put in for provisions at these two ports. After sojourning in the north, ships can explore the coast as they sail south, especially the Gulf of California that abounds in whales, and where there is no competition.

In these seas eight different species of whale are encountered. The largest, belonging to the cetacean family, is what the French term the true whale (*baleine franche*) and the Americans and the English the right, or black whale. This species supplies the whalebone used for corsets, umbrellas, and such articles. These whales, which are of tremendous size, are found during the summer season in the northern latitudes. When winter approaches they migrate south and frequent the local shores and bays. Frequently 200 barrels of oil can be extracted from one whale, and this explains why they are so highly prized by French whalers.

The Americans, on the contrary, prefer to hunt the species called cachalot, *Physeter macrocephalus,* known among the English and American whalers as the sperm, or white whale. This whale, which is distinguishable by its enormous head, which is one-quarter the size of its entire length, invariably remains far out at sea and in deep water. Although preferring warm water, it is usually found in the vicinity of the forty-fifth parallel, but can be caught upon returning south after hunting the true whale, even as high as the sixtieth parallel. This whale is somewhat smaller than the true whale and yields on an average 100 barrels of spermaceti.

Spermaceti is a stearic fluid contained in the cavity of the head, and has a value of 20 piasters a barrel, a price considerably higher than that of oil. In the United States where wax is scarce and costly, extensive use is made of spermaceti for lighting purposes; in France, on the contrary, candles of beeswax are preferred. Thus, when French and American whalers meet, they exchange spermaceti for common oil. The Americans also catch spermaceti whales, but only when an opportunity is afforded and to fill their ships rather than return empty-handed, for palm oil from the African coast is now beginning seriously to compete with the whale-oil market.

What are called by the English and Americans humpback whales, are invariably found not far from land and in all latitudes. They inhabit bays and when playing or fighting are frequently stranded on the shore. Occasionally when in port they fill the air with fetid gas which they exhale with a loud whistling sound. These whales, as their name indicates, carry on their backs, in place of fins, an enormous hump. They are fairly large and give considerable oil. However, they present the serious inconvenience of sinking when killed, and do not float on the surface of the water until a day or two after death. In ports, the place where they have disappeared is marked by a canoe or possibly a buoy, but out at sea where such precautions are impossible, they are never hunted.

The five other varieties of these cetaceans, known as the sulphur bottom whale has a sulphur-colored stomach, the finback whale, the grampus, the killer, and the blackfish, are less common and smaller than the first three varieties. They also plunge deeper in the water and as they produce less to compensate for the difficulties encountered catching them, whalers do not search for these species, but capture them only incidentally, when conditions are especially favorable, reserving their resources and energy for the true whale, the humpback whale, and the spermaceti whale.

Possibly this information, unknown to those coming to this coast for the first time, will encourage whalers to sail along the Northwest Coast and California. In these waters, which are seldom visited and which abound in cetaceans, ships can take on within a short time a full cargo and the owners will reap the dual advantage of shortening the length of the voyage and receiving back within a shorter time the funds advanced to outfit their whalers. The most important points in the laws and ordinances[13] actually enforced regarding fishing for whales will now be enumerated.

LAW OF JUNE 25, 1841

"Article I. The premium established by the laws of April 22, 1832, and July 9, 1836, to promote whale-fishing, shall be defined as follows and shall go into effect on March 1, 1842."

"Premium upon departure. Forty francs for standard tonnage upon departure for equipment wholly French, and 29 francs for semi-foreign equipment, within the limits defined by Article IV of the preceding law of April 22.

"Premium upon return. Twenty-seven francs for standard tonnage

---

[13]Extract from the **Bulletin des Lois** for the months of July and August, 1841. (D. de M.).

upon return for full French equipment, and 14 francs, 50 centimes for semi-foreign equipment, according to the terms of Article II of the law of April 22, 1832, if the ship has fished beyond Cape Horn, even if east of the Cape of Good Hope within the latitudes defined by the aforesaid Article II, and by Article III of the same law.

"Article II. Ships especially equipped to fish for whale in the Pacific Ocean, after a voyage of at least thirty months, during which they shall have traveled beyond 28° north latitude, shall be allowed an additional bounty on whale oil and by-products from the head that might be produced as the result of their fishing.

"This bounty shall be fixed as follows by the hundred kilograms;

"For ships leaving between the day the law is promulgated and December 31, 1845, 20 francs.

"For ships leaving between January 1, 1846, until the law expires, 15 francs.

"Article III. A royal ordinance shall determine the special conditions to be fulfilled by the owners who send ships to fish for whale.

"Article IV. The provisions of the present law, as well as those outlined by the laws of April 22, 1832, and July 9, 1836, which are not abrogated, shall remain in force until December 31, 1850."

The principal condition in the King's ordinance of August 10, 1841, defining the special conditions to be met by owners sending out whaling vessels are as follows:

"Article I. Every owner who wishes to dispatch a ship especially for whaling in the Pacific Ocean shall be required, in order to be eligible for the bounty, to make a preliminary declaration before the commission of the port where the ship is outfitted, guaranteeing to set a course for the destination for which he has outfitted and to carry only such products as result from his fishing."[14]

However, it is impossible to differentiate with accuracy between spermaceti whalers and ordinary whaling vessels. Each fishes for what he can find and exchanges with foreigners products that are mutually needed.

Ships of 500 tons are the best size to hold a fair catch and the necessary provisions for voyages that last as a rule thirty months. A vessel of this size, manned by a crew of 30, all Frenchmen, would receive the following bounty, whether returning empty or loaded with whale oil.

---

[14]See the **Archives du Commerce**, Vol. XXVIII, p. 132 ff., for the complete text, and the analysis of motives, as well as the report presented to the Chambers by the Minister of Commerce, April 19, 1841. (D. de M.).

Upon departure, by tonnage 40 francs x 500 tons—20,000 francs
Upon returning, by tonnage 27 francs x 500 tons—13,500 francs

Total bounty for a whaling vessel_____33,500 francs

Ships carrying a spermaceti whale oil would receive the additional bounty provided by the aforesaid law. Within the last ten years French fishing has had considerable development, and our nation now owns some eighty whalers, totalling 30,000 tons and manned by 2,000 sailors. Large premiums have been paid in certain years; in 1837, for example, these were in excess of 1,260,000 francs, but unfortunately these have not held at this level. The returns in spermaceti whale oil have shown a steady growth. In 1841 our ships brought in 66,000 kilograms, whereas six or seven years earlier this amounted to less than 3,000. There is reason to believe that the incentive of bounties will increase the number of expeditions sent out from our ports. The government, moreover, takes a personal interest in promoting such expeditions for whalers, and provides an excellent apprenticeship for training sailors for the royal navy.

The Americans have already sent a navy officer, Mr. Estabrook, to Monterey to act as consular agent. Information has also been received that the cabinet at Washington is about to appoint as consul one of two prominent merchants, Mr. Larkin or Mr. Jones, who previously served in this capacity in the Sandwich Islands. The local agent of the Hudson's Bay Company will probably be appointed English consul.

Despite the commercial and political aspect attached to the renewed interest in California that has been caused by conditions in Texas and the break that is imminent between the United States and Mexico, the recent creation of a French consulate at Monterey, a resident official, and the repeated visits of our own warships in these waters, affords our countrymen and the captains of our merchant and whaling vessels proper protection in the event of trouble or invasions, and also provides a way of disciplining insubordination and desertion on the part of sailors.